THE NEW YORK NOBODY KNOWS

THE NEW YORK
NOBODY KNOWS

WALKING 6,000 MILES IN THE CITY

WILLIAM B. HELMREICH

PRINCETON UNIVERSITY PRESS

PRINCETON AND OXFORD

press.princeton.edu

Sixth printing, and first paperback printing, 2015

Paperback ISBN: 978-0-691-16970-5

The Library of Congress has cataloged the cloth edition of this book as follows:
Helmreich, William B.
The New York nobody knows : walking 6,000 miles in the city /
William B. Helmreich.
pages cm
Includes bibliographical references and index.
ISBN 978-0-691-14405-4 (alk. paper)
1. New York (N.Y.)—Social conditions—21st century. 2. New York (N.Y.)—
Social life and customs—21st century. 3. New York (N.Y.)—
Civilization—21st century. 4. Neighborhoods—New York (State)—New York.
5. Community life—New York (State)—New York. I. Title.
HN80.N5H45 2013
306.09747'1–dc23   2013017223

British Library Cataloging-in-Publication Data is available

This book has been composed in Sabon with Helvetica Neue for display

Printed on acid-free paper. ∞

Printed in the United States of America

9 10 8

TO MY FATHER

CONTENTS

PREFACE

When I was nine years old my father devised a game to keep me entertained. It was called "Last Stop." We lived on Manhattan's Upper West Side. Whenever he was free on the weekend, we walked to the local 103rd Street stop on the IND (Independent Subway System) line. From that subway we would transfer to another train and take that to the last stop on the line. Upon exiting we would explore the neighborhood on foot for a couple of hours, sometimes taking a city bus to further extend our trip. When we ran out of last stops on the various lines, we'd move the destination point to the third-to-last or some other stop. We played this game off and on for about five years until I began high school.

That's how I learned to love and appreciate New York City. I would stand with my father, looking out on the marshes that were in Brooklyn's Canarsie section, and reflect, "So this is where my teacher told me he'd send me if I misbehaved." One time my father poked his head into a bar near Utica Avenue in Brooklyn and everyone scattered. I never found out why. Another time we took a bus to Throgs Neck in the Bronx, and I saw men fishing. I marveled at the sight, having never before seen anyone fish. I was a city kid. I played stickball, belonged to what passed for a gang on my block, and knew every chocolate bar in my local candy store. These experiences and the trips I took were the fertile ground where the idea for this book grew. As for my father, he continued walking well into his eighties, extolling its health benefits. He died of natural causes in 2011, three weeks shy of his 102nd birthday, so I guess he was right.

I have been teaching a graduate course on New York City at either City College of New York or the CUNY Graduate Center for forty years. It's a great place to do so because so many of my colleagues have done outstanding work on the city. Their collective works rival that of the University of Chicago scholars of the 1920s who went out and explored their city in similar fashion.

Besides reading extensively on the subject and writing papers, as part of my course my students go out walking with me for full days to explore the different boroughs. Many are from other countries, and it's a fascinating experience for them to see what I often refer to as the greatest outdoor museum in the world. They are invariably surprised and delighted to learn that all the boroughs are unique and interesting in their own right.

One day my chairman at CUNY Graduate Center's sociology department, Philip Kasinitz, remarked to me almost offhandedly, "You've been teaching about New York for so long. Why don't you just write a book about it?" I thought about what he said and suddenly realized that I had probably wanted to do just that my whole life. And so I decided to do it. I was also inspired by Joseph Berger's 2007 book, *The New New York.* As a journalist for the *New York Times,* Berger has covered the city for decades, and his volume is a marvelous travelogue through many of the city's ethnic neighborhoods, filled with information and fascinating insights about them and their people.

The fact that I've lived in New York for most of my life was a tremendous advantage. I'd walked much of the city many times before—by myself, with my students, for pleasure, or simply because I was going somewhere. But there was one huge difference between those walks and the journey I was about to undertake: I had never walked the city systematically, block by block, and for the purpose of writing a book. This greatly increased my focus, for now everything I did counted. It had to be apprehended, described, and analyzed. All my senses were alert and my brain was moving in high gear.

Another benefit was that not only had I grown up in New York, but I had also worked here in various capacities. In my younger days I had been a caseworker for the welfare department, a waiter and a busboy, a cabbie, and a researcher on various projects ranging from one on the homeless, to another on voting behavior, to interviews with people about food preferences, flooring, telephone use, and many other marketing studies. I have also lived in other parts of New York besides where I grew up.

Finally, there was the fact that I've lived in other cities too—Atlanta, St. Louis, New Haven, and elsewhere. This and brief stays in other cities around the world gave me a comparative perspective, the ability to see what made the Big Apple both unique and similar to other metropolises. Armed with this information and my personal background, I set out on what was to become a transformative journey, one in which I experienced and learned more than I could possibly ever have imagined.

ACKNOWLEDGMENTS

A large-scale project of this sort will inevitably have many debts to acknowledge and I do so with great pleasure. I want to first thank Peter Dougherty, director of Princeton University Press, for believing in this idea and giving me the opportunity to realize it. I am also indebted to my editor, Eric Schwartz, for his careful guidance, support, and enthusiasm, even to the point of traveling with me to various parts of the city. Jill Hughes, my copyeditor, played an important role in improving and polishing the manuscript, as did Senior Production Editor Kathleen Cioffi. Kudos too, to Jessica Pellien, Assistant Publicity Director, for her efforts on my behalf. Many thanks to all the other people at Princeton who helped me. It's a privilege to work with such a great group of people.

I'm especially appreciative of the past mayors of New York City, each of whom gave generously of their time and shared very valuable insights and reflections with me: Rudolph Giuliani, Michael Bloomberg, David Dinkins, and the late Edward Koch.

My gratitude to my colleagues and other knowledgeable people who evaluated and commented on my work at various stages cannot be overstated. I'm especially thankful to Roger Waldinger, Mitchell Duneier, Elijah Anderson, John Mollenkopf, Peter Moskos, Alford Young Jr., and Paul and Irene Marcus. Others who greatly sharpened my focus, saved me from errors, and enhanced my understanding of the subject include Richard Alba, Bill Kornblum, Phil Kasinitz, Nancy Foner, Herbert Gans, Cynthia Fuchs Epstein, Sharon Zukin, Mary Clare Lennon, Joseph Berger, Sheldon and Tobie Czapnik, Leslie Paik, Reuben Jack Thomas, Mary Curtis, Keith Thompson, Ramona Hernandez, Mildred Green, Alan Helmreich, Denise Helmreich, Danny Frankel, Jack Nass, Eli Goldschmidt, Joan Downs, Steven Goldberg, Allan Rudolf, Roslyn

Bologh, Esther Friedman, Sylvia Barack-Fishman, David Halle, Gabriel Haslip-Viera, Maritsa Poros, Lily Hoffman, L'Heureux Lewis-McCoy, Mehdi Bozorgmehr, Parmatma Saran, Howard Fuchs, Jim Biles, Katherine Chen, Chudi Uwazaurike, Iris Lopez, Francis Terrell, Robert Katz, Susan Tanenbaum, Arline McCord, Zach Dicker, Stephen Rabinowitz, Stuart Feintuch, Erwin Fried, Bill Green, Sanford Goldfless, Albert Weinstein, David Stetch, Jeffrey Wiesenfeld, Nomi Rabinowitz, Amnon Shiloach, Samuel Heilman, Jeffrey Gurock, Philip Jacobs, Sydelle and Robert Knepper, Archie Dykes, Ivan and Lisa Kaufman, Rona Woldenberg, Martin Werber, Edward Wydra, Gil Wachstock, Philip Fishman, Pearl and Nathan Halegua, Daniel Vitow, Stuart Rubenfeld, Patrick Sharkey, Cordell Schachter, Gwen Dordick, Jack Levinson, Laura Bowman, Jack Wertheimer, Ira Salomon, Lisa Helmrich, Tom Schott, Jenna Snow, Evan Nass, and Deborah Van Amerongen. Special thanks also to my photographers, Jesse Liss and Bob Marcus.

As they say, "We stand on the shoulders of giants." In that sense I'd like to acknowledge my early mentors at Washington University in St. Louis—Irving Louis Horowitz, Lee Rainwater, Jules Henry, Alvin Gouldner, Nicholas Demerath, Irving Zeitlin, George Rawick, David Pittman, and John Goering—who taught me how to think sociologically and out of the box. Through the early years of my career, there were colleagues who served as role models, especially William McCord, Joseph Bensman, Bernard Rosenberg, Gerald Handel, and Betty Yorburg.

Many others helped in a myriad of ways and I wanted to acknowledge them as well. They know what they did and what it meant to me and to the success of this undertaking: Karin Feldhamer, Suri Kasirer, Amanda Constam, Eric Creizman, Jeffrey Wiesenfeld, Nathan Goldberg, Avi Hadar, Marcelle Fischler, Edward Bader, Joe Potasnik, Thomas DiNapoli, Nicholas Di Marzio, Dennis Sullivan, Willie Rapfogel, Bill Helmrich, Gary Knobel, Judith Rothman, Aaron Freilich, Kenneth Cohen, Michael Nicolosi, Itzhak Haimovic, Gary Goldberg, Michael Pliskin, Arden Smith, Lizza Colon, Denise Major, Joyce and Ira Goldstein, Helen and Harvey Ishofsky, Harriet and David Schimel, David Werber, Judith

Connorton, Arnie Breitbart, Charlotte Wendel, Len Gappelberg, Neil Kalt, Billy and Nechama Liss-Levenson, Edward Auerbach, and Ramona Hernandez.

I'm blessed to have a very talented family of writers. All of my children—Jeff, Joseph, and Deborah—read the manuscript carefully. Their comments were incisive and very thoughtful and this is a better book because of their efforts.

Most of all, I owe a great deal to my wife, Helaine, an exceptionally talented novelist, biographer, and historian. As she has done with all of my books, she read every word that I wrote and made hundreds of invaluable suggestions, from both a literary and conceptual standpoint. It was as much a labor of love for her as it was for me, and she accompanied me on more than a few field trips. It has been my great fortune to have her as a wife, friend, and intellectual companion.

New York City

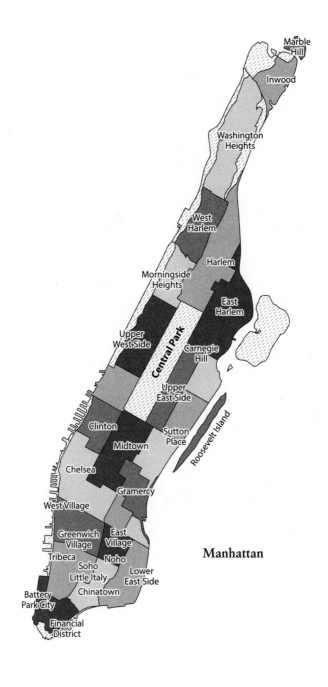

Marble
Hill

Inwood

Washington
Heights

West
Harlem

Harlem

Morningside
Heights

East
Harlem

Upper
West Side

Carnegie
Hill

Central Park

Upper
East Side

Clinton

Sutton
Place

Midtown

Roosevelt Island

Chelsea

Gramercy

West Village

Greenwich
Village

East
Village

Tribeca

Noho

Manhattan

Soho
Little Italy

Lower
East Side

Battery
Park City

Chinatown

Financial
District

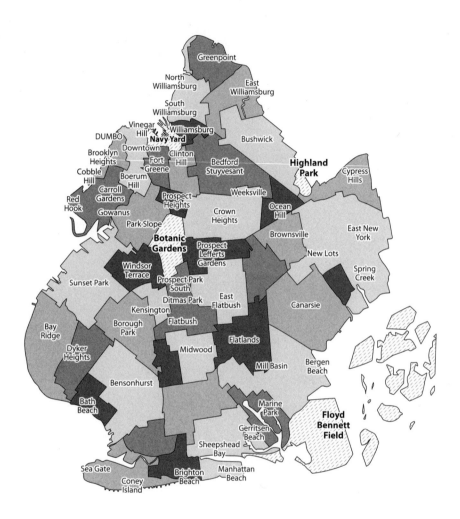

Greenpoint

North Williamsburg

East Williamsburg

South Williamsburg

Vinegar Hill
Williamsburg

DUMBO
Navy Yard

Downtown
Brooklyn Heights
Fort Clinton Greene Hill

Bushwick

Cobble Hill
Boerum Hill

Bedford Stuyvesant

Highland Park

Cypress Hills

Carroll Gardens

Prospect Heights

Weeksville

Red Hook

Gowanus

Crown Heights

Ocean Hill

Park Slope

Botanic Gardens

Brownsville

East New York

Prospect Lefferts Gardens

New Lots

Windsor Terrace

Spring Creek

Sunset Park

Prospect Park South

Ditmas Park

East Flatbush

Canarsie

Kensington

Bay Ridge

Borough Park

Flatbush

Dyker Heights

Midwood

Flatlands

Mill Basin

Bergen Beach

Bensonhurst

Bath Beach

Marine Park

Floyd Bennett Field

Sea Gate

Gerritsen Beach

Sheepshead Bay

Manhattan Beach

Coney Island

Brighton Beach

Brooklyn

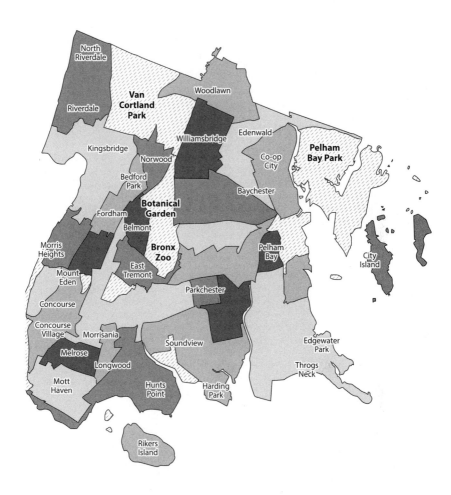

North
Riverdale

Van
Cortland
Park

Woodlawn

Riverdale

Edenwald

Kingsbridge

Williamsbridge

Pelham
Bay Park

Norwood

Co-op
City

Bedford
Park

Baychester

Botanical
Garden

Fordham

Belmont

Morris
Heights

Bronx
Zoo

Pelham
Bay

East
Tremont

City
Island

Mount
Eden

Parkchester

Concourse

Concourse
Village

Morrisania

Soundview

Edgewater
Park

Melrose

Throgs
Neck

Longwood

Mott
Haven

Hunts
Point

Harding
Park

Rikers
Island

The Bronx

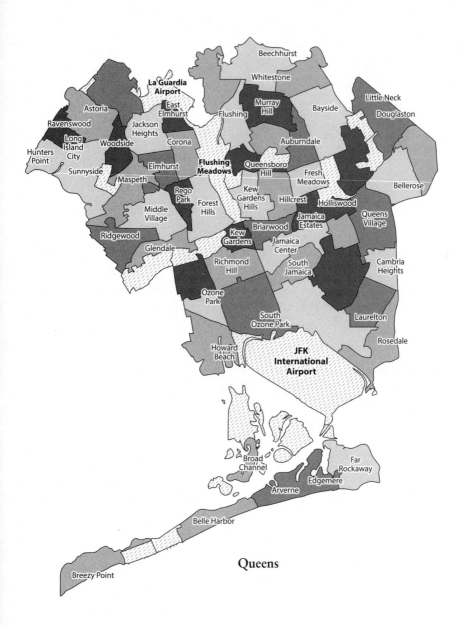

Queens

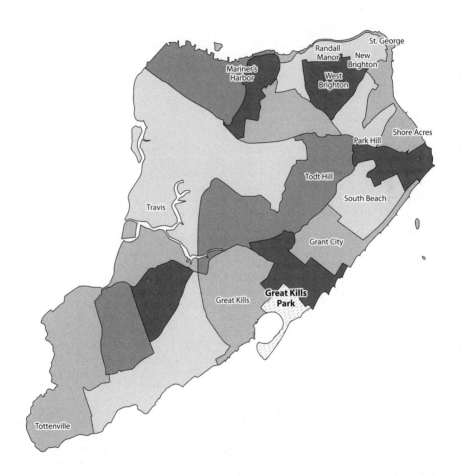

Mariner's
Harbor

Randall
Manor

St. George

New
Brighton

West
Brighton

Shore Acres

Park Hill

Todt Hill

South Beach

Travis

Grant City

Great Kills

**Great Kills
Park**

Tottenville

Staten Island

THE NEW YORK NOBODY KNOWS

1

INTRODUCTION

The ultimate aim of this book is to present a picture of the inner life, heart, and soul of New York City, to apprehend its spirit and make it come alive for the reader. I set out to do this by learning how the residents of the city experience their lives as people and as New Yorkers. The essence of the city is its people. By their actions and interactions they determine the shape it assumes, the flow of its daily life, and the aspirations and dreams it has. The relationships between those who live here, the joys and disappointments they experience and share, as well as the work they do and how they spend their leisure time, all constitute the lifeblood of the city itself.

But a city is not a static unit. It's a dynamic and constantly changing environment, adapting to the needs of its residents. And when that city has more than eight million inhabitants who come from every part of the globe, understanding how it works is a daunting challenge. New York City's immense size and scope and the tremendous variety of its people make it impossible to reduce it to a set of empirically verifiable observations and conclusions as one would do with a clearly defined neighborhood—any attempt to do so cannot succeed. Rather, New York must be viewed as a broad portrait in which the sum is indeed far greater than its parts. And the stories of the city's people and how they negotiate their lives are the vehicles that make it possible for us to enter and begin to comprehend this amazing world.

Walking New York City, block by block, brought into sharp focus a reality that I always knew was there but had never really articulated, because it was so much a part of me that I never felt a need to express it. It emerged time and time again as I spoke and interacted with people from every walk of life. To sum it up, *New York is a city with a dynamic, diverse, and amazingly rich collection of people and villages whose members display both small-town values and a high degree of sophistication. This stems from living in a very modern, technologically advanced, and world-class city that is the epitome of the twenty-first century.* That is both the major theme and conclusion of this intense and detailed journey to every corner of the five boroughs that constitute the city.

While these qualities reach a high level of expression here, they are by no means unique to New York City. They characterize people in other major cities too—Paris, London, Shanghai, New Delhi, and, in this country, Los Angeles, Chicago, and Boston. While these cities each have their own unique identity, all of them are places infused by new arrivals from everywhere who blend in with longtime residents, who are in turn energized and reshaped by the churning mix resulting from such contacts. This outlook on life and the patterns of behavior that emerge from such exposure are not expressed or realized to the same extent by all New Yorkers, yet they are present in varying degrees among the vast majority of its inhabitants. And this book is devoted to an exploration of that reality—how it reaches its full potential and how it informs the city as a whole.

Other important findings arose from this project, all of which are summarized in the concluding chapter. These include the critical ways in which gentrification and immigration have changed New York; the permanent impact of 9/11 on the city; the long-term trend toward ethnic assimilation as well as the creation of hybrid identities; and the broad sympathy toward undocumented immigrants.

New York City has never been scientifically studied as a whole by sociologists. In fact, none of the city's boroughs has even been investigated as a unit. What we have are many fine studies of communities.[1] I once mused aloud about this to a colleague. His response was, "Well, it's a huge topic. Maybe no one was crazy enough before you did it to walk the whole city." Perhaps he's right. You do have to be a little crazy to explore the city as I did, though not so much if you see it as healthy, fun, interesting, and as a challenge. It's also a matter of context. No one thinks of runners in New York City's marathon as crazy, because it's an accepted concept. They run about forty miles a week when training for the marathon, and as Abigail Meisel reports in the *New York Times,* growing numbers of cyclists are commuting from twenty to forty miles daily from the suburbs. But at least walking in Gotham is seen as an accepted form of activity. When I walked in Los Angeles, I almost never met anyone doing the same. For Angelinos, exercise meant only going to the gym, jogging, or swimming.

But the experience of walking the city is far more than that. Walking is critical to the task because it gets you out there and lets you get to know the city up close. However, you cannot merely walk *through* a city to know it. You have to stop long enough to absorb what's going on around you. And the only way to do that is to immerse yourself in it—spending as much time as possible in the streets; hanging out where others gather; attending meetings, concerts, sporting events, and the like; in short, doing what those who live there do. That is why the ethnographic method—direct observation, and sometimes even participation in whatever was going on—became the primary approach of this project.

My initial plan was to walk twenty representative streets of the city from end to end and use them as a basis for the book. But I soon realized that there was no way any particular twenty or even one hundred streets could claim to represent a city as large as New York. To do it right I would simply have to walk the entire city, a daunting but eminently worthwhile project. If nothing else, it would be great exercise!

This decision was crucial, for I now had hundreds of examples from what I observed to write about. The many stories and vignettes presented in this book were selected either because they were typical of phenomena I saw over and over again in many parts of the city or because their uniqueness enables us to learn something interesting about the city. When there is so much to choose from, you can pick the very best examples to make your points. Obtaining a general understanding of the entire city ultimately means you won't be able to present in-depth portraits of every neighborhood, but the benefits of getting a broader picture are well worth that limitation.

I ended up walking about 6,000 miles, the distance between New York City and Los Angeles and back to New York (4,998 miles), and then from New York City to St. Louis. I covered almost every block in Queens, Manhattan, Staten Island, Brooklyn, and the Bronx, including seldom-traversed industrial sections of the city. At the end of each walk I wrote down the number of miles I had traveled, as measured by my Omron pedometer. I averaged about 32 miles a week over four years, starting with Little Neck, Queens, in June 2008 and ending with Greenpoint, Brooklyn, in June 2012. This came to a grand total of 6,048 miles, an average of 1,512 miles a year, 126 miles a month, or 120,960 city blocks (twenty blocks equals one mile). I wore out nine pairs of San Antonio Shoes (SAS), the most comfortable and durable shoes I've ever owned. And all of the outer boroughs turned out to be much more interesting than I'd anticipated.

As I walked, I interviewed—you could also call them conversations because of their largely spontaneous nature—hundreds of people whom I met, and this too was critical to my efforts. Speaking directly with the city's residents was the second critical approach to my undertaking. Hardly anyone refused to talk with me. I asked no one their full names, so as not to invade their privacy, but quite a few people volunteered them anyway, and when they appear in this book, it's with their permission. Although I have changed a few minor details, most names and places are accurate.

Most of the time I did not tell anyone what I was doing unless they asked, because I wanted their answers to be spontaneous and relaxed. In keeping with that goal, I never began an interview with a standard: "Excuse me, could I ask you some questions about this community?" Instead I would say something like: "How come you're dressed like this?" or "Is this neighborhood safe?" or "What's a horse doing in that guy's backyard?" (That really happened, in Gerritsen Beach, Brooklyn.) Before they knew it (and most of them never did), they were being interviewed.[2]

I used a tape recorder whenever possible, and when asked why, I told people I wanted to remember what they were saying. Most of them didn't mind, and some were flattered that their words were worth recording. In situations when I thought taping wasn't a good idea, I summarized the conversation by speaking into my recorder as soon it was over. Many of these casual interviews yielded insights on a number of levels. Here's a good example of one. I approached a stocky, youngish Honduran man who was waving a plastic orange flag outside a Lower Manhattan garage, signaling drivers that the garage had space for their cars.

"Do you find this job boring?" I asked.

"This is not my main job."

"What's your main job?"

"Menten," he said in his limited English.

"What's that?"

"Menten."

Figuring I would understand what he meant if I asked him to describe his work, I countered with, "What do you do when you do menten?"

"I clean the garage, throw the garbage away, sweep up."

"You mean maintenance?"

"Yeah, menten."

Suddenly seized by inspiration, I asked, "Can I wave your flag for a minute? I wanna see what it feels like."

"Are you okay?" he asked, a worried tone creeping into his voice.

"It's all right. I'm a professor."

Of course, my line of work had nothing to do with my qualifications for this task, but I had learned that many people don't pay close attention to what you say as long as you say *something*. I would ask someone if I could use their bathroom because I was going to a wedding immediately after our interview, or I would ask if I could make a copy of something because I was leaving for a vacation. It made no sense, but the answer was often yes anyway.

Sure enough, the Honduran man said, "Okay."

And then a weird thing happened. After waving it for a minute, the flag curled up tightly around the stick and I could no longer wave it. Feeling sheepish, I handed it back to him. I learned from this that the simplest task can be difficult for those who don't know how to execute it.

My reverie was abruptly interrupted when he exclaimed, "I know who you are! You're the boss!"

I don't know whether he'd seen the CBS reality program *Undercover Boss*, where a boss goes among his workers incognito to see how they're doing their jobs, but I did take note that he wasn't in the least bit bothered by this possibility. In fact, after I responded enigmatically with, "You never know," he simply laughed and said, "Be good, my friend."

One important lesson from this episode was the realization that we have become a surveillance society. People accept with equanimity, it seems, the idea that others may be spying on them. Independent confirmation of this view came from many other interviews. Another lesson was that New Yorkers from every walk of life are, by and large, a friendly and open lot. That too was substantiated many times over.

I also conducted a number of formal interviews with key leaders in the city, those who headed community boards, religious organizations, and the like. The goal here was to address issues that my walking and impromptu conversations did not fully explain. Of particular interest were my interviews with former mayors Ed Koch, David Dinkins, Rudy Giuliani, and the current mayor, Michael Bloomberg. All were open and forthcoming and spoke about their role in the city and their thoughts about its needs and challenges from the perspectives of both history and hindsight. All of these people are identified by name in the narrative.

Normally sociologists take a more removed view of their work, even though they clearly have feelings and thoughts about it. However, since the research for this book consisted mostly of walking and engaging people personally, I felt it was important to tell what I was thinking as I did so. Thus, at many points I try to explain how I felt as I strolled through the streets. Maybe it would be good if researchers did more of that in general, but that's obviously not for me to decide.

This is an exploratory study, a first effort to understand the city. It does not pretend to be exhaustive or comprehensive. My hope is that other researchers will use it as a basis for doing more detailed work on the many aspects and topics introduced here. When you're the first one on the block, you have to be careful not to assume too much. This is especially true of ethnography, which is a qualitative, often intuitive approach that is most fruitful in providing insights and deeper understanding as opposed to statistical conclusions.

There are many ways to analyze the city of New York. One approach is to use its *geographical* division into boroughs and neighborhoods and carefully examine each of them. Another approach is to think of the city in terms of *categories*—Asians, whites, New Yorkers, Brooklynites, organizations, small stores, sports, seniors, children. The city can also be evaluated in terms of *issues*—immigration, gentrification, crime, and education. Yet another method is to look at New York City as a patchwork of physical *spaces*. These include streets, buildings, walls, statues, playgrounds, and memorials. All of these lines of inquiry are employed in this book, because each one helps us to better comprehend this complex metropolis.

The chapter topics were chosen because of their importance and because they were particularly suitable for observation. Immigrants have long been central to New York's history, as well as that of the United States, and walking gave me many opportunities to meet and engage them. Since the city is made up of many different communities, examining each of them from up close was a natural choice, as was looking at how New Yorkers spend their free time. It was also important to look at the city as a space, because how city dwellers use it speaks volumes for what the city means to them. Understanding the gentrification process was critical because it is the single most effective vehicle for learning about how New York City has been transformed over the last four decades into a vibrant and exciting place, both residentially and commercially.

Finally, how people do or do not identify ethnically tells us much about issues that go to the core of who they are and where they're heading, both personally and collectively. Throughout the book an effort has been made to consider how the city has changed since it hit rock bottom financially in 1975.

This was clearly a highly labor-intensive project, involving thousands of hours of hard, even grueling, work. Most of the time I walked by myself, with no research assistants to help me. There were times when I was willing to travel one and a half hours by public transportation in order to walk a neighborhood for two hours. You have to grab time whenever you have it. In the fall and the spring, summer and winter, weather permitting, you walk the streets. Then you listen to the tapes and transcribe what you need on rainy or very cold days. You also use that time to read, interview, write, and think. No time can be wasted. Otherwise, you can spend ten years doing a book of this size and still not be finished.

The end game—namely, writing the book—requires an ability and willingness to sit in a chair and work for twelve to fourteen hours straight, day in and day out. Single-minded focus is essential, so there's no checking your email five times a day. And if you're sick, you must do everything in your power to get well quickly. My body held up surprisingly well, and I suffered almost no health problems. I daresay that because of the steady exercise I'm in even better shape than when I began. My foot became inflamed just as I was walking Canarsie one early December day. In the interest of time, I went for a cortisone shot rather than taking a slower approach of ice and rest. Knowing that the snow season was fast approaching also influenced my decision, since you can't easily walk or interview in the cold months. The shot worked. Another time, after suffering a stomach virus, I went out as soon as I felt even a little better. Time can be a real enemy, for the longer the lag between the fieldwork and the writing of the book, the less alive it is and the more likely you are to forget things. Of course, you need time to reflect, so it's a trade-off.

When I came home I listened to and transcribed the tapes I'd made. Rather than use a transcription service, I did it myself. Listening to them helped me catch the inflections and nuances in the conversations and allowed me to decide on the spot what I needed to include and what I could exclude. I also read the scholarly and popular literature about New York, focusing heavily on the most recent writings, since I was familiar with older ones from having taught my course for so long.[3] Thus the information in this book represents both my own findings and the research of others. I ended up with 750 pages of single-spaced typed notes that were, in essence, the raw material for this book.

When doing ethnography it's important to remember that observations should be taken with a grain of salt if you're looking at something for the first time. For example, I see a number of beautiful vintage Corvettes parked in a lot near the Staten Island beach. The cars shimmer as they catch the waves of heat from the hot asphalt, baking in the sun. "How nice that these Corvette owners have a hobby and an affinity group through which to express themselves," I think. After talking with them I discover that they are not here just to socialize and show off their cars. Pointing to a box of toys, one of them says, "We're here because we're giving these toys to disadvantaged children. And that's what we decided to do as a club." Of course, many clubs may not do any good works as part of their activities, so it's best not to generalize or make assumptions about people.

In a similar vein, when was the last, or even first, time you saw a bar with a Jewish name? Well, I did. It was on Manhattan's Lower East Side, on the corner of Allen and Stanton Streets, and was called Epstein's Bar. It struck me as a possible sign that the idea that Jews don't drink was dying out, that a younger generation of Jewish yuppies was changing that stereotype, and that they were no longer the least bit embarrassed about it. But it really shows why it's important to ask and not assume.

Inside, I approached a non-Jewish bartender, a young woman with long, blonde hair who was polishing shot glasses with a damp cloth. Smiling at my question, she provided a clarification. "It's taken from the Juan Epstein who starred in *Welcome Back, Kotter,*" she said. "In the show his mom was Puerto Rican and his dad was Jewish. So the new owners named it that way. And it's also because the Lower East Side was once Jewish and then became

Puerto Rican too." Hanging on the wall was an advertising poster for Levy's Jewish Rye bread, reading, "You Don't Have to Be Jewish to Love Levy's." This particular variation of the ad featured a Hispanic-looking kid eating a pastrami-on-rye sandwich.

Many people asked me why I didn't save time and just drive through the city. I'll start by saying that driving via the highways that go through New York City is practically worthless. From that vantage point, you'll focus mostly on the tall buildings, like the public housing projects, and miss the gardens, trees, and smaller buildings that make up 80 percent of the area, and the storefront churches that often tell a story in their very names. From the Bruckner Expressway you'll see five-story walk-ups in the Bronx that remind you of *Bonfire of the Vanities,* but you'll miss the teeming life that is actually happening in front of them, on the stoops, and in the streets filled with playing children. Driving through the streets slowly is a little better, but not much.

You need to walk slowly through an area to capture its essence, to appreciate the buildings, to observe how the people function in the space, and to talk with them. Driving gives you nothing more than a snapshot. More to the point, it creates a physical wall between you and the neighborhood. By the very fact that you're *driving through,* you are making it clear that you are not from the area and are an outsider. When you walk through a neighborhood, although people may see that you're from the outside, the mere fact that you're walking suggests that you're at least visiting. More likely it lends plausibility to the appearance that you have some business there—you work in the area, or you're meeting a local resident who might be a friend, a business contact, drug dealer, whatever. You might be a cop. Or notwithstanding the fact that you don't resemble a native, you might be just too poor to live elsewhere. None of these thoughts (except for the cop scenario) are likely to occur to others when you drive through. Walking is infinitely more difficult, it is more time-consuming by far, but it is indispensable for anyone who is seriously interested in comprehending the city and gaining the rapport with the locals that's necessary for it. And that's why I chose to walk.

What about bicycling through the city? This method of exploring an area is no doubt better than motoring, but it's still a bit too quick for serious reflection. At the same time, it's an excellent way to take the pulse of the city if you lack the time to walk and want to cover ground quickly and with some degree of intimacy. And you're more likely to be seen as a possible local if you bike. In fact, if you want to engage people, you can stop and do so more easily than in an automobile, which is seen as far more intrusive.[4]

And then there are those who say, "Why do you have to walk through an area for four hours, especially one that's dangerous? Wouldn't an hour or so be enough to get the flavor?" I wish I could say that this is the case. It would certainly make my work easier. The problem is that you never know when you are going to see something really interesting or meet someone with a fascinating story or persona. It could be in the first hour, but it could just as well be in the fourth hour. I can't emphasize enough how many times I have had the encounter or insight that made the whole day worthwhile near the end of my walk—those twenty preschoolers listening to a story about Jesus; seeing a man walking four pit bulls in Bushwick, Brooklyn, with two boa constrictors wrapped loosely around his neck; and a black-and-white mural in the South Bronx telling a tale of life and death there. Had I not walked the eight or ten miles that day, I would have never seen such sights. Hard work is hard, but the results are usually well worth the effort. How do you know when you've walked enough? It's probably when the buildings, community centers, noises, smells, and, most of all, conversations, start becoming repetitive.

I walked the city mostly during the daytime, but I also traveled through its streets at night. Things change when the sun sets. The avenues throb with far more activity. People are out and about, standing, talking, and joking in front of the buildings, on street corners, and also enjoying the entertainments available after dark—the theaters, restaurants, and various squares where citizens congregate. Walking on weekends or holidays, as well as on weekdays,which I did, also makes a difference in what you see, as do the different seasons.

In my back pocket I carried little street maps of whatever neighborhood I was visiting. That's how I made sure that I walked all the blocks. Generally I traveled to the neighborhoods by subway, where I would often use the opportunity to read a book. I would travel by car only when the area I planned to explore was an outlying one. Not wanting anything in my hand while I walked, I used what I called the "Tic-Tac method." I'd buy a box of Tic-Tac mints in a small grocery store, pay for them, and then ask the clerk to hold the book I'd been reading on the subway until I returned, leaving both the book and the Tic-Tacs with him and saying jokingly (I hoped), "If I don't come back, you can keep both." They almost always agreed. On one or two occasions store owners even said to me, "You don't have to buy something for me to hold on to your book. I'll do it anyway." As for the tape recorder, it was in my pocket.

Until you do it, it's impossible to realize what walking six thousand miles really entails. If you walk west to east, just from the Hudson to the East River, down Fifty-sixth Street, it takes about forty minutes (including waiting for lights to change) and runs about two miles. Then if you go on to walk from Fifty-fifth to Fifty-first Streets, it comes to a total of ten miles. This gives you an idea of how big the city is. I walked anywhere from five to thirteen miles each trip, depending on the length of my conversations with people and the points of interest I discovered.

There are times when you just lose your "research voice." Maybe instead of writer's block you have "walker's block." You're not in the mood to talk to people, you can't think of any interesting questions to raise, what you see doesn't inspire any original thoughts. You start thinking, "Maybe I've just been doing this for too long." I do think that when ideas, themes, and so on start repeating themselves, it may mean that it's time to stop walking and write some more, but on the other hand, when you're in new territory, a part of the city where you've never walked, that isn't necessarily the case. You may simply need a temporary break. And if so, you should take it and fill up the time with more reading, or take a brief vacation. Fortunately, walker's block didn't happen to me too often, probably because New York City is just so interesting.[5]

Eating or drinking something while walking is a good idea if you want to blend in, especially if an area doesn't seem to be particularly safe. To others, the normal activity of eating or drinking shows you're a local. Who but a local would be eating while walking outside? Also it makes you look like you're not afraid or nervous. You're holding food and a bottle in your hands, which means you're not on guard in a "ready for anything" mode. I suspect middle-class people are less apt to eat while walking in the street regardless of where they are. Talking on a cell phone also works. It suggests that you're relaxed and that you don't feel a need to pay such close attention to your surroundings. Sitting down on a stoop or porch is also good, because that's what many residents do anyway. Just be careful where you sit. Try to choose a house that looks as though no one's home.

The most frequent question posed to me when I mentioned my research was, "How were you as a white man able to walk through the dangerous neighborhoods without getting hurt?" This is worth an extended discussion. To begin with, I dressed innocuously, no bright colors to call attention to myself. I wanted to blend in as much as possible, no matter where I was. I followed this rule even more carefully in poor ghetto areas, being especially careful to not wear bright red or blue, which are sometimes seen as gang colors.[6] People in these areas typically wear T-shirts and shorts, which often don't match at all. I followed suit. I would wear white socks and black SAS shoes. Generally speaking, I got no second looks, not even first ones.

Of course, people couldn't help notice that I am white, but I was far from the only white person walking around. There were cops, teachers, social workers, auto repair shop owners. Plus, many Hispanics could easily pass as non-Hispanic whites. Age worked against me (I'm in my sixties) in that I could have seemed physically vulnerable, fit as I might be for my age. But in my view the benefit outweighed the downside. I was seen as harmless, not a threat to the residents or their manhood. I wasn't worth challenging or attacking. Still, there were people who saw me as a cop. When I protested that definition once, a black man informed me that "a cop can easily dye his hair gray, so it doesn't mean anything." Still others may have thought it would be risky to harm a white person. As one put it, "If I did something to a white person, the cops would come down on me. It would interfere with my business." I did not inquire what that business was, since it was most likely illegal.

All too often, people who regard themselves as savvy New Yorkers think it's necessary to put up a tough front to show they're not afraid by projecting a no-nonsense demeanor that can include a tough-guy, unsmiling look accompanied by a purposeful stride. That is exactly the wrong thing for a visitor to do. It is often seen as a challenge and a sign of inner fear, not to mention proof that you don't belong, that you are ill at ease in the area.

Whenever I walked toward young, well-muscled people who looked tough, possibly gang members or drug dealers, I would wait until I was close to them, and if they made eye contact, I would immediately smile and say, "Hey, how ya doin'?" or some variation of that. The effect of that counterintuitive comment was immediate and almost always the same: "Fine. How you doin'?" Sometimes they added "Pops" in a gently joking, almost affectionate way. After all, I had been friendly, had shown no "attitude," nor any fear. In many cases my greeting wasn't even necessary, since people in the ghetto often avoid eye contact because a wrongly interpreted glance can lead to big trouble.[7] Another suggestion is to never quicken your pace if you see people ahead who make you nervous. You are conveying fear when you do that and therefore inviting problems. You can't run anyway, because those whom you fear are almost always going to catch you if they really want to.

Paradoxically, perhaps, you are safer deep inside a rough area than on the edge of one. Deep inside signifies that you are part of the neighborhood. On the edge you are seen as wandering in from the outside or moving about on the border. This is why City College students in West Harlem, for example, are in less danger than those who live near Columbia University, with its beautiful streets like Claremont Avenue and Morningside Drive, right next door to the dangerous Manhattanville and Grant public housing projects. The poor resent the wealth that the Columbia students represent. The City College students, on the other hand, are not perceived as, nor are they likely to be, middle or upper class. In fact, many are themselves local or from other poor communities.

Does this mean that walking through bad neighborhoods isn't that dangerous? Absolutely not! It is, and whoever does so is taking a chance. However, knowing what you're doing can definitely reduce the risk. Here's an example of something that could have gone either way. In Brownsville, Brooklyn, still one of the most dangerous parts of the city, three people—two black males and one black female—were walking ahead of me. In the ghetto, people turn around every so often to make sure they're not being followed or that someone isn't about to jump them. It's a quick, over-the-shoulder glance that is never aimed directly at whoever's behind them. A direct look might provoke a confrontation. I happened to be walking a third of a block behind this trio, and I accidentally kicked a bottle cap. As it skittered noisily up the sidewalk, they gave a quick look behind them, but without even pretending not to look at me directly. Why? Because the noise gave them a justification for checking me out. I knew it and they knew it.

These and a myriad of other responses are examples of street engagements that sociologist Elijah Anderson so insightfully portrays in his classic work, *Code of the Street*. The book describes an elaborate system of nonverbal communication that is a constant presence in the ghetto. Knowing what to do based on past experience is critical, but you can't really prepare for everything that might occur. When you encounter someone, certainly a stranger, you have less than a minute to size up the situation. How they look at you, the inflection in their voice when they talk to you, how they're standing, how they're dressed, the time of day, how you appear to them—all of these and more must be taken into account. And each case is unique. You just have to think on your feet and hope you handled it right. In my meeting with the trio described above, I paid no attention, didn't look directly at them, and just kept walking forward while they turned around, apparently satisfied that, given my appearance, demeanor, and the distance between me and them, I posed no threat.

Yet even for the savvy, danger lurks. You might walk an area 100 times and nothing will happen, but it might the 101st time.

And it could happen the very *first* time you walk it. In poverty-stricken areas, where opportunities are slim and serious problems are common, there's a greater chance that someone, especially a teenager, will act irrationally. Risk or fear of apprehension are not in the calculations made by such individuals.

Sometimes after walking through yet another poor section of the city, I felt that I was losing my normal sense of cautiousness. After walking thousands of blocks I was becoming habituated to my surroundings. Letting one's guard down like this can be dangerous. One Sunday afternoon I passed at least twenty clusters of youths in the South Bronx without giving it any thought. The problem is that each cluster is a new possible threat to one's safety and must be properly approached. Fortunately, my reality check worked in time.

Although I was never attacked or robbed while walking through the neighborhoods of New York, I did have some close calls. Perhaps I had more but was unaware of them. I was walking down a street in the early evening in Cypress Hills, Brooklyn, and saw striding toward me three large men in their twenties wearing dark clothes and low-slung shorts. It was too late to cross the street, and as they came nearer I couldn't help but notice that they were not leaving me any room on the sidewalk to pass. The darkening twilight sky, accompanied by large gray clouds, made the men look blurry and somehow more menacing. I reluctantly walked between numbers one and two, thereby invading their space, but saying hello as I did so. They did not respond. Rather, they had mean looks on their faces. But nothing happened, and my hello, however tepidly received, may have done it. It probably signaled to them that I meant no disrespect. But who knows?

One incident in particular has remained vivid in my memory. A friend of mine had asked me to take him to a "tough part" of the city. I was reluctant, not wanting to put him in danger, but he insisted and I finally agreed. We were near 182nd Street, in the Fordham section of the Bronx, and I was looking at one of the many wall murals that are so pervasive in the poorer areas of the city. The mural featured the image of "Big Junior," a dark-skinned Hispanic man who had died a few years back at the age of forty-seven.

From the way the mural looked, I got the impression that he might have been a gang leader. I read the poems and the names and appraised the artwork. My friend began making critical comments about the mural's quality, laughing as well.

"Be careful what you say," I admonished him."You never know who's watching."

"I don't see anyone," he responded. "Don't worry so much."

And then as we turned to leave, a burly young Hispanic man in a T-shirt and low-slung shorts approached us. By his rolling gait (sometimes called a "pimp walk") and the narrow set of his eyes, I sensed a challenge coming—and I was right.

"Yo, can I help you with something?" The words were neutral, but from the hard-edged tone the question was clearly "What are you looking at?" or "Why are you (whom I don't know) staring at this mural?" My response was deliberately nonchalant, designed to head off a confrontation.

"I was just admiring how beautiful the artwork was. How do they do that on such a big surface?" I said.

He then explained the technical details of how the mural was created, which was my goal. I had figured that once he began discussing it, his anger, whatever it was fueled by, would dissipate. And so it was. He calmed down.

"And who was Big Junior?" I asked when he finished.

"That was my father," he said, "and our family put up this up in his memory."

"Oh, I'm so sorry to see he passed away at such a young age," I replied. "What happened?"

"Oh, he had diabetes."

"Gee, that's really tough, but at least you found a really good way to remember him." And that was it. No conflict. No problem. But imagine if I had been laughing or smiling and he saw that.

Without belaboring the point, there's a stereotype of the average New Yorker as a person who can be cynical, hard, and distrustful. Moreover, he *must* act this way to protect himself from the sometimes unforgiving environment in which he functions. Some of the people I met were like that, but the overwhelming majority were friendly, engaging, open, and helpful. This was especially

noteworthy because they usually had no idea why I was even talking to them.

Overall there's a spirit of helpfulness in the city that is, by most
accounts, more prevalent than, say, thirty years ago, largely because of perceptions that the city is safer today than it used to be.
Personal observation confirms that. Leaving the Fifty-ninth Street
subway station in Manhattan, I spy an old man climbing the steps
slowly. A woman of about thirty-five or so, with a long ponytail
and wearing a red jacket, looks at him and asks, "Need help?"
"No," he says. What's striking is that *she's* dragging along a heavy
suitcase. A minute later a stranger helps *her* take the suitcase up
the steps and then walks off into the night, a silent act full of meaning in a city of millions. And it's infectious, I soon discover. Several
hours later I run across Third Avenue to help a woman secure a
cab. Was I influenced by what I saw earlier? I'm not sure, but it's
quite possible.[8]

I meet James Terry, a youngish-looking Parks Department employee at Harlem's Marcus Garvey Park, who originally hails from
Georgia, and ask if I can use the park's bathroom. "Sure," he says,
"but I'll have to take you in, because it's off-season." We enter a
subterranean area beneath the pool. It's dark and gloomy with
shiny brown and yellow bricks lining the walls. When his supervi-
sor walks by, James suddenly puts his arm around me and says
to the boss, "This is my cousin." He does this again with a broad
smile to someone else a minute later. Seeing the look of skepticism that greets this claim (James is black and I'm white), he adds,
"Adopted."

"Well, we're all brothers under the skin," I say, jokingly.

"Oh, you'd be amazed," James says. "When we have our annual
get-togethers in Thomson, Georgia, I meet all these white people
in the family—Italians, Scottish, you name it." James is a fount
of information about the community. He tells me there's a seven-
course, fifty-cent lunch available daily at the community center on
123rd Street and gives me tips about various local hangouts. The
park is safe, he asserts, "except for nighttime, when you get the
winos and the riffraff."

Yet there is an edge that residents have. It's a style of interaction that can be seen by outsiders as rude, rough, and "in your face." Natives take it in stride and usually give as good as they get. As I mentioned earlier, I've lived in other big cities, and you can't do that in most places without offending or confusing people. You make a sarcastic joke and they don't get it, largely because they have no experience with such humor.[9] The following conversation initiated by a black woman in Bedford-Stuyvesant, Brooklyn, probably in her thirties, illustrates the point. I'm walking my dog, and she says, "That's a nice-lookin' dog you got there."

"Thank you," I reply, "and she's friendly."

"Oh, you're trying to give her away?" she counters.

"Never, not a dog like this," I say with a smile.

"Naw, you wouldn't ever do that, would you?"

The banter continues in this vein for a few more minutes. In essence, this is a form of self-entertainment, New York–style.

Walking around the city is like being on stage. You can't opt out and just leave when people begin talking to you. To do so can be risky. I was speaking on my cell phone with someone as I walked down a street in Red Hook, Brooklyn, when I was accosted by a tall man wearing a black bandanna who began kidding around with me. I went along with it, and he laughed loudly and pronounced me to be "cool." He then asked, "Have you got any money you can spare?"

I responded with an incredulous look and said, "Are you kidding? Do I look rich?"

He laughed hysterically, bid me a good day, and took his leave. Ignoring him might well have provoked him.

Sometimes, though, the tack taken can be much cruder, usually when something's at stake. It's Good Friday and a young black man is trying to sell candy in Central Park, but there aren't many takers. A white man in his twenties wearing a Harvard sweatshirt strolls by and pays no attention to the younger man's refrain, "Wanna buy some candy, cheap?"

Angered with being ignored, the younger man yells, "Hey, I'm trying to get to Harvard too, dickhead. Buy some candy. Gimme a break."

Well, anything is possible in America, so perhaps the idea is not so far-fetched. People from poor areas sometimes do get into schools like Harvard. No one else reacts either.

I learned to expect the unexpected, or at least to be ready for it. You start out with an objective, you achieve it, but along the way something else happens. I was able to get a man I was meeting for the first time to show me his apartment in the projects. When I entered, I could immediately see that he loved the color red. Everything in the apartment was red—dishes, microwave, silverware, or, if you will, "red-ware," coat hangers, chairs, sofas, the very walls— all were in a bright red color.

"When did you fall in love with red?" I asked him.

"Ever since I was a child," he replied.

"Why?"

"I don't know, I just love the color." And he didn't appear at all embarrassed by it, treating it as a basic component of his persona.

Yet the way he had personalized his home was private until I walked in. Did he realize that to an outsider this color scheme might look weird? Perhaps he was proud of it. Maybe he wanted to see my reaction. What was the underlying meaning behind such a hobby? I can't say.

Thus, we see that when you are allowed access to someone's home turf, all sorts of things can emerge. And this is just another of the hundreds of examples I could give of why this was the most fascinating research project I've ever done.

And now we begin.

2

SELLING HOT DOGS, PLANTING FLOWERS,
AND LIVING THE DREAM
The Newcomers

Every day thousands of vehicles squeeze into the bottleneck on
124th Street between Third and Second Avenues that leads
onto the Robert F. Kennedy (formerly Triborough) Bridge. Traveling eastward the drivers of these vehicles are not likely to notice
the remarkable mural that covers six stories of a tenement building wall, for you must face west to see it. Called *Centro de La Paz*
(Center for Peace), the mural was sponsored by the Creative Arts
Workshop and painted by more than two hundred New Yorkers,
many of them poor neighborhood youngsters. (See figure 1.) Their
efforts were augmented by some one hundred artists from around
the world—Argentina, Ecuador, Nigeria, England, and elsewhere.
The names of the artists are duly inscribed on a two-story-high
scroll that is part of the mural.

Moses Chaszar, an administrator at Columbia Teachers College,
was fourteen years old back in 1995 when he volunteered for the
project.

> I grew up on 126th Street, and kids like me, we weren't always
> seeing the best things. So this mural represented our hopes and
> dreams. In it there's this one road through the whole earth, and all
> around it you have skyscrapers, igloos, pyramids, and the Grand

Canyon. And on the side you have Mount Rushmore. Only instead of American presidents, you have Indians. Many of the artists donated money as well as time. It took us two summers working on scaffolds, and we used special paint from Germany that's supposed to last for eighty years.

In a city with hundreds of murals, this one definitely stands out—in scope, design, beauty, and size. The many immigrant groups depicted and the themes of unity, diversity, and tolerance encompass the aspirations and hopes of the millions of immigrants who have come to New York City since its inception and who have shaped it into one of the greatest cities in the world.

Why is immigration such an important key to understanding New York today? Because more than three million newcomers have made their way here since the mid-1960s, largely in search of economic opportunities but also political freedom. In such numbers they have the power to truly change a city. Their very arrival is change. All new populations bring with them new ways of doing things, new ideas and perspectives, along with a variety of needs, hopes, and expectations that must be met by both government and the existing population. While immigration has slowed somewhat since the late 1990s, it is still growing. The size of these newcomers as a group also means they cannot be ignored. Describing New York City, one immigrant observed, "Everybody here is new at some point. That's what makes New York so great."[1]

Even aspects of the city that seem somewhat peripheral to the immigrants are not. Take gentrification, for instance. When areas are renewed or rebuilt, the somewhat wealthier people moving into these areas must have certain services available to them. The deliverymen on bicycles are often immigrants, both documented and undocumented, as are the laborers who tend the new residents' gardens, clean their buildings and apartments, and take care of their children. In the process the immigrants observe and learn from the gentrifiers what being a New Yorker can mean to its residents. In some cases the children of the newcomers may even attend the same schools as those of more successful longtime inhabitants. In this town, where the same block can have an inexpensive walk-up and a renovated brownstone, people share space with unlikely and often unequal neighbors and meet in venues ranging from schools and playgrounds to houses of worship and local shops. We do not know much about these interactions, but we should, because they are an integral part of how change occurs.

The immigrants have played a major role in the rebirth of the city. Their energy, drive, and ambition have significantly contributed to a belief that this city has risen from the dark days of near-bankruptcy, drug wars, rampant crime, and an inability to deliver basic services that characterized it in the mid-1970s. And this belief has been borne out by reality. However, the immigrants are not the only factor in New York's resurgence. The thousands of young and highly educated people who have streamed into Gotham in unprecedented numbers from elsewhere in the United States are an equally important part of the story. The willingness of the private sector to invest in the city, a dynamic government, and better protection for its citizens have all played an enormous and equally important role in New York's revival.

To walk the streets of this city and speak with its immigrants is to realize that these people, who have often struggled mightily just to get here, are generally hardworking, optimistic, and grateful for the opportunities that this city and the country in general represent. Moreover, their spirit and can-do mentality often carry over into the lives of their children, who, notwithstanding the usual angst and strain of generational differences, are forging ahead and achieving success in ways their parents cannot. The response by longtime residents to their presence is mostly favorable. The older children of immigrants are overwhelmingly seen as industrious and ambitious. Some people do gripe about their clannishness, different values, and seemingly strange customs. The reality is that when distinct and large ethnic and racial groups arrive, speaking a foreign language, fears of displacement, even engulfment, are quite common.

The conversations I had with the city's immigrants made it clear to me that the transition from their previous lives is complex. They look to the future but release their hold on the past with reluctance, because it is, and always will be, an essential part of their lives. The bifurcation is clearly brought home to me one day as I walk a street in Jamaica, Queens, and spy a man on a quiet block. He has created a beautiful garden along the grassy strip that runs next to the gutter. It's a small area, about four feet long and three feet wide, surrounded by a miniature white picket fence.

"These flowers are beautiful," I say by way of starting a conversation.

Small and wiry, with bright white teeth framed in part by a neat mustache, he responds with a soft smile, "They are flowers from my country, Guyana, which I love. I planted them to remind me of home. This way, when I look outside I always remember the beautiful place I lived in before I came here."

There's no way to know how many of the city's immigrants have used their gardens for similar purposes, but it's unlikely he's the only one. "Amazing," I think. We talk about remittances, transnationalism, visits to the homeland, and credit associations as markers of common identity. They are, but it's also important to see how a person's identity manifests itself in small yet deeply emotional and even personal displays. In this vignette it is apparent that home is never far from the thoughts of the immigrants. And is this any different from people like earlier generations of Italians who planted fig trees in their gardens that went under wraps every winter?

In this chapter we examine some important aspects of the immigration and adaptation of the newcomers to New York City. First we look at who comes here, where they have settled, and how they have changed the makeup of many neighborhoods. Included among the immigrant population are many undocumented residents who pose special challenges for the city, and these are the subject of a separate discussion.

We then move on to the kinds of work done by the immigrants, many of whom possess incredible drive and ambition. The reasons why they work so hard are also evaluated. This is followed by an examination of the larger struggle to adapt to life in this country while also trying to preserve their identity, and the challenge of what values and lessons to transmit to their children.

There are differences, some subtle, others distinct, *among* members of the same group. These differences and a discussion of how the immigrants interact with other groups are analyzed, concluding with a look at the possibilities of some groups forming coalitions.

Who Comes Here?

New York City has more legal immigrants and children of immigrants than any other city in the world, with almost seven hundred thousand new immigrants arriving in the last decade alone.[2] Together they make up a majority of the 8.3 million people living in the city, with most of them coming from the Dominican Republic, China, Jamaica, Mexico, Guyana, Ecuador, Haiti, Trinidad and Tobago, Colombia, Russia, India, and Korea, along with those from Puerto Rico, who have a unique status as citizens, plus an estimated half-million-plus undocumented residents. Of course, New York was always a city of immigrants, but the composition was different, with Italians, Jews, Irish, Germans, Poles, Russians, and other European nationalities predominating in earlier days.

Dominicans (12 percent of the total) are the largest foreign-born group, followed by Chinese (11 percent), Jamaicans (6 percent), and Mexicans (6 percent). Puerto Ricans are still the largest Hispanic group in the city, numbering some eight hundred thousand. Overall the Mexican population is increasing the fastest. Generally, among those who are here legally, Mexican females outnumber males, while it appears that more undocumented males than females are living here.

The diversity of the immigrants is truly amazing. They come from virtually every corner of the globe, including Nepal, Malaysia, Yemen, Egypt, the Philippines, Portugal, Ireland, Australia, and Burkina Faso, and they speak more than 170 languages. Dividing these people by, say, religion is not always revealing, because their country of origin frequently trumps their religion in terms of relevance. For example, Muslims from Arab countries like Syria, Egypt, and Iraq have little in common culturally with their coreligionists from Kyrgyzstan, Kazakhstan, Pakistan, Afghanistan, or

Turkey. In fact, very little is known in general about the immigration experiences of people from these countries.[3]

Grouping the immigrants solely by income is similarly of little help either. There are wealthy Persians, Indians, Western Europeans, West Indians, and Latin Americans. But except for individual cases, money is not the main criterion by which members of these groups select their friends. Even within countries there are sharp divisions. Guyanese originally from Africa have a strained relationship with people whose origins are from India. The former reside mostly in Brooklyn and the latter in Queens. Russian Jews from the southern republics of Uzbekistan and Tadzhikistan have little in common with Russian Jews from Ukraine and other European republics.

Where Do the Newcomers Live?

The greatest concentration of immigrants is in Queens and Brooklyn, followed by the Bronx, Manhattan, and Staten Island. Elmhurst, Queens, is the most diverse neighborhood, with representatives from almost 120 lands. But Queens also has some of the most homogeneous communities, like mostly Irish-Catholic Breezy Point and Broad Channel, both in Queens, or the black communities of Cambria Heights and Rosedale. To get a better idea of where the newcomers actually reside, let's look at a sampling of some of these areas.

Pakistanis and Bangladeshis are in Flatbush, Brooklyn, and in Flushing and Bellerose, Queens, where South Indians also live. Baychester, in the Bronx, is first in Jamaican immigrants, and the contiguous areas of Crown Heights, East Flatbush, Flatlands, and Canarsie in Brooklyn have major concentrations of West Indians. Sunset Park and Bensonhurst, both in Brooklyn, are home to a very large representation of Chinese newcomers, while Flushing has both Chinese and Koreans in significant numbers. Forest Hills and Jamaica Estates, both in Queens, have substantial numbers of Bukharian Jews and Jews in general, as do the Queens communities of Hillcrest, Fresh Meadows, Kew Gardens Hills, and the eastern part of Far Rockaway. In Brooklyn there are big Orthodox Jewish communities, many of them Hasidic, in Borough Park, Crown Heights, Williamsburg, and Flatbush. Russian Jews have long been in Brighton Beach, Brooklyn, but in recent years they have moved to Mill Basin, Bensonhurst, Borough Park, all in Brooklyn, and to southern Staten Island, near the beach. Filipino immigrants are most numerous in Forest Hills, with 44 percent of them calling that area home. The Irish, whose immigration has ebbed and flowed according to economic conditions, live primarily in the Woodlawn section of the Bronx (and adjacent South Yonkers) and to a far lesser extent Maspeth, Woodside, and Sunnyside, Queens. Their knowledge of English and the fact that New York has a large Irish population has always made the city a popular destination for Irish newcomers.

Hispanics, a very large group in general, live in every borough, but their largest concentration is in the Bronx. In an example of why "the devil is in the details," as they say, 93 percent of Morrisania's population is U.S.-born. Why is that? Because Hispanics, primarily Puerto Ricans, have been living there and in other sections of the Bronx for decades. Mexicans live predominantly in East Harlem, Sunset Park, Corona, and the Mott Haven section of the Bronx. An interesting statistic charts their progress. In 1985 New York City had one tortilla store; by 2001 Mexicans owned six tortilla factories, with a combined weekly output of *one million tortillas,* all produced in the "Tortilla Triangle," a small slice of Brooklyn between Bushwick and Williamsburg. Brownsville and East New York, Brooklyn, and the Arverne, Edgemere, Cambria Heights, Queens Village, Laurelton, and Jamaica sections of Queens are almost completely black, with a mix of native and foreign-born inhabitants. And the West Bronx has become a magnet for West African immigrants.[4]

Regardless of its well-deserved reputation for tolerance, New York is still one of the most segregated cities in the nation. One of the negative consequences of residential concentration for the various groups is that it has an isolating effect. Entire neighborhoods, like portions of Corona, most of Bushwick, and sections of the Bronx, are so monolithically Hispanic that they are essentially closed to non-Hispanic speakers. Most of these residents don't speak English, and the signs in stores and on billboards are in Spanish. Although New York is becoming an international city, it is also one where only group members can communicate in certain parts of it. This is true of West African neighborhoods in the Bronx, and for the Chinese, in Flushing, Queens, and Sunset Park. This language barrier slows down the adaptation of the incoming group even as it gives them a comfort level and sense of security. In short, it's a mixed blessing.

Population Changes

The speed and sheer numbers of the immigration patterns have created an ever shifting geographical map where change has become the norm. There are still some neighborhoods that haven't changed much, but they are increasingly unusual. Non-Hispanic whites, mostly gentrifiers and students, are beginning to replace Dominicans in Washington Heights, Manhattan, which has now been dubbed Hudson Heights by enterprising real estate agents seeking to profit from image makeovers. Inwood to the north and lower Washington Heights (between 168th and 135th Streets) are beginning to follow suit, with many students and less-moneyed whites moving there. In Queens more and more Indians are choosing to live in Briarwood and Richmond Hill, and greater numbers of Chinese are buying and renting homes in the formerly Indian sections of Flushing and Queensboro Hill. The Chinese are rapidly becoming more concentrated in Sunset Park, Bensonhurst, and Fresh Meadows. Their numbers are shrinking in Lower Manhattan and in Jackson Heights and Woodside as Indians and Bangladeshis replace the Chinese in these Queens communities.

The Korean move eastward from Flushing is truly breathtaking as they buy businesses along Northern Boulevard in a 120-block area stretching from Main Street all the way to about 255th Street by the Nassau County border. This was once an overwhelmingly Italian, Irish, and Jewish area. Take a drive up Northern and you can see hundreds of stores—nail salons, gas stations, restaurants, automobile dealerships, bookstores, and so on—most with Korean lettering (and some with Chinese writing) alongside (at least most of the time) English signage. And as you leave Little Neck and enter Nassau County, there's a giant version of the Korean-owned H Mart grocery chain. Is Nassau the next destination for the most upwardly mobile Koreans (and Chinese)? Yes, and it's already happening.

The past three decades have witnessed many shifts in where immigrants have come from and in what numbers. One of the most profound changes has been among the Asians. Today, for the first time, the city's Asian population exceeds one million, nearly one out of eight New Yorkers, larger than the Asian populations of Los Angeles and San Francisco combined. This is a 32 percent increase from 2000 and four times the Hispanic increase in the same period. By contrast, non-Hispanic whites lost 3 percent and blacks 5 percent during the same period. Those of Chinese origin, the first arrivals here, make up half the total. And, of course, South Asians are different from East Asians, and Filipinos are different from both. Some argue that their diverse origins have given the Asians less influence. For instance, in the political sphere only one Asian American, John Liu, has risen to a city government position; Liu is the city comptroller. There are only two Asian council members and only one state legislator. A smaller number of Asian Americans in the voting-age population, relative to others, may be part of this problem. Still, for a group this large, that's peanuts.Other inequities exist for Asian Americans as well. Despite their being 13 percent of the population, they have snared a mere 1.4 percent of the city council's discretionary funds. The fact that they are mistakenly seen as an overwhelmingly highly educated group masks the fact that many Asian Americans do not conform to this stereotype, with an income considerably below the city's average, not to mention deficient English skills.[5] Yet a portent of the future may have emerged with the 2012 election of Chinese American Grace Meng of Queens to the U.S. House of Representatives.

As to the native whites whom the new ethnics presumably replaced, that too has a rather surprising twist. Owing in part to gentrification, economic changes, and the general revival of the city, native whites are actually a slight majority in Manhattan. And they are increasing in certain gentrifying neighborhoods like Astoria, Queens, and in Bedford-Stuyvesant and Fort Greene, Brooklyn. Native whites have, nonetheless, significantly declined in other parts of New York, such as Bensonhurst and Marine Park in Brooklyn and, in northeastern Queens—Bayside, Beechhurst, Whitestone, Murray Hill, Douglaston, and Little Neck. This is due, in great measure, to large influxes of Asians into these areas.

Yet even within areas that experience ethnic succession, certain pockets hold up. In Ozone Park, Queens, between Rockaway Parkway on the north and the Belt Parkway on the south, and between Woodhaven Boulevard on the west and Aqueduct Racetrack on the east, there are some sections that, while mixed in with certain blocks including minorities, still have substantial numbers of white ethnics, largely Italian, I suspect. You know it from the proliferation of American flags, plastic-wrapped fig trees in the winter, and statues of the Virgin Mary in the front yards, and from talking to the residents themselves. In part the Italians have held out because of the boundaries that the roads clearly demarcate. But it's also due to the fact that, by their nature, Italians won't let others push them out of a neighborhood without putting up a fierce battle. How fierce may depend on their age and whether their children still live with them. There are even a few Jews living in Ozone Park, but their presence is mostly within mixed marriages, which you can see when Christmas decorations include a small menorah for Hanukah. Such resistance also lingers in sections of the North Bronx and South Brooklyn.

The houses in Ozone Park are mostly Dutch colonials. The neighborhood's Ozone Park Jewish Center seems to be run mostly by people from nearby Howard Beach, a primarily Italian neighborhood that also has a small Jewish population. Occasionally one does see evidence of a minority family in Ozone Park. West of Woodhaven the area becomes mostly Hispanic. Brooklyn isn't far beyond and may contribute to that, because the areas bordering this part of Queens have large concentrations of blacks and Hispanics. East of Woodhaven the Queens continuation of Brooklyn's still somewhat notorious Pitkin Avenue is a quiet, peaceful, almost bucolic place.

Besides shifts in lands of origin, there have also been changes *within* some of the groups in terms of class origins and the regions from which they originate. The earlier Indian community, whose members came in the '60s and '70s, was wealthier and more educated, settling mostly in Manhattan. Many eventually moved to the suburbs. Those who came in the '80s and '90s were more similar to typical third-world immigrants and generally moved into Queens. Moreover, while Indians have settled all over the United States, they see New York City as different, cosmopolitan, and therefore more like their homeland. One reason why Queens has traditionally been so attractive to Indians is the many apartment buildings with reasonable rents and close access to Manhattan, where many of them work, not to mention access to La Guardia and John F. Kennedy airports.[6]

Similarly, these days Chinese immigrants are often Mandarin speakers who do not comprehend the Cantonese dialect that predominated among earlier arrivals. And once more Chinese began coming here from mainland China, especially Fujian Province, new groups became part of the immigrant mix. This has consequences not only for the community itself but also for those who service its members and need to better understand it. In one case—which would be comical were its implications not so serious—an occupational therapist at a well-known hospital mistakenly assumed that a stroke patient was deteriorating rapidly because he could not follow basic commands. As it turned out, the therapist was translating her words into Cantonese, when the patient's native language was Mandarin!

The Jewish population of New York has also been undergoing transformations. In the 1950s the city had about two million Jews. The results of the most recent study, conducted in 2010 by the United Jewish Appeal-Federation (UJA-Federation), were reported in a June 12, 2012, article by Joseph Berger that appeared in the *New York Times*. The study found that the number of Jews in New York had decreased substantially, to 1.1 million. But there were profound shifts in their makeup. According to the study, the number of stereotypically liberal, highly educated Jews is declining, while the Orthodox are growing very quickly. About 40 percent of the city's Jewish population identify as such, compared with 33 percent a decade ago. This figure is likely to go much higher in the future, as 74 percent of all Jewish children in New York are Orthodox.

Two other important Jewish groups are Russian Jews, numbering about 185,000 in all, and Israelis, with about 29,000 living in the five counties within New York City and in Nassau, Suffolk, and Westchester Counties. According to the UJA-Federation report, most Russian and Israeli Jews reside in Brooklyn. Much of the population there is older than the Jewish community as a whole. The Russians came to the city mostly in two waves—one in the late 1970s, and the second in the early 1990s. Their levels of education and employment patterns generally resemble those of other Jews, and they are far more likely to identify ethnically as Jews and Russians than religiously.

Manhattan's Upper West Side, whose Jewish population had declined by the late 1960s, reemerged in the 1980s and 1990s as a Jewish area for younger people and remains so today, rivaling the Upper East Side's long established Jewish community. Parallel to these developments, Harlem, which is now perhaps one-third white, depending on how one defines the boundaries, includes among its new inhabitants many Jewish yuppies, artists, students, and homesteaders. Emblematic of its changing status, the Lubavitcher Hasidic Movement, which focuses on outreach to unaffiliated Jews, now has a Chabad house, or center there—two, actually, if you include the one at City College of New York. This is only one more indication of how the city is ever changing. Given the fact that Harlem was home to more than 150,000 Jews in the early twentieth century, it also shows how certain migratory patterns repeat themselves over time, though for different reasons. Back then people moved to Harlem because of a desire to leave the slums of the Lower East Side, and today it's because apartments there are cheaper than in other parts of Manhattan.

Discussing his classic work about New York City's ethnic and racial groups, *Beyond the Melting Pot,* that he and Daniel Patrick Moynihan, penned more than four decades ago, Nathan Glazer admits that he could not have foreseen the tremendous increase in immigration.[7] This is an important observation because one of the consequences of this influx was to significantly reduce the opportunities for many of the Puerto Ricans and African Americans who were already in New York City when the immigrants arrived and who were mired in poverty. Many of the new groups came with the social and economic capital needed to take advantage of the opportunities in a political, economic, and social climate that was changing for the better. They had networks within their own group, they had financial resources, and they had not experienced the discrimination and prejudice that had sapped the energy and hopes of the Puerto Ricans and African Americans. Understandably, the latter groups greeted the new arrivals with mixed feelings at best.[8]

Many of the immigrants who have entered this country over the past thirty-five years, especially from Asia but also from the West Indies, are educated and have skills that have enabled them to move quickly up the ladder. And even those like the Dominicans, Yemenis, and Ecuadorians, who are not well educated, have entrepreneurial abilities and a willingness to work hard, accompanied by a belief in the American dream that can carry them through the most difficult times.

The Undocumented and Their Impact

And then there are the undocumented immigrants, as those who are in this country illegally are known.[9] There are an estimated six hundred thousand undocumented people residing in New York City, but even that figure is a guesstimate, because it isn't in the interests of the undocumented to let people know they're here or where they are living. Most of them are people who overstayed their visas. Those who came here illegally in recent years are most likely to be Mexicans or Chinese. Walk into almost any restaurant in New York City and yell "Immigration!" and you will discover they are there as they race out the back door.

And if you're out for a late-night stroll on a quiet street in Queens or Brooklyn, they may ride past you on a creaky, rust-flecked bike with no light, one you would never buy for your kids. They are on their way to work or home and are likely to have ridden five or ten miles to get there. You can see them clustered on busy streets in the city, hanging out in front of a 24/7 bodega, clad in ill-fitting sweaters or sweatshirts that say Budweiser, Tommy Hilfiger, or Harvard. They chat and laugh among themselves, but always there is this uncertainty, almost a furtiveness about them, that you can see in their eyes and in how they stand. They can never be completely comfortable in this land, not until and unless they receive the green card seal of approval.

Anyone who lives in heavily immigrant-populated areas of the city can tell you stories about apartments or homes that house twenty to thirty residents where only six can live comfortably. They've seen the door down their hall open quickly to let someone in, and perhaps they caught a glimpse of a converted living room with five bunk beds, where all rules of safety and health are violated, where people even occupy beds in shifts according to the hours they work. There are streets in neighborhoods like Corona or Sunset Park where an entire block is made up of the undocumented, though you won't notice it if you're just driving through.

But the fact that they're hard to find does not mean they have no impact on the city's life. They do and in many ways. First, undocumented immigrants work at so many jobs that others don't want—dishwashers, unskilled factory and construction laborers, waiters, maids, cab drivers, car wash employees, to name a few. If they didn't do these jobs, who would do them? And what would be the cost and benefits to both employers and employees? When an undocumented housekeeper takes care of a family, for example, it frees the woman of the house to go to a Wednesday matinee or a museum. Every penny that she spends—tickets, train fare, lunch, taxis, and so on—sustains the city's economy. If such help were not available, there would surely be people who wouldn't have a housekeeper, at least not a live-in one. And if they had to pay more, they might not have the money to spend on entertainment or expensive clothes. This is just one of many examples, but the point is obvious. Mayor Michael Bloomberg declared in a 2006 Senate hearing that the city's economy "would collapse if they were deported." They are also involved in illegal activities—prostitution, black marketeering, gambling, and drugs—often just to survive.

The undocumented, especially in large numbers, have a profound effect on the economic sector, whether it's construction, maintenance, light manufacturing, immigration lawyers, the service economy, or many other areas. U.S. citizens who want to legalize the undocumented are well aware that to do so would drive up costs in many industries. But they also feel it's the right thing to do, that it will offer both protection and a future to them. This is true because their circumstances mean they don't go to doctors unless they're desperate, they don't report crimes committed against them, they avoid using bank accounts, they can't legally obtain a driver's license, and they are largely uninvolved in American communal life.

Without a solution to their dilemma, the undocumented will continue to resort to extralegal methods to gain legal rights, some of which actually work. One Central Asian college student explained it to me like this: "If I'm a full-time student, I can get a license. And to become a full-time student I don't have to prove I'm here legally."

"But what about those who aren't students?" I said.

"In my community everyone knows you have to pay a lawyer if you want to get political asylum."

"What kind of asylum?" I asked. "Nobody's fleeing from a war in Kyrgyzstan."

"Well," she answered, "you can say you're being persecuted because you're a Christian, or because you're a lesbian."

The system has many hurdles to overcome that encourage fraud by immigrants desperate to achieve permanent residency status. The annual green card lotteries, which began in 1990, have millions of applicants, with about fifty-five thousand winners each year. And although the government has not deported most of the immigrants who are already living here illegally, they are often terrified that deportation could happen to them. After all, even under the pro-immigration administration of Barack Obama, the number of those currently deported has been about four hundred thousand annually, although this may change in Obama's second term.

Another consequence of their illegal status is the fact that the undocumented use public services like hospitals and schools. Further complicating matters is the fact that all of their U.S.-born children are legal, which is, of course, one of the main reasons the undocumented risk so much to get here—to give their children American citizenship. Nationwide, an estimated 2.3 million families, about three-fourths of those here illegally, have at least one child who is born in the United States, thus making the families eligible for food stamps and other benefits. These children attend school, though not always regularly, and live in a sort of twilight zone where their parents cannot always help them if they have problems and where they must be careful that their parents' status as undocumented is not discovered. They are perhaps 11 percent of the total student population in New York City and cost at least $1 billion a year to educate. When these children become adults, they will have children of their own to support. What will happen as their own parents grow older and need more care but lack the social security, pensions, and other benefits that seniors in the U.S. typically have?

Undocumented immigrants are often treated as if they were a separate entity, but that is not really the case. Untold numbers of them have relatives who are in the United States legally. They may well live with those relatives. And while legal immigrants may sympathize with those who are undocumented, what about those who are here legally and are not related to the undocumented, who don't know them personally? Do some of them feel resentment because they believe the undocumented are taking jobs away from them? The undocumented who have no family here have an even more difficult time. They sometimes form affinity groups along the lines of living or working together. These people become "family" to each other.

On the whole, I found great sympathy for the plight of the undocumented among people from every walk of life and irrespective of whether they lived in neighborhoods where illegals resided or in other communities. District managers of community boards were basically of one mind, best expressed by a Hispanic manager in the Bronx: "I have no problem with them, because they're willing to work. Shame on employers for not paying them a decent wage. They're not working for themselves; they're working for their children. This country's been founded on illegal activity. End of story." A Jewish Queens community district manager said, "Why not legitimize people who are here? They're working hard. They're not committing crimes." Indeed there is little evidence of their engaging in criminal activity. If detected, such activities can result in deportation, which is the last thing the undocumented want.

At the same time, there are people who contend that the undocumented take away jobs from citizens and don't pay taxes. When I asked former mayor Ed Koch about the issue in a July 2012 interview, he responded with this:

> I am someone who believes that there should not be a broad amnesty. I am for immigration and believe it's very helpful to the country, and it's what has made New York City great. But I am not for illegality. I believe we should have compassion, and I support what the president did in saying we're not going to deport youngsters under the age of sixteen who came here. But as far as the eleven or twelve million illegal immigrants here, I think they have to go home with exceptions for compassion. There is no country in the world more generous than us with respect to immigration. We take in a million immigrants every year—750,000 regular immigrants [and] 250,000 seeking political asylum. I am for putting people who hire them illegally in jail. If you deprive them of jobs, they will go home. In fact, during the recent recession many went home. But as mayor I issued three executive orders, saying, "Don't hesitate to send your children to school. Don't hesitate if you are in need of treatment to go to a hospital. And don't hesitate to tell a cop if you've been subject to a criminal attack, because unless you've committed another crime, the mere fact that you're here illegally will not cause our police officers to turn you over to the immigration authorities." I was criticized for that, but I still believe it to be the compassionate way, and every mayor after me issued those same orders.

Koch's words highlight the guilt and ambivalence many feel about people who are in the United States without proper documentation. The undocumented and those who employ them are violating the law regardless of whether their presence helps or hinders the economy. On the other hand, people want to be compassionate to other human beings and cannot accept a denial of basic rights such as medical care and safety once they are here.

Making a Living in New York

Immigrants to New York City face an economic world of limited options. Manufacturing has declined for decades, and high-tech positions in a service economy often require skills that these newcomers lack. What's left are mostly jobs that reward hard work and long hours, including a good number that don't require much spoken English, that make it possible for entire families to be gainfully employed.[10]

According to the Bodega Association of the United States, New York City has twenty-five thousand bodegas, or delis, and counting. Their annual sales come to $7 billion a year, and they employ some sixty-five thousand people. While we often think of Hispanics and Koreans running these businesses, the newest group to do so is the Yemenis. They are highly adaptable, speaking enough Spanish in Hispanic neighborhoods to get by. They keep a low profile ethnically, being sensitive to how Muslims may be viewed in the post-9/11 era. As a rule, you can't tell that Yemenis operate the bodega unless you ask. An exception is an East Harlem establishment near First Avenue and 108th Street, where a big sign over the store reads, "Yemen King Grocery."

In general, certain ethnic groups dominate certain economic niches. Examples abound—Israelis in the car wash business; Indian, Pakistani, and Bangladeshi gas stations; Asian nail salons. Often these ethnic niches can be traced to individuals who entered the field and opened a path for their fellow ethnics. Other reasons include resources and skills possessed by group members, economic opportunities, labor shortages, timing of arrival, and their own preferences for various occupations. Sometimes their businesses reflect a style that is unique to their culture. For example, while

American-run beauty salons and nail salons emphasize friendliness and attentiveness to customers, Korean nail salons stress respect, competence, and efficiency.[11] This may also be a matter of necessary adaptation by the Koreans, since the language barrier doesn't allow as much for the touchy-feely relationships favored by the Americans.

Ethnic dominance in various occupations breeds the usual resentments by others who feel excluded, of whom the conflicts between Koreans and African Americans are perhaps the best known.[12] On more than one occasion I heard charges of clannishness from other immigrants. Sometimes it's not limited to a niche but can be a broader field that's open to all, but where group favoritism is perceived. What's interesting is that those who complain about this wax euphoric when it happens to benefit them. For example, I spoke with a Polish contractor in Brooklyn who expressed great bitterness about the Chinese immigrants in Brooklyn. He has lived in New York for twenty years, having immigrated from Bialystok, Poland. "When the Chinese do business, they only help their own," he said. "Nobody else can do business with these companies. They only use Chinese suppliers, Chinese builders, and Chinese workers. On the surface they are friendly, but they won't help you."

Then again, there is the Polish & Slavic Federal Credit Union, which blatantly appeals to people's ethnic backgrounds and loyalties. The bank supports Polish churches, Polish-language schools, and has branches in Glendale and Maspeth, Queens; Greenpoint, Brooklyn; and various Long Island and New Jersey communities, all of which have large Polish populations. This is called making a business out of ethnicity. "But what's wrong with doing that?" say supporters. Customers like it because it gives them a certain comfort level. They can communicate in their native language, and they feel a level of trust dealing with fellow Poles and Slavs. Even the Polish contractor I spoke with finds nothing wrong with it, ignoring the implied contradiction of his earlier comments.

Similarly, the enclosed African Market on 116th Street in Harlem is a significant commercial center for Africans. There are clothing stores, barber shops, electronic stores, and restaurants. And in the surrounding area there are other enterprises like Mohammed's Environmental Cleaners. Located between Fifth and Sixth Avenues, the African Market provides space for many artists and vendors selling African garb, jewelry, paintings, pocketbooks, and the like. Despite strong resistance, this group of merchants was moved from the far more widely visited 125th Street to its present location in Harlem. Were they catering only to tourists, they'd be finished. But having the market here means it's also in the main area where Africans meet and shop, so Africans can both patronize their own shops and develop a social community, with restaurants that serve as places for exchanging news and allow them a chance to watch TV shows beamed from their homelands. An African museum is also being planned on 109th and Fifth Avenue, on the first floor of a luxury condominium building.

Regardless of its benefits, such protectionism does limit the opportunities for less fortunate groups like poor African Americans and Puerto Ricans and the undocumented. For these groups, collecting bottles or working as an "automobile chaser" or "hustler" is often a decent alternative. Some of them try to steer drivers whose car windows are broken or whose taillights don't function to local repair shops. If they are Hispanic, possibly they'll have an edge with Spanish-speaking drivers. They will usually get $10.00 a car for their efforts, and in a good week they can earn $350.00. Where do they work? Where the shops are, around Citi Field in Queens, perhaps, or Hunts Point in the Bronx.[13]

In their struggles to find work the new immigrants sometimes end up in unlikely professions. Early one morning, around 7:00 AM, I greet a man fixing his pedicab in a garage for them on Fifty-seventh Street, close to the Hudson River. He hails from Honduras and is a pioneer of sorts, as pedicabs didn't exist until a few years ago. It's actually the bicycle version of the rickshaw. A permit costs twenty-six hundred dollars. The ride costs one dollar a block. Horse-drawn wagons are more lucrative, it turns out. On Houston Street I see a man, a Palestinian from Beit Iksa, near Jerusalem, who has lived in New York for over thirty years. He does sidewalk art, commercially, often as advertisements to announce events. He's painting the sidewalk in pastels. He's done hundreds and they typically last for a year. He has a website and he paints in many locations. "No one objects," he asserts. "And if they do, by then the message is out."

If you're an immigrant or thrifty visitor to the Big Apple, you might want to check out the enthusiastically named American Dream Hostel, a bed-and-breakfast place at 168 East Twenty-fourth Street. It's really a modest, converted four-story tenement building owned by a Peruvian immigrant who, in this offbeat way, achieved his own dream. It's dedicated "to the youth and teachers from overseas," according to a flyer in the lobby area. Actually, one of the reasons he chose the name, according to the clerk, is "because alphabetically it's one of the first names that comes up when you look for places to stay at." The rooms go for $119 a day, fairly cheap, and are single occupancy with a shared bathroom. Twenty years ago it was an SRO (single-room occupancy) lodging place for poor men in the city. Today, however, with so many homeless shelters, that approach is no longer popular, and there's other money to be made in the revitalized New York of 2013. In choosing this line of work, this Peruvian man joins thousands of immigrants in New York and throughout the United States who manage or own small hotels or motels.

Most immigrants to the city own or work in small businesses like grocery stores and cheap restaurants, where they often face daunting challenges as they try to make a go of it. Ben Howe describes the travails of surviving in the face of bureaucratic rules, many of which seem petty or, worse yet, make no sense at all.

This spring we've been visited by undercover NYPD officers trying to catch us selling liquor on Sundays before noon (11:57 AM, to be precise); Consumer Affairs personnel trying to catch us selling cigarettes and lottery tickets to minors; Consumer Affairs, again, seeing if we pad our scales or use a cat to catch mice; even the Drug Enforcement Agency, looking for contraband sales of cold medicine. . . . Okay, some of these are legitimate, but the enforcement seems to be a bit overzealous at times. And what about the following listed violations? "having spoons positioned incorrectly in the potato salad (for some reason they're supposed to be face down)."[14]

Why Do Immigrants Work So Hard?

Many Americans take it almost for granted that a prime criterion for a job should be something that makes them happy. Immigrants cannot afford such luxuries. They must think first in terms of economic survival. I speak with Patrick, a Ghanaian immigrant, who is a guard in a Bible museum.

"How do you deal with this job? Aren't you bored standing here all day?" I ask.

"Well," he answers, "I look at the paintings of Jesus and I meditate about life."

"But still," I insist, "it must be boring. You can't meditate all day unless you're a saint or a yogi."

"Well, yes, that's true," Patrick agrees reluctantly, "but I have to make a living. But do you know of another job I could get?"

I suddenly feel guilty. Maybe I'm sowing seeds of unhappiness in him that he was only dimly aware of before. "How long have you been doing this?" I say.

"About ten years."

"What would you like to do?"

"Fraud investigations," he answers without hesitation, fishing out a card from his pants pocket to prove his bona fides. It reads, "Fraud Investigator," and is for a company named Black Star Shipping. He knows that this was the name of one of Marcus Garvey's companies. He also has accounting experience.

"What's the most interesting experience you've had since coming here ten years ago?" I ask.

"Well, one time some Greeks came in here. They had an exhibit of the Greek Orthodox Church and they wanted to light candles. And I told them, 'You can't light candles here. This is a museum.'"

I suggested that the museum could have lit electric candles, an idea he found amusing. Patrick is a nice man. His example of the most interesting experience in ten years only confirms that many jobs, and lives, can be very uninteresting indeed.

Walking on a Bushwick street one bright sunny day, I pass a young Hispanic man wearing a T-shirt on which is emblazoned the slogan, "Every Damn Day—Just Do It." It exemplifies the struggle of life, one applying even more to the immigrants, perhaps—you gotta get up every day and just keep going. For them that's what life is all about.

Koreans are often associated with this stereotype of just plugging away until you make it. Nor are they likely to deny it. Listen again to Ben Howe's description of it in his funny and highly informative book, *My Korean Deli*: "the people who took over the deli industry from the Greeks and the Italians, the people who drove the Chinese out of the dry-cleaning trade, the people who took away nail polishing from African-Americans, and the people who made it impossible for underachievers like me [the author is a WASP married to a Korean American] to get into the same colleges our parents had attended."[15] A Korean American grocery store owner explained his twenty-eight-year record of economic success: "There is a supermarket two blocks from my produce store. But I have been able to successfully compete. Why? Because I go to Hunts Point Market four times a week and choose fresh produce items I like. But since the supermarket gets produce items delivered by trucks, it has little choice of items. My store can also compete with the supermarket in prices of items because each day I select produce items on special sales at Hunts Point Market."[16] So there you have it. The little guy bests the big guy because he's willing to work harder.

The Chinese can also match the Koreans in ambitiousness. Is there a shopping center anywhere in America without a small Chinese takeout establishment? On Eighteenth Avenue near Seventy-third Street in Bensonhurst, I come across the Brooklyn Center for the Musical Arts, featuring in its front window a large TV screen showing a young Chinese girl of perhaps seven or eight, dressed in a white blouse and a navy jumper. The girl is sitting on a stage, playing a baby grand piano. The repetition of this two-minute scene, looped to play over and over, effectively conveys the school's idea that practice makes perfect and that one must be totally dedicated if one wishes to succeed. I cannot hear the music on the street, but I know it must be great. In any event it's a wonderful way to sell the school, one of hundreds that, along with test preparation and tutoring centers, have sprouted as storefront operations in Asian neighborhoods throughout the city.

Parked on the corner of Fifty-fourth Street and Eleventh Avenue in Manhattan's Hell's Kitchen area is one of the city's ubiquitous Sabrett hot dog stands. The smell from the frankfurters floating in boiled water is at once familiar and pungent—just about every New Yorker knows it. I strike up a conversation with the hot dog vendor, an olive-skinned, dour-faced man named Ram. He is from Punjab and has been in this country for almost twenty years, during which time he has never taken a vacation. I think about what it means to have dreamed the immigrant dream of success in America and to end up in this job. Is this man bitterly disappointed that he has been doing this for nine hours a day, six days a week, for many years?

When I ask him this question, he responds, "What can I do? This is my life. I must make money for my family. I don't want to do nothing, to take for free, like some of the people in this building." He waves dismissively at a nearby, low-income apartment building where some people are hanging out, guzzling beer.

Only when he talks about his children, now attending college, does his face become animated, infused with expression. And I realize that Ram sees himself primarily as a bridge between his past and the future, one centering on those he has brought into the world. Having visited India and seen the widespread poverty there—much worse than in New York City—I suspect that this man truly appreciates whatever he has.

Other vendors with whom I speak tell similar stories. Ram's comments are strikingly like those of an Indian deli owner on Staten Island, who says, "I work very hard and open early, at 5:30 AM. I go sleep at 10:00 PM. On Fourth of July I took a small vacation and went with my kids to Canada. The really big vacation

I take is when we go back to India for a month in December/
January."

"Are your kids going to work in the deli?" I ask him.

"I hope not. I tell them, 'You do something better. Money no
problem. I do anything struggling. But you guys *gotta* do something better, because I don't wanna see you just standing here, slicing up the meat.'"

"How long are you here?" I ask.

"About five years."

"Did you think you were going to end up in the deli when you
came to America?"

His response is surprising. "Actually, I had a grocery store in
India, but I never thought I would do it here. Before Staten Island I
worked for seven years in a deli in New Jersey." And here we see by
his response that not everyone who takes this kind of job has never
done it before. This deli owner did the same job in India.

People think of the deli as a business that an immigrant can
make a living from, but it's like so many things: if you're willing to work hard—no, *very hard*—you can actually make a mint.
Sunny's deli operates on a well-traveled Brooklyn street selling
the staples of such businesses, lottery tickets and cigarettes. But
the real money is in the hot food. Sunny sells falafel, *shawarma*,
turkey burgers, cheeseburgers, you name it. He is a Palestinian, a
place best known to most New Yorkers for its struggle to establish a homeland. But like so many immigrants in New York, his
primary politics is business, which is why he enjoys good relations
even with his Israeli customers. His wife is Sicilian. What's most
remarkable is his volume. "Now this place is worth no less than a
million and a half," he crows. "You don't touch this place for less.
Not even a hundred thousand dollars less, you won't touch it. Because this is an eighty- to ninety-thousand-dollar-a-week business.
Twenty-four hours."

And that's the key—twenty-four hours a day, seven days a week.
But you have to be willing to work that hard. In the winter, Sunny,
the owner, works the lucrative night shift. That's where the big
money is. "In winter, I never see the daylight," he says. But most
of all, as Tug McGraw, of New York Mets fame, said, "You gotta

believe." Sunny has self-confidence up the wazoo. His words say it all. "Listen, I am a man with five languages, you know? I can make this business up to the sky." Sunny says that he takes home between eight and ten thousand dollars a week. That's almost half a million dollars a year. But in any case the trajectory of his family is classically American. Make the dream come true, offer the spoils to your children, and listen as they say, "No, Dad, I'm not going to work like that, no." Sunny says, "They want to go to be a pharmacist, or, like, a doctor, you know? Lawyers. They don't want to work. They want to go to school, college. You know?" To Sunny, the professions may have status. But they're not like *real* work.[17]

People like Sunny, if they don't take their profits and return to their homelands to live in splendor, move to the suburbs or to wealthy enclaves in the city. Mill Basin, in the southern part of Brooklyn, is one of these destinations. (See figure 2). In recent years it has become popular with successful immigrants, many of them Russian, and even an occasional mobster. Originally it was a Jewish, Italian, and Asian area with modest ranches, split-levels, and colonials, and there are still many members of those groups living there. Location probably plays a role in this decision, since Brighton Beach, an area of first settlement for Russians, both Jewish and non-Jewish, is not far away.

Today many of the homes in this area are large, beautiful, and lavish, much like the homes in the Italian American Todt Hill section on Staten Island, and often one of a kind. Behind the tall gates of one home I saw a Porsche, a Bentley, and a Maybach (about four hundred thousand dollars). Any one of these luxury cars would have been plenty, but all three? Over the top, screaming, "I made it!" Two menacing German shepherds prowled the property, growling and barking as I stood there. The house is a hodgepodge of styles, with a green mansard roof, curved walls made of white brick, a three-story-high entrance hall. Opposite, on the water, is another gorgeous home. This one is in the Romanesque style, with huge stone urns outside and a tiled roof. Yet another mini-palace features a guardhouse in front of it.

And so we see that beyond the need for economic survival is another level: the need or the desire to succeed. Those who have it possess a different personal makeup from people who are content with a reasonable income. They may also have certain talents or abilities. And what jump-starts their often Herculean efforts is undoubtedly the fact that, as opposed to the limited opportunities in their native lands, they see a chance to make it really big in this country. It's these two factors—necessity and ambition—that fuel their great energy.

To the neighbors of the newcomers these successes are often fascinating. They talk about the "new Russian millionaires" in the same way tour guides in Beverly Hills talk about celebrities, providing tidbits of gossip and stories about the people and the parties inside these homes. In its glorification of ostentatiousness, it is but the latest incarnation of the American dream that has captivated and motivated generations of past, and now present, immigrants. Why some groups have a greater need to flaunt what they have would make for an interesting study.

But some immigrants are not interested in this marker of success. They have other criteria in mind—namely, their position in society. Consider the following case: According to a knowledgeable woman in the South Indian community, running a hot dog stand can be pretty lucrative. "These are well-off people. They can easily make maybe seventy thousand dollars a year, and they pay very little in taxes. They declare maybe ten or twenty thousand in income. And if they make so little money on the books, they can then get free Medicaid and free schools. So it's a good job economically."

"Is your husband a hot dog vendor then?"

"No, he's an engineer."

"And how much does he make?"

"He only makes sixty-five thousand dollars a year."

"Is he angry about that?"

"Yes, but he wants to be an engineer."

"Would you marry a hot dog vendor or an engineer if you had to make that choice?"

"An engineer, and I did."

"Why?"

"Because of the status of being an engineer. My father's an engineer. It's not only about the money."

This, too, is part of the American dream—to be respected. Cab drivers may earn one hundred thousand dollars a year without paying a lot of taxes. But they lack status. Like Americans, the newcomers, depending on the cultural and economic levels of the societies or communities from which they came, are stratified not only by income but also by prestige.

Regardless of what jobs they do, the immigrants of recent decades have much stronger transnational connections than did earlier waves of newcomers. They send money home, travel frequently to their native countries, and, with varying degrees of seriousness, consider returning home one day. A newly emerging trend is a reverse migration of the second generation, the highly educated children of immigrants who are moving to their parents' countries of origin. This trend is fueled largely by economic conditions in the United States and abroad that have made it more attractive to work in nations like India and China than in the States. Just how many people are doing so and whether the trend is temporary or long-lasting remains to be seen, but it is a phenomenon that could not have been dreamed of in previous generations, when the overwhelming majority of immigrants came here for good. Not only economic conditions and a global economy but also the ease of travel in the twenty-first century as well as the Internet have made distances irrelevant and communication instant.[18]

Female participation in the workforce has greatly increased in the last thirty years among all groups, but there are variations from group to group. Jamaican women, for example, are more likely to work than Dominican women, largely because the Jamaicans speak English, have higher educational levels, and come from a society that already has high female participation in the workforce.[19] Dominicans are culturally proscribed from working once their conditions improve, because not working is seen as a sign of status—as in "They don't have to work." Besides, if they don't work, they can take care of their children. This, too, is changing. Children sometimes help out, but they are not a major presence. You may see them in a Chinese takeout joint, or they may accompany their housekeeper mothers to work, but these are often forms of day care when there is no one with whom to leave the kids.

Adapting to Life in America

For most immigrants the driving force behind their decision is economic, accompanied by a desire to reunite with their families. Some have even become the subjects of famous, if somewhat apocryphal, success stories that exemplify rapid and successful adaptation. Take the Kennedy Fried Chicken chain, a multimillion-dollar operation with about one thousand stores in New York City's poor areas and in other East Coast cities. It was started in 1979 by two Afghanis, Taeb Zia and Abdul Karim, who, the story goes, realized that their own names wouldn't carry much weight if tacked onto a store sign. So they looked for a familiar name and decided that a former U.S. president's surname would suit their needs perfectly. Their red and white colors and the initials KFC have sometimes gotten them into trouble with another famous name, Kentucky Fried Chicken. The New York chain has also spawned imitators, like Lincoln Fried Chicken, JFK Chicken, and even Obama Fried Chicken, the last of which has drawn some flack for stereotyping. The positive side of this story is that you can make it big here. The negative side is that there is usually envy from other immigrants, most of whom have not enjoyed such success.

Some immigrant groups have substantial economic capital. They often sell products imported from their native lands, but, despite their resources, the transition and adaptation to American norms and tastes can sometimes be awkward and literally "lost in translation." In the windows of a small, crowded discount store in Queens, owned by Chinese people who barely speak English, are some boxes that contain Barbie-type dolls. The dolls, which come with accessories, are named "Defa Lucy," and the description on the box succinctly reveals the gap between native and foreign. It reads, in part, "Here, are full of laughter and pleasure; Please, let joy go on. There are colorful flowers all over the earth. . . . Look! Defa Lucy is dancing with butterflies." The wording is not terrible, but something is clearly off. Just as it is when Chinese restaurants select names like Happy Broccoli, Eastern Strawberry, or New Golden Billion.

Economics is only one piece in understanding what it takes to succeed. In her network analysis of the Gujaratis, an Indian ethnic group, sociologist Maritsa Poros shows how immigrants employ friends, their native land, community organizations, professional associations, and business connections to help their people advance. But there are negative consequences too that result from using connections. When insiders do wrong, they're often forgiven, because ostracizing them could result in the leaking of confidential information about how the group operates, its sources of supply, how its members "cut corners," and the like. Giving them a pass also serves to prevent insiders from leaving to pursue business opportunities that involve contact with outsiders. In this way the group's insularity is enhanced, but then the social adaptation process slows down. And it is also a reason why outsiders are often excluded from doing business with Gujaratis. As outsiders they cannot be easily controlled. Ostracism means nothing to them. They cannot be shamed within the community, because they are not really part of it.[20]

Education has long been a key to successful adaptation. But many groups like to preserve parts of their ethos even as they acculturate, and creating private schools is one way of doing so. Catholics and Jews have long done this with their parochial, day, and afternoon schools, and so have Muslims. Many of the Muslim schools, like the Al-Noor School in Brooklyn on Fourth Avenue near Twenty-first Street, encourage their high school graduates to attend college. Education is separated by the sexes, and a religious program is offered too. The school motto sums up the combination: "Education for Life and for Hereafter."

On 134th Street and Rockaway Turnpike in Queens, I see the Ali San Academy. And, ironically, across the street is the Rav-Bariach security products store. It's a well-known Israeli company that makes door locks and keys. "Do they sell to the academy?" I wonder. It seems from appearances that the students there may be Guyanese Muslims, representing a fusion of nationality and religion.

Those from countries with few immigrants here—Malaysia, Norway, Bhutan, Uruguay—generally receive scant attention from immigration specialists, who understandably opt for examining the larger groups, whose impact on the city is greater. I'm reminded of this when I pass by the Manakamana Mai Deli & Grocery (named after a Hindu deity) on Myrtle Avenue in Glendale, Queens near Seventy-first Street. The young man working there is a twenty-two-year-old Nepalese named Laxu. He exhibits fascination and great pleasure when I tell him that his name is similar to the acronym for Los Angeles International Airport, LAX. I tell him to Google it.

He does and exclaims, "Wow!" in wonderment.

I joke with him. "Imagine," I say. "You're named after a huge airport."

He laughs appreciatively. I wonder that no one has ever told him this.

"How's your government doing these days?" I inquire.

"Bad," he says. "It's the Maoist guerillas."

He's been here two years and I ask him how he is able to speak English so well. He tells me he learned it in Nepal, and I'm reminded of how important knowing English is to the adaptation process. Some in his community live in nearby Ridgewood, near Myrtle and Wyckoff Avenues. The main Nepalese community is in Jackson Heights, Queens, where there are restaurants like the Himalayan Yak that serve as their gathering places. Laxu passes the time playing online poker with eight other players—for fun, not for money—using video poker chips. This is a minor way in which the Big Apple has changed in the last thirty-five years—technology. People can fiddle around on the Internet to relieve their boredom while they're working. Laxu plays every day for four or five hours, both at work and at home. Although he uses his computer to play poker, there's little doubt that those able to navigate the Internet in English will adjust faster to life here, as his ability to almost immediately find LAX online attests to.

One event that has probably had a significant psychological impact on how the newcomers feel about their new home is the election of President Barack Obama. As a result, people—black, white, and other—feel that race relations have improved. Obama's election (and reelection) speaks to the possibility of anyone rising to the top, irrespective of their origins. After the election, as I walked through various ethnic neighborhoods, I could see that the enthusiasm for the new president was both high and unmistakable, especially among teenagers of all backgrounds.

The adaptation of older immigrants is truly under-studied. Observations on this by sociologist Judith Treas suggest why this is so. "They never win spelling bees," she says. "They do not join criminal gangs. And nobody worries about losing jobs to Korean grandmothers." In other words, older immigrants are not an important group in terms of what sociologists investigate. But they are important to younger people. They are babysitters and important carriers of the old traditions with their families, as well as role models. They also experience the typical problems that all senior citizens have and that society addresses—depression, physical ailments, and loneliness. There are cultural reasons for their importance too. In Asian societies the aged are respected far more than they are in the United States. Devendra Singh, a seventy-nine-year-old Indian, ruefully reflects, "In India there is a favorable bias toward the elders. Here people think about what is convenient and inconvenient for them." And that can apply to the immigrants' own Americanized children as well.[21]

Difficulties in Adapting

At times outside events can seriously hamper a community's ability to adjust to life in New York City. One factor that greatly affected the Muslim community's ability to adapt and be accepted was 9/11. I found that many Muslims make it a point to disassociate themselves from what happened. A Yemeni bodega owner's response was typical: "I don't agree with Muslims who believe their religion tells them they can kill other people. If you kill a thousand, you're going to the hell fire. Anyone who does that must be a communist who doesn't believe in God. God does not want you to kill others. My kids are in school here, and I want them have a good life here as full Americans." As I listened to this man talk, his voice trying to rise above the cacophony of some Spanish speakers rummaging through a pile of socks on display near some plantains,

my mind flitted to his origins. Fifteen years ago, living in a Yemeni village, could he ever have imagined himself in a Washington
Heights bodega, declaiming loudly about his Muslim coreligionists
and 9/11? Like so many others, he is trying to piece together a new
existence, to reinvent himself, for his sake and that of his family.

Some Muslims go even further in their efforts to empathize with
how Americans feel about them. Following an attack on an Egyp-
tian-owned coffee shop in Astoria, Queens, after the World Trade
Center went down, the store owner declined to press charges, saying he understood the anger. The culprits in turn apologized and
offered to pay for the damages. An Arab cabbie discussed the incident candidly and insightfully from a broader perspective:

> Do we all have to be blamed for something we didn't commit? We
> cannot change our face. We can't make plastic surgery just for the
> time being and when the next terrorist is Chinese or a white guy, we
> can come back to our original faces. . . . I've been here since 1989
> and I never once been up in the World Trade Center. But that was
> where I make my living. Twelve times a day I was dropping people
> off, picking them up there. When a tourist comes to New York, the
> first thing they say, "Where is the World Trade Center?" If you're
> coming from Pennsylvania or uptown at 195th Street, you point
> with your finger and you find those two buildings. They were the
> same for me as the pyramid of Giza or the Sphinx. When you're in
> Egypt, anywhere you go you see them. After 7,000 years to see them
> collapse, it's like a part of my soul collapse.[22]

Today, more than ten years after 9/11, Muslims are still singled
out for special surveillance. Regardless of one's views on the matter, the effects on Muslims in the city are profound, despite their
general success in acclimating to their new surroundings. I asked
former mayor Koch what he thought were the permanent effects
of 9/11. His answer revealed how deeply passions can run on this
subject.

> I believe that we're in a war with Islamist fanatics, terrorists,
> and that this war will go on for fifty years, maybe more, and the
> question is, Will our country have the intestinal fortitude and the

courage to stand up in that war? I believe that the impact of that
catastrophic tragedy is great because there will be a reminder each
year in a memorial ceremony. It will strengthen the country. We're
a society—I'm talking about Western civilization—that loves life.
So the question is, Who will prevail? Those who love life or those
who want to die? That's a question that no one can really answer.
Obviously Muslims are not all terrorists, but even a small proportion, maybe 10 percent out of a billion, is enormous when they
support terrorism, even if [they themselves are not] committed to
terrorist acts. The police commissioner of New York City has units
to combat terrorism here, in London, and in New Jersey. And some
so-called civil libertarians want to stop it. That's nuts!

These are the challenges facing one group of immigrants. There
are also many who, for one reason or another, fail to adapt on an
individual level, and it happens within every group. Some return to
their native lands; others lead unsatisfying lives here, surviving on
the margins; and still others end their lives in tragic ways. Statistics
and patterns are important, but they do not even begin to tell the
human stories that highlight the aspirations, pain, and even disaster that are part of the immigrant saga.

I heard and read about many such cases during my research on
the streets of New York, but none were sadder and more poignant
than that of Hugo Alfredo Tale-Yax, a Guatemalan man who
came to New York in 2002 to make a new life and to earn enough
money to buy a larger piece of land for his family back home. His
family was made up of subsistence farmers who grew corn on a
tiny plot in the highlands. Hugo's dream died a most cruel death
on April 18, 2010, when he was stabbed in the stomach in South
Jamaica, Queens, reportedly after trying to help a woman having
a heated argument with a man. What was especially tragic was
that, as captured on video, Hugo lay bleeding on the ground face-
down for over an hour before he died as dozens of people walked
past him and did nothing. Maybe they thought he was just drunk
and homeless, but what about the blood that was oozing out from
under him? Was that not worth a second look and perhaps a call
to 911?

Hugo was a skilled carpenter, but, like many other people, the recession had rendered him jobless and unable to fulfill the family dream, even as he promised his father a month earlier, "I will get through the difficulties and carry out the plan." And there were real difficulties that he was embarrassed to tell his family about. His joblessness had led to excessive drinking and ultimately to homelessness, with a playground on Ninety-first Avenue near the Van Wyck Expressway serving as a makeshift home for him. After his funeral, Hugo's body was shipped home, "reversing a trek that cost him $6,000 and took him 14 days to complete; he walked through Mexico into Texas."[23]

And for what? Here was a good, hardworking man who wanted nothing more than to improve his life and that of his family. Back home Hugo's family and the village would have served as a support system. Even when he was down and beset by hardship, feeling, as his brother said, ashamed that he could not make it in America, Hugo died by showing kindness to another human being. That is something to be proud of, and for this reason alone he should not be forgotten. As of this writing, his murderer has not been found.

The Struggle to Maintain Identity

Immigrants try to maintain their group identity in many ways. The most common are through language, politics, religion, maintaining family ties, food, music and other forms of entertainment, sports, literature, ethnic media, educational and cultural programs, visits to the homeland, and living near one another. The importance of this and the many ways in which it manifests itself was brought home to me when at noon on December 3, 2010, I was walking in a neighborhood of African immigrants along 116th Street west of Malcolm X Boulevard. Suddenly I noticed a commotion outside a small restaurant. (See figure 3.) Young black men were bringing in food, shouting, and clapping one another on the back. Some of them seemed angry, others were happy, all were quite animated. I walked inside, where a number of men were eating rice, beans, and chicken gizzards, mostly at long tables. Their attention was riveted to a large-screen TV that was broadcasting the disputed results of the presidential election in Ivory Coast, and they ignored my arrival, even though I was the only white there. At one point the TV showed an official tearing up ballots of a candidate he didn't like. But just at that moment the official tally had been announced declaring the opposition candidate, Alassane Ouattara, the surprise winner over the incumbent, President Laurent Gbagbo. The whoops and shouts of joy and dismay made crystal clear the degree to which these African immigrants still identify with their homeland. For them, it was as if the election were being held in New York City.[24] Walk into any ethnic restaurant, bar, or barbershop—whether it's Polish, Dominican, Australian, or Uzbeki—and you will see TV programs of all kinds beamed from the homeland.

American sports, in particular, have a way of capturing the enthusiasm of the immigrants, perhaps because, unlike native music or language, sports are essentially not ethnic. To the millions of Americans from every background who avidly follow some sort of sport, the players' performance is far more important than their race or ethnicity. But for the immigrants, their children, and even their grandchildren, it's extremely significant, for it tells everyone that someone from their homeland has made it into a mainstream arena.

The following two stories—both about Dominican immigrants, but only by happenstance—describe identity maintenance but do so in totally different ways, each of which has the potential to expand our understanding of how identity is shaped. The first story concerns sports, whereas the second is what I would call imaginative and somewhat opportunistic.

I see and enter a restaurant on 191st Street and St. Nicholas Avenue in Washington Heights called El Nuevo Caridad. It features photos of the owner, Miguel Montas, with famous ballplayers, mostly New York Mets and Yankees. The Formica tables are laminated with photos of players. Baseball gloves and bats are displayed along the walkway leading into the place. Some forty-odd menu offerings, a mix of Spanish, West Indian, and generic food, are named after the players, most of them Hispanic and some of them eternally famous, like retired Giants pitcher Juan Marichal.

It reminds me of Larry David's Los Angeles deli, where the sandwiches are identified by the names of famous Hollywood actors and personalities. The vertical bars of the railing at El Nuevo Caridad are actually bats, interspersed with gloves. By eating here, customers get deferred status from the players who have also dined here and are reminded that at least some of their people have succeeded big-time in America.[25]

Identity is not only where you find it but also what you make of it. I stop in at 106 Fort Washington Avenue, at the corner of 164th Street, in Upper Manhattan, a building where my family once lived for a while. The building superintendent—or, as New Yorkers would say, the super—is Mike, a balding fifty-five-year-old Dominican man with three children. We strike up a conversation. I listen as he tells me how the area has improved and who's moving in, the long waiting list, his children, and what they're doing. Suddenly he says, seemingly out of nowhere, "Can you believe it? This building is called Samana Mansion. When you look at a map of the Dominican Republic, on the east side, on the northern tip is the Samana Peninsula. That's where a very famous whale came from Alaska, and the tourists come there. And this building is full of Dominicans! There's a Dominican province named Samana and a peninsula. There's even a mountain range there named Samana."

"It was called Samana when I lived here," I respond, "even before this became a Dominican area."

"Really," he says in a surprised but not defensive way. "All I know is what it means to me." His answer indicates a search for a connection to his own people. It's a way of showing that the Dominicans have a place here in the city, however tenuous the link may be. In this way meaning is extracted from a coincidence.

The name of the building is engraved into the white-painted concrete atop its entrance. Why was it named Samana? It turns out that Samana has other meanings too. Samana was the name given to a group of wandering Indian ascetics, one of whom was Gautama Buddha, of Siddhartha fame. It is also the name of a mountain range in Pakistan, as well as a town in the Punjab region of India called Samana. But we'll never know why the building carries the name. Beyond the fact that it was built in 1920, more than ninety years ago, no further information is available, so the mystery remains.

Religion often plays a major role in immigrant adjustment. Ministers counsel them, church services console them, and agencies affiliated with religious institutions assist them. The prominent role of religion in the United States creates an environment that is conducive for its propagation.[26] Here's an excerpt from a sermon given by a minister at a Nigerian Pentecostal church in Queens:

> I pray for the cab drivers, that you protect them from accident, from robbery, from receiving unnecessary tickets, and help them to keep their job. I pray for the nurses, that they will not give wrong medications, that they will not be sued or contract diseases. . . . I pray for all the children of this church that you will give them wisdom and understanding, that they will be grade A students. . . . I pray for those that are in business, that they will prosper, Lord, that you will be their business partner, that they will be safe on the street, that they will not be pushed into the subway track, that you will shield them from bullets and police that misunderstand who they really are.[27]

The minister apparently knows all the right notes to hit. She has an intimate understanding of the newcomers' struggles and the challenges they face every day, thereby making religion relevant to their lives.

Entering an African/Caribbean church in Brownsville on a Sunday morning, it's easy to comprehend the deep spiritual and emotional needs that religion fills for so many immigrants. The women wear traditional dress—gaily colored turbans and dresses. It's called Mountain of Fire and Miracles Ministry, located at 180 Blake Avenue near Amboy Street. Hundreds of worshipers are singing ecstatically, swaying in unison, gesticulating, hands pointing upward in delirium. The music and chanting is beautiful, and I am moved by the emotional involvement of the participants. Here again is testimony to the great power of religion in this city to attract its residents, both old and new, rich and poor, and many in between. It's what goes on in hundreds of churches throughout the city every Sunday.

When a white person walks into a black church, he or she is is noticed and, in this case, warmly welcomed. Members of the congregation so much want you to share in their happiness and feel their joy; they believe so much in what they do that they feel they must encourage you to join them, thereby validating their own faith. In this church color brings together people from Africa, Haiti, Jamaica, and elsewhere. It's an example, too, of Pan-Africanism, which is normally a political movement but can also manifest itself in the religious sphere.

The level of religious interest among immigrants is not limited by any means to Pentecostal-type churches. It's just as present in the larger denominations, albeit more formally expressed. The Most Reverend Nicholas DiMarzio, bishop of the Brooklyn Diocese of the Roman Catholic Church (which also serves the faithful of Queens), explained to me in an interview how important the immigrants are in the church's activities and their larger impact.

> The immigrants are critical to our work. There are so many of them and their faith is often very intense. Some groups are more involved than others. For example, the Haitians are very active. I have sixty-four seminarians, and maybe eleven are black and a good number of them are Haitians, which is incredibly high. Several thousand West Indian Catholics march in the parade as Catholics, proud to be members of the faith. The parade gets to be a little risqué. But [chuckling] we march in the front. We don't see that. It's a strong and very supportive culture. Next year we'll be reaching out to the Chinese in particular, because so many of them are unaffiliated.
>
> And a big change over the years has been that religion has become much more of a common denominator. When a Catholic Irish person marries a Catholic Dominican and they identify as such, then we've made it and they have too. It demonstrates one of the successes of immigration in this city.

Immigrants often breathe new life into dying churches. Where once the Catholic church primarily served the Irish, Italians, and Germans, today it's much more attended by Hispanics, Haitians, and Asians. Ditto for the Protestant churches, whose clientele has also shifted dramatically. For example, there's the First United

Methodist Church of Flushing. In 1986 it had 30 native English-speaking members but 450 Koreans. Even then there were already more than 300 Korean churches in New York, mostly in Queens. The English speakers credit the Koreans with financing the improvement of the building. "They have money and we don't," says one. But there are differences in worship, style, and outlook. The pastor has a different sermon for each group. The Koreans like long sermons that are almost exclusively devoted to biblical themes. The English speakers prefer short sermons focused on social and political topics. Today there are hundreds of churches throughout the city that advertise services being held in multiple languages: Spanish, Chinese, Korean, Polish, and Creole, along with English.[28]

New arrivals to New York frequently feel pressure not to reveal their origins, although immigrant efforts to retain their culture have become far more acceptable than they were fifty years ago. An article in the *New York Times* reports that Muslim deli owners often feel they must sell pork and alcohol and allow the sale of lottery tickets even though all of these violate Koranic prohibitions. The conflict is well expressed by Khairul Kabir, a Bangladeshi immigrant who owns a deli in East Harlem, who says, "Selling *haram* [forbidden] is the same as eating haram. I feel guilty, totally guilty. I want to sell the business and go home and not sell haram. Every day I'm thinking I should do that." Kabir acknowledges, however, that his "thinking" about selling is tempered by the recession. The fact is that options are limited for an immigrant who has found an economic niche. And so, instead, he gives his mea culpa: "I am doing a lot of bad things. I pray to Allah to forgive me." It's an example—one faced by uncounted numbers of immigrants over the past two hundred years—of having to choose between economic priorities and group loyalties or beliefs. Often, as in this case, the former wins out.

Kabir's imam, Mohammed Fayek Uddin of the Jackson Heights Islamic Center, took a decidedly liberal, even perhaps a separation-of-church-and-state, view of Kabir's quandary. "In this country everyone has to do something. I deliver my speech in front of the people; it depends on their choice. No punishment, not here. Allah will give punishment on the Day of Judgment; I do not have an authority to do that."[29]

Children of the Immigrants

The sociologist Philip Kasinitz and his coauthors carried out interviews, did ethnographic research, and conducted surveys over a decade and wrote the most definitive book to date on the second generation of immigrants to America. They note that New York City has more adult immigrants and children of immigrants than any other city in the United States. The parents worry that their children may become too American and lose their cultural ties to their communities. The most important finding from Kasinitz and his colleagues is that most of the children of immigrants are doing very well.

This optimistic assessment is not shared by everyone, however. Immigrants often reside in poor areas and have a high unemployment rate. As a result, their children could become what sociologists Ruben Rumbaut and Alejandro Portes have dubbed a "rainbow underclass."[30] In New York City the Mexican second generation is experiencing the greatest problems. As opposed to their hardworking immigrant parents, many of the younger generation are failing. Approximately 41 percent of those between sixteen and nineteen have either dropped out of school or never attended in the first place. And Mexicans are the fastest-growing immigrant group in the city: about 266,000 in 2007, compared to 61,722 in 1990.[31] Add the undocumented immigrants, who are not necessarily counted in U.S. Census data, and the numbers are even higher. Those who are here illegally are afraid to get help for their children; there are also problems with the language barrier, the need for several jobs to make ends meet, and the overall lack of social capital.

Discussing his childhood after coming here illegally from Mexico, Iván Lucero, a waiter, recalled, "You don't think of nothing else but having fun with your friends, meeting up with girls, having your boys with you. The last thing you think of is school."[32] This is borne out by conversations with people in the community who cite all the attendant issues of family conflict, teenage drinking, petty crime, and just hanging out aimlessly. If the problem isn't addressed, this "lost generation" of immigrants will become a much more serious problem when the children become adults.

Differences within Groups

To outsiders they may all seem alike, but there are often significant differences within nationalities, starting with class. I stop outside a restaurant on 100th Street, near Lexington Avenue, called LaGalette, which advertises "fine Senegalese cuisine." It's a cinch that, at the prices, Senegalese vendors of knock-off pocketbooks on Canal Street aren't dining there. A Haitian describes how the "higher-class" Haitians are more apt to attend Sacred Heart Church in Cambria Heights, while those of lower class will choose St. Ann's in nearby Queens Village.

Sometimes these class differences become intertwined with the group's priorities and perceptions. Listen to how the middle- and upper-class Chinese, known as the "Uptown Chinese," as opposed to the poorer "Downtown Chinese," express their disdain for American values:

> In the eyes of Chinese immigrant parents, American children, white as well as black, have no work ethic because the schools don't give them enough to do and American parents don't bother to teach them discipline. While white kids play sports after school, Chinese kids are typically enrolled in an activity with an academic component. "I think they have too much free time," Taiwan-born stay-at-home suburban mother Mrs. Chung explains her strategy, "and I hate to see kids waste their time. You know, I don't think life should be like that, you know, waste time. So then I heard some other friends, their children are learning music." . . . . American kids lack respect for their elders and authority in general, eat the

wrong things—particularly too much fried food—and spend too much time pondering deviant sexual behavior that can lead to their own gender confusion.[33]

Class differences can also lead to open hostility. Teju Cole, the Nigerian writer, tells of his encounter with an African cabbie, who says to him: "Not good, not good at all, you know, the way you came into my cab without saying hello, that was bad. Hey, I'm African just like you, why you do this?" Cole apologizes, but to no avail. The damage is done. The driver stares ahead at the road, his silence speaking for itself.[34]

It's worth noting that many immigrants may be poor upon arrival in the city but come from middle-class backgrounds and have middle-class values. They left looking for opportunity and often plan to return. Still others, like some of the Chinese and Koreans in Flushing, or Persian Jews who initially settled in Kew Gardens, Queens, moved rapidly to the suburbs. On the other hand, not all group members fit the stereotype. We're accustomed to thinking of Jews as highly educated—doctors, lawyers, MBAs—but the Bukharian immigrants have changed that perception a bit. They are predominantly shoemakers, barbers, tailors, contractors, a whole segment of working-class Jews, and very unlike the concert pianists, doctors, and computer programmers emanating from the European portions of Russia. Many are very traditional. You see a person with a *kippa,* or skullcap, running a shoe repair shop. There's something old-world about it as you watch him sitting by an old-fashioned gooseneck lamp, bent over a lathe, fixing what has to be repaired in a tiny shop on, of all places, Sixty-sixth Street between First and Second Avenues. You'll also find the Bukharian Jews in Richmond Hill or Middle Village, Queens, both non-Jewish areas.

In addition to class, there are religious, tribal, linguistic, and geographic distinctions within the groups too numerous to go into. But the issue is the same: the immigrants must navigate these shoals among themselves in addition to dealing with those on the outside. It's a daunting task, fraught with perils and challenges that must be overcome if they are to achieve parity with other Americans.

Living Together

The arrival of so many groups in a relatively short period of time has resulted in contacts of all sorts between peoples who have had limited or no experience with one another. America has always been a melting pot, but each new mix of peoples is unique, with its own tensions, challenges, and opportunities. Changing social attitudes, technology, and economic conditions further complicate matters.

I enter a grocery store, an Asian bodega, on Hillside Avenue in Jamaica, run by Sri Lankans. What attracted my attention was the sign outside: "We carry products from Sri Lanka, India, and the West Indies." This strikes me as an example of syncretism. True, the store caters largely to Asians, but the distance between Sri Lanka and the West Indies is several thousand miles and the cultural circumstances are not the same. I wonder also if the owner is carrying items specific to the different countries. It turns out he is. I pick up a jar of Maldives fish chips produced in Sri Lanka. The small collection of CDs available features music from all three areas. Among the different types of candles for sale is a Jewish *yahrzeit*, or memorial, candle. Curious as to what the clerk will say about this fourth group, there being no Jewish population in the area, I ask him what it is. "Oh, that; they're church candles that religious people sometimes buy."

I come across a similar establishment in Ridgewood, another part of Queens that is home to many nationalities. It's a deli, selling European, Balkan, and Middle Eastern specialties, with the innocuous and seemingly incongruous name of Parrot. Inside there are Polish, Hungarian, French, Romanian, Greek, and Bulgarian cheeses, to mention only a few of the many offerings. There's also Hungarian salami and the spicier Gypsy salami. All of these ethnic groups have settled in the adjoining areas of Greenpoint, Ridgewood, Glendale, Sunnyside, and Maspeth. In this Romanian-run establishment they sell two Israeli brands of hair shampoo, as well as German shampoo. You get the feeling that the whole world is represented here. "Everybody comes here," intones the manager in answer to my question of who the customers are. It's a common pattern—increase sales by appealing to as many groups as possible.

Another example of syncretism is on Westchester Avenue in the Bronx. Many stores advertise *halal* (sanctioned by Islamic law) meat, but this one says, "Musa's Halal Chinese Food." There's a drawing of a chicken on one side of the sign and a cow on the other side, meaning, by its absence, the store sells no pork.[35] And it is sandwiched (no pun intended) between a Veterans of Foreign Wars center and a Domino's Pizza. Two doors down is the Mexican El Texano eatery. That the owners of these shops are located cheek-to-jowl next to each other assures that they will have contact with and get to know each other, as will their clienteles. Sometimes the appeal is explicit, as in the sign I saw outside a Harlem pizza/chicken joint proclaiming, "No Pork on My Fork."

But there's more to a neighborhood's identity than food. These food stores identify an area as multiethnic, but the real contacts take place in the neighborhoods themselves—in the buildings, on the streets, in parks, community centers, schools, and sometimes houses of worship, all places where immigrants have met and mingled for more than a century. Visiting Intermediate School 194, built in 2003 on Waterbury Avenue east of Castle Hill Avenue, I learn that this part of the Bronx has many Muslim Asian immigrants, especially Bangladeshis, Pakistanis, Indians, as well as Guyanese. The school is about 50 percent Asian and 45 percent Hispanic, and it also has some whites and blacks, a good number of whom come from nearby Parkchester. It's a beautiful, spacious, and spotless institution. But most important, it's the perfect place for groups to learn about and appreciate each other.

Contacts do not happen only in these places, however. Sometimes they occur in locations that we don't ordinarily think of. I'm sitting in a kosher fast-food place on the Upper West Side and observing the Mexican workers. I find myself thinking that besides their daily problems of earning a living, when they send their kids off to school these immigrants often have no idea of the cultural groups their kids meet. What stereotypes about Jews are being reinforced or challenged here? It's especially true in this type of situation, because people have a way of treating fast-food workers, busboys, car wash attendants, and the like as if they were pieces of furniture, talking, arguing, and sharing secrets as though these people aren't there. Before arriving in New York City, the Mexicans, often coming from small villages, had never met Jews. And they are generally unfamiliar with American culture. The same bewilderment must surface if they're hired as maintenance workers in a Polish cultural center, or as dishwashers in an Irish bar. They certainly won't get the nuances. We do not explore this sufficiently. These experiences, occurring in many locales throughout the city, are important, both for what they tell us about the past lives of these immigrants and about how their future perceptions will be shaped.

When different ethnic groups live in the same neighborhoods, they often view each other in stereotypical terms, but the following comments by a longtime German-Jewish resident in Washington Heights, which is today largely Dominican, reveal how complex people's impressions can be. We also see how people struggle with each other's opinions, which they suspect may not be entirely fair. "It seems that the Dominicans and Jews here get along pretty well," I observe. The man, an Orthodox Jew and an accountant, responds:

> When the Dominicans came here, the German Jews were taken aback by the loud music, the graffiti, the noise, and the garbage. I don't want to be a racist, because I understand that in the islands that's what you do with garbage . . . . you dump it in the middle of the street. [This is certainly no longer the case today.] On the other hand, my mother was walking on 181st Street fifteen years ago and she was mugged, and this Hispanic shopkeeper came running out, ran after the mugger, caught him, and yelled, "Don't you ever come back to this neighborhood, or I'll knock the daylights out of you." [This is an example of an alliance among the "decent folks" that transcends ethnicity.] My wife will be riding in a train, and who will get up and give her a seat?—a Hispanic. Not only that, but my mother was sitting *shiva* [in mourning], and the Hispanic people in the building came out in droves. And we have other contacts

with them too. Orthodox Jews got involved in the school boards
because there were issues of concern to them, like you might not
want a school built next to the synagogue. Of course, the Hispanics
became upset, saying, "If you don't send your kids to the school,
why should you have a say in what happens to them?"

The contacts are uneven and sometimes situationally defined.
For example, when Leiby Kletzky, a young Hasidic boy, went missing (he was murdered and dismembered by someone who belonged
to the Orthodox community), about twenty Pakistani volunteers
participated in the search, demonstrating the solidarity and concern of Muslims who operate businesses in the area.[36] Was this
a way of gaining favorable publicity for them, as some cynically
observed, or simply an act of human compassion for neighbors, or
both? Regardless, it was noteworthy. As one Jewish resident told
me, "It was amazing and made a deep impression on me."

I pass by a Manhattan Jewish temple located across the street
from a Pakistani-owned government building. "Do you have
anything to do with the people in the temple?" I ask a Pakistani
employee standing outside, thinking there are tensions but also
friendly contacts between Muslims and Jews.

"No," he responds. "We're friendly, say hello, but that's it."

Is this an opportunity lost, or does it sometimes take a crisis like
the Kletzky case to energize people? How frequently do such open-
ings for communication emerge, and how often do people take
advantage of them? We simply don't know.

In general, many relationships that are strained in the homeland
become different in the Melting Pot Capital of the world. Indians
and Pakistanis seem to get along fine here.[37] Devout Muslims and
Orthodox Jews live and work together amicably side by side in
Flatbush. (See figure 4.) Their beliefs regarding modest women's
dress become one reason for working together, as well as the fact
that both groups take their religion seriously. Polish superintendents have found a niche in this area too, and one of the more
popular neighborhoods for them is Borough Park, home to many
Orthodox Jews. It doesn't matter that the Poles were regarded as
very anti-Semitic in Europe. Here it's irrelevant. In fact, Orthodox

Jews express preferences at times for Polish household help, a sym-
biotic relationship quite common in the *shtetls,* or small villages,
of pre–World War II Poland. A Polish contractor tells me of his
close relationship with Rabbi Menashe Klein, a prominent leader
in Borough Park, saying, "He wanted me to go to Israel to design
a synagogue for him."

Frequently the view appears to be that there's no room for such
conflicts in the new land. But more than that may be at work
here. One mitigating fact is that the basis for conflicts often lies
in land disputes that really have no salience here. Also, local issues like crime, jobs, and education take precedence for the immigrants. Third, groups with differences between them, like Chinese
and Koreans, may find themselves experiencing the same kinds of
prejudice, and that unites them. Finally, the groups are aware of
their past differences but may wish to seize a fortuitous opportunity to try to repair them. And in that sense the city becomes a
hothouse laboratory for conflict resolution, demonstrating that in
another context warring groups can live together in harmony. It's a
view that reinforces the most optimistic hopes of the immigrants—
namely, that they can leave their age-old conflicts behind them and
start over again. Whatever the individual motivations, by the time
second-generation immigrants have reached adulthood, they have
been here for most of their lives and cannot relate to conflicts with
which they have no real familiarity. At the same time, if group
members are taught prejudice, it may yet take hold.

But the immigrants are only part of the trend toward tolerance.
Rabbi Joseph Potasnik, executive vice president of the New York
Board of Rabbis, gave me an example of such interactions when I
interviewed him in January 2013. He's an articulate, charismatic,
and engaging man with an excellent reputation for reaching out to
people of all backgrounds.

> Some years ago I was invited to the installation of Archbishop
> Edwin O'Brien, who is now at the Church of the Holy Sepulcher
> in Jerusalem. He sent me two tickets—we had been cohosts on
> my weekly show on WABC Talk Radio/770, *Religion on the Line.*
> When I arrived that day, there was an elderly Catholic woman who

desperately wanted to enter, but she had no ticket. As I had an extra ticket, I offered it to her and she said, "Who are you?" "I'm a rabbi," I told her. "Only in America," she said, "does a Catholic need a rabbi to help her get into St. Patrick's Cathedral for a ceremony." This reflects the current reality. It is commonplace in the city today for people of different faiths to see each other as members of the human family. And I see it all the time in the depth of human relationships we share with the diverse faith communities.

Forming Coalitions to Achieve Goals

What about coalitions that meet true needs? Alliances are often forged as a matter of convenience, even necessity, motivated by common needs and interests. But because of real differences, jealousies, suspicions, and the fact that that there's just so much available for each contending group, these coalitions have often foundered or have prevailed only in small geographical areas. Look at the tensions when Hispanics and blacks tried to work together in the '60s and '70s.[38] Today, differences often occur *within* groups such as West Indians and African Americans or *between* Hispanic groups like Dominicans and Puerto Ricans.

Hispanics can at least claim a common language and, very broadly speaking, a common geographic origin. Asians cannot so easily do so. Koreans, Chinese, Japanese, and Vietnamese share a similar East Asian heritage and geographic location, though they speak different languages and have had negative experiences with one another in the past. Still, they would seem to have more in common than they do with South Asians. But the South Asians also have strong differences among themselves. Pakistanis, Bangladeshis, and Indians may have a common geographic origin, and they look indistinguishable from one another, at least to outsiders. But Indians are predominantly Hindu while Pakistanis and Bangladeshis are overwhelmingly Muslim. And relations between Pakistanis and Bangladeshis are strained, despite their common religion. And where would we categorize the Guyanese? Fifty percent of the Guyanese in the United States are of Indian heritage. Yet they come from a South American nation, have not lived in India for generations, and are divided into Christians, Hindus, and Moslems, with some incorporating elements of all three faiths.

Hispanics share similar problems. Those from Peru, Colombia, and Ecuador, as well as Bolivia, are culturally separate from Caribbean Hispanics. Yet within that grouping, Dominicans, Puerto Ricans, and Cubans are also different from one another. What all this means is that lumping Asians, or Hispanics, or blacks, into one large group may be of limited value, because alliances between such disparate peoples may be very tenuous, just as they have been among other groups. And that includes another unmentioned group—those from Africa. The cultures and histories of countries like Kenya, Angola, Nigeria, and Liberia, are quite dissimilar.

These grand, all-inclusive alliances often work better in theory than in practice, it would seem. Yet without large coalitions, none of these immigrant groups will have real political and economic power. Nonetheless, it's important to remember that the group's identity is often shaped from without rather than from within, and this may provide a rallying cry around which different groups can coalesce. Just look at the modern civil rights movement of the 1960s or how the Irish, Slavs, and Italians became the "unmeltable ethnics" that Michael Novak wrote about.[39] And in the end, even the Jews frequently came to be seen merely as whites by blacks and Hispanics. It's complicated, to say the least, but the shifting mosaic does illustrate the vast changes in the makeup of the city's population mix, with the outcome remaining to be both defined and determined.

3

DINERS, LOVE, EXORCISMS, AND THE YANKEES

New York's Communities

Up near Fifth Avenue, opposite Marcus Garvey Park, is a place set up in a garage with a sign proclaiming, "Halem Bike Doctor." (The missing "r" was a misprint that they decided to keep; see figure 5.) The bike doctor turns out to be Donald Childs, a man who actually uses a stethoscope to detect and diagnose why your bike is so unhealthy or, to put it simply, broken. He explains to me how he does his thing: "I listen for the bike's 'pulse,'" says "Little Donald." (Everyone in the area, it seems, has a nickname—one, I'm told, that sticks with you forever once it's given.) "If I hear a 'whoosh,' then it's okay. But a creak, then the frame is cracked somewhere, or you need bearings." Lined up outside are dozens of shiny bikes selling at bargain rates that reflect the store's low overhead, attracting enthusiasts throughout the metropolitan area. Every Father's Day, Little Donald, a longtime past sponsor, helps organize a bike race of maybe thirty-five laps around Marcus Garvey Park, with free bikes loaned out to kids with "good report cards."

According to an article in the *New York Times,* it is the oldest continuously held bicycle race in New York City, the 1973 brainchild of David A. Walker, a former community police officer. Above all, it's one of thousands of events that gives the city's neighborhoods a sense of unity and purpose.[1] As for the park, it is one of the crown jewels of the Mount Morris neighborhood. It feels safe, as described by both white and black mothers who push their kids back and forth on swings. In the summer the large swimming pool is crowded, and the amphitheater features concerts by well-known stars like Quincy Jones and Aretha Franklin, attended by people from all over the city.

While New York City is a collection of many separate communities, it is also a unified whole. Obviously the city has a multiplicity of neighborhoods. Both in reality and in the minds of its citizens, New Yorkers view the places where they live as tiny but vibrant countries, governed by unique norms, bound together by distinct value systems, and subject to external control only in matters of functional necessity. In short, the city is a balkanized collection of towns, villages—call them what you will—almost as if they were taken from a large nation and compressed into fixed spaces.

Why is this so? First, it reflects certain elemental and primal needs to bond together, to feel secure. Second, it is part of a need to gain control over the spatial environment, to know the limits and boundaries of a place that they call home. It is also a reality created by choice. Most of the city's communities, in terms of their physical and group makeup, are there because the majority of those inhabiting them want it that way, either out of perceived necessity or because it's where they want to be. And that is why they voluntarily elect to live in a particular neighborhood. As for those people who are thrown together by different preferences for the same community—whites, Asians, senior citizens, gays, Hispanic domino players—they either learn to accommodate or move elsewhere.

And then there's the other side of the equation: New Yorkers are also acutely aware that they reside in one of the greatest cities in the world. This way of thinking is reflected in their daily conversations, in how they pepper them with references to the city: "I'm a New Yorker; what do you expect?" "Welcome to the Big Apple," and so on. It's embedded in the connection they feel to the Metropolitan Museum of Art, the Bronx Zoo, Times Square, Riverside Drive, to the hundreds of parades in all the boroughs that tell the stories of its peoples and their aspirations as well as what gives meaning to their inner selves. And it's a connection to an idea, embodied in a space and a state of mind that is far larger than themselves. It's there, they know it to be true, and so does everyone else who lives here.

Because safety is so basic to making a community livable, it's the first topic we look at in this chapter. It's also the top consideration when people decide which neighborhood to settle in. While there may be differing views of just how safe the city is today, most of those with whom I spoke agree that it is a much safer place than twenty or even ten years ago. As we shall see, reality supports that perception, though for those who live in unsafe areas, life can sometimes still be very precarious. In fact, even safe areas are not immune from crime or danger. And why crime in New York City has declined turns out be a combination of many factors.

Feeling Safe: Reality or Illusion?

This is one of the greatest changes in the city over the last thirty-five years. If people do not feel safe and are afraid to walk the streets, it is impossible for the city to attract business investment and the highly educated young talent that can make it thrive. In the 1970s and 1980s thousands of people were murdered in New York every year. The worst year was 1990, with 2,251 victims. Although this happened during Mayor David Dinkins's tenure, Dinkins hired five thousand additional police officers right before Rudy Giuliani took over. Today the city's murder rate hovers around 500 annually, a decrease of more than 75 percent. In fact, in 2012 a new modern record was set, with only 414 murders, most of them involving people who knew each other. According to city authorities, among the reasons for the decline that year were the "stop and frisk" policy, deploying police to "hot spot" areas, adding more police officers who focused on domestic violence, and monitoring social media to prevent gang-related murders.

By contrast, in 1977 truck drivers refused to make even daytime deliveries to certain areas without police escorts. And when police entered the building, one officer stayed outside to protect the squad car. In addition, during this era, countless buildings were set on fire in poor areas of the city by landlords, tenants, and criminals for all sorts of reasons, contributing greatly to the sense of lawlessness that pervaded the city.[2] Community district manager Jon Gaska described to me the situation in Far Rockaway's Edgemere Houses in the late 1970s and the 1980s: "After 11:00 PM the cops would let people run red lights on Beach Channel Drive [a major local thoroughfare], because if not, people would pull you out of your car, rob you, and steal the car. There were 'animals' who would stand on the roof of the project and shoot at the nurses coming out of Peninsula Hospital across the street, just for fun. That's how bad it was." While this was an extreme situation, large segments of the city were considered dangerous at the time.

Today the dramatic improvement can be seen in all five boroughs. The Soundview area of the Bronx features middle-class apartment complexes like Lafayette Estates, the Brittany, and the Deauville (sounds like Miami Beach!) with diverse populations. The same is true of Parkchester and Co-Op City. With 15,372 residential units as of 2007 and about 55,000 residents and still growing, Co-Op City is the largest co-op housing development in the world. It's a diverse community too, with 55 percent black, 25 percent Hispanic, and the rest non-Hispanic white and a few Asians. These places, with their parking garages, manicured lawns, and large balconies, have a decidedly middle-class feel to them even though there are also poor people residing there.

In poorer areas, however, residents often do not believe that the crime rate has gone down. Two elderly black women told me it couldn't be true, because they had just seen a report on TV of a rapist who was attacking women. People in these areas aren't sociologists. They don't read about trends. They believe in their gut. If the media writes about a crime, then in their view crime is up. A black resident of the projects told me his area wasn't safe because New York has so much crime. When I told him that the murder rate had gone down from about two thousand a year in the '80s and early '90s to five hundred today, he was very surprised. I say the same to another woman in the Jackson Houses, by 149th Street in the Bronx. Her reaction? "Oh, yeah? Well, if the murder rate went down to five hundred a year, then four hundred of them is happening right outside my building. You can do what you want with numbers, but people are getting killed right here all the time."

In truth the picture of crime today is both varied and complex. In many instances it's a relative issue. A woman tells me, "Oh, it's pretty safe anywhere in Bushwick."

"Even at night?" I ask.

"Oh, God, no. Certainly not late at night."

So then why does she feel it's safe? Because fifteen years ago you couldn't feel safe in Bushwick even in broad daylight. As noted before, compared to 1990, crime is down by 75 percent. Still, you can't call a community that had thirteen murders in 2010 "safe" by today's admittedly higher standards.[3]

I'm walking down Livonia Avenue, east of Pennsylvania Avenue, in the East New York section of Brooklyn. The area is about as dangerous as it gets today, and a policeman with whom I speak confirms it: "Of course, it's not like in the '80s or '90s, but it's bad. It's rated the worst precinct in New York City. And there's no way in hell that you'd wanna be walking around here at 1:00 AM. And I don't care if your car is stolen in Arkansas, Massachusetts, Texas, Missouri, Pennsylvania, or Indiana. No matter where it's stolen, it'll end up here in East New York." This is not accurate, of course, as cars end up in many places, but the point about the area being a center for such activity is correct. A few blocks later I see a sticker on a nice-looking car: "East New York's Finest Auto Racing Club." It seems a paradox, but perhaps the club is home to the stolen cars mentioned earlier!

Safety also has an ethnic/racial component. An Orthodox Jewish woman who works in a Canarsie preschool says, "It's safe during the day, but as soon as it starts getting dark, I leave. After all, I'm white."

"But it's not like Brownsville, is it?" I persist. Brownsville is known to be a dangerous neighborhood.

"No," she responds, "but there was a shootout here a block away two weeks ago."

The shootout is definitely evidence of crime, and her color makes the woman vulnerable. Whites working in other poor parts of the city expressed similar views. But the same question asked of an elderly black man, also employed by the preschool, a man originally from Georgia who resides in the Glenwood Houses across the street, elicits a different response. "It's pretty safe," he declares as he enjoys a quick Kennedy Fried Chicken lunch while on a break. "I came here from Crown Heights and I feel safe, even at night, though you always have to be careful." The reality? The crime rate in the precinct has dropped by over 70 percent since 1990.

Regardless, one issue that has greatly upset minorities throughout the city's rougher areas is stop-and-frisk policies, which are seen as targeting minorities. It became a more public issue in 2012, with a bill introduced in the state legislature to force changes in the policy, one that has been vigorously defended by the police.

Life in Unsafe Areas

To live in a bad neighborhood is to live in a world whose concerns probably seem surreal to outsiders, but they are real nonetheless to its residents, as the following exchange with a Bronx man reveals.

"Why does that house down the block have all the iron bars around it, top to bottom?"

"It belongs to an Indian guy from I don't know where, Guyana or Pakistan."

"Why does he live on the block, imprisoned like that? That's not a life."

"Because he owns three-quarters of the friggin' block. He's protecting his investment."

"Does he also have to come to an agreement with the gangs here?"

"Everybody does. It's a matter of unspoken respect and understanding. He has to come around and have papers signed and shake hands. And the gangs know that."

And so, in the end, you do what you have to do to survive.

This is by no means the only reason for bars on windows or doors. It is interesting that on the same block one house will have bars covering its windows from the first floor to the top floor, giving it the appearance of an impenetrable fortress, while another home directly across the street has no iron bars protecting it whatsoever. Do the unprotected just refuse to worry about being burglarized? Do they simply find it too distasteful to live behind bars, almost as if they were in a prison of their own making? Are they powerful people whom others will not mess with? Do they have differing perceptions of crime? Are those with the fortress look drug dealers protecting their stash, or people making it hard for enemies to attack them, or both? Any one of these is possible. Moreover, these days the bars on homes could even be an ode to earlier days when the neighborhood was much more dangerous, although a good number of people have been removing them as the city has become safer.[4]

There are still parts of the city that have stubbornly resisted all efforts to make them safe. The police crack down—the cherry-picker truck with the NYPD logo is a tell-tale sign—crime ebbs, the police leave, and a month or two later they're back. One such neighborhood is in the Fordham section of the Bronx, especially around Tiebout Avenue and 184th Street, where a large, intricately drawn, and fascinating mural adorns the wall of a Verizon building. Ubiquitous through the city's more dangerous parts, this one reads:

> *To my beloved husband Wilson.*
> *Your love I miss every day of my life.*
> *For all I have now is those precious memories that will always be in my heart forever.*
> *For I know we lived together in happiness and will rest together in peace.*
> *Your Wife, Mitzi.*

It has not been defaced at all and is cosigned by many people, who are identified as family members. There are no fewer than thirty-five names up there—Emily, Joshua, Robbie, Sergio, Olga, Yvonne, Papo. These are all normal names, and I think of this as an exception to the gang member murals, with the usual R.I.P.s. "How nice it is," I think, "that a woman, her children, and her extended family chose this way to memorialize her life partner."

But then I see a list of people on the right under the words "The Shirt Boys CC Mob," who have also signed on to this. Also part of the mural are entries for the "The 184th Street Posse," "The 156th Street Beck Boys" (probably Beck Street), and the "L.A. Boys, West Coast." So there's a national support group too. Altogether the names of what seem to be gang members and affiliates on the mural number about twenty-five more people. These are likely gang names, so it's certainly not a simple personal family presentation. In fact, it's probably just another gang mural in which the gang and the family are rolled into one group.

According to Verizon employees, the company has a tacit understanding with the local gang: the mural stays and the gang leaves the workers alone. That's the price of doing business in the city, and they're not the only ones to cooperate in such a way. Businesses of all types throughout the city have similar arrangements, though employees are understandably reluctant to acknowledge them. Others with whom I spoke on the block insist that Wilson was a good man who ran a T-shirt business and helped local kids stay out of trouble. According to them he died in an automobile accident. Whom to believe? One can't be sure, but it's possible that Wilson belonged to a gang at one point, or at least had friends who did, and that he was also a businessman.

There is no question that management must often walk the proverbial extra mile in these dangerous neighborhoods. This can include giving bonuses to people—one referred to it as "urban pay"—to entice employees to work in highly unsafe neighborhoods. People who want or really need the money may go for such deals, but they don't feel any safer. I spoke with a Hispanic man who was traumatized by a shooting in a nearby bodega that left two men dead. "I never feel safe here," he said, "not in a hundred years. Maybe nothing happens for two years and then, bam, bam, you're dead." This is a sobering thought. "It could happen to me," I think. But I put it out of my head. To believe that is to stop walking in these parts, and thus to limit the scope of my book.

While gang activity is less citywide than it was twenty-five years ago, it's still a problem in the more troubled neighborhoods. Even the local version of poetry reflects the continued existence of a gang culture. I use a bathroom in a Laundromat by Vermont and

New Lots Avenues in East New York. Scrawled on the wall are the words, "Let it rain, let it flood; let a Crip killah Blood." Everything in this area is poor, poor, poor, a forlorn community—Louisiana, Georgia, Pitkin Avenues, and many others. There are lots of store-front churches, signposts of poverty. No fancy brownstones like in Bedford-Stuyvesant. Many young, seemingly aimless youths gather on the streets, invariably dressed in gray or black hoodies and low-slung pants. It's a very rough area.

There is also a general acceptance of behavior in these areas that makes them different. Bushwick is one of the poorest neigh-borhoods in the city, with a high crime rate and very little gentri-fication. Fittingly, I saw a person there, the likes of which I have never seen before. A black man in perhaps his early thirties, clad in a red shirt and dark brown pants and wearing sunglasses, he was walking four large pit bulls on leashes down Broadway near Jefferson Street. Broadway is the border between Bushwick and Bedford-Stuyvesant.

Passing by a woman walking with her seven-year-old daughter, the man proclaimed, "Here, your child can pet these dogs." When she demurred, he said, to no one in particular, "Now, you're not being a nice New Yorker." As I took a closer look at him (I was walking sort of alongside him), I saw that he had two large boa constrictors wrapped around his neck. A minute later he stopped and encouraged a man to let his daughter, who seemed about the same age, pet the snakes. The man obliged and allowed one of the boas to wrap itself around his daughter, who showed only the slightest bit of apprehension—more like curiosity, it seemed.

Only in an area like this could one see such a sight. For one thing, pet boas are illegal, and four pit bulls tell you the neighborhood is not safe. Most revealingly, the casual reactions of people signify that this is not an unusual scene in Bushwick. What it means is that there's a general tolerance of such behavior in the neighborhood, because people know from personal experience that law enforce-ment in this area is minimal, so they feel and act like forgotten people. In other parts of the city, a crowd would probably gather, or people would give the man and his menagerie a wide berth. And the police would likely be summoned. But not in Bushwick on a sunny Mother's Day afternoon in early May 2011.

Nonetheless, within these areas a different model sometimes emerges. People get tired of lawlessness and take concerted action to remove the troublemakers. They organize patrols, work closely with the police, and form or reinvigorate existing community groups. In his book *Code of the Street,* sociologist Elijah Anderson shows how effective such efforts can be when those who take action are generally respected in the community. He describes how the "old heads" make clear their opposition. But because they respect the "code of the street," they know that to be credible to drug dealers they must make it clear that they will stand their ground physically to enforce their view. This is adherence to the code of "Be a man." In this way, and only in this way, the "decent" people win against the "street" people.

All too often, however, their victories are fleeting. The shootings or drug dealing in a park or on a street corner might stop, but the culprits haven't disappeared; they've simply melted away and moved their operations to another location. Walking through these sections, I sometimes feel like a visitor to another land. Only it's not another land. It's as much part of the city as Manhattan's Gramercy Park and Upper East Side, or Brooklyn's Cobble Hill or Bay Ridge. There are no walls or guards on the boundaries. When crime occurs in the tonier enclaves, those who commit them often come from the poorer areas. For that reason alone their existence matters to everyone.

Is Any Neighborhood Completely Safe?

No area, no matter how crime-free it seems to be, is completely safe. This was brought home to me one day in a sudden eruption of mayhem in one of the quietest communities in New York—bucolic Tottenville, located on the southern edge of Staten Island near the Outerbridge Crossing to New Jersey. Walking there with a photographer one spring day, I heard and almost simultaneously saw five police cars, sirens wailing, lights flashing, moving at high speeds down Hylan Boulevard, heading for a small park that jutted out to the water's edge at the end of the road. We raced two blocks on foot down the street to see what was going on.

The scene was wild. A crashed car lay across a guardrail. There were, I would guess, about fifteen patrol cars, along with several unmarked vehicles. At the left of the scene a burly man lay face-down on the ground as officers stood watch over him with their guns drawn and pointed close to his head. An apparent jurisdictional disagreement broke out between two officers. It threatened to become violent, but this was averted as other cops intervened and restored calm. To the right, officers raced into the park trying to find and capture a second man. We assumed that a major crime had occurred. Perhaps one was in the offing, but the chase had actually started when two men were seen driving a stolen vehicle and refused to stop when commanded to do so.

Thus the influence of big-city problems resonates. And why not? It's part of the same constellation of police precincts that include Brownsville, South Jamaica, and the West Bronx. No doubt there are officers in Staten Island who've done duty in high-crime, high-profile parts of the city. No matter where you are, you're never far from the big, bad city. That it could happen in our presence exemplifies it to the nth degree.

By the way, you can't always tell if an area is dangerous just by looking. According to police sources, 188th Street between Audubon and Amsterdam Avenues was at some point considered the street in Manhattan where one was most likely to be shot. (Such "facts" fluctuate, depending on police responses.) But there's a huge caveat: the shootings happen mostly to drug dealers and at night; if you're a regular citizen, it's unlikely that you'll be a victim. I walked the block several times to see how it felt. And while there were a few toughs hanging out, everything seemed quiet and like any other block in the area. In fact, one side of the street consisted completely of a public school. Several newly arrived students from Yeshiva University, located a block away, also live on the block, oblivious, as I discovered, to the street's reputation.

Quality-of-Life Crimes

The homeless are also an issue, because they sometimes commit crimes and violate a range of laws ranging from disorderly conduct, to public urination, to loitering. Sometimes they threaten and harass others. Policies toward them have changed but have always focused on two major issues: how to treat and take care of them and how to either integrate or separate them from the general population.

In the 1980s they were allowed to be in the public eye. They could beg, wash windows, and sleep on the streets. There were even areas set aside in Penn Station where homeless people could get a night's sleep on the cold floor, albeit with a blanket covering them, as commuters gingerly stepped over their inert bodies. Mayor Rudolph Giuliani changed all that after taking office in 1993. They were forced into shelters and arrested whenever they imposed themselves too heavily on the public. Regardless, they are a permanent part of the collective conscience of New Yorkers, who interact with them in all sorts of ways. Many are sympathetic to them, many are not, and most cannot understand why they want to live this way.

Despite the challenges of dealing with the homeless, the situation has improved considerably since the 1990s. In the Bronx between 1995 and 2011, the number of homeless people was reduced by about 80 percent. Citywide, it's also down by a smaller but still impressive 40 percent, with Manhattan having the largest population. Much of this change stems from the establishment of smaller and more welcoming shelters that have replaced the older, barracks-style, more impersonal, and often unsafe places.[5]

In his pathbreaking book *Sidewalk,* sociologist Mitchell Duneier expands our understanding of the homeless by focusing on a group of black men who sell books along the sidewalks around Sixth Avenue and Eighth Street and often sleep there as well. They urinate in public, use drugs, and talk loudly to passersby who want nothing to do with them. Yet they sell the locals what they want, and they watch the neighborhood. Moreover, Duneier argues, they are essentially legitimate business entrepreneurs in terms of the merchandise they offer. However, living as they do on the margins of society, and given their checkered histories, they could easily become criminals if deprived of this veneer of legitimate work.[6]

As a regular subway rider over a five-year period (2007–2012), I can confidently say from personal observation that there has been a significant increase in the number of panhandlers and performers of all sorts in every part of New York City. Many of them are intimidating, though the majority are so only in the sense of the feelings of unease and guilt felt by those declining to make a contribution. One night, however, as I was traveling on the IRT's number 1 subway train (IRT is the Interborough Rapid Transit system), I witnessed intimidation of a different sort. A man announced that he was too old to dance or sing and just wanted a quarter for food. Then, becoming more specific, he said, "And if just one Asian person sitting here would give me some money, that would be really nice." Turning to me, sitting immediately behind him, he stage-whispered, "It ain't gonna happen." I wanted to tell him that singling out Asians was unfair, but the sociologist in me won out. I remained silent so that I could be the proverbial "fly on the wall," waiting to see what happened. The six young Asian women near me stared glumly at nothing, clearly uncomfortable, but neither they nor anyone else gave the man anything. It's also unusual these days to see a police officer even shoo away a panhandler. This may be due to transit police cuts in recent years as well as new laws protecting the rights of panhandlers who aren't making a real nuisance of themselves.

"Familiarity breeds contempt," said Mark Twain. And that's another aspect of these encounters. New Yorkers have become so inured to the homeless, to panhandlers, that they do not see them as individuals, nor even as human beings. They're just annoyances, things to be ignored. At the same time, many with whom I spoke believed that stopping and questioning the panhandlers would net at least some, possibly many, who have committed more serious crimes. It would also reduce the number of panhandlers, many of whom make people nervous and sometimes even frightened.

But there's another side to this issue, a human one. Once you get to know them, as the following conversation reveals, homeless people can be complex, entertaining, and even unique. I speak with James, a black panhandler on Cliff and Fulton Streets, who is nattily attired in a white straw hat, sort of a Panama hat, black shirt, and a multicolored tie. Somewhat jarringly, he's wearing matching sweatpants with a white stripe down the sides and sneakers. Nothing looks expensive, but it all matches, weird as the combination might seem.

I ask him, "Why are you dressed up so nice? People are gonna think you don't need any money."

"It makes you more better," he says. "I'm lookin' for work. I'm a printer and an artist. I was an offset printer for years. And when they came in wit' Staples and the like, they knocked printers like me outta work."

"Where did you grow up?"

"In Harlem on 116th. Now I live in Coney Island."

"About how much can you make in a day?"

"I average sixty to seventy dollars a day."

"That's pretty good. How do you get all these people to give?"

"I get 'em when they come to me. They all know me."

"Do the police ever come over here and say, 'What are you doin' here?'"

"No, they know me and they see I'm not causin' no trouble."

"How many days a week do you work?"

"About seven."

"Then you can make about twenty-five thousand dollars a year tax-free. What time do you come in, and when do you leave?"

"Anytime I want to."

"That's a job!"

"Yeah," he says, chuckling.

"Do you do better when your hat is empty, or when it's full?"

"Empty."

"Why? If it's full, don't people think, 'If everybody's giving, I wanna get in on the action?'"

"No, they don't think that way at all. People are lookin' at your hat and sayin', 'I can do better than that.'"

"What's the biggest amount you ever got?"

"A hundred dollars from some older woman. I was just askin' for some change. I was shocked. I went and paid my rent."

"What type of people are most likely to give you money?"

"There's no type. There's no strategy in that."

"How about a brother?"

"No matter. People are people and money is money. Some people will carry change in their pocket all day and never think about giving anything to anyone."

"Is there a benefit to this location?"

"Oh, yes. Because of this little street barrier, which slows the people down so they can give you somethin'. And when they see Mc-Donald's behind me, they can think they're givin' me money so I can eat something. It's not a good idea to be standin' in front of a bar."

"Great conversation we've had. I'm writing a book about New York City."

"Yeah, good. Put me in as 'Vagabond Lover.' Love the world and the world will love you. That's my motto."

"Do you belong to any church?"

"No, I don't go to church. I don't belong to no organized religion. But I'm a spiritual being. If you go back to one million BC, man probably worshiped the volcano."

This seemingly kind, gentle, yet resilient, street-smart man has carved out a life of sorts for himself. He has his location, people who support him, and cops who protect him. He has a philosophy of life and he has skills, even though economic changes have now rendered them useless. When he tells you why his hat is deliberately kept empty, why he stands where he stands, and who is likely to give him a donation, it becomes apparent that he gives careful thought to his job, that he has a strategy. He is also part of a unique community, unique because those who pass by his station are doing just that—passing by. They work there and live elsewhere. To the extent that they're a community, it's because of people like James, who has molded them for his purposes, into a fluid but real community of givers.[7]

Explaining Crime's Decline

As noted earlier, when former mayor Dinkins hired five thousand additional police officers, crime dropped to some degree under his watch. Like all New York City mayors, Dinkins has had his detractors. So on a windy and cold Thursday morning in February 2013, I travel up to Columbia University, where he's a professor at the School for International Affairs, to get his view of things, including crime in Gotham.

He greets me warmly. I tell him about my research on black militants in the 1960s, that I grew up in Manhattan, and that I teach at City College of New York. He smiles in acknowledgment and relaxes almost visibly. The city is in his blood and you can feel it as he speaks.

In his eighties, Dinkins still looks pretty good. He is immaculately dressed, wearing a navy blue jacket with a matching bow tie. He drives up to his office daily, "honking his horn at times," as someone who knows him says. Dinkins is soft-spoken, measured, and careful in his responses. It belies his tenacious nature, one reflected by the fact that he ran for Manhattan borough president three times before he succeeded. "When people asked me what I do, I told them, 'I run for borough president,'" he says with a twinkle in his eyes. He does not, as a rule, criticize or blame others, though he does feel the press has treated him somewhat unfairly. Even there, he implies that history will ultimately regard him in a better light. And, I guess, to make sure of it, he's writing a memoir, which he modestly refers to as "my little book," his own version of what really happened. As I listen to him, I find myself thinking that this is a genuinely nice man who tried to do what's right while holding down one of the toughest jobs in the world. He inhabited for years an environment where people are often both unforgiving and unrelenting in the pursuit of their version of justice. Looking back on his days as mayor, Dinkins says:

> Whether they're for or against gun control or stop and frisk, reporters will often say, "Let us not return to the crime-ridden days of the 1990s when Dinkins was mayor." It always annoys me, because it's written as though on December 31, 1989, when I took office, there was no crime, just the next day, when I became mayor. In truth, crime went down in most major categories during my tenure. [The murder rate during his term went down from 2,245 in 1990 to 1,946 in 1993.] When we took office we had fiscal difficulties.

Ray Kelly was my deputy police commissioner; Lee Brown was the commissioner. We had more cops, more assistant district attorneys, and more probation officers than before. And we did all that, in part, by putting a surcharge on all New York City income tax. We hired five thousand police officers, and one of the beneficiaries was Rudolph Giuliani.

New Yorkers from all walks of life, rich and poor, black, Hispanic, or white, cited Rudy Giuliani as the main reason why crime dropped so sharply. Even those who intensely disliked him grudgingly gave him credit in this area. Giuliani enthusiastically adopted the "broken windows" theory of George Kelling and James Q. Wilson, which argued that arresting people for petty crimes often netted those guilty of bigger crimes. William Bratton, hired as police commissioner by Giuliani in 1994, strongly believed in it too and had used it when he headed the transit police under former mayor David Dinkins. It was he who first used the term "zero tolerance" for breaking windows and for other "quality of life crimes" like jumping turnstiles, washing windows of cars stopped for red lights, and panhandling. Between 2003 and 2009 crime in New York City declined, and so did the number of broken windows. About 23,500 windows were broken in 2009, compared with 156,900 six years earlier. The murder rate went down very significantly from 1,946 in 1993 to 649 in 2001, when Giuliani left office.[8]

Bratton also developed COMPSTAT (COMPuter STATistics or COMParative STATistics), which targeted high-crime areas and held local precinct commanders responsible for reducing the crime rate. Some believe that other factors lowered crime, such as a larger police force; cameras; the growth of the informal economy, which provided a safety net for immigrants, both documented and undocumented; more community organizations; new homes built in ghetto areas that engendered pride in the residents; and even the reclassification of certain crimes to less serious categories.[9]

To get a better perspective on Giuliani's own thoughts on his contributions in this area, I met with him in early January 2013 at Giuliani Partners, a security firm he now runs. Looking fit and trim, he greeted me cordially with a firm handshake. He seemed relaxed and thoroughly at ease, wearing a tie but no jacket, speaking animatedly about the city and the current state of political affairs. He wondered aloud about the chances of the various mayoral candidates and wanted to know if I thought Joe Lohta, his former deputy mayor, had a chance to win it all. Like Ed Koch, he seemed to have mellowed over time, though the bluntness and sharp-edged wit was still there. He seemed fascinated with the idea of my having walked thousands of miles and wanted to know what I had discovered, listening intently as I described some of my experiences.

When I asked him about what he saw as his greatest contributions as mayor, he responded: "Reducing crime, encouraging business investment in the city, increasing tourism, controlling spending, all these were accomplishments I'm proud of. But my greatest pleasure came from *changing the attitudes* of people toward the city. Both political experts and intellectuals had claimed the city was ungovernable. People had simply given up. My attitude, as a leader who loved the city, was, 'It's unacceptable to say that. If we can't do it one way, then we have to find another way.' " Then, returning to the crime issue, he concluded: "It was crystallized for me by a man who wrote a letter to one of the papers saying that as a Columbia University graduate from another era he was worried about sending his son to his alma mater, that it would be too dangerous to walk around there. However, the recent changes in the city had convinced him that now he could, that the city was now a safe and vibrant place."

Other theories—more immigrants, shifting attitudes of the young, a decline in the murder rate due to more lives saved in operating rooms, the waning of the crack epidemic, changes in public housing, legalizing abortion, and less illegal drug use—are either unproven or have been debunked by various experts. As Berkeley law professor Franklin Zimring admits, only better policing seems to have some validity, but then just in some of the bigger cities, not nationally. Whatever the debate, all agree that no one theory answers it. Some say that not enough money is being spent to find out.[10]

Liberals generally argue that education and jobs are the answer, but there are few takers for mostly menial jobs when those with little hope can make much more money in illegal activities. Conservatives favor tougher enforcement. This works to some degree, but there are always others ready to take chances because their lives seem so hopeless.

In my conversations with people, I found that community leaders, police, and criminals give the presence of cameras a great deal of credit for reducing crime. Notwithstanding complaints about poorly placed or malfunctioning cameras, their very presence is a significant deterrent. As one Brownsville drug dealer told me, "Even if nobody saw you doin' something, the camera did, and you never know who's gonna watch it." There are thousands of buildings in the poorest areas of the city that have cameras outside and inside the buildings. Who watches the film footage? Building superintendents, of course, but also landlords from their offices. Moreover, films can always be reviewed even if supers, guards, or others weren't watching it live.

This is a huge shift from the past. New York City has become one big surveillance center. In a 2006 survey the New York Civil Liberties Union reported that in Manhattan alone there were over four thousand surveillance cameras in use, and I'm sure there are many more today.[11] Civil liberties advocates object to these cameras. One scholar, David Madden, views it as indicative of the end of public space. Using New York's Bryant Park as an example of "publicity without democracy," he sees it as an "uncoupling" of public spaces concerned with citizenship, democracy, and self-development and oriented instead to consumption, business interests, and a "big-brother" idea of control over the public.[12] But Madden's view clearly does not reflect popular opinion. If it did, protests against the policy would be far greater and cameras far less prevalent. Most people, some reluctantly, feel that to keep crime rates low and to protect the public from terrorist attacks, safety trumps privacy.

Another approach to crime reduction is a spatial/ecological one advanced mainly by architectural scholars. Their solutions are to build commercial spaces and residential housing that do not have narrow hallways with poor lighting. They advocate better visibility, prickly shrubs in front of reachable windows, elevators close to lobbies, doors that swing outward, graffiti-resistant paint, and much more. They also favor long and thin parks that feature regular and frequent maintenance, with well-marked exits and entrances.[13]

When all is said and done, there are many theories about why the crime rate dropped in New York City and nationwide. Regardless of which theory you subscribe to, crime is down in the city and has been for well over a decade. And no one can deny the enormous impact this has had on the lives of its citizens and on the rebirth of the city.

Once safety is achieved, many other considerations come into play for people when they think about which New York neighborhood they want to live in. To understand what communities are all about and why they are so integral to the life of the city, it's necessary to break down all of their components. And the best way to do that is to look at these components or characteristics as reasons why people choose, or do not choose, to move into a particular community.

Among the most important criteria for deciding on a place to live are commonality of background, values, interests, and a sense of community, a factor sometimes augmented by certain individuals living in the area. Amenities like parks, recreation, nearby houses of worship, shopping, and transportation also matter, as do restaurants, nightlife, and health issues. Community gardens and their role are important for some people and merit a separate discussion. A community's status, or cachet, is yet another consideration.

Interestingly, the city block one chooses can matter almost as much as the overall neighborhood. The organizations within a community, politics, business interests, and education also play a significant role in where people elect to live. We then turn to two separate and important issues relating to communities: (1) the projects and the relationship between Manhattan and the outer boroughs; and (2) determining how these communities are all united under the city's banner even as they maintain their separate identities. We end with some thoughts about technology and community.

Shared Backgrounds, Values, and Interests

A main consideration in selecting a community is living among people who are somewhat like you. Thus people frequently base their choice on ethnicity, race, or religion. One Irish American man moved to Gerritsen Beach, Brooklyn, after becoming familiar with the neighborhood because of his route as a United Parcel Service driver. "We'd been living in Midwood nearby, but most of the neighbors were Orthodox Jews. They were okay, saying hello, but we had nothing in common with them, nor did our kids. So we came here. I had grown up in Huntington and in Wading River, Long Island, and I liked the similar village feel and the water nearby." On the other hand, a certain segment of New Yorkers, like the residents of Ditmas Park, Brooklyn, deliberately choose a community because people from a variety of groups live there.[14] For them, the values that matter most are openness, tolerance, and judging all people as individuals.

To really understand what these choices mean and how they play out, you have to walk a neighborhood block by block. Some are very insular, almost isolated. One of them is Edgewater Park, just off the Throgs Neck Bridge, in the Bronx. (See figure 6.) Most of the homes are enlarged bungalows. There are no sidewalks, so the homes face narrow, mostly no-name streets with sections named with letters of the alphabet. Everybody knows everybody, and most of the people are either of Irish, Italian, or German descent, overwhelmingly Catholic, and generally they work for the city as policemen, sanitation workers, or firemen. Some of the homes along the shoreline have beautiful views of Long Island Sound, and many of the residents own boats. Express bus service to Manhattan is available from Edgewater Park. As I walk through the neighborhood, I find myself wondering what I'll say if someone challenges me with "Can I help you?" I'm not sure, but based on my half century of walking the streets of New York, I know I'll come up with something spontaneously, so why worry when it hasn't happened yet? Such an attitude is necessary if you want to walk everywhere in the city, not just where you feel comfortable.

Most of the isolated or gated communities in the city are over-whelmingly white.[15] One notable exception is the mostly Puerto Rican area in the Bronx by the water called Harding Park, about five miles from Edgewater Park. (See figure 7.) It's very rustic with mostly small, bungalow-style homes but also some nice ranches, split-levels, and colonials. Many of the residents have been here for decades. Those on the water have a great view of the Manhattan skyline in the distance. In the foreground is Hunts Point and Rikers Island. One annoyance is the noise of planes taking off from LaGuardia Airport.

The area reminds me of Puerto Rican villages I have seen—small houses, lush gardens, birds chirping, and even chickens occasionally running across the road. Puerto Rican flags flutter in the breeze alongside those from the U.S. Army or Marine Corps in front of many homes. There are also a few Dominican flags. The people are friendly and seem to all know one another. Roberto, who works for the city, says, "This is a beautiful neighborhood, mostly Puerto Rican. It's one community. We all know each other."

I chat with Esmeralda, who has a house right on the water. She and her husband are playing outside with their grandchildren. "This is a wonderful place. We live here for twenty-four years. Go look at the garden we have here." I walk about one hundred yards and come to a small grassy area with rocks by the edge of the water. It's a public place and her house is right behind it. "On the Fourth of July people come here to see the Manhattan fireworks. It's jammed with people picnicking and taking in the view. You can't beat it," she concludes as she gazes at the gentle waves lapping up against the uneven shoreline. New York City seems far away, even though it's clearly visible.[16]

Sometimes communities with shared values evince signs of living in their own world and even make rules that cannot be legally applied to public establishments. For example, the posted dress code outside a Hasidic-owned takeout-food shop on North Williamsburg's Lee Avenue, warns, "No sleeveless, no shorts, no low-cut necklines allowed in this store." I wonder if these rules are enforced, since the outsiders most apt to violate them would be shocked that they can't dress as they please. A sign next to another store orders, "Stockings whose color closely resembles the skin are not to be worn." (See figure 8.) It's a legal ruling by the Lakewood, New Jersey, rabbinical board. Apparently even the old approach of permitting the wearing of flesh-colored stockings so long as the seams are visible is no longer good enough.

Occasionally the borders of different communities appear to be clearly demarcated but are actually so only in portions of an area. For example, Flushing Avenue seems to divide the Hasidic neighborhood of South Williamsburg from that of mostly black Bedford-Stuyvesant. (See figure 9.) If you stand on the avenue where it runs between Nostrand and Marcy Avenues, it appears to starkly set off two distinct communities. On the south side is the New York City Housing Authority's Marcy Houses, low-income projects, predominantly black, where the rapper Jay-Z (the J and Z subway lines ran nearby) grew up. Here black kids shoot hoops in the park while adults sit on nearby park benches, engaged in casual conversation or simply relaxing. On the north side of Flushing Avenue is the Hasidic community. The recently built red brick apartment buildings have terraces from which I can see youngsters wearing large black skullcaps and with side curls dangling by their ears, standing and animatedly talking and laughing. Some are intently watching the basketball game in progress. Do they harbor a secret desire to join the game? What a chasm between the two sides of the street, both culturally and economically! They're in different universes. We know from what has happened in Crown Heights with blacks and Lubavitcher Hasidim that the gap between these two groups can be narrowed somewhat. But these are the very insular mostly Satmarer Hasidim, not the Lubavitcher. They're not into outreach.

Yet to look at this street as if it were a real dividing line is a distortion. True, the New York City Housing Authority policy is not to tear down a project, but rather to rehabilitate and renovate it, and that's why Marcy Houses remains. The Hasidim have large families and need space, but they would not move into a project that's completely black and Hispanic. So what happens is that the Hasidim go *around* the project, picking up again several blocks south of Flushing Avenue, and build new housing and even yeshivas (Jewish schools) beyond it, in Bed-Stuy itself. Here the two groups do have contact on the streets and on building sites and in playgrounds, where the children meet on neutral ground. Tiferes Bnos school is at 585 Marcy Avenue, well south of Flushing Avenue. And there are people coming back from morning services a block farther down. In this way it's possible for a community with shared values to remain so, even if it's separated by a few blocks.

Whether this movement into mostly black Bed-Stuy has any impact on how the various groups perceive one another would make for an interesting study. When members of a group are outnumbered, they tend to reach out more to their neighbors in a desire to be more accepted. This would apply even to the very distinctive Hasidim. Some may ask, why is this any different from the situations that existed in the '60s, '70s, and '80s when blacks and Puerto Ricans moved into white Brooklyn areas like Brownsville and Canarsie? The answer is that attitudes are quite different from those times, times when a popular observation was that integration is what happens from the time the first black moves in and the last white moves out. Not so today when greater numbers of blacks, Hispanics, and whites reside in the same neighborhoods (see chapter 6). There is far less tension and greater general contact now, even between Hasidim and other groups. In fact, I've encountered Hasidic Jews in the South Bronx, East New York, and elsewhere where they build, buy, and manage properties, working closely with the local residents. As we'll see in chapter 7, Hasidim even teach in public schools that are 100 percent made up of minorities. Their interactions with the locals in many situations merit closer examination.

Finally, there are circumstances when common values and interests can unite an ethnic group throughout an entire borough that cuts across many communities within it. As I walk the South Bronx, I see many New York Yankee flags and decals on cars and pasted onto apartment windows. The fact is that South Bronx residents are highly loyal to, and proud of, the city's baseball team. But it's more than what they do for the team by being fiercely partisan about it—it's what the Yankees do for *them*. Sure, the Yankees are known for their well-heeled fans, and indeed most of those residing in the impoverished Bronx neighborhoods that stretch out beyond the gates of Yankee Stadium could not afford anything but the cheapest and most remotely situated seats. But this does not matter nearly as much as the fact that the Yankees have chosen to remain in the South Bronx. That beautiful stadium gives standing to the borough. It means that the Bronx is their true home, and this presence says it all.

Against this backdrop is it any wonder that the elderly Puerto Rican homesteader and Korean War vet in Mott Haven can say to me as he stands outside his home, with Spanish music blaring from an outsize boom box, "I *love* the Yanquis. They are my team and part of my life. I go to all the games I can, and I get discounts because I was in the army." And in the larger sense, this is also what makes a community a community—shared loyalties, shared memories, and a bond with a team that has always made the Bronx their home. This is especially true of the team's Hispanic players, demigods like Mariano Rivera and Alex "A-Rod" Rodríguez, even as they gripe about how much superstar Rodríguez is paid. Yankee Stadium is an essential part of what makes these people proud of their community, one that outsiders must dutifully trek to if they want to see the one of the world's greatest baseball teams play.

A Sense of Community

Community is a critical and complex component, and one with many aspects. Above all, community means friendliness. I'm reminded of this as I pass a church in the Morrisania section of the Bronx that has expressed this idea, but has done so by borrowing from a commercial ad used in the motel industry. Outside Mother Walls AME Zion Church, a very old, one-story brick building with large windows, is an invitation familiar to millions of American travelers. A sign reads, "Come home to Mother Walls and be with the Father. We'll leave the light on." Are you listening, Motel 6? And, appropriately enough, it's actually on Home Street, right where it intersects with Intervale Avenue. In this context it seems as though the subliminal message being expressed is truly sublime.

One place where such feelings are palpable is Staten Island, which really doesn't feel like the rest of New York. Because they are not connected by subway to the rest of the city, and their borough has a smaller population than others, Staten Islanders feel neglected and have even wanted to secede from the city at various times. My conversation with Dan and Louise, who have lived on the north side of the island near the ferry for more than thirty-five years, gave the impression of people who live in a community that's its own world. Everything—the restaurants, the artists groups, the fights, the history—suggests a town that is on its own culturally and spatially and has been so for many years. But what's most impressive is the degree to which residents of the island interact with their neighbors and each others' children and the degree of solidarity they feel. "That's one of the reasons I moved here, this incredibly strong sense of community," says Louise.[17]

To really grasp the degree to which New York City's neighborhoods are, by and large, hospitable places, at least to those who live there, one needs to see them in the evenings and on the weekends, when people are relaxed and outside. One summer evening I walk up Westchester Avenue in the Bronx around 8:30 as darkness settles over the hot asphalt street. It is a warm and muggy night. Far fewer women than men are walking by. Some of them are carrying bags of groceries, others clearly returning home from the St. Lawrence Station of the 6 train. People sit outside the bodegas, again almost all men, on folding chairs, chatting, smoking cigarettes, enjoying the evening breeze. Walking along the service road of the Cross Bronx Expressway, I pass a small club and peer through the open doorway. Inside, four men sit around a folding table playing dominoes. The light, simply a naked yellow bulb, hangs from a cord coming out of the ceiling. It swings wildly back and forth, propelled by the breeze from a metal fan, and casts shadows through the room. When the light falls on the table I look at the middle-age Hispanic men wearing sleeveless under-shirts. Their foreheads glisten with beads of sweat from the heat as they move the dominoes to and fro, laughing and joking with each other, the banter of their conversation punctuated by hand motions and heads nodding, as if to accentuate the points they are making. It is clear that they feel totally relaxed and completely at home.

There are, however, drawbacks to living in a close-knit commu-nity. For example, an older woman living on East Ninth Street in Manhattan's East Village observed:

> This is a strong community, like a small village. We look out for each other. And we care, too. The friction here, when it comes out, is political, not racial or social. I mean, it's all about whether you're a Marxist or an anarchist. I mean, there are only two registered Republicans that I know of on the entire street. But it's not an ideal world by any means. There's a lot of gossip. Everybody knows what kind of car you have, if you do; who had a fight with who; who has a boyfriend. Everybody knows everything, just like in a small Midwest town. And sometimes, I hate to admit it, you just get tired of saying hello to someone you passed by for the seventeenth time in a week.

Others with whom I spoke had similar criticisms about the neigh-borhood, but the consensus was that the good far outweighs the bad. Why? Largely because when you need your neighbors, they know you and they're there for you.

Another area that has a very strong sense of community is East Elmhurst, Queens, a black, Hispanic, and Asian middle-class community right next to LaGuardia Airport. Blacks began buy-ing homes there in the 1970s. I remember visiting the ranch-style home of Ernest Kaiser, who at the time was the director of Har-lem's Schomburg Center for Black Culture. He was an outstanding bibliographer and historian at the Schomburg for forty-one years until he retired in 1986. We sat in his backyard drinking lemonade while he gave unstintingly of his time to help me with a book I was writing on African American and African relationships over time. The community was a Shangri-la, he told me. And in fact this was the feeling for many people in the neighborhood, a good number of them black. According to the U.S. Census Bureau, out of more than two thousand census tracts, East Elmhurst is *first* in the city in terms of people remaining in one community for a period of time. The median number of years living there is an incredible thirty-six. Among its more famous past residents have been Willie Mays, Harry Belafonte, Attorney General Eric Holder, and Dizzy Gillespie.[18]

For some people, "sense of community" is rooted in a perception, sometimes idealized, of suburban living in the city. One thinks of the white areas of New York as static in terms of who lives there. They are often perceived as once vibrant communities where forty years ago young families raised their children, but where they are now aging out, their offspring having long since departed for the suburbs, as chronicled by historian Kenneth Jackson in his classic work, *Crabgrass Frontier*.

But that is too simplistic a portrait. As Kenneth Kearns, district manager of Community Board #10, which includes areas like Throgs Neck and Pelham Bay, told me:

> This is not a gentrifying area, with yuppies coming. Right now it's more young white families who are looking for suburban living within the city limits. It's a bedroom community—namely, Pelham Bay—whose people work in Manhattan. Many used to live elsewhere in the Bronx—Co-op City, Fordham, Soundview, or Kingsbridge. This is a move-up destination community. In some cases they bought their parents' house. In Westchester they would pay a fortune in taxes, at least ten thousand dollars a year. The average tax bill here is about three thousand dollars a year. They're people who want to put down roots.

This non-yuppie group is one that's under the radar screen. They want an affordable mix of urban and suburban living that can be found only in certain locales, among them Little Neck, Bayside, and Cambria Heights, all in Queens; or in the Brooklyn communities of Marine Park, Mill Basin, and Bay Ridge. Like the Hasidim in Williamsburg, they could be an interesting group to look at more closely.

Community Characters

Virtually every community has individuals who can make a real difference in terms of its fortunes and who enhance feelings of unity. I speak with Douglas, a forty-two-year-old black man who looks younger than his true age. He is riding an all-terrain vehicle in Skyline, a New Brighton park near the West Brighton, Staten Island, community border. At first I thought he worked for the park, but it turns out that he's just one of these self-appointed community types. As he explains it, "I just live here, but riding around I see a lot of stuff, and I report it to the proper authorities so they can take care of it." Douglas is the sort of person who contributes in important ways to a community's quality of life. Such people can lower the crime rate through their vigilance, help people to feel part of a "real" community, and lobby effectively for community services. This type of voluntary activity is clearly not risk-free. The seventy-three-year-old woman raped in Central Park in September 2012 was attacked by a man angered that she had photographed him masturbating in the park. As it turned out, she was in the habit of reporting people who violate park rules like walking unleashed dogs and riding bicycles in areas where they are banned.[19]

Another type is the "public figure," a staple of life in many of the city's neighborhoods. These are the people who make life interesting and give places that difficult-to-define adjective—character. There was, for example, the mysterious street performer named Moondog. Wearing a horned Viking helmet and a flowing cape, and holding a spear in his hand, Moondog, whose real name was Louis Hardin, was stationed on Sixth Avenue near Fifty-fourth Street. Most of the passersby who gave him money never knew that this blind fixture on the street was a published composer whose music was on labels like Angel and CBS and who had written the music for more than a few radio and TV commercials.[20] This is the stuff that legends are made of. It is also what makes a place like New York special, because there are so many people like him. Even without Moondog's achievements, these unique characters add flavor to people's own lives. People talk to them and about them. Whether it's a cantankerous store owner, a street dancer, a man on a soapbox, a naked cowboy, or just a street-corner group, these people shape a community. They are often the glue that holds things together.

There are also people who give a community character by dint of their craft, be it a pottery maker, a designer of unique floral arrangements, the owner of a special restaurant, the "Harlem Bike Doctor," and many others. A perfect example is Louis Palladino, a pizza pie maker in the extreme. He has been making pizzas at various places in the Throgs Neck part of the Bronx for almost seventy years, and according to Palladino, that makes him the longevity record holder. Most recently he has been ensconced in the kitchen of an Irish restaurant on Philip Avenue called P. J. Brady's, where he serves up his creations on Sunday nights. The workers have his recipe for the other days.

Listen to Palladino describe how he makes a pie. He says that first it has to be cooked to an equal thickness from tip to base. "If it starts out thin and then gets thicker, you've got an amateur making the pies." Stretching the dough just right is also important, as is working the edges, but not the center, which "takes care of itself." There are key differences in how the ingredients are distributed too. He seasons sausage pies by sprinkling oregano on them, but for mushroom pies the flavoring of choice is garlic powder. "I must've made over a million pies and I put my heart in every one. I like to make my pies. I'm a pie man, that's what I am. I might be ninety years old, and if I can still make 'em, I'll make 'em." Louis Palladino is no itinerant worker or tradesman. He's an artist, a craftsman—that's what he is.[21]

I tracked Palladino down in his culinary lair one Sunday. He was friendly but quiet, almost shy. "Yeah, that's me," he said. "I love what I do." In his eighties, he still seemed healthy and alert. "I got customers who been eating my pies for many years, and with God's help they'll keep on eating them." The pizzeria is a pleasant place, with shiny booths and wooden bench chairs and young waitresses with a ready smile. Walking by it you would never know it as anything other than a nice-looking tavern where the locals watch the Yanks, Mets, Rangers, and Knicks, loudly criticizing or complimenting their performance as they drink beer and ale. But in the next room a pie man does his thing, and the people keep coming back for more.

And here's a rather unique community figure of an entirely different order. I stop outside a church on 2112 Grand Avenue between 180th and 181st Streets. It's in a semi-attached, three-story brick house with a metal cross hanging outside. It's called the Eclesia Catolica Cristiana. And on the announcements board outside is a very interesting statement. (See figure 10.)

> Thursday, 9-25-97, at 7:11 AM, the Most Holy Virgin Mary appeared to me and said, "You are St. Delfin I. Do you know who I am? I am Mary, Mother of Christ. I know that my Son visited you, and that he proclaimed you Second Savior and Messiah, for your love of the black, the white, the yellow, the mulato, the American Indian, and [others]. I am with you now and always. Many blessings will I give you for all who believe in Jesus and in you—my second most beloved son."

This is followed by a schedule:

> Exorcisms, Friday, 8:30 PM
> Sundays, Holy Mass, English 9:00 AM, Spanish 11:00 AM
> Everyone is Welcome.
> Rev. Fr. Delfin Rodríguez Rector

Delfin Rodríguez has been dead for seven years. Yet the story of how he became a saint remains on the board, almost as if it were frozen in time. It speaks of a time when this man was vibrant and alive. I talk with a black woman sitting in a small van outside, a lifelong resident, and ask her what this announcement is all about.

"His wife carries on," she says, "but they just have a few people that come every Sunday. He was a nice guy who helped people a lot. He had a long white beard and was always in white attire."

"Did you believe he was, like, a real saint?"

"I believe there was something special about him. Like whenever you needed him he was there. And whenever people walk by the house where the church was they remember him."

The woman passes no judgment on the truth of Rodríguez's claims to be a saint. But in the long run she seems to feel it doesn't matter. What matters is that he was a good soul who cared about others, and therefore there's no desire to challenge his claims. Who can know the truth about such things anyway? A man has a dream. There can be only one version of what happened in that dream—his own. And we can choose to believe or disbelieve it. As for the story itself, it's highly unusual—there aren't many exorcists in New York City's communities.[22] What isn't unusual, however, is the ubiquitousness of community characters in general.

As for me, I find myself wishing that I could have met and talked to Father Rodríguez. It's a not unusual feeling for me, because cities are dynamic in so many ways, forever changing. What's left are stationary reminders that have outlived those who created these places, whether they are buildings, restaurants that have moved but have left their signage behind, murals that lasted a few years and were replaced by buildings or simply erased by new owners of the spot. I also think about how much less I would have learned about Delfin Rodríguez had this woman not been there or if I had decided not to talk with her.

Union Turnpike ends at Myrtle Avenue, and right there the last block has the sub-name Frederick A. Haller Way, sponsored by Greenstreets, a New York City beautification initiative, which has also erected a little mall here, adding the familiar name Frederick T. "Bud" Haller Jr. "for his many years of dedication and commitment to the Glendale community." Naming vest-pocket parks and streets after local people who've contributed to a community enhances solidarity; makes people think, even momentarily, about what community means; and, most importantly, gives those living there a hope that they or their friends will be remembered by future generations for what they have done voluntarily. But getting it done means there have to be people who care enough about the person to see the idea through. Of course, sometimes the communities change. The Mexicans, Chinese, or other, more recent arrivals don't recognize the name on the plaque, but at least those who lived there can return, look, and remember.[23] Every neighborhood has hangouts—barber shops, beauty parlors, bodegas, parks, or even corners where people gather to talk. These activities are critical to maintaining a sense of community, to making people feel that they have a place they can call home, besides their apartment or house.

I sometimes go to a Bukharian barber in Queens. Alex is friendly, like most barbers, but he also respects his customers' boundaries. If I want to talk, he talks. If I want to read the paper, he doesn't talk. One difference about his shop is that he has a large-screen TV where he and his fellow barbers watch Russian soap operas or movies, exclaiming loudly in Bukharian at murder, sex, or whatever else takes place. He also has several buddies who hang out in the back of the shop, drinking and eating, and who are a fixture there, sort of a mini-community.[24] Sometimes when they laugh, gesticulate, and slap each other on the back, I wish I could understand what they're saying, but that's life. You can't speak every language!

The feeling of community in a neighborhood can also be enhanced by certain types of professionals, especially physicians. A neighborhood with caring practitioners living within it is all the more desirable for their presence. These people define a community, and they personify and articulate its values. A doctor who delivered hundreds of babies in a community, or one who took care of you or your parents for decades—they make a difference. Another category of people whose presence can add to a sense of community is police officers and firefighters. These individuals can and do save lives. Their relationships with the locals affect the community's self-perception and how outsiders view it.

Amenities

Amenities such as playgrounds, museums, libraries, and swimming pools all play an important role in decisions of where to move. An outdoors type may be influenced because of parks in the area. A devoutly religious person will put a vibrant church, temple, or mosque at the top of his or her list. Communities can also be attractive because they revolve around a certain activity.

Neighborhoods like Gerritsen Beach, Edgewater Park, Sheepshead Bay, City Island in the Bronx, and others near the water are
distinguished by the number of boats in both the nearby water
and in the driveways of many homes. Mill Basin, with lots of waterfront property, is typical. It is home to more than two hundred
private docks, the Bergen Beach Yacht Club, and the Mill Basin
Marina.[25]

Sometimes shopping districts determine where the action is. It's
a significant factor, but one with different meanings for different
people. For some a Fairway grocery or an IKEA home furnishings
store can tip the scales. For others it's shopping malls that contain
stores with low prices. Still others want to be a twenty-minute
ride away from department stores like Macy's, Bloomingdales,
or Bergdorf-Goodman. Others are more impressed by an indoor
mall like King's Plaza in Brooklyn. Stores geared to various ethnic
groups are a prime attraction for their members.

Often, given the city's polyglot nature, the shopping districts are
multiethnic. An extreme case can be found on Roosevelt Avenue
in Queens, where Korean, Indian, and Chinese stores are joined
by seven Colombian, Dominican, and Argentinean businesses. Not
far away, opposite William Moore Park in Corona, one Jewish,
one Korean, two Greek, and two Dominican stores coexist among
fourteen Italian businesses.[26] As I looked at these places, it suddenly hit me just how complex New York is. How many cities have
stores like this all in one location? A more common pattern is for
ethnic stores to all be located on one shopping avenue or street,
something that the city also has.

Those who reside in the more hardscrabble parts of Gotham
have their own shopping areas that bear little resemblance to the
Kings Plaza Mall in Mill Basin; the shopping center in Douglaston, Queens; or Manhattan's Fifth Avenue, Broadway, and various other streets. There's certainly no Macy's or Lord & Taylor.
Typical is Jamaica Avenue in Queens, where you will find a mix of
cheap carpet stores, used furniture places, beauty salons, and many
small delis. The main shopping area is from 169th to 160th Streets
with well-known chain stores like Rainbow, Marshall's, Old Navy,
and Zale's, the last of which appears to have few shoppers—it's

just too fancy for the area. The nearby King David Jewelry store, by contrast, is filled with shoppers. Most of the stores, some quite large, are not well known at all and they reflect the lower income level of the neighborhood—Electronics for Best, Don't Panic, Porta Bella Shoes. The Jamaica Center neighborhood even has people with a sense of humor, as attested to by a half-century-old tavern called the Blarney Bar, whose sign outside warns, "Hot Beer, Lousy Food, Bad Service."

There are similar shopping centers on 149th Street in the Bronx, where Westchester and Third Avenues meet, popularly known as "the Hub," and in Brooklyn, on Broadway, Fulton Street, and Sunset Park's Fifth Avenue. What they all have in common is low-end stores that reflect the poverty that surrounds them. The local population is not happy with the choices, or lack thereof, or the depressing atmosphere, but it's what they can afford and it's nearby.

Reflecting on this I wonder what those who live here must feel when they find themselves walking along Manhattan's Fifth Avenue. Envy of those who crowd into Lord & Taylor? Curiosity? How often do they go in just to window shop? Do they ever splurge for a special occasion like a birthday or anniversary? Or do they just hurry by, not even wanting to gaze at what they can't have. Certainly those who work in the area, as vendors, maintenance people, or even as security guards inside the stores, must think about this world, so far removed from Brownsville and East New York's cut-rate shopping boulevard, Pitkin Avenue.

Lack of good transportation generally makes an area less attractive. One example is Greenpoint, where having only the G train, which doesn't go into Manhattan, reduces the area's attractiveness for those working there. But there are those who see a lack of public transportation as an *advantage* in terms of safety. People feel that if they live in a two-fare zone (taking a subway and a bus), it makes it harder for criminals to reach and target their neighborhoods.

All of these factors are of prime importance in deciding where to live. There are other criteria that aren't as basic but may nevertheless be the tipping point. Among these are choices in where to eat. Success for restaurants often depends on their ability to connect with their communities. In Harlem customers at Sisters on East 124th Street seem especially fond of the roti dishes and of their signature offering, Brown Stewed Chicken. I ask Ricky, the chef, how it's made.

"It has a sweetness to it," he replies, in the lilting accent native to his homeland, St. Kitts. "It's not too spicy or smoky, and we use many ingredients, including brown sugar and onions. As all chefs will tell you, cooking's an art, not a science, and the trick is the amounts and the timing."

"But is there a special ingredient?" I persist.

"Well, yes," he says, with a soft chuckle. "It's called love."[27]

Because of their huge menus, moderate prices, and casual atmosphere, diners are often community anchors. They're truly for everyone—kids, seniors, businessmen, ladies' and men's groups. You can talk business; have a good time hanging out for a while; or have a heart-to-heart with your child, spouse, girlfriend, or mistress. You can have a big dinner or just a cup of coffee. Paradoxically, because of their size and division into booths, as opposed to a small restaurant where everyone glances at you as you walk in, patrons of diners are guaranteed a modicum of privacy. When a local diner closes, many in that community are affected because they associate it with so many important and perhaps life-changing events: "I remember exactly where we were sitting when I told them that if your daughter keeps on harassing my daughter, I'll see to it that you never . . . ." or, "She asked to meet me at the Moon Bay Diner because it was private."

So it's not surprising that in a *New York Times* article about the closing of the Scobee Diner in Little Neck, Queens, after an existence of some seventy years, the place was described by writer Joseph Berger as being "its neighborhood's social hub, the place where parents brought their uniformed children after Little League games, where teenagers took their first dates and where the end of another year was celebrated, whatever the report card said." And, I might add, it was only fitting that the Little Neck community's annual Memorial Day parade down its section of Northern Boulevard would pass right by the diner.

Interestingly, the Scobee Diner was owned, for a time, by the parents of former CIA director George J. Tenet, who spent five years working there as a busboy so that he could pay for his first car. Like so many other establishments, the diner bragged about the famous regulars who ate there—Richard Tucker, Telly Savalas, and Alan King. Highlighting the long hours involved in running a diner that was open 24/7 and featured some three hundred items on its menu, the last owner's daughter offered the following poignant observation as it was about to close: "This is the only place I knew for Thanksgiving. I didn't know you sat around a table."[28]

As with restaurants, nightlife is something many people take into account when deciding where to live. A local tavern where one can gather to imbibe while watching sports at the end of a long day or on a weekend has great appeal for some. It's even better if you can meet new people or just hang with friends and enjoy a friendly game of eight ball or shoot darts. Ditto for the wine bars and nightclubs that attract so many of the young. Walk along Broadway in heavily Hispanic Upper Manhattan, or on Roosevelt Avenue in Jackson Heights, Elmhurst, and Corona, Queens, and you will see them, one after another. The crowds in such places can be huge, just as they are in the throbbing nightlife areas of Chelsea, Noho, Soho, and Tribeca, in Lower Manhattan.

Finally, health considerations can influence one's choice of residence. Several Polish people in Greenpoint told me that they are moving to nearby Ridgewood because of pollution problems in the industrial parts of Greenpoint. For decades "garbage dump" was one of the things that first came to mind when people said "Staten Island," and that's because of the Fresh Kills Landfill. The garbage of millions of New Yorkers—during a fifty-year period, some 150 million tons of garbage—was disposed of there, making it the largest municipal landfill in the world. Today, however, Fresh Kills is being transformed into a park featuring wetlands, picturesque creeks, kayaking, horseback riding, and great views of the city. There is currently an idea up for consideration, the Mierle Laderman Ukeles proposal, calling for a million people to participate in an artwork for the newly created Fresh Kills Park. When completed, Fresh Kills will be the second-largest park in New York City after Pelham Bay Park, meaning it'll be bigger than Central or Prospect Parks. This makes it a particularly striking example of going from ugly to beautiful.

The Attraction of Community Gardens

Community gardens are another way to make people feel more attached to their neighborhoods. The largest number of such gardens, 316, which is almost half the entire total in the city, are in Brooklyn, and East New York has 88 of them. They are tended by locals and volunteers from outside, like high school students from Stuyvesant High. The rural roots of many of the area's Hispanic and black residents contribute in no small measure to their popularity. The areas with the fewest public parks tend to have the most gardens. Under New York City's Green Thumb program you get a one-dollar-a-year lease if you open up the garden to the public for a minimum of ten hours a week. And it's not permanent. In fact, if the city or a private group wants to develop the land, you have thirty days to vacate. This has caused conflict, of course.[29]

As I meander through the South Bronx, I pass a well-kept, white-shingled colonial home at the intersection of Tinton Avenue and East 158th Street. The house has a beautiful manicured garden that includes tiny spruce trees and a small waterfall gently flowing over round, smooth, beige stones arranged in a descending pattern. Religious statues are scattered throughout the garden, and a Puerto Rican flag flies over them. A sign in neat script proclaims, "Our Garden," and the flowers are just beginning to bloom beneath the sunny sky. You have the feeling that behind the iron fence a family has created its own little piece of heaven on earth, complete with a small plastic Adirondack chair on the porch, where they can imagine themselves being far from the hectic pace of city life.

My reverie on peace and tranquility in the city is suddenly interrupted by the familiar sound of the nearby subway heading toward the North Bronx on the elevated tracks above Westchester Avenue. When you realize that there is quite a bit of this subsidized housing, it becomes evident that the South Bronx in no way resembles the "Bonfire of the Vanities" of yesteryear, when the area was rife with crime and violence. In fact, on a weekday at noon there's almost no one in the street.

At the Grove Hill Park on 158th Street a sign announces, "A Garden Awakening Event." Local students from the elementary school up the block sit on the ground with their teacher and role-play as vegetables—an ear of corn, a tomato, and a pepper. Nearby is a riotous display of tulips, petunias, and daisies, which the teacher points to as she explains the concept of pollination. As I look at her, a young, earnest-looking, and enthusiastic woman in her thirties, I would guess, I'm reminded that without a veritable army of people, so many of them idealistic, who are reaching out to those less fortunate, these activities wouldn't be happening. These gardens also suggest the direction of the trend in the Bronx—improvement. There are fifteen-story-high construction cranes everywhere in this area where tall, brand-new residential towers are under construction and the sounds of bulldozers and ear-rattling jackhammers fill the air.

Then I see the El Flamboyan Garden on East 150th Street, one of so many community gardens that make the neighborhood beautiful. (See figure 11.) A boxy miniature school bus with Bozo the clown in the driver's seat sits in the garden, and along the side is a small, set-to-scale picket fence with alternating red and white colors. There is a statue of Jesus next to a Puerto Rican flag. An announcement invites people to a Father's Day celebration at the garden. In this way community and family are melded together and strengthened. There are probably two or three gardens per block in this area. The idea of using empty spaces this way was really brilliant.

The gardens have a personal feel to them because their designs are so eclectic, sometimes even haphazard, with freedom of expression the seemingly unifying factor. There are religious statues, ethnic flags, Yankee banners, ceramic art objects, and sailboats made out of tin with flowers incongruously placed on top; a bright bubble-gum-pink tractor sits atop a small mound of earth.

One celebrity who is involved in the city's gardens is Bette Midler, founder of the New York Restoration Project (NYRP).

It's a nonprofit group that has created sixty-four gardens to date. There are, in fact, hundreds of corporations, churches, museums, and other groups that donate money and time for a vast array of projects, beautifying, educating, and renovating. Without them the city would be much impoverished. According to people in the NYRP's Ogden Avenue office in the Bronx (the other is in downtown Manhattan), Midler comes up a lot and is personally involved. The young woman working in the office does this as part of her service for AmeriCorps, a domestic version of the Peace Corps. She informs me that vandalism is a problem in the gardens. NYRP's latest project, Million Trees NYC, an effort to make the city greener by planting a million trees in the Big Apple, is being carried out in conjunction with the New York City Department of Parks and Recreation. The project was announced on October 9, 2009, near Bette Midler's rose garden on Teller Avenue in the Bronx. I find myself wondering if there's room in the city for so many trees.

There probably is, if demand is any indication. And the phenomenon isn't limited to low-income areas. Gary Giordano, head of Queens Community Board #5, which includes middle-class, largely white Middle Village, Ridgewood, and Glendale, says, "We're proud that we've planted more trees through city funding than any other district. It makes all the difference when you look down a block and see it's lined with trees." The view is echoed by Marilyn Bitterman, head of Flushing's Community Board #7: "We have many parks, but we need more green space in the neighborhoods themselves." Contrast this with the bad old days of the 1980s, when people feared that a tree could be a hiding place for a mugger!

To sum up, the community gardens contribute to the essence of communities in many ways. Created mostly in poor areas, their presence beautifies the often monotonous sections of the city that contain block after block of tenement-style buildings interspersed with empty lots. They provide a comfort zone for those residents with rural roots, giving them a touch of home, if you will. Their eclectic nature, frequently featuring a potpourri of homeland flags, religious statues, children's toys, and other items, allows the residents to express themselves. Finally, they are a welcome venue for parties and celebrations that give people the all-important sense of community that so many of them seek

Community Cachet

Most communities want it, but not all can get it. Even if it's a reach, you have to create a hook. On the Upper West Side, emblematic of the neighborhood's intellectual bent, you have Eighty-fourth Street between West End Avenue and Broadway. It has been named Edgar Allan Poe Street as well. But what catches my eye is the coffeehouse near Broadway called Edgar's Cafe. (See figure 12.) I walk in and engage the Ukrainian waitress—a City College student, as it turns out—in a conversation. I see that some of Poe's poems adorn the walls, as well as a drawing of him. It seems he lived in a farmhouse on this location for a short time in 1844, penning his famous poem "The Raven" here.

Looking around at the young crowd, I ask her, "Do the people here know who Poe was?"

"Not really. Hardly any. In fact, people call up here asking to speak to 'Edgar.' They think he manages or owns the café."

I give her a skeptical look.

"I swear it! I swear it!" she exclaims, almost gleefully.

"So what do you tell them?"

"I tell them he's not in," she says, laughing. "And then I ask if I can help them."

And so we see how a Ukrainian waitress, in the United States for just three years, can trump native-born Americans in the knowledge game! Owing to a steep rent increase, Edgar's has now relocated to Amsterdam Avenue, and it's still a pretty cool place.

I pass Pete's Tavern on Eighteenth Street and Irving Place. It's also referred to on the sign outside as the place "O. Henry made famous." It turns out that the author lived nearby at 55 Irving Place and was a frequent patron. He also wrote "The Gift of the Magi" there. Inside, I'm shown his booth, which has photos and newspaper stories about him. Many famous people have been to this place, including James Dean, Natalie Portman, John Leguizamo, George Stephanopoulos, Jacques Chirac, and Daniel Patrick Moynihan. Founded in 1864, it's New York City's oldest continuously functioning tavern, thereby conferring status on both the place and the community. I vow to bring my wife, a writer and big O. Henry fan, here one evening as a surprise.

We go there a week later, only it's me who's surprised. I had imagined our having a quiet, contemplative dinner, discussing literature, and thinking of how we're in the company of greatness even if it's only O. Henry's table rather than the writer himself. To my dismay, when we enter, Pete's Tavern is no longer the quiet locale it was on the morning I had stopped in. It has been transformed into a raucous singles bar, with hordes of young people, most of them so inebriated they wouldn't have recognized O. Henry or paid him any mind even if he showed up. We can barely hear each other speak above the din.

What I do get out of the experience is a sharp reminder that one must try as much as possible to see New York City in the same locations at different times, because *when* is often as important as *where*. Day or night? Weekend or weekday? Winter or summer? It can be, and often is, very different.

In the East Village, Mud, an Internet café at 307 East Ninth Street, also happens to be where the Beastie Boys recorded their first album, *Polly Wog Stew.* That's clearly cachet. And number 321 was once home to Jimi Hendrix. A sign in front of the building tells passersby to feel free to write letters to Jimi and place them in the orange mailbox, where they will go "directly to heaven." And, unexpectedly, out in Staten Island, in the small village of Travis, I come across a red and gold New York City Fire Department truck. Written in gold script along its side are the words "Splendor in the Grass." Curious, I ask the driver what it means. Is it that someone just liked the movie a lot? "Oh, no. It's that they filmed much of the movie here in a house on Victory Boulevard." The house is no more, nor is Natalie Wood, but memories of the film remain alive. It gives the community a bit of status even if it cannot compare with the hundreds of movies made in Manhattan. Travis also has an annual Fourth of July parade, which former mayor Rudy

Giuliani and the current mayor, Michael Bloomberg, have both attended in the past.

Sometimes people aren't entirely happy with the way history is recalled. Malcolm X was assassinated in Washington Heights in the Audubon Ballroom, at 166th Street and Broadway. An educational center with an imposing entrance has been created in his memory. It's an interactive museum and an event space. I show up on a weekday at noon, the only visitor besides two French tourists, and speak with someone affiliated with it. "We have some visitors," she says, "but it's not promoted enough. Money has been a problem. And so we're forced to rent it out for straight-up parties—you know, drinking, cocktail dresses, Sweet Sixteens, you name it. I don't like it. I mean, this is like sacred ground." As a product of the 1960s, I strongly sympathize with her. To those who grew up in this era, the man was an inspiration, a person who overcame great hardship, only to be gunned down in the prime of his life.

I go upstairs and enter the ballroom. Beautiful murals on the walls movingly present Malcolm X's story. It is a somber place, one that invites reflection as you read the highlights of his life and his impact. A statement by Malcolm X under the last known photograph of him, dated February 18, 1965, reads, "I am only facing the facts. And I know that any moment of any day or any night could bring me death." People are always interested in that sort of thing, because it makes them feel that they're in the know, that they know how prophetic his statement was just a few days before his untimely death.[30]

On the bright side, no community in the city does as much to remember its history as Harlem. The neighborhood is home to plaques, street signs, plazas, buildings, all named after the greats—Frederick Douglass, Duke Ellington, Martin Luther King, W.E.B. Du Bois, Thurgood Marshall, and so many others. This attention to roots is one of the main reasons why Harlem as a place and a name has so much cachet.

Until now the focus has been on the past—Hendrix, O. Henry, Poe— but status is also bestowed upon neighborhoods where the glitterati live today. As with residents of Beverly Hills, it is a common practice of New Yorkers to make note of the countless VIPs who live near them. Walking one day in Greenwich Village, I enter World Class Cleaners. An award for quality service hangs behind the counter, signed by Donald Trump. A store employee proudly tells me, "Donna Karan, Liv Tyler, and Uma Thurman all come here. I can't give their addresses, but they're all in the area." Or how about the Park Slope owner of a brownstone who said, upon learning that Barack Obama and his girlfriend had lived there in the mid-1980s, "Is it possible that Barack walked on these stairs?"[31]

Not only does proximity bring status to the neighborhood, but the personal anecdotes that the locals tell make the celebrities more human and approachable. Residents can tell you what they're *really* like. A Greenwich Village resident confides, "Dorothy Rabinowitz, the *Wall Street Journal* columnist, was walking by one morning, and two people were having a domestic fight right in the middle of the street. In a way, with their loud voices, it was almost comical. And without missing a beat, she said, to no one in particular, 'They're probably Obama supporters.' That's her. She's really crusty."

In the eyes of the locals these public personalities are fair game. You don't need permission to tell stories about them. A woman walking her dog confirmed actor Christopher Noth's resident status and pointed to the building where he lived. "He was kind of snooty," she said. "I met him in the building—my son lived there too—and I said, 'Oh, you're from that cop show.' And I had the wrong one. And he said to me in a really cold tone, 'No, it's *Law and Order*.' And I said to myself, 'That's the last time. . . . ' " This example is vintage New York. Joe Citizen asserts his or her freedom to criticize and to control the situation by deciding never to talk to him again, no matter how famous he is. *She's* deciding, not him.

A neighborhood's status is also raised when sitcoms or films are made on one's block. As long as the filmmakers are considerate of the residents, most people seem to like the idea that their block is "film-worthy." But not everyone is enamored when cameras surround their area. The architecture professor Michael Sorkin criticizes the tendency toward the "Disneyfication" of the city, turning it into a set rather than a setting, and complains about the inconvenience caused to locals. "The inauthenticity is galling but so is the inescapability of performing in a drama of somebody else's devising, whether it means being charmed by architectural mendacity or just crossing the street when the production assistant asks you to."[32]

Those living in the more undesirable parts of the city are less likely to feel this way. They have bigger issues to contend with, like crime and poverty. I was with my students on a class tour when the Denzel Washington film *American Gangster* was being filmed in Harlem along Malcolm X Boulevard. No one—not the students, nor nearby Harlemites—seemed to mind. To the contrary, they were thrilled by the fact that a major studio was using the area as a setting. In that sense these neighborhoods have an advantage. They serve up authenticity galore.

The Block

Describing a neighborhood like the Upper West Side in general terms doesn't tell the full story. If it's 105th Street between Columbus and Amsterdam Avenues, a block of tenement houses no higher than six stories, it's very different from 106th Street between the same avenues, which is a two-way, broad block with pricier buildings and a large nursing home. Neither bears any resemblance to the very upscale and beautiful, brownstone-lined Seventy-eighth Street between Columbus and Amsterdam. This is one of the enduring paradoxes of New York City—tremendous variation *within* many neighborhoods.[33] One block can look peaceful, bucolic, and the next will be a hive of busy activity, with bodegas on the corners, people hanging out and talking, along with litter and graffiti. The behavior of the people on each block and their propensity to gather on it or not are generally determined and maintained by the common consent and habits of those residing there.

My conversation with Ray, a homeless man, demonstrates how prevalent these judgments are. I ask him if the block he's on, Ninth Street in Manhattan, is a good block from his point of view. "Yes," he says. "It's a lot better than Tenth or Eleventh, where more people got private homes and are a lot snobbier, and don't give you nuthin'. It's more down to earth. And it's definitely better than Third Street, where the homeless shelter is."

I peer into Ray's cart, which seems to be a beat-up rusted reject from a supermarket. There are Pick-Up Sticks in a cylindrical-shaped container, a game I remember from my childhood, along with crumpled-up tissues, broken pencils, a few cloth caps, empty soda cans, a discolored head of lettuce, a single glove with a hole in the middle of it, several rags, some paper cups, and other assorted detritus, fragments of a perhaps disintegrating life.

The block association, which is ubiquitous in Gotham, is a critical part of urban life. It is the closest thing to a formal village that New Yorkers have. The block's annual party, usually a potluck eating ritual, serves to reinforce the concept, because it emphasizes a certain commonality as well as conviviality. The street is closed to all traffic that day, which makes people feel unique, however briefly. The foods served, the music played, the conversations, and the photos taken, all serve to enhance a collective commemoration of the experience that grounds the block historically and gives it added meaning. Of course, since it encompasses both sides of a street, the party is really made up of two blocks.

The social dynamics that play out in these associations vary not only according to their needs but also according to the personalities that belong to them. A block association is a spontaneous organization and a voluntary one in an interesting way. Everyone on a block is eligible and therefore a member, but you can also choose to be totally passive and do nothing. An association's success varies because it depends on having the right mix of people or certain crucial players who have skills, talents, and political connections, or even political ambitions, the latter of which may motivate them to be more active in achieving its goals. I wonder how many people actually move out of a building because of disagreements with others on the block, personal or political. After all, if they have a major fight, they have to continue seeing these people all the time. But that's an issue for another study, I guess.

Finally, mention must be made of the "eyes and ears of the community," a phrase made famous by Jane Jacobs in her classic work

The Death and Life of American Cities. These eyes and ears are most often those of the residents themselves, and if they do their job of watching everybody on the block, the neighborhood will be both safe and vibrant. But they must do it in tandem with local business owners, the sidewalk vendors studied by Duneier, delivery people, building superintendents, porters, and doormen.

However, these individuals' roles can change suddenly and in unexpected ways. Consider the fuss made when a building porter from the Bronx married a model who lived in the Manhattan building where he worked (340 East Seventy-fourth Street). The porter was fired by the building's board, which reportedly tried to throw them out of the building "all for violating a social taboo." As the building's super, Irwin McSweeney, put it in a *New York Times* interview, "If they made a connection, they made a connection. Isn't that what America's all about? They should have just wished him luck." Apparently McSweeney didn't mind letting the board know that he had expressed this view.

And yet, reflecting the ambivalence about this situation, a doorman had a different reaction to the marriage. Asked by the reporter if it wasn't wrong to say "that a person who opens the door is on a different level than a resident," he responded with "a big uncomfortable smile," saying to the reporter, "Me and you, let's say I make $40,000 and you make $4 million. We go to a restaurant. I'm scared when we get a drink. You're going to order the $100 drinks." In his view a relationship was okay, but only at arm's length. "But for longer life, you're talking something, I'm talking something else. Nothing together—pffft."[34] In short, the "eyes" can exit in a second. A super is fired, a vendor is arrested, a shopkeeper goes out of business, and a porter marries up—and out.

Communities Organize

It's not enough for a community just to have a sense that it is one. It needs organizations, both formal and informal, if it is to succeed and attract people. Reflecting this, the city has hundreds of youth programs. In addition to their many activities, the overall goal is to instill pride. Thus, the mottos of those belonging to the Brotherhood/SisterSol, founded in 1995 and located at 512 West 143rd Street, are statements like, "I will be a man," and, "Sisterhood isn't just a word. It is a state of mind. It is a crown that is earned and must be worn proud. You have to rock it right." A member sums it up: "This was the first place that I ever felt like people were paying attention to what I had to say because I was smart, talented, and had something relevant to say. . . . I thought, finally a place where I could be me and be important."

The sad reality is that so many of these kids come from homes where no one ever says positive words to them. The confidence they gain at Brotherhood/SisterSol can change their lives. Indeed, the organization is a success story, as 88 percent are high school grads, and 85 percent were accepted into college. And the following statistic is not only impressive, but it also tells us what matters in this community: only 2 percent of those who have taken advantage of the organization's services became a parent before age twenty-one. This in a community where over 70 percent of black children are born to unwed mothers and more than a third of children live in poverty. No Brotherhood members are known to be incarcerated. These organizations are critical, but unfortunately, more are needed.[35]

Many programs, like JustUs, founded in 1979 by Bill DelToro, and part of the Out-of-School Time program, provide tutoring and take the kids to museums, plays, and to see shows at places like Radio City. Art and culture are also brought to the community in unusual and innovative ways. For example, until fairly recently the Museum of Natural History had a large mobile truck that brought exhibits to neighborhoods all over the city. Upon seeing it parked outside an elementary school in Mott Haven, I thought it must be because the school couldn't afford to take the students to Manhattan. But it turned out that it was because the museum's main location is very crowded, and it doesn't pay to travel from the Bronx and wait so long on line.

When I happened upon it, the truck was bringing an interactive dinosaur exhibit, *Dinosaurs, Ancient Fossils, New Discoveries*. The exhibit was supported by the city in partnership with Keyspan

Energy. Children went up a few steps and enthusiastically crowded around a number of gaily colored mini-dinosaurs, evidently enjoying the lesson given by museum employees, one of whom was a young man in his early twenties from Ohio. There were four such vans that visited public and private schools around the city as well as community organizations and libraries. They could accommodate up to about 120 kids a day and maybe 8,000 a year combined.

"It's a lot of fun," the young man said.

"Why are you in New York?" I asked.

"I want to be a writer, but I'm doing this in the meantime."

"Unsolved Mysteries," said one enticing sign. Another truck had an anthropology exhibit showing the homes of other cultures, and a third featured astronomy, helping the students explore and navigate the stars. It may not have been the real thing, but for these youngsters this was definitely "the museum."[36]

Religion permeates the lives of the city's communities, especially in the poorer neighborhoods. But it's not just that the many churches, synagogues, and, increasingly, mosques and temples literally almost envelop the neighborhoods. It's that children are exposed to them very early and directly. Throughout the city there are local religious organizations that provide day care and other programs, especially for seniors.

As I walk down 149th Street, well east of the Hub, near Trinity Avenue, I see a group of about twenty-five youngsters, roughly between the ages of four and eight, sitting on a drop cloth right on the sidewalk. Their mothers or siblings are standing nearby, clustered around some park benches in front of a public housing project. They come here once a week—in this area it's Wednesday at about 4:30—and willingly give their kids over to a privately funded religious group.

A young, earnest woman of about twenty-five is telling the children a story as they listen raptly. "A lot of people base their lives on magazines and on what other people say, on what their friends say and on what the music says they have to be. But I'm telling you today that all these things, they're gonna pass away. That's what the Bible says. 'Everything will pass away, but His word will never pass away.' God will always stay the same." For these impoverished children, the words she speaks have true value. In a world marked by absent and abusive parents and the dangers of the street, it is really important that there be something they can count on. And if that's Jesus, so be it. How do they know it's true? This young raconteur has told them so, just like any other sidewalk preacher.

> Jesus is the Rock. When hard times are coming, you can rely on Him and you won't be swept away, like in a big storm. Gilbert told his friends. "We need to go to the big rock where the houses are still standing." And all his friends, the Gekkos, started laughing at him. They laughed and laughed. "Gilbert don't be stupid." But Gilbert said, "I want to find that rock. I don't want to be swept away." Finally they got to the rock. And all the houses were still standing because they were built on the rock.

The moral is obvious. She shows pictures. The kids love it. They are spellbound. She asks, "Who has had bad things that happened in their lives?" Half of them raise their hands. On a nearby truck's side is a large picture of Yogi Bear. The woman dances in front of the kids, crying, laughing, gesticulating, acting out the story. "Everyone, say after me: 'Jesus is the Rock!'" And then goodies are distributed with religious gospel music in the background.

The following week, on a Tuesday, I see the truck parked elsewhere, by another project. The activities are sponsored by a Protestant church (Metropolitan Ministries, with support from churches as far away as Belfast, Ireland) operating out of a Brooklyn church on Menahan Street and Bushwick Avenue. They've been bringing religion to people for thirty years, mostly in poor communities, and they are warmly welcomed by the locals. The parents believe religion is good for the kids, and indeed it can be in terms of structure and stability. And so the kids are exposed to religion at an early age. It's a free Sunday school on a weekday afternoon. One mother tells me, "This is one reason why I moved here. It's close to this program, which my kids and their friends love."

Then there are programs for adults, like the one in the Bronx described by District Manager Ken Kearns: "They have simulcast versions at the Bay Plaza Theater in Co-Op City. One of the

fourteen AMC theaters was dedicated to the Met Opera's performance of *Aida.* So for just fifteen dollars we saw for three hours
the same performances that people at Lincoln Center pay two hundred dollars for. We also saw a performance with no time delay at
the Royal Opera House in London."

The senior citizens centers are the nucleus of life for the elderly
in New York, especially in the poorer areas, providing compan-
ionship, activities, and other services. I enter the Betances Senior
Center on St. Ann's and 144th Street in the Bronx. In a nod to
the local population it serves, it's also called the Institute for the
Puerto Rican Hispanic Elderly, its sponsor, and is funded by the
New York City Department for the Aging. You see elderly Hispanics shooting pool in one room, playing bingo in another, dominoes
in a third location, or lined up for an early lunch.

Some senior citizens often feel quite isolated. In one case an elderly Chinese immigrant, Robin Hu, spoke of his efforts to reach
out to newer Russian émigrés: "We don't know why the Russian
people came here. And they don't know why the Chinese people
came here. Because they can't ask us questions. We say hello. What
next? There's no next step. So you don't get close." But give him
credit. Mr. Hu tried inviting neighbors to his home to sing Russian
songs with his karaoke machine. Alas, no one came.[37]

Many seniors in the city were sort of left behind as children
grew up and either didn't help their parents move out, or the seniors were too attached to their neighborhoods to leave. Yet even
as their numbers dwindle, there is a strong desire for community
that is no different from the newer and more numerous arrivals.
And for them the focus is often the church or synagogue where
they gather on a daily or weekly basis to pray, chat, reminisce,
and enjoy the fellowship of like-minded people. Their children are
long gone, but the cherished memories of how they were raised,
the days when their house of prayer was filled with hundreds of
worshipers, remain in the minds of the parents. For them it's what
gives the community a feeling of still being alive.

When we think of people in need, Hispanics, blacks, and Asian
newcomers usually come to mind. Yet in New York City Jews make
up a large proportion of poor seniors. The most active agency that

assists them is the Metropolitan Council on Jewish Poverty, directed by Willie Rapfogel. A full 25 percent of the city's Jewish population is classified as poor, up from 20 percent in 2002, and the Met Council has an array of services for them, including home care, legal services, food programs, affordable housing, and crisis counseling. The majority are Russian Jews and larger Orthodox Jewish households.[38]

Every community has problems and here organizations are equally crucial. If there's a problem with prostitution, as was the case in the Hunts Point industrial area, the affected community can, through its community board, organize demonstrations against such activity. Or, as I observed at a meeting in the Melrose section of the Bronx, it can enlist Legal Aid and the Civilian Review Board to ensure that residents are treated fairly by the police.

Naturally politics also plays a major role in the city's neighborhoods. But, as John Mollenkopf argues, the process is very complex. Political leaders' fortunes depend on votes, and community leaders know that. Grassroots organizations, local agencies, and community boards pressure them to improve conditions for the people. One of the most influential groups in the city is Moviendo Juntos, based in Bushwick and Williamsburg, a coalition of 350 neighborhood leaders including members of tenant associations, block groups, low-income cooperatives, parent-teacher associations, and nonprofits. In this case ethnicity shapes politics, since the group is described as "the largest group of Latino leaders in New York City." Other groups, like the Hasidim and white ethnics, employ similar tactics. In Queens, where immigrants make up 47 percent of the population, Queens borough president Helen Marshall has established an Office of Immigrant Affairs. It sponsors events, brings together immigrant services providers and advocates, and funds various programs. Her office has also created the Queens General Assembly, which brings together longtime residents and immigrants to discuss problems of mutual concern.[39]

Starting with the Koch administration, the city began actively encouraging the corporate sector to invest in the city's communities. Today this has become big business. Hundreds of corporations provide financial support to the parks, to thousands of community organizations, and to cleanup campaigns. On a bigger stage, business interests, in conjunction with real estate developers, have also become involved in large-scale developments like the Atlantic Yards commercial and residential project, in Brooklyn, or various plans for developing Coney Island, which would include a year-round refurbished amusement park and a variety of commercial business enterprises. These corporate sponsorships create goodwill, financial entrée into communities, and even tax write-offs. The project has also created concern that the corporations may have too much influence in the community and use their leverage for personal gain.[40] But most people with whom I spoke—local leaders and people in general—felt that the good overshadowed the bad.

Walking by a Pret a Manger restaurant on Seventeenth Street in Manhattan, I saw a sign in the store window: "Every night we give our fresh food to the homeless in New York, rather than selling it the next day." Could they really sell it for a profit, or would they simply throw it away? Do they get enough customers with this practice to more than make up for the loss of not selling it? Do they simply want to let people know that they sell only fresh products? Naturally, the highest form of charity would be to give the food to the poor without letting people know about it. Then again, this *is* a business.

Education

Schools are of critical importance and a major factor in where people decide to live. First, it's the place where their children spend much of their lives. Second, there is much greater awareness today of how important education is. As Ralph Salamanca, manager of District #4 in the Bronx, put it, "People have become educated to the idea that if you want a good job, you have to go to school."

Still, it's a struggle in communities in or near other communities where crime and poverty dominate. Take Cypress Hills, Brooklyn, a community bordering East New York that is trying to survive. The eastern part, bordering Queens, is in pretty good shape; the rest of it, pretty dicey. I spot an old, small public school behind two Corinthian pillars on Richmond Street; it's P.S. 65, with a distinct shade of red brick. That color means it's really old—and quaint too. A pair of decorative cement shields above the entrance indicate that the school was built in 1889, over 120 years ago. It is the proud "home of the Golden Lions." Immediately to the right of the building, a lonely pair of kids' sneakers dangles on a telephone wire. On the stairs, where feet climb every day to presumably new heights, are various exhortations: "Work hard to be nice," followed by "It takes hard work to achieve," then "Raise the bar," and finally, "We are climbing the mountain to college." And a mountain it is, indeed, in a place like Cypress Hills.

There is still much dissatisfaction with the city's public schools, but things have improved a lot over the years. One sign is that the racial gap in education is narrowing. Black students in 2009 still trail white students by 17 percentage points, but this is far better than the 31-point gap that existed in 2006. While some critics have dismissed these results, saying score inflation and other issues might be involved, the overall direction is positive.[41]

One new development in New York City's education system is the growth of charter schools. Many receive aid from corporations and owners of hedge funds who see them as a real breath of fresh air. The public schools, however, as embodied by the teachers' unions, regard them as an implicit indictment of the public school system and as taking their jobs away. Maybe so, but these are publicly financed and privately run schools, with many nonunionized teachers, and they are responding to a feeling that the regular schools are not doing enough to educate the children. Many parents like charter schools. They strongly approve of the uniforms, the discipline, the programs, and the highly motivated teachers, who typically earn more there than in the public schools. On the other hand, there is a tendency by many to assume that charter schools are automatically better. This view has been challenged by some education scholars, who argue that there is a good deal of evidence that they often fail to perform as well as traditional public schools. In their view, success or failure often depends on the particular institution.[42]

Another option is, and always has been, parochial and nondenominational private schools, the latter located mostly in wealthier
neighborhoods. These types of schools matter just as much as the
charter schools in people's choice of communities. In low-income
areas the predominant choice is Catholic schools. A Puerto Rican
Bronx mother's explanation, while perhaps somewhat overly harsh,
represented the views of many in terms of what the poor like about
the parochial schools: "I send my kids to the Catholic schools because my kids aren't learning anything in the public schools. In one
class the teacher told the kids to put their heads down so she could
send text messages the whole time. This ain't education. It's a joke.
Catholic school costs me about fifteen hundred dollars a year. I
pay half because I got a scholarship. They teach values. And when
there's a problem they call *me,* the parent. They take pride in their
kids and truly care." The woman has her fourth-grade son's report
card with her. She pulls it out of her pocketbook to show me the
As. "Look how good he's doin'."

In May 2009, according to a *New York Times* article, Sean Keaton, principal of P.S. 20 in gentrifying Fort Greene, was removed
from his position after being accused of assaulting a school union
representative who was also a teacher at the school. The incident
brought into the open a long-standing dispute between parents of
the school's students. There was no question regarding the school's
achievements. Under Keaton's leadership over four years, troubled
students were given direction, test scores went up, and new cultural programs were created. One group of parents—mostly affluent and white, recent arrivals living in the handsome, often
renovated brownstones of Boerum Hill and Park Slope—felt that
Keaton was too rigid and unwilling to tolerate anything more than
minimal parent involvement. The other group, made up mostly
of working-class black parents, liked Keaton's stricter and more
structured approach. He and most of the students are black.

It was basically a clash of values and priorities, with one side
seeing Keaton as "firm and fatherly" and the other regarding him
as "tyrannical and abusive." In an interview the principal defended
his approach, saying, "I've never understood what parents wanted
except to be able to come in when they want, to come in and sit in

the classroom. And you can't do that in Park Slope, you can't do it on the Upper West Side, nor on the Upper East Side. Why should you be able to do that at P.S. 20?"

There is a hint of something else in this last statement. Keaton may feel that because he's black and because the school isn't in as fancy a neighborhood as some other schools, the parents think they can push him around and demand things they wouldn't dare ask for in a more established community. But what's really at issue here is differing value systems rooted in the different backgrounds, needs, and expectations of working-class black parents and middle-class white parents. The latter believe in a nurturing environment, not in a no-nonsense approach. But that's because there are two parents in the home and the mother does homework with her kid every night. And she probably has more time to come to the school. The black student has a mother who most likely can't hang around the school. Therefore she expects the school to be both educator and disciplinarian, to give her child the tough love that often isn't available because only one parent, generally the working mom, is the only one there. And as gentrification increases and more whites move into black areas, these clashes are going to happen time and time again.

Another part of the narrative is the accusation that Keaton assaulted a union representative and was removed from his position for doing so. First of all, accusations like that are damning enough, and when the offending individual is removed from his position, the allegations gain instant credibility. Thus, Keaton was seen as guilty by most people following the incident. Even his most ardent supporters had difficulty backing him, since they couldn't support assault. His alleged actions went against the image of an educator as a role model and as a person who stands for reason, patience, and leadership.

Two years later Keaton was "cleared of all charges," according to a *New York Times* article. Asked whether the principal would be offered his old job back, Margie Feinberg, an Education Department spokeswoman, would say only, "We're reviewing it."[43]

The original article was a lengthy piece on page A14 in the *Times* print edition. The follow-up article, appearing on page A22, was considerably smaller, so how many people noticed it? And how many people who read the first story saw the second one? And, of course, it was an embarrassment to the Education Department, which rushed to judgment and left this man hanging for so long. While his detractors said Keaton could be a hothead, ultimately he was an educator who had accomplished a good deal, so it's sad that he was convicted in the court of public opinion and permanently damaged. Regardless, the lessons in the larger sense are that education is a very important issue in communities, that there is a great divide among different groups over how to best implement it, and that it is brought into much sharper focus when different classes and races live in the same community.

Finally, it's worth mentioning that New York City has many excellent colleges and universities like Columbia and New York University that are attended by many New Yorkers. Among them, City University of New York (CUNY), especially under the dynamic and visionary leadership of Chancellor Matthew Goldstein, has played a critical role because of the large number of immigrants and their children who are attracted by both its low cost and rising standards. The school has also seen an increase in middle-class students, who feel it's a great bargain. In 2012, for example, students snared a record sixteen National Science Foundation awards worth $126,000 each for graduate study in the sciences. Not as well known but equally important is the existence of another tier of schools, mostly business and technical, that flourish in the less advantaged parts of the city. Monroe College, on Jerome Avenue in the Bronx, is a good case in point. Everyone has dreams, and Monroe, unheralded as it may be, but in existence for close to eighty years, tries to fulfill them.

In a nearby vest-pocket park I notice a Hispanic youth wearing a gray T-shirt, sitting on a park bench. Next to him is a shopping cart, inside of which is a large, green plastic garbage bag. "Hey! Ice-cold water, one dollar, come get it!" he calls out in a singsong fashion every minute or so. I watch him and see that no one is buying. Even though I'm not at all thirsty, I stroll over and purchase a bottle from him. He is enormously gratified with making the sale and thanks me profusely.

"How do you keep these bottles cold out here?" I ask.

"Well, first I freeze them at home. That way they stay cold a long time."

"Where are you in school?"

"I just graduated high school."

"What are you gonna do next?"

"I'm going to Monroe College."

"For what?"

"I'm going to be a rich businessman. It's a great college."

It begins humbly enough with bottles of water, this entrepreneurial spirit. Who knows where this young man's journey will end? Right now this is his horizon. He does not think about an Ivy League university, or even CUNY's Baruch College. This is it, but for him it's more than enough.

In former mayor Dinkins's view, education, along with helping immigrants, is perhaps the greatest challenge facing New York City today. As he put it, "We must see to it that all of our children are well-educated. I argue that we don't own this planet. We hold it in trust. I love kids. I'm a nut for kids. I say to my friends, 'As much as I like you, if you don't take care of the children I'll report you to the authorities.' And they laugh, but I'm crazy about kids."

The Projects: A Special Case

As is true in the majority of big cities, the presence of low-income governmental housing projects in New York significantly affects the poorer neighborhoods surrounding them and can be a factor when it come to choosing a place to live. Residents with whom I spoke repeatedly said that their greatest fears concerned teenagers in the projects, where drugs are often sold openly and the police are barely a presence. The cops' attitude is that as long as such activity takes place within the project confines, it's not a priority. However, the areas that now surround the projects have new subsidized housing that contrasts sharply with the projects themselves. The projects are still good structurally, but there is often a stigma of failure that surrounds them. And so those who can have left for the newer housing, and those who can't are more problematic families as a rule. As for the teenagers, they are frequently envious of the nicer living quarters enjoyed by those not in the projects.[44]

I walk into the Betances Houses on East 146th Street in the South Bronx. People who live in public housing often just become habituated to it, and it is not unusual to see more than one generation of residents in them. The building is reasonably clean, but there is a pervasive odor of stale urine in the elevator. There are no groups of people loitering in the stairwells when I exit and walk thru the halls of the twenty-first floor. The doors are not scratched and there's no graffiti on the walls. But everything is bare-bones style, with the typical naked yellow bulbs and grated windows. And yet the people living there still have hopes and aspirations, at least for their children. I talk with a woman who has lived in Betances all forty-three years of her life. She's standing with her neatly dressed nine-year-old son, whom she describes as "a gifted child in a gifted program. And," she adds, "my daughter also scored in the ninety-eighth percentile. So she's gonna go in kindergarten. Now she's in preschool."

New York City's housing projects are among the best constructed and managed in the country and have been so for seventy years. This is one reason that projects are rarely taken down; instead they're renovated. Keeping the projects in good shape is a huge enterprise that involves about 2,600 buildings, officially housing some 420,000 tenants; however, most put the actual number at about 600,000. Still there are plenty of problems, according to Nicholas Dagen Bloom, author of *Public Housing That Worked*: "Many New York City Housing developments, housing a high percentage of very poor tenants and concentrated in the poorest sections of the city, remain under siege. Aluminum flashing is often stolen, tenants inexplicably urinate in hallways and elevators, security systems are frequently sabotaged, garbage is dumped from windows every day, graffiti is constantly applied to glazed brick, and shockproof glass is frequently shattered. Not long ago a tenant was even mangled by an adolescent tiger he kept as a pet."[45]

Despite this somewhat gloomy assessment, there is still high demand for project apartments, because of the often tight market for lower-end housing and because the apartments are basically sound. Since the 1990s the New York City Housing Authority has built new community centers, fixed up the parks, and invested in better security. On the average about fifty-five hundred apartments come on the market annually, and approximately one hundred thousand people on a seven-year waiting list apply for them. The average New Yorker thinks of the projects as a place mostly for welfare tenants. In truth, however, it's a two-tier system—welfare recipients and working-class people, with the latter generally going to the head of the list.

As I stand inside a Bronx project apartment, it's easy to see why these apartments are still there. They're rock-bottom solid. The walls are made of plaster, not drywall. You cannot hear your neighbors unless they're really loud. The rooms are of a decent size. The showers and bathroom and kitchen fixtures as well as appliances are certainly good. And, of course, the price is right. They may look grim on the outside, but they're better than expected on the inside.

Given the lackluster nature of the projects, it's not surprising that people will seize on anything to make them look better. Thus Bronxdale Houses along the Bruckner Expressway has been renamed Justice Sonia Sotomayor Houses to commemorate her humble origins in that project. (See figure 13.) No one is under any illusions that the renaming will have a significant impact. But her status, and the fact that she's Puerto Rican, must give a certain measure of pride to the residents, though it does not change the reality of their poverty and cannot bring them riches, only hope. Similarly, the nearby parochial school from which Sotomayor graduated has a sign congratulating her on her elevation to the Supreme Court. A deacon with whom I speak says, "She came here in June 2010 to visit us and the kids. She was a good student, quiet. It's great she made it. It tells the kids that you can be anything you want to be." She may have been "a good student," but, as her autobiography makes clear, she grew up in the same rough-and-tumble circumstances as any ghetto kid, and the sisters whacked her as much as they did any other student.

This overview leads to an inescapable conclusion. The projects are not really an answer to people's desire to improve their lives.

Sure, they're well built, in better shape than those elsewhere, but at the end of the day there's nothing exciting, hopeful, or even interesting about them. There's a certain stigma attached to living in them. The problem is, what do you do with so many people? People who reside in three- or four-family brick homes built with generous loans from the government in the last twenty years or so in the Bronx, Brooklyn, and Queens are, by contrast, a resounding success story. People take pride in maintaining them because they have ownership. On the other hand, those in the projects own nothing. If the homes they were renting were attractive, that would be one thing, but they aren't. Paradoxically, their limited success— namely, the fact that they're habitable—has led to a far greater failure: the failure to tear them down and build more attractive housing because city government has concluded that they are adequate. This is exacerbated by increased demand for housing by the gentrifiers, a demand so great that they're willing to live literally across the street from the projects. If they weren't, then pressure from the private investment sector would mount to dismantle the projects.

The Outer Boroughs and Manhattan

Our discussion of why communities are selected by people would be incomplete without touching on this relationship. While not specific to a particular neighborhood, it affects all of those who live outside of Manhattan in varying degrees. In other words, because of Manhattan's centrality in terms of work and play, and its image around the world, not living there represents a conscious decision to live in a community outside of it. And people have reasons for that, ranging from not being able to afford Manhattan to simply wanting to live in a quieter, less crowded place. But there's another side too, and a very important one: despite the differences between Manhattan and its surrounding neighborhood, there are also unifying factors that transcend the individual communities inhabited by New Yorkers.

Those living outside Manhattan have an ambivalent relationship with it, though less so than thirty or forty years ago. Because of proximity to the area, and since they recognize what it offers by way of entertainment, tourism, and its status as a world financial center, they do identify positively with it. Moreover, so many of them shuttle back and forth to Manhattan because they work there. Yet they are also fiercely loyal to the communities in which they reside, touting them as oases of quiet and friendliness, near yet far from the bustling city center. And those living in the gentrifying parts of Brooklyn and Queens frequently delight in knowing that their neighborhoods have gained in popularity because they've been "discovered," and by Manhattanites, no less!

Ask someone who lives in the outer boroughs if they consider themselves New Yorkers, and the answer will almost always be a resounding yes. After all, isn't the city defined as five boroughs? And aren't they only thirty minutes to an hour away from Manhattan? These realities do contribute to a sense of oneness among people wherever they reside. Yet there is variation. Those in upscale, better-known, and nearby neighborhoods like Forest Hills, Brooklyn Heights, and Riverdale, are more apt to identify with it than those in Brownsville, Woodlawn, or Gerritsen Beach. As one plumber caustically observed, "No one's ever heard of Gerritsen Beach."

Staten Island in particular is viewed by many New Yorkers as a backwater of sorts—provincial, not classy, home of landfills, inaccessible, and bigoted. The following comments in Ben Howe's book about a Korean deli sum up the stereotype pretty well:.

> Deep shame attended our moving into Gab's mother's household, but it was not as bad as moving to Staten Island, New York City's pariah borough, a place where once-hot trends like Hummers and spitting go to die, a place so forsaken that not even Starbucks would set up a store there, nor even the most enterprising Thai restaurant owner—only immigrants from the former Soviet bloc, people fleeing environmental disasters and the most involuted economies on earth. (Perhaps they found something homelike in the smoldering industrial landscape, a familiar scent in the air.) As Gab and I quickly discovered, friends were uneasy about visiting us in our new borough. "Can you smell the dump where you live?" they would ask. "How long does it take to develop a Staten Island

accent?" We promised they wouldn't have to go back to Park Slope wearing velour sweat suits or smelling like garbage, but still they wouldn't visit us.[46]

It's a harsh description, but it's one that Staten Islanders know is out there in varying degrees. I walked the borough from end to end and found that Staten Islanders often have a bit of a chip on their shoulder when you first approach them. They're defensive, on guard, waiting for you to say something that will confirm their own opinion that people think of Staten Islanders as a bunch of dummies. But once they determine that you're okay, that you're not looking down on them or making fun of their community, they often become friendly and helpful. They're fiercely partisan to the island and its way of life, but they're also acutely aware that others may see them as provincial.[47]

There is one thing, however, that genuinely unites all New Yorkers: the memory of 9/11. In her comprehensive edited volume on the subject, *Wounded City,* anthropologist Nancy Foner referred to it as a "dispersed tragedy," because people from every part of the city and the surrounding suburbs were killed or injured. Add to that all the people who knew them, and the tragedy's far-reaching effects become clear.[48] Many streets are named after the victims, and there are signs on almost every firehouse in the five boroughs that read, "Never Forget," often accompanied by the names of the victims.

I walk by a firehouse on Dean Street, in Brooklyn's Prospect Heights section. The name Henry Miller, a firefighter, is prominently displayed among those who perished from this firehouse on 9/11. I think to myself that Henry Miller is a very well known writer, but here in this community it's a different Henry Miller who's known. They may have heard of the other one, but he's not the one who counts in their lives. It reminds us again of how central 9/11 became to so many New Yorkers.

Besides the numbers of people directly affected, there is the fact that the burning Twin Towers were seen by hundreds of thousands of horrified spectators. From Belle Harbor to Throgs Neck, from Hunters Point to Harding Park, as well as from New Jersey to Long

Island, people saw buildings filled with human beings collapse. Let's face it, a skyline is almost static and you get used to it. In that way its sameness gives the viewer a sense of security. So when the skies filled with flames and smoke on that sunny September day, it was a stunning and profound change .There was a feeling of shock, awe, and even perverse wonderment. "How could such a thing happen?" People stared in amazement at the unfolding tragedy as what they heard on the radio or saw on TV came to life. And then later they told everyone who hadn't seen it what it looked like to them. Like the 1963 Kennedy assassination, to this very day people ask, "Where were you when it happened?" All this and more is why 9/11 unites New Yorkers in a powerful and enduring way.

Everyone remembers Rudy Giuliani's role in the catastrophe. His strong leadership of the city during those trying times became virtually synonymous with the image of a city that refused to be crushed by what happened. My interview with him also revealed that he had a long-standing attachment to the World Trade Center.

> I enjoy photography and used to take photos of buildings and other points of interest in New York City—the Empire State and Chrysler Buildings, Yankee Stadium, and the like. But I was especially fond of the Twin Towers. The way they stood out, and their symmetry, framed against the sky seemed beautiful. I had watched them go up back in the '70s when I was working nearby as an assistant U.S. attorney. During the time I was mayor, the Leica Company heard about my hobby and suggested having an exhibit featuring pictures taken by me with their new camera, the Leica R7. I agreed and an exhibit was put together with photographs of the city, including my "Twin Towers." The proceeds from the exhibition—it was held in 1998—went to a charity that helped abused children. Also, when I worked with Guy Molinari, the former president of Staten Island, on financing for the Staten Island Yankees baseball team, I had an-other opportunity to express my feelings about the towers. What Molinari and I really liked about the location was the Manhattan skyline in the background. This meant that a ball hit over the left field wall would almost literally go sailing into space toward the Twin Towers.

A Final Thought: Technology and Community

Entire books have been written on the topic of increasing technology—ATMs, cell phones, advanced video games, iPods, and laptops and other computers,where you can instantly find the answer to almost any question—they have all impacted our communities, and that's true worldwide as well.

Consider, for a moment, just one of these: the cell phone. As I walk through New York City, I am constantly passing people who are speaking on their cell phones, whether strolling on the street or sitting on a stoop. In the old days they would have just been hanging out. In addition to providing a way to communicate, cell phones also relieve boredom by giving people something to do while they're on their way to the corner grocery or bus stop. Years ago you had to return home or find a phone booth. Today the phone booth has become a relic of history. In a sense the cell phone reduces the importance of community, because it means you can mentally "leave" or "zone out," since you can talk to anyone anywhere. On a more mundane level it also gives people a feeling of safety when danger lurks, since they can call the police or someone else if necessary.[49]

Here's another example of how technology has changed life over the last forty years. I meet a man who used to own DiMaria Restaurant, now defunct, but once a pretty good eatery located in Little Neck, Queens, until 2012. He's nostalgic about Cypress Hills, Brooklyn, where he lived until age eight, when the family left for the greener and safer pastures of Whitestone, Queens. "I remember the house very well," he says. "I have great memories of it because my grandparents lived there, and the backyard was big and beautiful and green, grapes, vines, and olive trees, all that 'guinzo' stuff" that my grandfather brought over from the old country."

"Have you ever gone back since then?" I ask.

"Just once or twice. It would be—how should I put it—too depressing to see how the house went down. It's a pretty rough area now, mostly Hispanic, and back then it was almost one hundred percent Italian. But wait," he says. "I can get it for you."

He finds a photo of the house on his cell phone, and together we peer at a very clear picture of his former home—and the whole block no less, Sunnyside Court. He gazes fondly at it. In the picture the bad neighborhood is not a factor. No one's on the street hanging out. In short, with technology you *can* go home again, without having to directly encounter the new reality, a changed block with none of the old bunch there.

4

DANCING THE BACHATA, PLAYING BOCCI, AND THE CHINESE SCHOLARS' GARDEN
Enjoying the City

On East Fifty-first Street between Third and Second Avenues I come across a most beautiful little park created by the Rockefeller family in 1971. Called GreenAcre Park, it's privately owned but open to the public. It opens in the morning and closes at 7:45 PM. Its main feature is a stunning waterfall, where the water cascades over several large boulders. (See figure 14.) The water fairly roars as it rushes over the top of the rock formation. Off to the side is an ivy-covered wall and some potted plants. A number of trees dot the area, providing both luxuriant foliage and ample shade. People are seated beneath them, usually at small tables, enjoying a cup of coffee with a croissant, talking, texting, reading the paper, or listening to music on their headphones.

If you sit right in front of the waterfall, it will literally drown out every other city sound—trucks passing by, horns honking, construction activity—giving you the feeling that you are hundreds of miles away, deep in the forests of the Catskills or Adirondacks. The waterfall can become mesmerizing if you stare at it long enough, the streams of flowing water hypnotizing the viewer into staying longer than he or she intended. In the beginning the water had to be heated in the winter, but today that's no longer necessary, perhaps because of climate change. Those gathered in the park are a mix of older and younger people, tourists and natives. One person, a doorman, tells me, "I come here every day on my lunch break and relax in front of the waterfall. It's the gem of the neighborhood."[1] And how many thousands of people walk by the park every day on this very busy street, not knowing the beauty that lies just steps away?

Reflecting on his comment and on the scene in general, I am struck by the importance of what he says. New Yorkers are an energetic lot. They work hard and they lead busy lives. Even getting to their job is often a challenging and tiring experience. The sights, sounds, and smells of the city assault them at every turn, and living here can sometimes seem like residing in a giant obstacle course. Nowhere is this feeling greater than in Midtown Manhattan. The fact that in its midst there exists a popular oasis of peace and quiet highlights the fact that people need opportunities to relax. Without them, life becomes virtually intolerable. When people speak about their night off, their weekend at the beach, their vacation, they think of such time as a reward for all their labors, one that makes it all worthwhile.

Walking through the city and observing the myriad ways in which New Yorkers enjoy life—the parks they sit in, the ball fields they play on, the restaurants and taverns they frequent, the movies they go to, the museums they visit, and the streets they congregate in, passing the time—it becomes clear that leisure time is a central part of their lives, measurable not by how much of their existence it takes up but by the contrast between it and the rest of their lives and by the degree to which they enjoy it.

As it turns out, leisure-time activities such as entertainment, religious and ethnic events, sports, parks, and social gatherings can also be prisms through which other critical facets of life are refracted. Through them it becomes possible to understand what it is that unifies New Yorkers, how they identify, what they value, and how this crucial aspect of their lives enhances the communities in which they live. It also serves as a stage for both social life and the conflicts that inevitably develop when competing groups vie for often scarce space. Finally, the evolving ways in which New

Yorkers spend their free time can sometimes be a harbinger of future trends that will ultimately gain acceptance.

Entertainment

Throughout the city, people of various ethnic, religious, and racial groups attend concerts, comedy shows, dance performances, and the like, many of which are geared toward their heritage and identification. It can be an Irish folk music trio, a Yiddish or klezmer concert, a Polish polka troupe, an Iranian singer, or a parade like the West Indian one in Brooklyn or the Puerto Rican one in Manhattan. The crowd, usually made up of "tribe members," is not only entertained but also sees it as a chance to reinforce and take pleasure in who they are.

One spring evening, to capture the flavor of such events, my wife and I attended the Beres Hammond concert at CUNY's Herbert Lehman College, located in the northwest Bronx. The crowd was "99.9 percent West Indian," as people in attendance told us. There was an especially heavy concentration of Jamaicans there because that is where Hammond, a reggae and pop megastar, is from. The crowd was really into him, with people on their feet, dancing the entire time, except for two-minute rest breaks. The luckier ones stood by the stage as Hammond shook their hands and hugged them.

Each immigrant who comes to the United States leaves behind ways of life that need to be adapted to fit in with their new circumstances. Yet they also wish to preserve their identity. Yes, they're now in America and hearing American music, but also important is the music of the homeland, accompanied by lyrics that express yearning, memories, shared values, and forms of cultural expression—how the houses looked, how the foods tasted, and how the people lived and related to one another. And of course the lyrics speak of the challenges of making it in their new homes. This is how the people reconnect, a connection made much more powerful by the fact that they are a crowd of over a thousand experiencing this together, in one place. That is why, when Beres yelled into the mike, "I'm proud to be a Jamaican," the crowd roared with approval. He said, "You gotta have feeling, you gotta care, and you have to fight in the workplace." The last comment really resonated with the values and aspirations of this hardworking community, whether it was made about job discrimination or just work in general. They responded equally enthusiastically when Beres said, "There's always someone waiting to take your job."

The crowd was about 65 percent women, and people were dressed about two steps above what you would call casual. Many women wore brightly colored sundresses and decorative jewelry. Other bands preceded Hammond, one of them, the Inner Circle, quite well known. Yet while people applauded, they didn't stand up and dance when the other bands were on. Hammond was who they were really into. He has a very nice voice, strong and resonant, with maybe a hint of a rasp in it. The crowd knew the lyrics, and many times he would let them finish the words of the verses. To look at him, he has a rather unprepossessing, though certainly presentable, appearance. He doesn't look like a Brad Pitt or Denzel Washington, yet to his audience he's a heartthrob. In short, he has a presence; he has charisma. The crowd absolutely loved him, laughed with him, swayed to his music, with many filming his performance. In short, he spoke to their hearts and souls.

Harlem has always been a national venue for music, dance, and art, and with its resurgence in recent years the area's popularity in that regard has also gained. These cultural venues include the Apollo Theater, the Schomburg Center, the Poet's Den Theater, City College's Aaron Davis Hall, the Dance Theatre of Harlem, the National Jazz Museum of Harlem, Jazzmobile, and the Dwyer Cultural Center, as well as the Manhattan School of Music, and much, much more. Unlike the Beres Hammond concert, these groups attract both outsiders and insiders, unifying them through music. Let's look at one of the many individual clubs and see what it offers the community.

Tommy Tomita, seventy-one, regularly holds court at St. Nick's Jazz Pub in Harlem's Sugar Hill section. He has lived in Harlem since 1987 and has made a point of bringing Japanese tourists to this famous watering hole for jazz music. "I want them to see typical Harlem with local people. I want them to feel the real atmosphere, not prepared for tourists." And indeed this is the real deal, since the place has been there in one form or another for over seventy years. One enthusiast attributed its appeal to "the authentic jazz that is in the walls."

It's a funky, idiosyncratic joint, starting with Tomita, who favors a suit, white shirt, and a gray silk tie, all the way to the Christmas lights that brighten up the place throughout the year. Though Tommy may be from Japan, where he owned jazz clubs, he has the moxie of a real New Yorker. On at least two occasions, both in the rougher era of the late '80s, he literally dodged bullets. One nicked him in the back as he was standing outside Perk's Restaurant on Manhattan Avenue and 123rd Street. The other time was in the East Tremont section of the Bronx. He was not deterred. Why? "I like jazz," he says.[2]

Bullets aside, what's important here is that Tomita and others, like the tourists his business attracts, open up Harlem to others, and they do it through the medium of music. In so doing they expose visitors to the cultural life of Harlem, one in which jazz has been central. This breaks down stereotypes on both sides, since Harlemites come to see Asians as people who aren't simply store owners but are also individuals who value Harlem's history and culture. This in turn enhances their own feelings of self-worth. And it's not only tourists who do this. New Yorkers—doctors, architects, budding musicians from everywhere, college students, and others looking for the "real Harlem"—turn it into a place where different types of people come together.

Walk through any Hispanic neighborhood in New York, and you'll find clubs and restaurants featuring music from a variety of foreign lands. One Saturday night I went to such a club on 138th Street in the South Bronx with my wife and some friends. On the ground floor the music was Dominican and the patrons were doing the *bachata*, a sensuous yet lively dance that originated in the Dominican Republic, to the accompaniment of a four-piece band. No one seemed to mind that the musicians had arrived an hour late. The atmosphere was happy, if not joyous. Nor did they mind my attempts to do the dance too, one I didn't know. "As long as you're game," I thought, "it's cool."

Upstairs, the space had been rented out to a Mexican group. The contrast was stark, with those in attendance, mostly couples, sitting around tables and drinking beer while a band played background music from their homeland. Some were slow-dancing in the dim light, and overall the atmosphere was far more subdued than downstairs. Their faces looked somber, and it felt like they had come here mostly to talk and relax after a hard week. Several conversations confirmed that impression, as well as the fact that those present were mostly undocumented workers.

On any given weekend there are hundreds of such events taking place. In Long Island City, Queens, you can spend an evening watching flamenco dancers do their thing. You can hear German music in Glendale; Irish ballads in the Woodlawn section of the Bronx; do the polka in a Greenpoint, Brooklyn, Polish club; and attend a Jewish music festival in Flatbush, Brooklyn, where men and women sit separately, as required by their religious beliefs. What is distinctive about the city is the variety. It's almost as though you don't have to travel to another country, because so many cultures are represented in one place. And each of these places welcomes outsiders. All this, of course, is in addition to Carnegie Hall, the Metropolitan Opera, and other well-known venues.

The subway system is a showcase for many musicians who play songs from their native lands. Examples are Chinese players of instruments native to their culture; Mexican mariachi singers who stroll through subway cars, dressed in their distinctive outfits; and Ecuadorians, Colombians, Peruvians, and Bolivians who play the haunting yet joyful music native to the highlands of their countries. For the average New Yorker these are opportunities to become familiar with other cultures. In truth, subway and street performers are and always have been part of the New York City scene. This phenomenon is true of any big city, but with its large number of immigrant groups, New York is especially colorful and varied. These entertainers have been here for decades, but enforcement of the laws regulating whether, where, and when they can perform has been stricter since the 1990s.[3]

Schools throughout the city play a critical part in bringing the arts to the community, and they use any kind of hook to draw people in. For instance, the Shakespeare School, P.S. 199 on Shakespeare Avenue, built in 1929, presents *The Taming of the Shrew* (or another Shakespeare play) every year in June for the parents and community—because it's the Shakespeare School. In essence, its name provides a convenient reason for bringing literature and culture to the school. In communities like this one in the West Bronx, few people can afford tickets to Broadway shows, so this is often their only chance to see a real play.

The development of programs in the arts frequently energizes and enhances a community. One of the larger art groups in the city is on Staten Island where hundreds of artists, musicians, writers, poets, and filmmakers, led by Joyce Goldstein and other community leaders on the northern part of the island, have created programs, art walks, and the like. There's also a summer music festival, with perhaps forty musicians participating. The annual Art by the Ferry Festival attracts thousands of visitors. Participants have included the Staten Island Songwriters Circle, Guys in the Band, Hot Monkey Love, and poetry by Ira Goldstein, Lorna Martell, Adam Waring, and others. There have also been art exhibits, shows by contortionists, puppeteers, break dancers, and many workshops, with free admission to everything.[4] Multiply this by the hundreds of art festivals that appear elsewhere in the five boroughs, and it becomes easy to see the crucial role they play in the city's social life.

Sometimes the art is on the walls of the community's buildings. On East 180th Street and Arthur Avenue in the Bronx, I see a mural created by the SoBro Poetry Project. A sample: "My family is the water in the ocean; My family is the music on my iPod; My family is the cheese in my cheese doodle; My family is love." It is penned by "Milnalis" of P.S. Middle School 3. And here's another one, titled "Friends": "My friends don't call me names; My friends are there when I need them: My friends make me happy; They make me smile when I am sad; My friends are my family; My friends tell me the truth." It's by Martha. Is this really good stuff? It's certainly original, especially the cheese doodle verse. What the mural accomplishes is that it gives these kids a forum, some recognition, and a feeling of self-worth. On the street the mural is seen by a lot more people than if it were hanging on a wall in a school hall. In a way having your words on a wall along a public street means you've been published. It's not exactly entertainment, like attending an event, but when people walk by it, they can stop to appreciate what's there.

Clearly we think of social life in a city as parks, theaters, street fairs, and so on. Yet there's also the idea of the city itself as a happening tableau of activity. So much can occur in the course of a typical urban day—a police chase or filming for a TV series, something that brings together strangers who feel they have witnessed or shared in something special.

I'm walking up Ninety-sixth Street on Manhattan's West Side, between Central Park West and Columbus Avenue, when I spy ahead of me, but across the wide, two-way street, a man on a ladder propped up against a building, breaking the windows of an apartment. Dark smoke is billowing outward from the window, and fire trucks have arrived. Most people walk by, putting on their blasé, "nothing impresses me" faces, though here and there several knots of people are gazing unabashedly at the unfolding scene. Some are taking pictures and filming the event.

This does represent a form of entertainment for those on their lunch break, and I often saw groups of people who were watching things happen—a man wearing a sandwich board proclaiming the end of the world, a domestic squabble, police arresting demonstrators, or others simply enjoying their retired status. I suddenly remember from my childhood a scene of two women on West 104th Street near Manhattan Avenue, then a poor area, fighting and shoving each other in the gutter. No one standing there claimed to know what the altercation was about, but since neither of the combatants seemed to be getting seriously hurt, the crowd simply stood and watched as though it were a prearranged match designed for the pleasure of the local residents.

Religious and Ethnic Events

Processions, parades, and street fairs are another form of social life that present opportunities for expressions of unity and identity. Religious processions are held at various intervals in different neighborhoods throughout the city. Catholics, Jews, Hindus, and other religions all have them. In areas where they do not take place, it's because the neighborhood is either too diverse or doesn't have strong local religious institutions that push for them.

One Sunday, late in the day, I chance upon a feast celebration in the still largely white Pelham Bay section of the Bronx, along St. Theresa Avenue and in honor of St. Theresa (not Mother Teresa). It is sponsored by the church of the same name, and there are at least two thousand people in attendance. Such events typically take place in neighborhoods made up of older Italian, Irish, German, and Slavic residents. To better understand and possibly capture the mood of the celebrants, I join the procession and walk behind a statue of the Virgin Mary. Despite the large throngs of people milling about, the scene feels strangely peaceful, perhaps because of the somber music played over a loudspeaker and the slow gait of the marchers, whose gazes suggest peace and reverence. The avenue is lined with stands on which are displayed sausages, pizza, and other delectable foods, the aromas filling the open air. There are also games of chance, as well as Hit the Dummy and Sink the Basket. All of these stands stop selling and enticing people as the religious procession passes by.

In front of the church are various church functionaries dressed in robes of various colors, one of whom begins speaking. "I think you will agree with me," he says, "that St. Theresa was very anxious to do this procession. And I think she was nice to cool things off a little for us. There is much to give thanks for, which is what we're all about. The greatest gift, of course, is the gift of our faith." With these opening comments he humanizes her to the audience. He invites all to hear the choir after he finishes. He prays for the assembled and acclaims Theresa as the greatest saint of modern times and then asks for a moment of silence. A shower of rose petals, red, white, and yellow, rains down, seemingly from the sky, but actually they've been tossed from the roof of the church. Everyone oohs and aahs appreciatively, perhaps imagining it as a miracle.

As I survey the scene I'm reminded once again of the centrality of religion in the lives of millions of New Yorkers. There are many other feasts, with multitudes winding their way through the Catholic neighborhoods of New York City, drawing thousands of devotees, but largely unreported by the mainstream media. They bind the community together, providing opportunities for religious expression and venues for social life. Yet there are also many people in the city for whom religion is irrelevant, even meaningless.

And when large numbers of both groups live in the same neighborhoods, conflict can occur. This was the case not long ago in Williamsburg, Brooklyn. An article by David González that appeared on June 7, 2010, in the *New York Times,* titled "Still Taking to the Streets to Honor Their Saints," zeroes in on the gap between the two attitudes about religion. One view, adopted by the Italian and other Catholic residents in New York, was for people to pay their respects to the process and join in or at least pause and watch. The other was characterized by "curious hipsters whipping out cellphones to take a snapshot."

This does not go unnoticed. In the words of Lucy D'Alto, a North Williamsburg resident, "It used to be the whole street was waiting to give money. We don't see that now. They don't understand. They see it as something superficial. They don't respect us, all these young kids—artistes, whatever you call them." The article describes the outrage felt by Antonio Curcio, president of the Society of Saint Mary of the Snow. "Two years ago when we were doing St. Cono, one of these yuppies dropped his pants. It's something I never saw in my lifetime. As a man, I wanted to grab him and smash him against a wall, but you got to be a better person." And if you asked him where he got that idea from, to be a better person, he'd probably give his faith, his Christianity, at least some of the credit.[5]

This is what happens when cultures clash in two communities. North Williamsburg is becoming gentrified. And if the groups are to live in harmony, each side must demonstrate tolerance and respect. In the Pelham Bay section, however, gentrification is not taking place. The community is still pretty homogeneous and, predictably, conflicts of this sort don't surface. Which way is better? That depends on one's own background and perspective. But the North Williamsburg example clearly highlights the deleterious effects of social contact between different groups in parts of the city. Usually the clashes are between religious, racial, and ethnic segments, but in North Williamsburg it's more of a class thing, mixed in with generational differences, though the young, in the Pelham Bay example. at least, still buy into what the older ones revere.

The difference can be seen in the size of the processions, with the one in the Bronx drawing thousands and the Brooklyn one attracting little more than one hundred of the faithful. The chasm is there, plainly reflected in the comment by Chris Tocco, an actor whose name suggests his own Italian Catholic roots. "It was a tiny parade and they shut down Graham Avenue. There was one float and a horrible marching band. It was very ironic. The Latino parades are more festive." That's the verdict. Priority should be given to those with better music. For Tocco it's all about entertainment and not at all about tradition. The rejection of what *was* is given voice by Jon McGrath, twenty-seven, who observed, "It seems very old-school. It's kind of like a vestige of the old neighborhoods of Brooklyn."

But aren't the new urban classes interested in "authenticity"? González observes that the twenty or so annual processions that occur just in this ten-square-block area "reaffirm not just faith, but ties to the old neighborhood and the old country."[6] Yes, the newer classes like the idea of authenticity, but within limits. They want it their way—quaint, with an old-timey feel, but never in a way that cramps their own lifestyles. And they are not likely to know that the processions are deeply personal to those who live there. For example, the devotees of St. Cono immigrated to Williamsburg from the village of Teggiano, Italy. St. Cono was a twelfth-century saint who is honored for having rescued Teggiano from an earthquake and a siege.

One new resident, Jack Szarapka, is getting ready to open a juice bar. He'd gotten a statue of St. Francis Xavier and was thinking of naming his new place St. Francis Xavier Juice Bar. Would that be considered irreverent? Perhaps, but to him it's probably a way of connecting to the past. Irrespective of how you look at it, religious events of this sort can and do bring into sharp focus the beliefs, feelings, and attitudes of people toward faith and their impact on the lives of the city's residents. Bishop Nicholas DiMarzio, while condemning disrespectful behavior, nevertheless adopted a conciliatory view, remarking to me, "These are kids who have no history in the community and who are often disconnected to religion—we're trying to reach out to them. That's the first step."

Religious and ethnic parades like those celebrating St. Patrick's Day and Puerto Rican and West Indian culture often highlight different points of view. A typical case in point is the Israel Day Parade, held every spring, with perhaps one hundred thousand marchers, mostly Modern Orthodox students from the New York metropolitan area's religious day schools, who stride proudly up Manhattan's Fifth Avenue. Since Jews are both an ethnic and religious group, supporting Israel must be seen as an expression of ethnic and religious identity and loyalty. It is a joyous event for the participants and onlookers as the sounds of music and singing fill the air, and as people on the sidelines cheer and clap, also using the event as an opportunity to bond socially with one another. Many have been coming for years and treat it as though it were a camp or school reunion, catching up on things with friends.

But it's not that simple. There are perhaps a million Jews living in New York City, and the overwhelming majority do not attend the parade. Why? First, they have no children of their own who are marching and don't feel an obligation or desire to do so. But more than that, many Jews today are secular and don't feel a particularly strong connection to Israel the way previous generations did. Adding to the ambivalence about the parade, if not occasional hostility to it, is the feeling that, as one person told me, "it has been hijacked by the Orthodox." This was probably truer ten years ago when private Orthodox sponsors dominated the event. Today the Jewish Community Relations Council, under the aegis of UJA-Federation of New York, is in charge of the parade, but the bitterness of injustices in years past lingers. One flashpoint back then was the refusal by those who ran the parade to allow Jewish gays to march. Today that's no longer the case—they are welcomed along with Bikers for Israel and anyone else who wants to join.

Because they are public, parades can provide a great deal of publicity to fringe groups. Every year a tiny band of perhaps five or ten Hasidic Jews belonging to a group called the Neturei Karta stand on Fifth Avenue at Sixtieth Street and unfurl large banners proclaiming their opposition to Israel and their support for the Arabs. For those who don't know any better, it's shocking to see Jews clad in religious garb that's supposed to represent Jewish spirituality seeming to side with those opposed to Israel. Then again, they're demonstrating their rights to free speech and freedom of assembly.

Immediately after the parade ends there's a concert in Central Park, sponsored by the Israel Concert Committee. This group strongly supports the settlers on the West Bank and has its own bands and singers who express devotion to that cause. The people who agree with the committee drift over and listen to both music and speakers exhorting Jews to support those living in Judea and Samaria, the biblical names for the West Bank. Such events bring into relief the divisions not only between members of the same group but also among them, and they demostrate how a supposedly fun event on a nice Sunday afternoon can become much more than that. On the one hand, the concert articulates and even magnifies the conflicting views, but on the other, it gives people a chance to let off ideological steam, if you will, even if those who disagree with the concert committee regard the event as just so much hot air. New Yorkers are a highly opinionated lot and revel in their right to say and do as they please in almost any setting.

Social activity in New York clearly encompasses internal sightseeing by both residents and tourists that's quasi-religious. This includes Little Italy's San Gennaro Festival, community events, fairs, and other smaller events. One of the more unusual happenings is visiting Brooklyn's Dyker Heights, set between Bay Ridge and Bensonhurst. It's an upscale, largely Italian neighborhood with the usual American and Italian flags side by side, accompanied by Virgin Mary statuettes and nativity scenes. Unless you drive, it takes some effort to get to Dyker Heights, as the nearest subway is a mile away. In an area of gracious private residences, during the Christmas season people lavishly bedeck their homes with beautiful and expensive decorations—reindeer, wooden soldiers, elaborate wreaths, trees, in a true festival of dazzling displays and multicolored lights. Some of them are even motorized, and one wonders if the owners are attempting to one-up each other. The area is roughly between Eighty-third and Eighty-sixth Streets from Thirteenth to Eleventh Avenues.

Cars drive slowly up and down the streets of Dyker Heights, their occupants gazing, often gawking, at this million-dollar extravaganza. Many have seen it before but delight in watching the faces of their friends who are experiencing it for the first time. Others willing to brave the cold walk the streets, their feet tripping gaily up and down the stairs in front of these million-dollar homes, a good number of them palatial with circular staircases, marble surfaces, and Roman columns and arches. I have spoken with people from all over the world—Norway, China, Argentina—for whom this neighborhood is part of the itinerary on their visit to New York City, an insider's journey that is becoming less so as the word spreads. Is touring the area a religious experience or simply a fun, touristy type of thing to do? Conversations with attendees suggest it's a little of each. A young man from Taiwan, visiting with his wife, said, "We love the lights and the way the houses look. But it's also a way of getting into the holiday spirit, and feeling the joy that Jesus brings into the hearts of those who believe."

Even sports can have a religious patina. Do we take note when a team kneels and prays before a game? What about a Hail Mary pass in a football game, described as such by spectators and broadcasters? One of the more interesting, perhaps unique, connections between sports and religion I ever witnessed occurred at a bocci game I was watching in the Marine Park neighborhood of Brooklyn. One participant watched another player make a beautiful shot, the ball nestled tightly between the wall and the other ball. "Wow," he exclaimed. "He nailed it to the cross!" And then he repeated it verbatim for emphasis. The speaker knew that those in the game were almost surely Catholic, predominantly of Italian heritage, and would appreciate his metaphor, though some Catholics with whom I spoke found it a bit off-putting. In this way he expressed and demonstrated the group's solidarity and identity, linking them ethnically and religiously and declaring it to be a comfort zone for all of them. As such, his comment was more than "just a way of talking." I found myself thinking, 'Here's a guy who's really comfortable in his own skin. He knows that I, an outsider, am watching the game and I'm standing two feet from him. It makes no difference to him, perhaps also because he's with his friends.'

Sports and Games

So much about New York is about sports. And on a Sunday it's impossible not to notice it, as people everywhere are glued to television or radio. Typical is a huge sports bar and eatery called 200 Fifth on Fifth Avenue in Park Slope. There are small TV screens at every table tuned to Jets or Giants football games. People are eagerly consuming burgers and fries and washing them down with beer and soda amid the loud din of fans exclaiming loudly and shouting at the screens, seemingly trying to will their teams to victory. When the home team scores, the roar of approval as the people explode in joy can be heard halfway down the block. It's a beautiful, warm, sunny day in early fall, but for these people the action is definitely inside, not outside. And I too am caught up in the excitement of being at one with the crowd.

Rooting for a citywide team can unite its residents. It can also be the focus of one borough. Staten Island has its own baseball team, the Staten Island Yankees, as does Brooklyn. Tickets for Yankee games cost as little as nine dollars, and there are activities in the ball park that, as one resident told me, "make things interesting." Yankee games have a small-town feel to them, the hot dogs are cheap, and you can easily get to the park. Unlike the Mets-Yankees annual series, there are no Mayor's Trophy games, but over the years a fairly intense rivalry has developed between the Staten Island Yankees and the Brooklyn Cyclones. Compared to Yankee Stadium and Citi Field, the price is certainly right.

The neutrality of sports has an equalizing effect on its participants and spectators, whether it's basketball, baseball, football, or soccer. While this objectivity doesn't prevent ethnic pride in a tribe member's success, its overall effect is to unify. Thus, a Hasidic teenager can easily ask a Hispanic or black youth watching a game, "Who's winning?" Take bowling, for example. Like many other sports, bowling is an opportunity to cross social class and ethnic boundaries. In the words of John LaSpina, a past president of the Bowling Proprietors Association of America, "This is an old code of mine—if the United Nations put a couple of lanes in, people would get along. Forget black and white, that's easy. It's Hasidic, Asian, Muslim kids from high school gym class. For whatever reason, it works."[7] One reason may be that it offers the opportunity to develop friendships, minus the risks of rejection as on a dance floor or in a nightclub. Nor is there any obligation. You start a conversation with someone and ramp it up or take your leave.

Certain sports and games are favored by specific groups. Tons of people play Ping-Pong, but it is a sport identified with Asians. Not surprisingly, then, it's a big deal in Brooklyn's Sunset Park, where the area surrounding the park (also called Sunset Park) is heavily Asian. The park boasts six world-class Ping-Pong tables contributed by a Chinese donor. On a Thursday morning when I visited, all of the players were Chinese, and the same is true on other days.

Or take dominoes, which is to the Latino community what basketball is to the black community, what bocci is to the Italian community, and so on. Walking through the Hispanic areas of the city in the summertime, one finds people, mostly men, seated around folding tables on the sidewalk, in parks, and even inside stores, concentrating on the ivory, black, or red tiles as if their lives depended on them. And in a way they do, because for so many life isn't worth living without the game and the highly enjoyable bonding banter and macho posturing that accompanies it, all reflecting aspects of their identity and culture, including language, geographic origins, and insider jokes. And, of course, it's a game most have known since childhood. It looks easy—just connect the dots on your pieces with those on the table—but it's not. There's a high level of skill, because you have to have a good memory. You also need to intuit the decisions your opponents are going to make based on their past performance. The game is also characterized by ethnic loyalties and divisions. Puerto Ricans, Cubans, and Dominicans generally play with their own group, with each one having particular styles and variations on the rules.[8]

In my travels through the city I noticed a large number of black people playing chess, from Times Square, to the streets of Harlem, to Starbucks, to the city's public parks. What stood out as I watched them was not only the enthusiasm they displayed but also their commitment to the game. I would walk by a park at night and see people playing with a portable lamp placed over the board. Speed chess is a particular favorite.

An article on the topic placed the game of chess in a racial context, asserting that blacks are acutely aware that whoever has the white pieces moves first, not a coincidence in their eyes, seeing it as "a life lesson." The article focused on the Washington, D.C., area and reported that thousands of blacks there play the game, suggesting that this is a national phenomenon, not merely a New York thing, though the first black grandmaster, Maurice Ashley, is a New Yorker. "Black chess is not like European chess," said one insider, "where everybody sits there all quiet and doesn't say anything. Black folks talk trash. You gotta have sass to go along with the game."

Is there a cultural reason for this love of chess? A black Maryland state senator, Ulysses Currie, offered the following explanation: "Chess defines us in ways other than the way we are often defined in newspapers and on television with the negative images. . . . Chess knocks the stereotypes and shows that we are intellectual, cerebral people and that we are interested in something other than basketball."[9] This, then, is a value—namely, to be respected for one's brain power.

This argument would not apply to Jews, a group overrepresented in chess, who, if anything, are stereotyped as being too smart—words like "shrewd" and "clever" are often employed in reference to Jews. Yet Jews and blacks share in common something else: a history of marginality, of always being on the outside, looking in, and feeling endangered. Such groups may therefore feel a need to be one step ahead, just a bit smarter, merely to survive.[10]

Other issues, like safety, and stereotypes about it, can enter into discussions about sports and complicate matters too. Much as chess seems like a peaceful pastime, some people are not thrilled about it, albeit for different reasons. In 2010 a story appeared in the *New York Times,* provocatively titled "Police! Drop the Pawn! Step away from the Table!" Inwood Hill Park in Northern Manhattan, was the scene of a police raid on chess players enjoying themselves at chess tables that just happened to be within a playground area. This is against the posted law—you can't be there unless you're with a minor.

Certainly this law presents a dilemma in terms of how space is used and negotiated. One can understand the safety concern, but what if you're a person who just wants to enjoy watching kids play because they remind you of your grandchildren now living in Los Angeles or Pittsburgh? And what if you're only there because the chess table is there? But here's the rub: chess players as a group pose no threat as a rule. Thus, one of the chess players who was issued a summons, Yacahudah Harrison, a forty-nine-year-old black man, asked, "What is so harmful with chess?" The problem is that he's homeless—in other words, unsavory. Harrison claims he was invited to the park by a resident who asked him to teach the game to children. If we care so much about the homeless that we create organizations to help them, give them money, and try to find homes for them, can't they contribute in other ways to society? Or does being homeless mean they can't be trusted to interact with children? Are they bad role models? Does race enter into the picture? Remember the Chicago Seven of 1960s fame? The chess players who were cited for breaking the law that day were playfully dubbed the Inwood Hill Seven, at least by the reporters who wrote the article.

Harrison took issue with the stereotype of drinking men when he said, "We drink jasmine tea and have some muffins, nothing decadent." For what it's worth, a fence separates the playing area from the playground itself. And they had their local supporters. One woman wrote the mayor and the police that her seven-year-old son learned to play the game from one of the men who used to hang out there.[11]

The police defended their actions as part of an effort to respond to complaints about crime in the park. The problem is that it's hard to draw the line. I was walking along Morningside Park in Harlem and stopped to observe men playing chess at some tables that were not in a playground. What drew my attention was that it was nighttime, and people had brought portable fluorescent lamps to the park to illuminate the boards and pieces. "They must really love this game," I thought.

I noticed a tall, younger man wearing sunglasses and a black leather jacket who was standing by the table. Perhaps he had been watching or playing earlier. But at that moment he was talking on his cell phone, intensely engaged in, from what I could overhear, the details of a drug deal he was apparently making. He ignored my presence, even though I was a stranger and white, in contrast to the minority makeup of the five other men present. Could he be a regular player when he wasn't dealing? Of course, many people have multiple roles in a variety of contexts. But was it fair to assume that because he was standing there he was a drug dealer *and* a chess player? Maybe not, but perhaps these roles coexist, so to speak, in an environment where these activities are often commingled.

Another sedentary game is bingo, but the players, venues, and its dependence on luck make it a whole different ball game, as they say. Bingo is very big among members of a specific group— senior citizens, mostly older, working-class women—and the game helps bring them closer together, even to unite them. Like bocci, bingo has Italian antecedents. The original version was invented in Italy in 1530 and called Lo Giuoco del Lotto D'Italia (meaning "The Clearance of the Lot in Italy"). It entered the United States in the 1920s and was first called beano, after the beans players used to mark their cards. In describing the Nostrand Bingo Hall in Brooklyn, *New York Times* writer N. R. Kleinfeld refers to it as "one of the enduring relics of a fading game long cherished by those long done working." These are the same people who get on a bus to Atlantic City, but in this case they don't even have to do that. For many of these old-timers bingo is almost a religion. Their lives revolve around it—the play, the camaraderie, the possibility of a thousand dollars or more in winnings—and a good number of them were invested in the game many years before they retired. As Kleinfeld puts it, "It's an analgesic for the yawning emptiness of old age."

Bingo even has intellectual forebears, most notably Carl Leffler, a Columbia University math professor who figured out six thousand combinations and reportedly lost his mind from the stress of doing so. Despite that pedigree, since success at bingo rests totally on luck, many think it's a game for idiots. At least in horse racing you can speculate about the horse's abilities as described in the racing sheets.[12] One place that I visited is the bingo hall in Richmond Hill, a cavernous former movie theater where enthusiasts gather on a regular basis. Their conversations focused on health, politics, and the economy, as well as on the changing neighborhood. Several of those present avidly discussed stock tips that had panned out, as well as some that didn't.

Reflecting the large West Indian and South Asian populations in the city, there are cricket fields in the areas where they reside, in the Bronx, Queens, and elsewhere. Lots of times it's informal, but sometimes it's the opposite, with people dressed to the nines. One case in point is in Staten Island, at Walker Park, between Bard and Davis Avenues near the harbor. A cricket game is going on, with the players dressed in white uniforms. Nearby, people are sitting with their families, watching the game, picnicking, and listening to music. The soft strains of calypso music fill the air, mixed in with the smells of curried goat and roti, a flatbread. The crowd is mostly West Indian and South Asian, and this game is sponsored and run by the Staten Island Cricket and Baseball Club, which is about 140 years old, having been founded in 1872.

At that time British people lived on the island, and cricket was played by British army officers who had immigrated to New York. As was the case then, those who come to Walker Park today view the club as an outlet for getting together socially and for validating an important aspect of their identity and culture. Casual games are played here on Saturday and more competitive ones on Sunday.[13]

Interestingly, while you might think of Queens and the U.S. Open when you hear the word "tennis," in New York the sport was actually first played in 1874 on Staten Island, where it was introduced by Mary Ewing Outerbridge, who got the idea of bringing it to the city after watching a game of tennis in Bermuda. Parenthetically, most people probably think the Outerbridge Crossing from Staten Island to New Jersey is so named because it's a bridge on the edge or outskirts of both locations. But as it turns out, it has to do with Mary's brother, Eugenius Outerbridge, the first chairman of the Port of New York Authority, after whom the bridge was named.[14]

One of the most unusual sports in New York is rooftop pigeon flying. In the past this activity was engaged in primarily by Italians and other white males, hailing mostly from Brooklyn and Queens. Today's flyers are predominantly African American and Puerto Rican. What's interesting is that the remaining older white ethnics mingle with the minorities and develop relationships across group boundaries through this activity. All this is chronicled by Colin Jerolmack, who spent three years studying the group in Brooklyn's Bedford-Stuyvesant and Bushwick neighborhoods.[15]

The YMCAs and YMHAs (Young Men's Christian Association and Young Men's Hebrew Association, respectively) throughout the five boroughs are of great importance to community life. Their programs vary, but they are there for those unable to afford high-priced gyms or private recreation clubs, as well as to reinforce religion. Typical is the Twelve Towns YMCA in Cypress Hills by Jamaica and Force Tube Avenues near Highland Park. The center has racquetball, swimming, a fitness room, basketball, and dancing. What's amazing is the price: $429 annually for adults between twenty-five and sixty-four, and $780 for a family with two or more children. Not all Ys are so cheap. At the other end of the scale is the Vanderbilt YMCA in Mid-Manhattan's East Side, where the annual cost for a family is $2,000, still a bargain compared to a private facility.

Last among the sports and games important to the city, but certainly not least in terms of the number of participants, are the informal games played by children. Regardless of where they grow up, kids like to have fun pulling pranks, whether it's throwing water balloons from windows or ringing people's bells in apartment buildings and running away. Their Halloween pranks, featuring potato and egg throwing at cars, are also good examples of this. In Gerritsen Beach, Brooklyn, a favorite pastime is giving wrong directions to drivers who wander into the community and get lost. The driver ends up facing the water on a dead-end street. Such amusements have the effect of binding residents together in later life as well as they reminisce about their youth.[16]

Parks

Easy access to good public parks, the best known being Central Park and Brooklyn's Prospect Park, are a major reason why people consider certain communities worth living in. Their offerings, some of which include zoos, generally reflect the communities' interests and group identities, based largely on who lives there. Thus, Riverbank State Park at 145th Street and Riverside Drive, has gospel concerts. And there's a Halloween party and a parade with costumes, DJs, the works. There's a kids' carousel at a dollar a ride. And park-goers celebrate the neighborhood's Puerto Rican heritage.

The involvement of private corporations and wealthy individuals in New York City's parks is accepted today as a fact of life, though many professionals are uncomfortable with the influence wielded by outside interests that results from such connections. This pattern began in earnest during the Koch administration under the energetic leadership of then parks commissioner Gordon Davis. The parks are exceedingly important to New Yorkers. Despite the high demand for construction of every type in this urban metropolis, 14 percent of the city's land area consists of parkland. What's remarkable is the variety of parks that exists in the city and the different uses to which they have been put.

Sometimes through its offerings an entire park that is officially open to the public at large becomes a venue for a particular group to reinforce its identity through various activities. Sunset Park in Brooklyn anchors the largely Chinese community in which it is situated. It appeals to people of all backgrounds, yet Asians seem to find the park particularly enjoyable. On one recent visit I saw middle-age men and women doing yoga or tai chi there. One man explained to me, "This is part of my culture and it is also very healthy. You should try it." Groups of Chinese men have a hilly area near the park's north end, where they gather just to talk and exchange stories. Set high on a hill, the park boasts a terrific view of the Manhattan skyline, the Statue of Liberty, and New York Harbor.

Notwithstanding the pattern in Sunset Park, integration is clearly the norm in multiethnic neighborhoods or if the area is transitioning from one group to another. Sometimes several ethnic groups play basketball together, sometimes they don't. It depends on many factors: Do they know and/or personally like each other? Do they live on the same block? Do they attend a nearby school together? Sometimes a park displays ethnic coexistence and actual mixing. For example, on several trips to DeWitt Clinton Park, on Eleventh Avenue between Fifty-second and Fifty-fourth Streets, I saw basketball games featuring only black teenagers, while at nearby handball courts the participants were exclusively Asian. Yet the kids mingled freely around the water fountain and interfaced along the benches. From comments made in answer to my questions, it would seem that the issue of who was playing what was simply a matter of game preference.

Hundreds of parks of all sizes throughout the city serve as places where people of different socioeconomic groups meet and socialize on a level playing field. Skyline Park in northern Staten Island is known as a place where people from the poorer community, lower down the hill in New Brighton, meet with those who are better off, from West Brighton. Reportedly, everyone gets along, and my own observations and queries confirmed that. The adults tend to cluster in their own ethnic or class groups, but the children mix freely on the monkey bars, in the water flumes, and in the sandboxes.

Most city parks are public, but there are exceptions. One of the most beautiful is the two-acre Gramercy Park in Manhattan, complete with aesthetically pleasing gardens and flowers along winding paths, even birdhouses. Alas, it's private, requiring a key to enter the grounds. Only those living near it can use it. Of course, the gardens that exist in the interior grounds of many city apartment buildings are also off limits to the public, but these are not on the street itself, where those walking by are apt to feel particularly frustrated at not being allowed access to what is easily mistaken for a public park. As a result, Gramercy Park has a certain elitist air, with the casual stroller vaguely feeling that there's something wrong about it. Conversely, the park unifies the residents who share and enjoy it.

For those who are annoyed at being excluded from private parks, there are some great and relatively unknown parks in the city, and they can be found in every borough. The Chinese Scholars Garden in Snug Harbor, part of the Staten Island Botanical Gardens, was created at a cost of $5 million. (See figure 15.) It is one of the most exquisite and beautiful gardens you will ever see, and it reflects the community's strong belief that such a garden is an important project and that it adds greatly to its social life. It is well worth the trip to see the stonework, lacquer work, statues, engraved designs, gazebos, latticework, goldfish ponds, and many other artistic creations. Everything is beautifully done, and walking through it makes one feel particularly contemplative, relaxed, and even scholarly. Garden guide cards inform visitors that plants stand for ideas and certain floral arrangements represent poems or philosophical concepts. For example, a description near some flowers reads: "The flowering plum, bamboo, and pine are the three friends of winter. The plum blooms in late winter and is therefore a symbol of the loyalty of a scholar's friends even in the harshest of political times." The small stairs of the garden's One Step Bridge are designed to make visitors walk one step at a time, allowing them to contemplate a different view from each point along the way.

Another park deserving of special mention is Von Briesen Park, also in Staten Island. Although it lies right in the shadow of the Verrazano Bridge, most New Yorkers have never even heard of it. A place where gentle winds blow from the east, it was founded by a prominent German immigrant, Arthur Von Briesen. It's situated on ten acres located on the water, and despite numerous attempts to build recreational facilities in it, they all failed because the Parks

Commission felt strongly that it should remain what they deem as "the most beautiful passive park in the city." The park still has unusual trees like the horse chestnut and the red oak.

Von Briesen was a big supporter of democratic ideals, believing that immigrants would become better citizens if treated fairly, and with that in mind he created the German Legal Aid Society in 1876. This eventually morphed into the famous Legal Aid Society that has lasted until this very day and helps thousands of indigent people in New York City every year. What unites these two activities is a concern for both the unprotected trees and flowers and the indigent. What makes this story relevant for our purposes is that, based on my own observations, the park elevates the social lives of residents and others by providing a beautiful setting for walking and socializing.

A park, I discovered, can be both tiny and special. Deep in the South Bronx, on Fulton Avenue at the edge of the Cross Bronx Expressway, I enter a tiny, beautiful park, perhaps a quarter of a block in length. Nestled against the wall of an apartment building, with a soft black gravel surface, it is called the Uptown Sitting Park, and that is basically what it's for. You can sit on one of several contoured benches with room for three or four people. There are also a few concrete chess or checkerboard tables by some of the benches. The park is very shady, with a number of trees and a beautiful, flower-covered trellis. There's no playground, no sports facilities, and no litter. The garbage cans, lined with plastic bags, are virtually empty. On three visits I found no one present except, on one occasion, a young African couple who live up the block and who told me it's a favorite spot for "people in love." Indeed, the feeling is one of peace and solitude.

Immediately behind the park is a busy gas station that sits on bustling Third Avenue, obscured mostly by the evergreen trees that border the park. I walk over to the station, point, and ask the gas attendant, "Do you know what's up there?"

"No," he replies.

"It's a beautiful little park," I tell him.

"Oh," he says in a bored tone and goes back to pumping gas. He has been toiling at this job for three years.

Most amazing, perhaps, as you sit on the benches is that you can get a clear view, through the branches, of the Cross Bronx Expressway. As I gaze at the passing ten-wheel tractor trailers, buses, and cars, I am struck by the contrast between the quiet of the park and the busyness of what goes on around it. The contrast is heightened by the fact that people walk by on the sidewalk seemingly unaware that there is a park there. It is camouflaged by the trees. I feel almost as though I'm dreaming, contemplating the city from a distant vantage point—that I see it, feel it pulsating, but am not at all part of it.

As I leave I notice a sign listing the usual restrictions against loud noise, cooking, and littering in the park, but it is the first admonition, "No Monopolizing," that catches my attention. What does it mean? No monopolizing of space? Of conversation? No financial monopolies? No Monopoly games? Who knows? Two blocks up the hill I see one of the many public housing projects in the Bronx, rising into the cobalt-blue afternoon sky. "Does anyone from there ever come here to escape their grimness?" I wonder.

Although most people don't think about it, New York City is home to many streams, ponds, forests, and even wildlife within its boundaries. Coyotes love it because it has lots of rodents and no large predators like bears or mountain lions. While the coyotes tend to hang out in the Bronx, herons, snakes, and wild turkeys are flourishing on Staten Island.[17] Many of the parks have forests and meadows. For example, Inwood Hill Park in northernmost Manhattan stretches north from Dyckman Street to Baker Field. It's quiet and heavily wooded, aside from the tennis courts and ball fields near the eastern edge. As I walk along the shaded paths, not many people are around, and it feels as though I am a hundred miles outside of the city. This is equally true of Bowne and Cunningham Parks in Queens, Prospect Park in Brooklyn, and many others.

Staten Island also has a large greenbelt area where one can hike for miles and miles. And there is a beautiful beach to the left of the Verrazano Bridge, with reddish sand and a four-mile boardwalk that's in excellent condition. (See figure 16.) People sunbathe, play volleyball, walk, jog, and bike, just like they do elsewhere. Known as South Beach, the area features free kayaking, a carousel, puppet shows, and fireworks in season. The beach was there 150 years ago, and in its heyday it was like Coney Island, with a roller coaster, games, rides, food vendors, and other amusements. During the 1890s more than one hundred Westerns were filmed at Fred Scott's Movie Ranch in the South Beach area. Many film stars of the silent era got their start here, people like actress Lillian Gish and director D. W. Griffith. Far Rockaway has the only surfing beach within the city limits. On a sunny day in early April, I see two surfers in the water, their surfboards arcing over the waves, hitting them just right, becoming one with the cresting waves. Surfers come from all over the tri-state area (New York, New Jersey, and Connecticut) and clearly enjoy themselves.

The crown jewel of what nature has to offer in New York City is Jamaica Bay Wildlife Refuge, which is also a great recreational site. It's part of the National Park Service and is the only wildlife refuge in the country accessible by subway. In an in-depth *New York Times* article describing people's increasing awareness of its ecological importance, Alan Feuer points out that Jamaica Bay is "the city's largest open space." He describes the bay as sitting "at the literal and figurative edge where the natural and manmade worlds collide."

The bay is utilized in many ways by the various groups in the surrounding area. The Guyanese have the Curry Duck Festivals there at Floyd Bennett Field and at Jacob Riis Park, and the Native American Pow-Wow Festivals attract thousands of visitors every year. It is also the site for hundreds of community gardens. Naturally, people living by the bay use it most often, usually for fishing, boating, swimming, and hiking, and have been doing so for generations. At one time many residents earned their livelihood from the bay—namely, with commercial fishing and, in places like Sheepshead Bay, charter boat fishing.[18]

The millions of folks who annually take advantage of the city's parks, preserves, and greenbelts, plus the large amounts of space devoted to them in a city where even an eighty-by-one-hundred-foot lot can cost a million dollars, speaks for itself. These spaces are critical for the physical and mental well-being of New Yorkers and visitors alike by making available opportunities for relaxation, reflection, and spending time with one's families and friends as well as meeting new people. Moreover, by observing the activities that go on in these places, we can learn a great deal about people's social lives, values, needs, and their priorities.

Social Clubs and Gatherings

Along Eighteenth Avenue in Bensonhurst, in an ode to a generation past and sandwiched between the storefronts of more recent arrivals, is the Loyal Order of Moose: "Members Only." They're offering Christmas music by Phil Anthony for Thanksgiving Day, a whole turkey on every table—carve your own. And not long after, there's the lodge's New Year's Eve dance. It's really the Knights of Pythias, which claims to be a nonsectarian organization dedicated to friendship. These orders are most often populated and run by Christians and serve to unify them as a distinct group. Once the kids have grown up and moved away, these nostalgic gathering places of bygone days are what's left, along with some Italian delis, a bocci court in a local park, and always the church, smaller and sharing space with new ethnic groups, but still a crucial stabilizer, even an anchor for the old folks. Jews, mostly working-class types, also belong to these orders, especially the Masons and B'nai Brith lodges. In such cases the membership, relatively speaking, is mostly Jewish.

Like social lodges, senior citizen centers are important meeting places and give their members opportunities for socializing and participating in activities. As one director in Brooklyn said, "We give them a reason to get dressed in the morning and put on lipstick." Elderly liberal Jews gather at the Sholem Aleichem Cultural Center on Bainbridge Avenue in the Norwood section of the Bronx, or at the Workmen's Circle MultiCare Center in the nearby West Kingsbridge area, off Sedgwick Avenue. Why do they come? Because this was once a neighborhood for left-wing Jews who lived in the nearby Amalgamated Houses.

Seniors frequently gather in restaurants, parks, and on streets. Physically, Bensonhurst is quintessentially Brooklyn. Its mix of Art

Deco, Art Moderne, and hodgepodge architectural-design apartment buildings, joined by one-, two-, and multifamily houses of every description—two- to four-story, Kreischer-era, yellow brick houses with bow or bay windows, built in the 1880s, split levels and ranches, colonials—remind the visitor of what is meant when people conjure up images of old Brooklyn. The Kreischer Brick Works factory was located in Staten Island. Some streets are tree-lined, others are bare, most are in between. In the neighborhood, middle-age and elderly men hang out in front of the buildings, sitting on stoops or folding chairs, or in nearby coffee shops and Burger Kings, where they have their favorite tables.

Typically they are dressed in flannel shirts and plain pants, wearing windbreakers that may read "Korean War Vet" or "Mets," and thick, square work shoes. The words on their caps often reflect where they worked, the beers they favored, and the teams they loved, most often the standard white *B* for Brooklyn Dodgers on their blue, often faded caps. They speak in animated tones, gesturing, laughing, and jabbing each other playfully to emphasize their points. The conversations most often revolve around their families, their work, past and present, and, most important, which team to bet on—the Lions, the Patriots, the Jets, as well as on the ever-changing fortunes and abilities of their Yankees and Mets.

And yet the new Brooklyn is there too, pushing its way into the consciousness of these oldsters. They can't help but notice the passing crowds of Asians and Russians thronging the Eighty-sixth Street shopping area: the ethnic stores; the multilanguage signs; the travel agencies advertising low fares to every corner of the globe; and the restaurants, a United Nations of New York, offering Turkish, Russian, Japanese, Mexican, Peruvian, Chinese, Korean, Vietnamese, and Afghan food. The future, if not the present, is clearly theirs. Overall, the Bensonhurst area is today mostly Chinese, Russian, a bit Albanian, coupled with the remaining white ethnics—Italians, and some Irish and Jews. Change has indeed come and the oldsters know it. Yet for now they do their best to hold on, clinging to each other for comfort.

In smaller cities or in the suburbs and outer boroughs of New York City, bars usually serve as places to meet friends. The locals know each other. In Manhattan, however, that's often not the case. There bars often serve as a destination point for those living elsewhere, especially the young. An almost carnival air of excitement prevails as the subways disgorge revelers, especially on weekends and holidays, at Times Square, Penn Station, Union Square, Astor Place,and West Fourth Street, all bent on having a good time. This is seen by many as one of the benefits of living in the Big Apple—you don't have to go far to feel like you have done so. In forty-five minutes you can go somewhere and meet new people, listen to great stand-up comedy, eat in a five-star restaurant, or just go to a dive and see a new and different slice of urban life.[19]

Naturally the most ubiquitous form of social gatherings is people getting together in one another's homes for an evening of dining, drinking, and conversation. Occasions like birthday parties and anniversaries give them special meaning. Formal commemorations, like Mother's or Father's Day, also cement the social glue that holds society together. Walking the streets of Bushwick on Mother's Day, I saw many parties that were typical of those going on throughout the city. The holiday is one that brings families together. Houses were festooned with balloons, many of them silvery, heart-shaped ones proclaiming "Happy Mother's Day!" In poor areas like Bushwick, people especially welcome the opportunity to be happy about something. I passed by one two-story, newish brick dwelling where a crowd of Hispanic people, probably family members, had gathered. The music was loud, the atmosphere convivial. Parked in front of the house, looking incongruous in this impoverished part of Brooklyn, was a regular-size (not limo), bright red, gleaming Rolls Royce. A rich relative? A rental? A drug dealer? A lottery winner? Who knows?

A Final Thought

One general emerging trend that manifests itself when the social life of New York City is examined is a greater concern with health and environmental issues, and it turns up in sometimes unexpected ways. New housing construction projects are beginning to advertise their emphasis on such issues. A subsidized housing development called Via Verde has opened in the South Bronx at Brook Avenue and 156th Street that emphasizes healthy living as the rationale for much of its design. The main health problems in poor areas are obesity, poor diets, and asthma. The ground floor of Via Verde is occupied by a medical clinic. There are ceiling fans to discourage the use of air conditioners unless it's really necessary. Staircases are built to encourage people to use them, buildings take advantage of natural light, and there are fitness centers too.[20] These features aren't earth-shaking, but they reflect a new consciousness about health and the environment from a business where developers are usually focused on how many apartments they can build in a particular space. They also suggest that builders think it's a good selling point.

The health trend is also evident in leisure-time activities. Conservation groups have always promoted safeguarding the environment, but their level of activity has increased significantly in the last decade or so. The Bronx River Alliance, founded in 2001, is dedicated to cleaning up the once very polluted Bronx River, which had many abandoned cars and other debris dumped into it. The alliance works closely with the Parks Department and many community groups. It is amazing what such volunteer organizations can achieve. Since 1997 the Bronx River Conservation Crew and thousands of volunteers have removed 250 tons of debris and trash as well as 72 cars and almost 16,000 tires from the river. Their goal is to create a twenty-three-mile-long "Central Park" for the Bronx, with an entire network of parklands running alongside the Bronx River, a greenway. To that end 45,000 shrubs and trees have been planted. The organization has even developed a canoe program for students and the general public who want to do urban exploring. This kind of planned approach for the future has become more common.

New also is the temporary closing off of twelve streets in New York and their designation as "play streets," for the express purpose of promoting health through activities like running, yoga, jumping rope, tennis, and rugby. The effort is particularly designed to combat childhood obesity. The evidence gathered so far suggests that the plan has been a success, attracting children who previously spent most of their time watching TV and playing video games indoors.[21] Of course, the city is full of parks and they are used, but having a play area just outside the house will at least tempt those who don't want to walk far, who want to be near home, and whose families wish to supervise them from close by.

In 2011 New York City began rating restaurants for cleanliness, using a letter grading system. This too is a reflection of heightened concern with health throughout American society. The grading system has a Zagat-like effect, even though it doesn't deal with the quality or taste of the food. Its effects have not yet been studied in depth, but preliminary results are encouraging.[22] Certain assumptions about the rating scale can be made, however. First, a grade of "B" might make one think twice, and a "C" or "Grade Pending" would certainly be disturbing to the average diner. After all, a restaurant might serve delicious food, but if it makes you sick, then what's it worth? Subliminally "A" is always seen as synonymous with quality: one thinks of an A average, bonds with a triple-A rating, and the like. Evidence of just how ghastly, or costly, such a judgment is can be inferred from the strenuous efforts of more than a few eateries to hide the placard stating their grade by placing objects like a table or large potted plant to conceal the offending letter.

In short, when you look around the city, from the explosion in health-oriented eateries, to bans on smoking, to campaigns for better living, paying attention to health is more popular today, and it's a trend that's beginning to permeate every aspect of society.

5

TAR BEACHES, SIDEWALK CARVINGS, IRISH FREEDOM FIGHTERS, AND SUPERMAN
Spaces in the Big Apple

To enter the world of a Bronx or Brooklyn bus—it's fair to call them spaces—is to join a world populated in large measure by the poor, the black, and the Hispanic, with an occasional Asian and an even rarer elderly white person who was apparently left behind in the various eras of white flight. Except for teenagers, nearly everyone looks tired, bored, and, in many cases, worn down or defeated by life's hardships. Their clothes tend to be shabby, and children tug impatiently on their mothers' dresses, pants, or arms and legs. There are people with canes, others in wheelchairs. A few read books in Spanish. Some talk listlessly or listen to music, but most just stare out into the distance.

My presence on the bus goes unnoticed. I'm wearing a nondescript outfit designed to hopefully blend in—blue shorts, a non-matching khaki-colored polo shirt, white socks, and black shoes. Indeed, no one favors me with more than a furtive passing glance, if that. The only riders who draw serious attention are four adventuresome young tourists from Germany, Scandinavia, or wherever, who've decided the bus is the *real* way to explore New York City. Their dress, language, demeanor, and foreignness seem to make people feel they have a right to stare at them openly, almost as if to say, "If you weird-looking and strange-talking people are on this bus, where you don't fit in at all, then we have a right to look at you for as long we want." And, of course, people do stare at the foreigners. It's a public space and, in a sense, their territory, though only until they get off. But staring is not something they would ever do so openly to their fellow residents.

The city has thousands of spaces and here we look at them in detail. We begin with larger spaces—neighborhoods, industrial and commercial areas, and parks. We then focus on the streets and sidewalks themselves. Next we turn our attention to shops and malls, as well as the signage on stores, advertising spaces, and the signs on houses of worship. The next areas to be examined are buildings and walls. We conclude with shrines, plaques, statues, and views.

These spaces teach us a great deal about the people living here. We learn what space means to them; how they use it for living, work, and play; and how it expresses their beliefs, values, priorities, and matters that concern them. Among these are territoriality, artistic expression, identities of various sorts, advocating for various causes, bonding, sharing stories and jokes, remembering people or history, giving to others, and solidarity in protest. The spaces are mostly outdoors and public, but occasionally they are private spaces that can be seen in public. Missing from the discussion, though not entirely absent, are the private worlds behind locked doors, but there is more than enough going on in the unlocked world to provide insight and understanding of how this great metropolis survives and thrives. Let's begin by focusing on neighborhoods, not so much as communities, but as spaces.

Neighborhoods

When I was a kid, my family lived in Washington Heights for several years. There were certain blocks I always walked on and others I never walked on. This is true for just about everyone. You have blocks where your friends live and others where they don't. A church you attend is on one street, a school is on another. Your favorite stores are on one shopping block and not on another. There were also blocks I didn't walk on because they had a reputation among youngsters of being unfriendly to outsiders. This rarely applied to adults, who blithely walked these streets unaware of such dangers. For them, danger usually meant being mugged. Thus, residents often have a truncated view of their own neighborhood, almost as if they live in a "sub-neighborhood."

I lived for several years on 164th Street, one block west of Broadway, in Manhattan's Washington Heights, and I never set foot east of Broadway on 164th, 163rd, or 162nd Streets, though I did on 165th and 161st. I strolled along 157th Street, but not on 158th or 159th. My friends and I regarded the entire area as our "home turf," but, in truth, only portions of it were. Now that I've systematically walked almost every street in the city, including those in my old neighborhood, I traverse these blocks like a first-time visitor, which, in fact, I am. I never noticed them back then, but now I do, because I'm seeing them for the first time.

What this means is that people's spatial boundaries are often narrower than their statements about "my neighborhood" or "where I grew up" would seem to suggest. Thus, when they generalize about the "West Side" of Manhattan or "Flatbush," Brooklyn, those terms might be far less applicable to the entire area than their comments imply. And since different people consider different parts of their neighborhoods important, people can grow up in the same part of the city and have widely divergent opinions about its attractiveness, people, safety, and even its main points of interest. These are self-imposed boundaries owing to networks of friends, preferred activities, and the like.[1]

In general, when we think of residents "controlling" a neighborhood block in a territorial sense, what comes to mind is block associations, friendship networks, the "eyes and ears" discussed by Jane Jacobs, or the presence of gangs on a block. One extreme negative example of the last category happened on a one-way street, Undercliff Avenue, in the Morris Heights section of the West Bronx, which fell under a gang's control. An apartment building on the street, number 1571, was the gang's "guarded fortress," and from their vantage point they could spot every approaching car and "brandished guns when they sensed trouble." It was, by all accounts, a "brazen operation," based in ten vacant apartments. The leader, born in the Dominican Republic, was José Delorbe. Delorbe also enjoyed the complete cooperation of the superintendent, one José Jiminez. The authorities described it as a "long-running" operation that they had under surveillance.[2] One wonders why it wasn't stopped earlier. The answer is probably that residents were, and are, too afraid to testify. What this demonstrates is that, when not challenged by the law, undesirables can actually control a public space as if it were their private property.

Very few public spaces in the city can be sacred, impervious to the outside world. New Yorkers can and do walk in every neighborhood or other public spaces. Even as an outsider you can stand on a block and sing or dance, or you can sell lemonade. This is brought home to me as I pass through the byways and small curving streets of the exclusive, upscale neighborhood of Todt Hill, in Staten Island. I am with my students on a Sunday afternoon. Trips throughout the city are part of the graduate course I teach about New York City. There are huge gated mansions, or palazzos, here, and the homes exquisitely represent the beautiful styles of Gothic, Georgian, Romanesque, and Greek Revival. Some are ultramodern, and many have spectacular views of the city. The streets are empty on a Sunday afternoon in October. We come to a corner and suddenly I spy, tacked onto a telephone pole, a neat, hand-lettered sign in black lettering on a plain piece of paper. Its simple message says it all, direct and unambiguous: "Single and Ready to Mingle," followed by a local phone number.

As I peer up and down the street, I have the feeling that space and privacy have somehow been violated in this redoubt of the rich. But, of course, they haven't, because this is the city and the streets are, in fact, anything but private. These people may feel they have a private community, but if so, it's private only in their imaginations. The wild life, as it were, beckons just beyond the edge of their property. "Will anyone be enticed by that offer?" I wonder. "How long will it stay up there? Will an angry resident tear it down?" "You never know," I conclude, and as I do so, I remember that many years ago this area was in the public eye in another way.

It was identified as the community where Paul Castellano, a Mafia mobster, lived before he was gunned down.[3]

It's important to understand that the space that defines a neighborhood is not limited to its residents but can also include those who regularly work in the area. Thus, the Café Clementine in upscale Tribeca, by West Broadway and White Street, has about a dozen, mostly Latino employees who deliver meals locally to the residents. Outside is a rack for about fifteen bikes used by the delivery people. But there is little meaningful interaction with residents beyond these transactions, since the delivery people are largely defined by their specific role, nothing more.

The Westside Coffee Shop, also in Tribeca, located on Church Street between Canal and Lispenard Streets, serves primarily Dominican food to the immigrants who work in the area. Surprisingly, in the evening most of the customers are not Latinos, but African men who work nearby on Canal Street as sidewalk vendors. The place is a hangout for the men, mostly Senegalese, that allows them to stay inside and avoid the cold weather, to use the restroom, and to just socialize. The few Latinos who come there use the restaurant for what it was intended—to eat Spanish food. During the daytime hours the customers are pairs or individuals, both white and Hispanic, who come in mainly to eat lunch. Thus, the space usage changes according to what's happening at different times of the day, and this is true of many city neighborhoods.[4]

The battles over public space in neighborhoods play out in a variety of venues, from parks, to buildings, to street corners. Richard's law office is across the street from an apartment building on Ninth Street, the Brevoort. As he tells it, "There was this woman from the Brevoort with a dog, and every day the dog would cross the street right by my office and do its business there. Of course, she picks up, but still, why here? So one day someone asked her what was wrong with the area in front of the Brevoort, and she said, 'Oh, the co-op rules don't allow it.'" Richard laughed as he told me this, but added, "It's okay."[5] What this shows is how a private board's authority can extend into the public square without more than a perfunctory challenge. There are many other examples of such behavior. People put their feet or bags on empty subway or bus seats; they reserve parking spots on the street by standing in them until the driver arrives; they attach a basketball hoop to a utility pole; and so on.

The spaces of New York can also become battlefronts when filmmakers use the various neighborhoods as stages or props, something that both thrills and repels local residents. The architecture professor Michael Sorkin is outraged at what he views as a gross violation of public space, which, as he sees it, is also *his* space:

> I feel my blood pressure rise as I pass the ranks of mobile dressing-rooms and supply trucks, all with their exhausts belching and their noisy generators to keep overpaid stars cool or warm. I hate the officious production assistants asking—insisting—that I cross the street so the filming of some moronic commercial can proceed without interruption. I especially hate the groaning catering tables spread with nutritious snacks placed curbside in case anyone involved with the production wants a nosh: but none for you! To me these spreads always suggest Reaganism, abundance for a few, illusory trickledown for the rest.[6]

Allowing for the hyperbole—production assistants make nothing, as anyone knows; some may even be his neighbors' children working as interns—Sorkin has a valid point. Who owns public space? And what limits are there to the rights of those who own the space?

And shouldn't those residents whose space is being commandeered, even with approval from the Mayor's Office of Film, Theatre, and Broadcasting, be compensated in some way, perhaps with a neighborhood party? Free tickets to the film? Yes, there is evidence of some class and cultural bias in Sorkin's comments, like when he refers to "moronic commercial" or "Reaganism." But isn't there also a lack of consideration on the part of those who make the films? At first these shoots are fun, conversation pieces for residents, but after a while they're seen as disruptive. For Sorkin, the overriding condition is, or should be, the extent to which the presence of filmmakers hinders or encourages public access to these spaces. In a city as diverse as ours, such sharp differences are guaranteed to emerge. And they often require Solomonic wisdom to resolve.[7]

Industrial and Commercial Spaces

The city has many areas, especially outside of Manhattan, that are devoted to industry. Suppliers of goods and light manufacturing predominate in these spaces, and residential housing zones are few and far between. Typically these districts are near bodies of water. People from nearby residential areas become familiar with the industrial zone because there are places in it or bordering it that they use. For example, Barretto Point Park sits at the end of Tiffany Street in the industrial area of southern Hunts Point. It seems out of place, this somewhat barren park, one-half mile from any residential section. But it is used for basketball, swimming, and picnics. Those who frequent it may walk past the White Rose Tea Company, marble and granite companies, or the point of origin for the city's Sabrett hot dog wagons. In doing so they learn to see the city as a place of industry, not just a place where people live, shop, and play.

Life in these spaces also has its own rhythm, to which others must adjust when they visit or come to stay. The restaurants in these areas, generally modest establishments, must keep long hours. I enter one called the Oasis and am told by the Greek American manager, as she takes phone orders in a rapid-fire stream of New Yorkese English, that running a business here in Hunts Point is not easy. "You gotta be open 4:00 AM to 9:00 PM at least. And you can't charge too much, because these are workin' people." I look at the menu, and, indeed, she's right. A burger is $4.00 with fries; an egg sandwich goes for $1.45. It is a clean-looking place and gaily decorated with large potted plants.

On Jerome Avenue north of the Cross Bronx Expressway is a long commercial stretch, extending north for over a mile, all the way to Fordham Road, and populated almost exclusively by automobile and auto accessory and repair shops of every type—radios and radiators, mufflers and motors, windshields and wiring, tires and towing equipment, speedometers and seat covers, you name it. But these businesses are not simply for the locals. People come from Staten Island, from New Jersey, and from Connecticut, looking for bargains and offering cash to eager takers. The same is true for the auto repair places and junkyards that sit in the shadow of Citi Field in Queens. Aside from their dedicated light-industrial uses, such spaces serve to introduce people outside the community to various neighborhoods where they otherwise might not ordinarily spend any time.[8]

Another type of commercial enterprise is the moderately priced chain hotels—Holiday Inn Express, Comfort Inns, and Days Inns, and others—in the outer boroughs, which serve as cheap lodging for foreign tourists who want to be near Manhattan without having to pay $400 a night. Typical locations are Long Island City; downtown Brooklyn, like the Gowanus neighborhood; and even the small village of Travis on Staten Island. These places advertise abroad in media read by the European and Latin American markets. Customers can get a room that runs from $150 to $250 a night and which is often a half-hour subway ride to Manhattan. These hotels are temporary dwellings that serve a larger purpose having little to do with their immediate neighborhood—namely, to make the city accessible to visitors. In that sense they're not really part of the community; they largely just take up space there. Those who stay in them typically rise early and head for Manhattan, though they will sometimes dine locally.

One unusual place that doesn't fit the chain enterprise mode is the Box House Hotel on Box Street. I came across it on a walk through industrial northern Greenpoint. It looked pretty ordinary on the outside, but inside it was a different story. It's a boutique hotel, one of a kind, and was originally a window and door factory. The lobby features French Provincial chairs and cartoon-like paintings of Victorian houses as well as prints of birds and flowers. Nearby is an old upright piano and a glass display case featuring antique paperweights, clocks, and other odds and ends. The hallways are painted in a soft yellowish color, with white moldings, and have gleaming wood floors. The unusual rooms are spacious and beautiful, with sixteen-foot-high ceilings, modern kitchens, and flat-screen TVs. Like the standard-looking hotels, the Box House Hotel caters to a foreign clientele, the room price is about $250 a night, and you can be in Manhattan by subway in fifteen minutes. These moderately priced hotels in the outer boroughs of New York may become a trend if visitors from abroad begin gravitating to them.

Another unusual place to visit is the Akwaaba Mansion in Brooklyn's historic Stuyvesant Heights area, on tree-lined MacDonough Street. It's an 1880s historic mansion with an Afrocentric emphasis. There's the "Jumping the Broom" room, the "Ashante," and another referred to as the "Black Memorabilia." The rooms are beautifully appointed, the breakfast is Southern style, and you can have it all for half the price of a nice Manhattan hotel. In the back is a large lovely garden suitable for parties, and Manhattan is only nineteen minutes away by subway.

Parks

Typically one can think of streets and neighborhoods as expressions of territoriality, but this is equally true of parks. Groups of people—young mothers, Asians, Hispanics, seniors, or friends from the neighborhood—frequently stake out spaces for themselves. At Jacob Riis Park in Queens the beach is divided into fourteen bays. One is used primarily by gays, two by blacks, and still others by Latino and Caribbean groups. Unlike gang territory, no one is harassed if someone from another group strays into the "wrong" area. The spaces maintain their boundaries more by common agreement, one that, nonetheless, makes allowances for "tourists."[9]

Parks are often lightning rods for conflicts between contesting groups over space. A debate at a public hearing in May 2010 highlighted that issue. A city proposal had been made to cut the number of artists and craft vendors allowed in Battery Park, High Line Park, Union Square Park, and in heavily trafficked portions of Central Park by 75 percent. The question was how to choose between two core urban values: an oasis of tranquility and a venue that allows one to select and purchase works of art.

Artists were highly visible at the public hearing, some wearing shirts proclaiming, "Artist Power." "A park without art is like eating spaghetti without spaghetti sauce," declared one partisan who sells oil pastels. (The logic of that analogy could clearly be challenged, since those who didn't want the art might prefer a different "sauce" or no sauce at all.) Indeed, those opposed largely objected to the whole scene, with one person adding, "We don't want to make a mall out of our parks."[10]

The highly popular High Line Park (at least twenty thousand visitors on weekends) was born amid considerable controversy. Developers wanted to demolish the old West Side railroad line where the one-mile-long park now sits and build on it, but in the late 1990s there was fierce resistance to the plans, and a group formed to oppose them. Called Friends of the High Line, the group sought to convert the space to a park in a unique location, even organizing walking tours of the area. Although the old tracks were overgrown with weeds, the place had a strange, peaceful, almost haunting beauty, one accentuated by its lofty perch above the ground. The High Line had originally been used by railway freight lines to deliver goods door to door, since the tracks literally ran through the factories and warehouses they serviced. The last rail delivery, a load of frozen turkeys, had been made in 1980. A key victory in the battle between preservationists and developers came when Mayor Bloomberg threw his support behind the park idea in 2002.[11]

The High Line is one of New York's most unusual parks. It runs from Thirtieth Street and Tenth Avenue down to Gansevoort Street, which is near Twelfth Street. Because it runs along unused elevated railroad track, it's more of an open space than a park, though it does have landscaped flora and fauna. It's really a promenade, as opposed to a park, and it's about as high as the third floor of a building. You feel as if you're walking through an urban forest of buildings, because you're slicing through the city, much as you would if you could traverse many blocks via alleyways, which you can't. The elevation gives you a chance to view where you're walking against the scale of the larger space in which it is found—namely, the city as a whole. Up here I spy graffiti that I wouldn't see on the ground floor level.[12] The presence of High Line Park has also positively affected real estate values in the general area.[13]

The best-known, longest, and largest protest over space that became parkland in recent times was the controversy over Westway, a proposed but unbuilt highway. Perhaps because New York City is the example par excellence of high-density urban living, attempts to remove parkland or to create it frequently generate fierce struggles. The 1972 plan envisioned replacing piers, warehouses, and other unused structures with new housing, commercial space, and parkland on about seven hundred acres. Since there was funding available for federal highways, city leaders also wanted to rebuild the old West Side Highway in the area. It would be set back far enough from the shoreline so that up to eighty-five thousand housing units could be built between it and the water.

But the plans became mired in controversy for years, generating the type of opposition engendered by the proposed Lower Manhattan Expressway, opposed earlier by Jane Jacobs and her allies. Too many people were viscerally opposed to anything that smacked of the big projects engineered in the past by the then much reviled builder Robert Moses, who was instrumental in creating New York City's highway structure.[14] The Environmental Protection Agency's conclusion that rebuilding the highway would lead to significant pollution did not help. In 1990, bowing to reality, the federal government ended its efforts to gain approval for Westway. The preservationists, casting themselves as "the little guy," had won again. It ended up as a very pretty park along the Hudson, with bike paths in the downtown area and with some piers and streets being renovated and improved. Federal approval for the park was finally given on May 31, 2000.

Streets and Sidewalks

While streets and sidewalks are clearly public spaces, the minimal degree of privacy that walking through New York used to afford has been eroded by the thousands of cameras that blanket the city, most prominently in heavily trafficked areas. For example, at last count there were eighty-two city-owned cameras in the seventeen blocks between Thirty-fourth and Fifty-first Streets. And that does not include the private cameras used by stores, building owners, and the thousands of people who regularly video whatever they see, including—whether inadvertently or intentionally—you. So if you think you can scratch yourself in private in a public space, think again. One consolation is that they probably don't know you personally. Moreover, these cameras, usually monitored by former FBI or Secret Service agents, are set up for review only after some crime has been committed, like a bomb scare or a theft. In addition, people who watch the videos live often become deadened to what they see after a while.[15]

Presumably, the ubiquitousness of these cameras makes criminals think twice, and that makes the city a safer place. Is it worth the tradeoff? To a degree that depends on how important privacy is to you. Maybe you want to feel that you're walking down a street with your lover in blissful anonymity. Or possibly you don't want the lie you told about where you were that evening to be discovered. Perhaps you just don't like the idea that someone's looking at you from somewhere in the basement of an apartment building as you pass by, even if it's for your own safety.

Regardless, what we do know is that even when people realize they're being observed, it's unlikely to affect their behavior in the long run. Why? Because most people are far more interested in whatever it is they're doing than in who's watching them do it. Sociologists who require informed consent when they do studies involving observation or taped interviews know this all too well. After a brief period people become less self-conscious and go back to what they're doing. Nevertheless, the outcome is that public space becomes far less private.[16]

The city's streets are going to be changed, says the New York City Department of Transportation. It will encourage streets with European-style trajectories, mini-islands in the middle of the streets, with landscaped greenery that will slow down automobile traffic and will be friendlier to cyclists and pedestrians. The goal is to get people "to think about streets as not just thoroughfares for cars, but as public spaces incorporating safety, aesthetics, environmental and community concerns."[17] The approach, supported by Mayor Bloomberg, is very different from the way Robert Moses saw things. But some people are worried that such plans will slow down commerce and prevent them from getting to their destinations efficiently. Nevertheless, as part of the move, portions of Broadway have been closed to vehicular traffic, and the overall reaction to the concept has been favorable.[18]

It's amazing how even a temporary event can provoke a fight over space. The city had ordered permanent chairs and tables for the pedestrian section of Broadway. When it belatedly discovered that opening the area months before the seats arrived meant that people would mill around with nowhere to sit, cheap, folding lawn chairs were ordered. That went over like a bathing suit in the Arctic. People, including Hizzoner, said the chairs cheapened the space and looked low-class and very unappealing, not suitable for the greatest city in the world. Many, however, liked them and thought they were cool and "campy." Besides, the situation was only temporary, they asserted. Tim Tompkins, the Times Square Alliance's president, best summed up the range of opinions when he remarked, "I've had people say to me both that it's a stroke of genius and that I'm the king of trailer trash. The lawn chair decision is far and away the most controversial decision I've made in my seven years as head of the alliance."[19]

In a *New York Times* opinion piece, Susan Dominus wrote that the pedestrian mall "looks a little unworthy of New York," arguing metaphorically that it looks like the city is "already letting itself go, like some Lehman Brothers wife who has not just forsaken her golden highlights, but given up on grooming altogether." Dominus says the problem might be the image of people sprawled out in the already sagging plastic chairs. "New York City is a city of walkers, not sitters, a city of motion, not repose." True here, but clearly not in all cases, like parks. The Sheep Meadow in Central Park regularly features hundreds of people lying down on the grass. Rather, it's a sense that the pedestrian mall is just a tacky-looking place, not fit for the Big Apple. Dominus describes Times Square as "half-defined by the city and half-defined by tourists." It's clearly the city half that she feels was encroached upon, and the controversy demonstrates how space is defined by vision, class, perception, and geographical identity.[20]

The fact that the chair issue generated so much heat shows how important public spaces are to so many people. When you walk in places like Times Square, you feel they're yours. Why? Because Times Square is a quintessential representation of the city. After all, when people talk about New York, they don't think about your block in Washington Heights or Lefferts Gardens. They think of the Statue of Liberty, Central Park, Fifth Avenue, and we all know that; thus what goes on there is a central concern to New Yorkers. Besides, people in this town have strong views about lots of things, and space is a great venue for playing them out, especially when your tax dollars are involved.

I have my own opinion too. When I first saw the offending chairs, I thought people had brought them there to sit on, but when I saw hundreds of the same type, I realized that this was unlikely, though it did cross my mind that perhaps the chairs had been rented. Actually, some people treated the folding chairs as if they were their own, with about fifteen of them reported stolen. Ultimately I supported the idea, because people get bored or tired after an hour of just walking in the pedestrian mall, and they need to sit somewhere to rest. In a way the area is like a park.

Streets are clearly public spaces. And so are the signs indicating their names. Street names can provide teaching moments about New York City history, and there is much information available about the thousands of streets in the city and how they received their names. Let's take a curious-sounding example. I'm walking on Force Tube Avenue in Cypress Hills, Brooklyn, a street that also extends into Queens. How did it acquire such a strange name? It refers to the cast-iron pipes through which water was pumped up, or forced through tubes, to the Ridgewood Reservoir, completed in 1858. Not only that, but the path of these pipes actually runs along Force Tube Avenue, which may explain why it's the only diagonal street in the neighborhood. The pumping station was nearby, on Atlantic Avenue and Logan Street.[21]

I ask a Pakistani homeowner who lives on the street if he knows why it's called Force Tube Avenue. "I have no idea," he responds. He's only been living there about a year. But it's an address he uses every day—on letters, job applications, drivers license, and so forth. Wasn't he curious? And the answer is no. Should he be? Who can say? But his attitude may reveal an interesting perspective—namely, that it doesn't matter in his eyes, because it has no effect on him. He's too busy trying to make it in America to worry or even think about such things.

I pass a Bronx street called Cottage Place off 170th Street, just east of Fulton Street. It is a short block, dead-ending into a school whose property is marked off by a high fence. On the left and right side of the street are the backs and sides of apartment buildings, none of which has an entrance facing it. In short, it's something of a nothing street. There are many other such blocks in the city, like Kluepfel Court in Ridgewood, Queens, or Bonner Place off Morris Avenue in the South Bronx. Hardly anyone's heard of them. These are literally tiny slices of the Big Apple. Yet to those living on such blocks the space matters, because it's theirs. It's home. In fact, it's almost private because of its size, the small number of people who live there and who usually know each other, and because you wouldn't normally be on it unless you lived there or knew someone who did. Why do I insist on walking these tiny blocks? Because I feel it's unfair to neglect them just because of their size. Real people live on them, and, besides, I want to truly be able to say I walked all of New York.

Short streets exist even in the busiest, most traversed parts of New York, like Cliff Street, near Wall, John, and William Streets, and Maiden Lane, the financial heartland of this town. What is Cliff Street? It's a block long with one or two buildings on it; a couple of bars; the headquarters of the Uniformed Sanitationmen's Association, Local 831; and a McDonald's. There's also an office for rent. You want to be on Cliff Street? It's available. Another short street is the curvy Doyers Street, off of Pell Street. But it's not unimportant, because the Chinatown station of the U.S. Postal Service may be found there. In fact, this branch was a crucial scene in the 2012 film *Premium Rush,* an underappreciated flick about the world of bicycle messengers working the streets of Gotham.

Sidewalks are an important part of street space. Though used primarily for walking, they are also home to sidewalk vendors of all sorts, including men like the ones described in Mitchell

Duneier's *Sidewalk,* who live on society's margins. The vendors sell everything—pocketbooks, apple cake, sunglasses, books, apple cider, CDs, vegetables. People believe that the prices of these sidewalk goods will be lower because the vendors have no overhead, and, indeed, they usually are. Coordinating organizations like Greenmarket have sprung up to license and monitor many of the food purveyors. In 2010 Greenmarket listed fifty-one areas in all five boroughs, from the Staten Island Mall, to Hunters Point in Queens, to Broadway, by Columbia University. A progressive group called Sustainable Table provides questions to ask local farmers (the emphasis is on locals) who participate. Questions include "Are your cows ever given antibiotics?" "Are your hens ever force-molted?" "How much time do your chickens/turkeys spend outdoors each day?"

New Yorkers are forever expropriating public space for themselves. In fact, as Elijah Anderson demonstrates in his book *A Place on the Corner,* hangouts along the sidewalk, often in front of stores, are an integral part of many a community. Above all, they give those who frequent them a sense of self-worth. It's almost an aggressive sort of thing that relates to feelings of territoriality. I come across a group of middle-age Puerto Rican and Dominican men wearing sleeveless, ribbed undershirts and Yankee caps, seated on metal folding chairs and playing dominoes at a card table on the sidewalk in Williamsburg. Nothing new there. What's different is that where they're sitting is only one small part of the space. Behind it is a grass lot that the men call their park. It's where they barbecue and party on weekends and holidays. A Halloween-type skeleton dangles at a crazy angle from the high wire fence, behind which is the men's park.

About five feet from the table on the sidewalk, next to a metal closet containing a baseball bat, some beige duffel bags, and a tan raincoat, is a four-foot-high bookcase along the wall of a brick building. The bookcase is lined with a bound set of legal volumes, inside of which are the proceedings of hundreds of cases brought before the New York State Court of Appeals. The men jokingly tell me, "These books could get you out of jail," as they offer me the whole set of twelve volumes for twenty dollars. I guess it's an example of a *Fiddler on the Roof* item, there "just for show." As further evidence of their entrepreneurial mind-set, they offer to teach me how to play dominoes for just five dollars an hour. I plead a previous engagement and continue on my way. It's clear to me that this space is an important quality-of-life place and that they treasure it. Like the men in Anderson's study, they will defend it. Rather than tear it down every night, they pay a homeless man to guard it.

Sidewalks can also be used for artistic purposes. I walk along Wadsworth Avenue and stop in front of a typical apartment building on 192nd Street. What has attracted my attention is actually the ground in front of it. Usually, as I tell my students, people look straight ahead, sideways, and occasionally upward as we walk, but rarely do we look down. There are about twenty squares on the sidewalk, basically the length of the apartment building's front section. Carved into these squares are beautiful and delicately drawn trellises and vines as well as tulips, roses, and leaves. The designs alternate. (See figure 17.)

I ask people walking out of the building who made them, but they don't know. It doesn't even seem to interest them. I find the Dominican super and ask him. "Me and my brother did it in 1992, when the sidewalk had just been made," he tells me. Even though he has been in the United States for twenty-seven years, he speaks almost no English. His eleven-year-old daughter translates. He drew them using a plastic mold pressed into the wet cement. Why? "I did it to make the place look nice." It turns out he's an artist, with paintings he made hanging proudly on the wall inside his apartment. The sidewalk carvings demonstrate how people take pride in where they live, as well as how the creative impulses they have can find a way to be expressed. These works of art are anonymous, just a little space the man and his brother have literally carved out—that is, until somebody shows up and makes inquiries. But for this immigrant the space has great personal meaning, and perhaps ethnic meaning as well. It is a more or less permanent symbol that he was here, that he made his mark, one that he can be proud of it, even if he has the modest job of superintendent. And he's not finished yet, because he's planning on painting the artwork soon.[22] What is amazing to me is that this individual can meet me, a stranger whose language he doesn't speak, invite me into his apartment with his young daughter there, and give me a tour simply because I expressed interest in his artwork. This trust, or relaxed attitude, if you will, was repeated hundreds of times in my many forays into the city. People opened up much more easily than I anticipated.

Spaces can be both permanent and temporary. The sidewalk is permanent, but its uses change according to the flow of human traffic and how people opt to use it. William H. Whyte, the urban planner and sociologist, describes how people have public conversations on the street in New York City and in other metropolises. Surprisingly, many conversations seem to almost always take place in the middle of the crowd instead of near the street or the walls of buildings, thus forcing pedestrian traffic to flow around them. "Just why people behave like this I have never been able to determine," he says, wondering why people would choose to block traffic and not mind being jostled by it.[23]

One possible explanation is that these meetings are invariably unplanned, the product of people who know each other meeting accidentally. They are on their way home, to work, another meeting, dinner, an appointment, whatever. Regardless, the chance encounter is not on their schedule, which creates a conflict: they want or feel obliged to have a conversation, but are loath to give up on their planned activity. They feel pressured by time constraints. To move to the edge of the sidewalk would be to admit defeat—namely, that their plans have been disrupted and amends may not be possible. So in order to keep alive the hope that they can accomplish what they set out to do while not offending those with whom they are speaking, they retain their position in the center, the place where they were walking originally.

Thus, we see yet another instance of how space is deployed to express territoriality, only in this case the physical boundaries are invisible, permeable, and temporary. Yet they are very clearly delineated psychologically and even, perhaps, subconsciously in the human mind. Conceptualizing space in this manner helps explain human behavior in public spaces where intentions are not obvious. Other examples of asserting control over a space would be standing near a park entrance or sitting on the stoop of a building.

Shops and Malls

Although a store is a public space, store owners have the right to adorn or embellish their business any way they want to and many do just that, sometimes in pretty idiosyncratic fashion. Here are two unique instances of such efforts. As I was walking by a Washington Heights pharmacy, my attention was drawn to an ancient-looking Underwood typewriter in the window. The owner of the store, the Hilltop Pharmacy, located on Fort Washington Avenue near 187th Street, has made a display in his window that features memorabilia from the 1940s and 1950s of mostly drug-store-related items. Included are medicines like iodine in a blue-tinted bottle and a weight scale from the period. The scale proclaims, "No Springs," suggesting that it provides honest, accurate weights. Next to the scale are a box of Sucrets, a container of Cashmere Bouquet talcum powder, Dr. Sheffield's Oral Pain Reliever, and other old brands like a radio made by Grundig. I ask Bill, the pharmacist, why he decorated the window this way, and he says, "I don't know. The forties and fifties looked more vintage to me. I like old stuff. I have customers who give me their stuff from those times. It's a quirky thing, I guess. My best friend's father was a doctor, and when he died he cleaned out his office and gave me the stuff. I'm not gonna do anything with it. It's more of an aesthetic." Bill doesn't really have a clear-cut reason for his hobby, other than liking "old stuff," but it's obviously something he values.

In this next case, the rationale behind the décor is much clearer, though the reason isn't readily apparent. I notice some books piled high in a window of Le Veau D'or, a pricey French restaurant on Sixtieth Street just west of Lexington Avenue. (See figure 18.) Some of the volumes are novels by Danielle Steele, one book is a travelogue, another was penned by Oleg Cassini. A third is titled

The United States of Arugula, and there is *Moneyball* by Michael Lewis. Mystified by this intriguing use of space and the seeming haphazardness of the literary selections, I enter and inquire. An older man says, "No big deal. I have no idea."

"What do you do here?" I ask.

"I'm the owner, but my daughter runs the place. Ask her; she'll be here soon."

She shows up five minutes later and immediately clears up the mystery: "These are all books written by customers who eat here and who have mentioned my father's name or that of the restaurant in their works. My father was in the restaurant business for fifty years. People come in here all the time, wanting me to put their books in the windows, and I explain the conditions and they understand, of course. And if you mention us in your book, then you'll be in the window too." Obviously, the owner, Robert Treboux, a man in his eighties, knew exactly why those books are there. He was merely being modest. Problem solved—and an interesting use of space for sure, not to mention a novel way (no pun intended) of publicizing the establishment.

And here's a territorial appropriation of space that's as weird as it gets, because it's a secret to the owner of the space, a deli, at least until he stumbles upon it. Fed up with the TV watchers who are clogging the aisle for customers who want to buy something, he looks for a quiet place or space. It's shortly after he has taken over the deli.

"Maybe I can hide in the stockroom and read," I think wishfully. But as I venture back, I hear voices there too and smell something pungent and sickly sweet, like an air freshener—except it smells as if it's on fire.

"What's going on back here?" I demand, sweeping aside the stockroom curtain. . . . No one answers, so I squint, and in the smoky haze I begin to discern bodies: three, maybe four, seated on milk crates.

"Can I help you guys?" my mouth says, not because I want it to but because sometimes my mouth says things without asking me first, to fill up awkward silences.

"I don't know," someone finally says. "That's not the question."

"What's the question?" I ask the figure, who appears to be made out of smoke.

"The question is, Can we help *you*?"

It's at this point that the owner of the deli realizes that the men don't know who he is. "Clearly I interrupted something," he concludes. "Who am I anyway?" he asks himself. He suddenly discovers that he has invaded their space—theirs because they've been using it all this time, given permission to do so by the owner's clerk, who hasn't told him about the arrangement. To the outside world, it's a deli owned and operated by the owner. In reality, though, it's a store for customers and, he has discovered, a hangout for potheads and drinkers who constitute a sub-society in the back of the store, unseen and virtually unknown to shoppers and even the owner.

Dwayne, the clerk, is in the stockroom and tells those gathered, "That's Ben, the new owner." . . . . "You mean the owner *of this store*?" a large man described as "a human Brinks" asks incredulously. "Everyone looks at me as I nod dumbly, feeling as if I've just been identified as the perpetrator of an unspeakable crime."[24]

One lesson to be learned here is that you can think you own a space and be shocked to find out that in some ways you don't, because the place you lock up every night has areas you've never been to and aren't particularly welcome in. In truth, space is often what we make of it—in short, how and whether or not we use it. Until we do so we may *formally* own it, but we really don't.

The line between the private and public uses of space can be quite porous at times. The same deli owner observes wryly that some customers walk through the door five or six times a day, acting as if it's their home, "wearing pajamas or stroking an iguana." The attitude seems to be, "'This is New York. Get over it.' And, of course, they're right. What would New York be without bad behavior? And where would people exhibit it if not in delis?"[25]

The deli owner is obviously being facetious, but is he right to feel this way? These people have broken no law, and while they're taking the concept a bit far, isn't the customer always right, even in this sense? The real problem here is that when you own a public establishment, there are limits to how much control you really have over it. Sure, if customers are unruly, you can toss them out. But having a long and loud conversation on the phone (another complaint of his) doesn't come close to that description.

Unfortunately for you, the proprietor, the customers know you need them, so they can take advantage of that fact. Ultimately this is a casualty of shared space. Of course, if it were a private restaurant, the rules and customs would be different, although there, too, ambiguities would exist. For example, could you eat mashed potatoes with your hands if you wiped them on your napkin just as if you'd eaten barbecue ribs with your hands? Could you sing at the same decibel level that characterizes a loud conversation while eating alone?

Spaces can have multiple uses. Boutique shops can be built in a neighborhood to sell their wares but also to give people the feeling of quaintness and intimacy. This is how areas like Chelsea or Hunters Point in Queens brand themselves. Some customers will object, of course, preferring low prices and large stores that have more variety. Some shops can also be used as places where different groups can meet, like the farmer's market in Union Square.[26]

Shopping malls in general are related to the communities near them and are considered part of them. Reflecting that reality, the Queens Center Mall celebrated twenty years of existence with four weekends of free entertainment, featuring klezmer music and songs from the Andes Mountains, from Greece, and India, as well as flamenco and Irish dancing. All of these offerings reflect their location in the multiethnic Elmhurst, Corona, Jackson Heights, and Rego Park areas.[27] In the more "passive mode," such activities serve a lot of other purposes too, such as demonstrating the many different types of uses the same space can have. They're teenage hangouts, socializing venues, opportunities for market research, a chance to see American culture as it plays out in shopping options, eateries, and the like.

Signage

Signs on stores, houses of worship, and advertisements in subways, along walls, and on buildings abound in New York, just as they do everywhere in America. This use of space has many purposes, and what they are tells much about the city's people and what's important to them.

Names given to stores are supposed to inform and entice people to come in. They frequently take the name of the community or street, and sometimes they extol the virtues of what they're offering—delicious, tasty ("Hi-Class," said one sign) pizza, or "Golden Bubbles" outside a Laundromat. No community, rich or poor, is immune to such appeals. Sometimes they refer to what people generally look for in life. For instance, there are many stores with the word "lucky" in their names, especially corner groceries and delis, perhaps appealing to lotto players. There's the Lucky One Deli on Adam Clayton Powell Boulevard between 147th and 148th Streets and so many more, but, tragically, the businesses themselves are not always lucky, like the owner of a "lucky" deli who was robbed and killed in Brooklyn.

"Lucky" may well be the most popular name for stores in general, perhaps in large part because so many people come to this country to try to change their luck. While I'm walking on the Lower East Side, I see a Chinese-owned seafood shop on Forsyth Street, between Rivington and Stanton Streets, called Lucky Fish. (See figure 19.) Hopefully the owners are lucky, but the fish that end up here certainly aren't. They're the opposite—dead, chopped up, and ready to be eaten. "Lucky" is one of a small number of words that have special importance in Chinese culture, and indeed many Chinese stores bear that name. Another such word is "Happy," also popular among Chinese immigrants.[28]

On Vermont Avenue, in the hardscrabble Cypress Hills area, you'll find the Survival Grocery Deli. Maybe the name refers to economic survival, since the deli advertises food offerings called "Recession Specials." Then there are stores with grandiose names, like the hole-in-the-wall Manhattan Grocery on the corner of 161st Street and Amsterdam Avenue, which actually looks pretty ordinary, or the small Upper East Side duplicating shop with the name Copyland. On Bergen Street in Crown Heights, I spot a bodega with a more intellectual name—Economic Deli and Grocery. The graffiti on the wall has a strange demand: "Say economic to drugs!" Is that a no? I guess so.

Some signs evoke subliminal, though not necessarily sublime, connections. On Columbus Avenue near Ninety-sixth Street you'll find the Sing & Sing Market. Most people, especially New Yorkers, think of the state's Sing Sing prison. Inside I ask the Hispanic woman behind the counter what the name means. She's heard of the connection, but insists, as though I thought otherwise, "It's not a jail. It's a market." I thank her for her assertion and depart.

Perhaps these unusual names are a sign of the times—namely, the constant stream of arrivals from foreign countries who open businesses yet have difficulty with English. A kosher breakfast nook on Cliff Street advertises "Fish & Cheeps [Chips]." Nearby on Broadway a cafeteria offers a "plan [plain] baked potato." Signs can also attempt to appeal to community loyalty, as in a pet store in Park Slope named Pup Slope.

Signs can also address people's fears, as in the following sign I spotted just off Flatbush Avenue: "Advanced Dentistry." Now, what do they mean by that? "Quality, Painless, and Affordable," the sign continues. But what caught my attention was, "We Cater to Cowards." Most dentists seem to be annoyed with cowards; this one caters to them.

Some store signs don't seem to make any sense, like one I saw in Bay Ridge on Fifth Avenue and Seventy-sixth Street: "Tap House—Great Pub Food," says the first part of the sign on the awning. But the next words are really sort of contradictory: "Same as Always, Better than Ever." Was the Tap House "always" better than ever? Then what is the "Ever" referring to? Then again, perhaps the strange wording is nothing more than an attention-getting device.

The Chabad/Lubavitch Hasidic movement is also very consumer- and advocacy-oriented. In the Gramercy Park section of Manhattan I see a tiny movie marquee with small, round yellow bulbs surrounding it. The black letters read, "Chabad of Gramercy, Now Praying," instead of the usual words, "Now Playing," and rated "G." Anything to draw attention. By the way, the Chabad menorahs, which are visible outdoors wherever Chabad puts down roots, are iconic. Possessing silver metallic, streamlined, angular lines extending from the center in a *V* shape, they remind me of the chevrons that often adorn Art Deco buildings throughout the city.

Signs in, on, or for stores, past and present, can also be used, just as bumper stickers or graffiti are, to communicate sentiments or emotions. I pass a shop in Staten Island with a sign over it, reading, "From Another Time: Antiques, Collectibles—USED." Well, that seems obvious. But when I peer in through the open door I see that it's a social club, with people watching TV and playing cards. A man sitting on a slatted wooden chair outside the store confirms it, adding, "This used to be an antiques store."

"Why did you keep the sign after you took it over?" I ask.

"Because this is a place that's especially for veterans, those from the Vietnam War, and even World War Two, and they, well, you know, feel like they're really from another time."

Private businesses sometimes make use of space not only for business purposes but also to deliver social messages, expressions of what New York City is all about, and other communications. These messages, seen by thousands of tourists as well as residents, can have a powerful impact if delivered in a compelling fashion. A good example is the advertising of Manhattan Mini Storage, which uses large outdoor signage stretching up several floors of its building, to both advertise and express its views. Here are some examples: "Nobody becomes famous in Des Moines," thus meaning New York is the place to be. (And, of course, you can store your stuff with the Manhattan Mini Storage Company.) The ad not so subtly implies a lack of concern for the feelings of Des Moines residents, as well as the thousands of smaller communities across America. Another themed message, which demonstrates awareness of both current events and its Chelsea location, is the statement: "If you don't like gay marriage, don't get gay married." In other words, no one's forcing you to, so mind your own business. In addition to the sentiment, the approach embodies the tough-guy, big-city attitude to a T. Besides, it could bring the company some local business in this heavily gay community.

Buildings

As I'm walking in Grant City, Staten Island, I pass some garden apartments and notice that on the balconies of both the first and second floors are some beautiful little gardens. People have made maximum use of the tiny amount of available space to grow hanging plants and flowers; one even has a trellis. Everyone wants their proverbial "place in the sun." They're not for show; they're for their owners' own pleasure. These uses can be discerned wherever in the city there are garden apartments. On the other hand, some people have nothing on the balcony, save for an upturned bicycle. Across the street is a private home with a large area suitable for a big garden. Ten balcony spaces could fit into it. And yet, paradoxically, there's no garden at all. Instead the owner has filled it in with gravel, perhaps so he'll never have to mow his lawn again. The common denominator here is that people reserve and exercise the right to do whatever they want to in their own spaces and use it as a way of expressing themselves.

Walking on Lower Manhattan's Henry Street, I look up at two buildings that are next to each other but seemingly as different as night and day. One's a five-story tenement built a century ago. The other's a sleek, gleaming structure that looks very new. The tenement has fire escapes and the new age structure has glassed-in terraces. Yet both reveal identical uses for their outer spaces—sit on it, store bicycles, potted plants, and the like. In the end, though it may look different, space is space if you have a particular use for it.

Perhaps the most common use of city rooftops is for sunbathing, and those who do so call these spaces "tar beaches." But they are increasingly being used to create gardens as well. The *New York Times* reported on this trend nationally and cited efforts locally by apartment dwellers on the Lower East Side to create a four-hundred-square-foot rooftop garden. Among the reasons for creating such gardens are that they're good for the environment, it's good to grow and eat local food, and just for the fun of it. But often the reason is simply having an emotional attachment to the concept.

New Yorker Paula Crossfield reflected on her decision to plant a roof garden: "The bottom line is that I harbor a secret desire to be a farmer, and my way of doing that is to use what I have, which is a roof."[29] Indeed, for many people the roofs of their apartment buildings are part of what makes living in the city so great; rooftop views connect them to the city. As Richard Goodman gazes upon the city, he exclaims, "What a sense of promise this view of Manhattan gives!"[30]

The stoop is a long established feature of New York life. Generations have hung out on the steps outside their apartment buildings and have made those who come out of the building feel as if they're walking a gauntlet and intruding on a private conversation. Teenagers have been fond of playing stoop ball, which involves aiming the ball (usually a "Spaldeen," otherwise known as a Spalding brand) at one of the stoop's steps. Perhaps only residents of the building and their visitors can legitimately hang out on their building's stoop, but it does have a public feel to it and strangers do occasionally sit on it.[31]

In Richmond Hill, Queens, I sat down briefly on the stoop of a private home whose steps bordered the sidewalk. Even though it was a private home, I saw nothing especially wrong with what I did, because, having grown up on a Manhattan side street, I'd always thought that steps accessible to the public could be utilized by the public. Five minutes into my rest, the owner, an Indian, who probably hadn't grown up in the city, if one could judge by his heavy accent, showed up. "I hope you don't mind, but I just want to rest my feet for a few minutes," I said.

"Oh, that's quite all right," he said. "Relax and enjoy yourself."

Stoops and sometimes the edges of sidewalks are increasingly used to give away items that are no longer needed. People use space to give to others. Most commonly they put used clothing, toys, and furniture on the street, but in recent years there's a new trend. Books, especially in neighborhoods where people are readers—Brooklyn Heights, Park Slope, and the Upper West Side—are often placed in neat piles on the stoops. These range from novels to dictionaries to unusual categories, like Swedish/English grammar books.

There are literally hundreds of ways that buildings make their mark on the city. They come in many styles, shapes, sizes, and colors. People frequently express concern about a neighborhood's character, and it's often an important talking point at community organization meetings and those of the New York City Landmarks Preservation Commission. On East Fifty-first Street between Second and First Avenues is a townhouse that is literally clad almost entirely in metal. Behind the metal is glass, and although it's possible to peek into the house through the small spaces, you really can't see anything. It's a private house, so you can't do anything about the design.

On the other hand, people have the right to criticize—and they do. A doorman says, "I don't like it. I know these people. They're a nice couple, but they got too much money. They don't know what to do with their money. It's out of character with the regular, normal townhouses on the block." In this case the couple isn't listening, but you can see how public pressure can act to change private space, simply because the block as a whole is public. The issue also involves a value judgment—namely, whether or not you think a house should fit in with other buildings in the community.

Another interesting example of a house that makes its mark is a most unusual private home, unique in its design, located in Brooklyn's Mill Basin neighborhood at 139 Bassett Avenue, where it intersects with Arkansas Drive. On the left as you face the house are three large American flags flying in the wind. The house, four stories high, is made of cement, light gray, with a tubular design. There are squares and rectangles on the walls of the house. There are also silver-colored, metallic, abstract sculptures in front of the home. On top of the home is a sculpture consisting of graceful, flying silver birds. The windows feature wavy-looking lines on frosted glass. The grounds are decorated with various Calder-like stabiles, as well as statues of children frolicking in the grass. A large boat sits in the back, next to the water, framed against a brilliant blue sky.

Viewing this extraordinary home is a surreal and memorable experience. Who owns it? An Italian American family who purchased it from the mobster Anthony "Gaspipe" Casso. The family members, the Turanos, are sort of "private community characters," since they also have a very close relationship with former state senator Carl Kruger, who was convicted of corruption. Kruger is reportedly a frequent guest at their home. I ask several neighbors about the unusual design. No one seems to object, or at least no one is willing to say so openly. Typical of the responses: "Anyone can do what they want when it comes to designing their homes even if someone else doesn't like it. They paid for it and it's their own business, not mine."[32] (See figure 2.)

Sometimes the design of a building may be deliberately muted when a group or organization wants to be accepted in a community. One example is when the managers of group homes buy houses and try to make them look like any other private home in the neighborhood, despite the number of people living in them. Clearly the hope is that if they blend in physically, acceptance will follow.

There are also instances where a structure may be designed so that it will go unnoticed. A great example of this is a synagogue in the Richmond Hill, Queens, area. It's only a few blocks away from the Kew Gardens border, an area that's heavily Jewish, but the location is definitely not Jewish and, in effect, crosses a border into a section that has many Muslims, Hindus, and Christians. The synagogue is a one-story affair that has almost no markings to identify it as a Jewish house of worship—not even a mezuzah— even though it is an Orthodox synagogue. The building's Art Moderne glass blocks make it virtually impossible to see inside, and there are no windows. The entrance has a combination lock and a small sign with English letters above a door of plain heavy metal identifying its name. But those letters would not give away what it is except to a knowledgeable observer. Most startling, there's no address on the door, no Star of David, no menorah, nor any of the usual markers of temples.

A conversation with one of the synagogue's members establishes that the users don't want to attract attention at all. "We try to keep a low profile. It's not a Jewish neighborhood, and we were advised that it's best to not make waves." This is clearly a beachhead, since young Jewish families have been moving into other parts of Richmond Hill in search of less expensive housing for their growing families. This place means a shorter walk to a synagogue. I ask a Sikh neighbor, owner of the house next door, and he corroborates the member's comments. I ask him if the congregants are afraid that the building will be bombed by Muslims. He laughs uncomfortably. "They just don't want any trouble, no rocks thrown by kids passing by." I notice that there is a camera aimed at the building.

On my walking trips through the boroughs of New York, I rarely observed this level of concern. In changing neighborhoods where there were only a small number of Jews living in the area, no attempt was made to hide the religious identities of buildings, though there were sometimes high fences and cameras. When I did see it, it was always a mosque in a mixed community, most likely because of political or security considerations. At the other extreme is a synagogue on Amsterdam Avenue at 105th Street that makes no bones about its existence despite its sensitive location. It shares spaces with the old, established West End Presbyterian Church headed by Reverend Alistair Drummond. The congregation is called Kehilat Romemu and is run by David Ingber, a well-known hip rabbi with an Orthodox background. The space also houses the New York Piano Academy.

I'm standing in front of a typical ten-story apartment building at 59 West Seventy-first Street, built in 1924. In the middle of the structure, between the fourth and fifth floors, surrounded by bricks and clearly visible from the street, is a large concrete *M* with an engraved garland extending from its sides. (See figure 20.) Why?

I see two women exiting the building. Approaching them, I ask, "What's the meaning of this *M*?"

One of the women looks up and, in a surprised tone, says, "Gee, I never noticed it."

"How long have you lived here?" I ask.

"Over forty years, but I guess I never looked up and I didn't notice it."

"What floor do you live on?"

"First I lived on the ninth floor and now the fourth, right below the *M*, I guess. It must have been the architect who did it."

She has a point. Architects and builders in all boroughs often name buildings after themselves, though usually, like Trump Towers, it's the full surname. Or they may name the building "The Laura" or "Theodore Arms," after a child, parent, sibling, or spouse, or for some other reason known only to them. It's far less common to see a place identified boldly with only a letter. The origin of this practice is uncertain, but what's most interesting is how a person living in the building for decades has never even taken notice of it. The single initial expropriates space on the front of a building in order to draw attention, but it hasn't registered in anyone's mind. Was it worth the effort? I ask a few more residents about the M, and not one of them is aware of its existence. The current superintendent and the management company don't know what the letter is doing there, though the super thinks it may be named after the architect or builder. He informs me that at one time the apartment doorknobs all had the letter M on them. If I were an advertiser, I'd stop paying for the ad.

On Bushwick Avenue in Brooklyn, near Grand Street, I come across a most unusual display. Its lack of clarity makes it similar to the M story. Draped over a wire hanging from a utility pole fifteen feet from the ground is a plastic doll, about sixteen inches tall. The doll, with long, light-brown hair that looks and probably feels like smooth straw, is a scantily clad woman wearing what appears to be a bathing suit. In her hand is a green bottle of what looks like ginger ale. Gazing at her smiling face, I find myself wondering whatever possessed someone to put it there. It's almost certainly not a matter of territory. Perhaps it's just a prank, done for no other reason. There's a redbrick public school at this location, but the children standing outside the building have no clue as to why it's hanging there. Eighteen months later I walk by and the doll is still there. That's a long life span for something like that. It reminds me that we can't always make sense of everything we see, because we weren't there when it happened.

Buildings can have a life of their own that extends beyond past usage and affects the present. They can evoke thoughts and feelings in people's minds. In Washington Heights, on 157th Street between Amsterdam Avenue and Broadway, I come upon a Seventh-Day Adventist church that has taken over a site where an Orthodox Jewish synagogue previously existed more than a half century earlier. In New York City, due to ethnic succession in communities, churches often buy and redo synagogues they have bought. But there was a difference here. The Adventists' form of Christianity has many similarities to Judaism. They take the Bible literally. Thus, they do not work on Saturday, observing it as the Sabbath. Nor do they eat pork. So taking over a synagogue meant something to the Adventists. It was a sanctified place. Indeed, as I enter the sanctuary, I see that much of the original interior has been beautifully preserved—the pews, the windows, even the social hall.

I speak with a Hispanic member who is modestly dressed in a long skirt, just like Orthodox Jews. She tells me, "Every Friday night we eat dinner together in the social hall. We don't work on the Sabbath, we don't cook, and we don't buy anything, although we turn on lights and we drive. We follow the Old Testament. Whatever it says, we do. We eat only kosher food—no pork, no shrimp or lobster. We have two hundred members, mostly Dominican and a few Puerto Ricans."

I ask, "Since you have many Jewish practices, how do you feel about the fact that this was once a synagogue?"

"Well," she says, "we feel a special holiness about this place because it was a synagogue before, and many of the customs and laws we have are the same as the Jews. They also observe the Sabbath. And I heard they were more comfortable selling it to us because of the common customs."

One of the most unusual church-related stories I heard on my long expedition through the city's streets involves the Church of All Saints. The beautiful, large stone building is on Madison Avenue between 129th and 130th Streets. It's an imposing-looking structure and as I gazed upward, I noticed several smallish but clearly visible Stars of David in various places. Unlike so many churches in New York that retain signs of once having been synagogues, this one had clearly never been a synagogue. In fact, the Venetian Gothic building was designed as a church in 1893 for the area's Irish immigrants by James Renwick Jr., who was also the architect for St. Patrick's Cathedral. So what were these symbols of Judaism, which have been used as such for centuries, doing there?

Intrigued, I contacted one of the ministers, who told me the following: "This church has been around for well over a century. The story that's been passed down is that a Jewish man owned the property and was uncomfortable selling it to a church. He asked that if a church were to be erected on the site, it should contain several Stars of David to memorialize the fact that it was once a Jewish-owned piece of property. I've never been able to verify it, but it's as good an explanation as any since it was never a synagogue." If this story is true, it's a most unusual use of space, one where a person might have made his mark on property, but most people who pass by have no idea as to what the architect did and why. I say "might have" because there's no hard evidence to support this story.[33]

Walls

Making all sorts of grinding, squealing, and squeaking noises best known to regular subway riders, the number 7 train slowly snakes its way through the Hunters Point neighborhood, past the Citigroup Building and the Sunnyside Yards as it heads toward the city. As you hear the whistle of the adjacent Amtrak train, the groans of subway cars, trucks passing by, engines in full throttle, and walk under the subway trestle past a nearby bus depot with graffiti all around you and Shannon's Tavern on the corner, you get a distinct sense of being deep in the bowels of this great city.

Davis Street is virtually empty of people, save a lone Japanese tourist with a camera hanging from his neck as he peers into a Japanese guidebook. The Empire State and Chrysler Buildings are clearly visible across the East River, so near yet so far from here. The new condo buildings are also metaphorically far removed from this area, though they are physically only eight or nine blocks away on the Queens waterfront. John Coe runs a truck parts company here on Davis Street, inherited from his father. I ask Coe if he ever gets tired of looking at the graffiti. "No," he says, "because it changes every year. People come here all the time, put black paint over an existing piece of art, and then create their own work there." Next to him is a place that supplies fireplaces to penthouses. Now, there's a specialty store!

This is the home of 5 Pointz, centered at the intersection of Twenty-third Street, Davis Street, and Jackson Avenue.[34] People come from everywhere—Korea, Sweden, Venezuela, and California—to put up their own versions of art. It's open to the public and there are always camera-happy tourists walking around, snapping photos, as well as occasional fashion and film shoots. Tour buses make 5 Pointz a regular stop in Queens. One artist whose name appears frequently on these murals signs his work "Meres One." There are superheroes galore, monsters, stick figures, and nearly naked women. One mural, filled with clowns, asserts, "We don't clown around." The building on which most of the wall art appears is home to many art studios. Across the street on Davis, Manhattan Ignition Company has two trucks painted on the wall outside its offices. The area's culture seems to have rubbed off. The neighborhood even had a slight brush with notoriety when the Weather Underground placed a bomb under the Jackson Avenue courthouse in October 1970.

Street art is one of the most interesting aspects of New York City's industrial areas, home to some of the most creative murals and graffiti you'll ever see. Unfettered by limited space, industrial areas are a great location for experimentation and expression, and one of the best places to see it is in East Williamsburg. In general, these parts of the city come closest to what New York City used to be as a manufacturing center. Here you'll still find granite factories, electrical parts centers, makers of heavy machinery, dried-foods producers, building materials suppliers, brick inventories, bus garages, shoe factories, pipe supplies, and the like. When manufacturing occupied more of a center stage fifty years ago, these types of artists didn't exist in the area. While the artists may find that the large outer walls of old factory buildings provide an ideal canvas for their work, their presence in these industrial areas may also be an attempt to reconnect with the city's former inner soul.

Nearby, at, and around the intersection of Meserole and Waterbury Streets in East Williamburg, Brooklyn, are some astounding artistic displays. (See figures 21a and 21b.) Those in the know come from all over the world with cameras to view and photograph the murals, many created by world-famous graffiti artists. A sign indicates the breadth and scope of the work: "Over 100 artists from 11 countries for eight days in three galleries between two cities," signed, "Paper Girl New York, 2010." There's one exhibit in the form of trompe l'oeil (French for "fool the eye") down both sides of a street, depicting, it seems, the era of the 1930s or 1940s. The exhibit becomes smaller as you move away, so that it appears as though you're looking down a street when it's actually a flat surface. Another display features a sculpture of a small child pointing at a globe of the world. His entire body from head to toe is covered with small army toys—tanks, missiles, helicopters, soldiers, and trucks.

You can gaze at a metallic structure whose gigantic metal claw reaches out over the edge of a nearby building rooftop. The sculpture has a huge misshapen head. Another mural has a black man with a knitted cap on his head that reads *HP*. There are old-fashioned portraits of movie stars from earlier eras. Another section of art has vibrant paint from seemingly every color of the rainbow that is made to look as though it's dripping down. There's also a face of an orange and pink bear. By accident, most likely, one wall mural incorporates the shadow of a pair of sneakers on a nearby telephone pole wire swaying gently in the air. The effect is sort of psychedelic. As the displays constantly change, at least some of what one sees at any given time may no longer be there a year later.

Some coffeehouses have sprung up in this rediscovered area, and one barista at the Newtown Cafe on Waterbury explains when and how things got started: "I guess it began about two or three years ago. People just came here. Some moved in and others made the old buildings into studios. And now there are concerts on Saturdays in the buildings. There's a guy, Shepard Fairey, who did the mural across the street. He's like the Michael Jordan of graffiti art." Indeed, he designed the famous Barack Obama "Hope" poster. Another great location for graffiti is at Troutman Street and St. Nicholas Avenue in nearby Bushwick.

Graffiti murals also adorn the walls of the low-rise businesses that line Boone Street in the East Bronx. Though not of the same quality as East Williamsburg, they're elaborate, colorful, and evocative, featuring comic book and movie heroes. Moreover, they are seen by the outside world, as tour buses come by every so often, filled with visitors, many of them foreign tourists from China, Japan, Spain, and other lands. Why do the owners of these businesses grant permission to the artists to use their outer walls? Aside from the fact that the artwork looks nice, if permission is not given the kids may vandalize the walls, and supporting art is a far better alternative. There are different types of murals here—political, religious, gang-related, those that memorialize people, and simply works of art.

Although there are many books on graffiti, this form of art has never made it into the mainstream except for an occasional exhibit of photographs in the Hamptons or in Los Angeles. It may be because the avant-garde graffiti types do not fit into the establishment art world with its galleries, art shows, and exhibits. Moreover, how do you commercialize graffiti art? Charge admission by turning the space into a private property? You certainly can't sell it, though one could imagine building owners paying for it. Regardless, street art is in a different universe from that of the commercial art scene.[35]

Murals are often used as teaching tools. Some community projects emphasize large themes like diversity, unity, and peace; memorials to the neighborhood fallen; political movements and protests like that of the Irish hunger strikers; and Hispanic or black heroes. Some of these are created by well-known artists like James De La Vega or Chico. I pass by a typical mural in Harlem, on Edgecombe Avenue and 165th Street, visible inside the lobby of a West Harlem public school through an open door. It was created by children with the help of teachers. The people depicted, all of them alumni of the school, include an unlikely trio: Diana Sands, a black actress who starred in *A Raisin the Sun* and other plays, and who graduated from the New York High School for Performing Arts; singer Harry Belafonte; and Alan Greenspan. The last image indicates that the children are given not only black role models but white ones too—and a leading economist at that! Similarly, in East New York we have P.S. 149, the Danny Kaye School, on Sutter Avenue near Vermont Street, named after the comedian.

When we think of art space in subways other than advertising billboards, the murals in certain stations come to mind. They are examples of how artists expropriate public space. It's their work, but it's overseen by Arts for Transit, a New York Transit Authority division. And now comes something new, also under the purview of Arts for Transit—"chirping birds, rustling leaves, a burbling brook." The plan is to pipe these new sounds into a rebuilt IRT station house on Ninety-sixth and Broadway via hidden speakers. The concept stems from "the ideas and iconography of Asian pop art and contemporary graphic design." It will be the backdrop for a display in the turnstile area consisting of about two hundred stainless-steel flowers hanging over the turnstiles. The flowers will even sway a bit, giving the appearance of a "shimmering garden." No one will be fooled, to be sure, but hopefully commuters will be lulled into a feeling of calm and peace. There's even a connection to the past, since this part of the Upper West Side was known as Bloomingdale (Dutch for "vale of flowers") when the station was constructed in 1904 and was actually a relatively rural area then.[36] Today many subway stations contain artistic representations of one kind or another.

Standing on 168th Street and Amsterdam Avenue, rediscovering Washington Heights, I am struck by a very beautiful six-story mural painted on the side of an apartment building. It depicts a man with his arms wrapped around vegetables, and a woman holding a baby and standing next to an elderly lady. It's by the Groundswell Community Housing Project and is titled *Live in the Environmental Area of Your Destiny*. The mural is an example of the tremendous creativity in these neighborhoods by people hell-bent on expressing themselves. Artworks like this are one of the many things that beautify a city. Seeing them in the middle of a drab neighborhood is always unexpected and a pleasant surprise.

The people who helped make the Groundswell mural possible are duly listed on the wall: Manhattan borough president Virginia Fields; the Rush Philanthropic Arts Foundation; Lowe's, Modell's, Valspar Paints; and special thanks to the 33rd Police Precinct and the Washington Heights-Inwood Community Council. So, to paraphrase Jimmy Durante, everyone gets into the act—the politicians, police, community groups, and private industry. They need to be recognized so that they can justify their positions, their funding, and their tax breaks. It's "pay for play," a common phenomenon in other communities too, often depending on how important it is to those whose names are to be invoked. Whether such involvement is good, bad, or in between is a hotly debated topic that comes into sharper focus in the next chapter.

Not surprisingly, political expressions of support or opposition for various figures, local and national, are widespread. A bit more strident, but still typical, is a wall poster on St. James Place near Gates Avenue in Clinton Hill, Brooklyn, titled *Axis of Evil*, with drawings of Henry Paulson, Ben Bernanke, and Christopher Cox. It looks like a series of wanted posters. The statement has been made on the wall of an abandoned house. On the more conservative side of the political spectrum is a wall mural in the small parking lot of the American Legion Post on Eighth Street in Gowanus, Brooklyn, near Third Avenue. The mural includes the Statue of Liberty and the emblems of the various armed forces, plus a portrait of an American eagle. A cartoon-like balloon depicts the eagle saying, "All gave some. Some gave all," meaning the ultimate sacrifice of one's life for their country. There's hardly a legion post or fire department company in the city that doesn't have a patriotic message emblazoned on its outside walls. And tucked away on Mosholu Avenue in the Riverdale section of the Bronx, you can find Shcharansky Square (Russian spelling), named after the Jewish Russian dissident Anatoly Sharansky, right in front of the Russian embassy. This in-your-face decision was made in 1982 by the then Bronx borough president, Ruben Diàz Jr.

What grabs my attention in all this is the diversity of issues covered. Throughout the ghetto areas you can see plenty of R.I.P. murals memorializing gang members, but others are messages of antiviolence. In Crown Heights opposite the western edge of Brower Park, a mural exhorts people not to use guns. It features many overlapping paintings of people carrying guns—children, pilgrims, a man whose tongue is like a snake representing the National Rifle Association, and the Second Amendment on a scroll dripping with blood. A sign painted into the mural reads, "Gun Show Today: No ID Required," and there's an image of a pipe with weapons pouring out of it. Another mural in East Harlem comes from a totally different direction. Purporting to be modern art, it is identified as *Picasso and Van Goh,* clearly missing the second *g.* The art, however, is in the Picasso style. A sign on it says, "Support Graffiti," almost as if it's taking on the lofty mantle of a social movement. This exhortation is common throughout the city.

And here's a mural advocating for animals on the northwest corner of 103rd Street and Third Avenue. It has beautiful paintings of dogs and cats. I notice that it was completed on September 9, 2001. Little did those artists know what would happen to redefine this city just two days later as the Twin Towers collapsed. My noticing this date is another example of how everything in our thinking is affected by that day. The mural urges people to spay and neuter their pets and includes a contact number to call and learn how to do so cheaply. But not everyone notices or cares. A street vendor in front of the mural has his regular stand there, and he didn't, telling me, "I'm not interested in this."

Sometimes there are statements on walls where people attract attention simply by articulating social problems. Here's a message shaped like a small billboard: "92% of all women who are newly diagnosed with HIV in NYC are black and Latino." The information is from a report published by the New York City Department of Health and Mental Hygiene. "For free HIV testing contact. . . . " And beneath it somebody has scrawled, "Who cares?" The sign is on Audubon Avenue and 168th Street, across from Columbia Presbyterian Hospital. The fact is that walls are interactive spaces for communication, not just one-way advocacy.

One of the most unusual, imposing, and, given its subject, incongruous, displays I saw was a four-story-high mural on 124th Street, just west of Second Avenue. It was made of woven, canvas-like material attached to the side of a building, and painted on it were the faces of Bobby Sands and other IRA members who participated in the Irish hunger strike of 1981. (See figure 22.) Why here, in Harlem? Why not in Woodside, Queens, or in the Wood-lawn section of the Bronx, both still Irish neighborhoods with lots of immigrants from the Emerald Isle? Several people in the neighborhood surmised that the mural was an effort to show solidarity with black people in Harlem. To learn more I tracked down and spoke with Brian McCabe, a retired New York City detective who is vice president of Federal Shield Security, an investigative firm, and who was instrumental in bringing over the artists from Belfast, Ireland, to create this memorial.

"That's not the reason at all, though I'm sure there were people in Harlem who identified with our struggle," McCabe said. "We put it here because hundreds of thousands of drivers use 124th Street to get onto the Triborough Bridge [now called the Robert F. Kennedy Bridge]. And as they're waiting for the light to change, they have ample time to reflect on what they see." And what do they see? First, an inscription that reads, "This is dedicated to the ten brave Irish hunger strikers who sacrificed their lives in 1981. Their cause is ours. freedom . . . ." Besides images of the strikers, there are those of Martin Luther King Jr., Mahatma Gandhi, Leonard Peltier (Native American activist), and Nelson Mandela, plus the symbols of the four ancient provinces of Ireland. "Ideally, I would have liked the mural to be on Houston Street," laments McCabe, "but space is very expensive there."

Sadly, this beautiful canvas is gone, a casualty of gentrification. A brand-new apartment building has risen in the space. I don't know where the mural is now, but its disappearance is silent testimony to the ever changing nature of the city. If old buildings can be torn down and replaced, how much easier it is to remove something from a wall.[37]

Shrines, Plaques, Statues, and Views

I chance upon what could only be described as an amazing shrine to Brooklyn's history and culture, with all the icons it reveres. Were I not walking every block in the area, I would not have discovered it. It's in the form of a private house at 2056 Eighty-fifth Street, right down the block, paradoxically, from Brooklyn's only Kabbalah Center. I assume the two do not have more than a passing acquaintanceship. The unique house is a striking example of the borough's richness and diversity.

The bronze sign in front reads, "This property has been placed in the National Register of Historic Places by the U.S. Department of the Interior." It's a white brick colonial with a porch attached to the second story, vinyl siding on the third floor, and many plaster statues arrayed in front of the house and along the driveway. There's a garbage can with a small monster peering out near a red and yellow sign that reads, "Welcome to Steve's Place." (See figure 23.) On the right is a three-foot-tall brown statue of a man dressed in a trench coat and a black hat. In the middle is a fifties-era gangster clad in a black leather jacket and a hat pulled down low. He has long sideburns, sunglasses, and a cigarette dangling from his mouth. There's also a biker mannequin with a guitar. Then there's a cigarette girl wearing a scanty outfit and a little hat. She's carrying a small tray of fake tulips. Next to that is a seated Godfather-type figure, leisurely reclining and holding a cigar in his hand. And in case you didn't suspect it, the sign says, "Original Capone Gangster." At the top it reads, "Jury Convicts Capone." By contrast, next to Capone's likeness is a symbol of the U.S. Army. On the window behind it are several gremlins. Nearby is a statue of a marine standing at attention, and alongside him is a statue of a derelict. Above that is the famous photo of the marines planting the American flag on Iwo Jima. An assortment of jungle animals dots the area as well.

Jutting out from the second floor is a statue of Superman appearing to break out of the house. On one side of him is a Batman poster, and on the other is one of Robin. Above a knight in armor is a face attached to the wall. There's also Betty Boop near a barber shop pole and a sign encouraging the viewer or customer to "ask for Wildroot," a famous hair lotion of the old days. There's Elvis and his guitar, the song title words "Don't Be Cruel" etched behind him, along with a scale of red-colored notes. He is next to Marilyn Monroe, who is standing above the famous grating where the wind is blowing up her skirt.

At the back of the driveway is a brightly colored garage door with a dotted stripe down the middle, just like a road. It's done in 3-D trompe l'oeil style so that it looks as if you're driving into it.

And where are you driving into? Why, the Brooklyn Battery Tunnel, with signs reading, "EZ Pass," "CASH," and, "Leaving Brooklyn." There's also a statue of Humphrey Bogart. And then Superman makes a second appearance as Clark Kent emerging from a phone booth after a quick change of clothing. I almost feel as if I'm spying on him, especially when I see the famous quote from Perry White, publisher of the *Daily Planet,* exclaiming, "Great Caesar's Ghost!" There's a pirate of a Captain Kidd type, Dracula, Frankenstein, Forrest Gump, and Arthur Herbert Fonzarelli, aka the Fonz.

There's much more, including iconic photos of Brooklyn, like one of Ebbets Field. All in all, the scene is a rich tapestry of the borough's history as well as the era in which it played out, depicting characters and real people that residents of Brooklyn liked. It's also an effort to demonstrate that despite all that's happened in the last thirty-five years, Brooklyn has hewed to its cultural trappings and its history, unique in some aspects and tied into the larger society in others. To sum up, this unusually decorated home is a part of America and at the same time apart from it. If there are such complex exhibits elsewhere in the five boroughs—other than Christmas displays—I'm not aware of them. It's an amazing space on private property but there for all who pass by to see.

Another shrine, this one in Queens, exists on a much smaller scale but is interesting and unusual nonetheless. A man in Hunters Point, Joe Colletti, seems to have converted his home into a shrine memorializing the 1912 *Titanic* disaster. He has created a museum dedicated to telling the story, located at 47-08 Eleventh Street. It's in a two-story house, and when you step into the vestibule a buzzer goes off, presumably alerting the owners or implying that you are being watched. In the front window is a replica of the famously doomed ship. This is Joe's chance to ensure that one of history's great tragedies is not forgotten and to indulge in an activity that interests him.[38]

"Live Life in a Way That Leaves No Regrets," reads a sign outside a simple house in Bushwick covered in pale yellow aluminum siding. It's part of a memorial to a man's mother. People were falling into a hole around a tree outside his home. So the Puerto Rican man living there put what he called a "lucky bunny" in front of it. He tells me, "She died at eighty-four, but I also did it because in her old age when she looked out the window she always saw the tree. I also took a miniature baby crib, which I painted in blue and white, to cover the hole. It's also a design just to show that she wasn't forgotten." My expression of interest in his project is instantly rewarded with some lighthearted banter. "There's a club across the street wit' dancing, but you can't get in, because you gotta have ID, and you're too young." We both laugh heartily. In truth, thousands of New Yorkers have taken city-owned sidewalk spaces and converted them for their own uses.

I come across a very interesting place on Eighth Street between Fourth and Third Avenues in Gowanus, Brooklyn, the only one of this sort that I found. On the first floor of a three-story, brick row house I see in gold letters the words " P. De Rosa, 180 1/2, Grocery" on a window with white vertical mini-blinds on the inside. (See figure 24.) Underneath and off to the sides are neon signs, unlit, advertising Schaefer and Rheingold Extra Dry, two old beers of an earlier New York. The commercial signs look out of place on this completely residential block, and I wonder why the store is there. It certainly appears closed, and I cannot see any sign to indicate that it's a functioning establishment. I spy an elderly woman sitting on a stoop across the street and ask her about it.

Her answer clears it up. "The grandfather owned the store forty years ago when I moved in here, and then it was open as a store. They're an old-time Italian family, been here a hundred years, and the grandson lives there now and he keeps it that way. And every Christmas and Easter he lights up the beer signs."

I cross the street again and ring the bell, but only a dog responds, the deep bark letting me know that he or she is on duty. It is a rather unusual use of space. The grandson has maintained this permanent shrine and tribute to his grandfather and has shown filial loyalty and respect for his forebears. And his deed is known by his neighbors and all others who stop and inquire about its meaning.[39]

Let's look at cemeteries for a moment, which are shrines too. People think of a cemetery as a place where your loved ones are buried. But they are often located in places far from where you live, quite possibly in a neighborhood that you wouldn't visit except for that purpose. Often the area has changed ethnically over time, but since it's much more difficult to move dead people than live ones, the cemetery remains. And so the cemetery trek becomes a way that people can learn about other groups. You see a community that you know nothing about, you walk around, and you stop for a snack or even a meal there. In this way people broaden their knowledge of different communities and the city as a whole.

This applies, of course, to other nostalgic visits to the old neighborhood. These spaces invariably change, but they are a treasure trove of memories for those who return for one reason or another. You look at a church you attended in your younger days, and as you stand there you wonder what happened to all those kids who attended its youth groups, its religious school. What about the adult members, the committees on which they served? Lives were lived here, political intrigues were played out, and religious events were celebrated. And lifelong friendships began inside its walls. For those who have revisited their old neighborhoods, such a trip is filled with memories. And the church, to the extent that it remains intact, is the vehicle that lends special meaning and even comfort to them. In that sense, the old building, even if it has been transformed into a bingo hall or community center, keeps alive the past that its former occupants yearn to preserve.

Sometimes even a building that is not in the neighborhood serves to awaken memories. Space is often a vehicle for evoking what once was, and a classic example is that of the still-standing Sears, Roebuck Building in Brooklyn, the first one located in the city. Located on Bedford Avenue and Beverley Road, it is an Art Moderne structure built in 1932 that literally towers over the two-story homes and small apartment buildings in nearby East Flatbush. And anyone who lived through the 1930s can appreciate that period when they reflect on the large blue, red, and white letters atop the building that read, "Sears, Roebuck and Co." Eleanor Roosevelt was in attendance when it first opened. Today the building is shuttered, but those in the know who walk by realize that they're looking at a monument to a forgotten era. As I ponder this building's meaning to those who see it, I realize that New York City is sort of like a time machine. Look at the Sears Building and you're in the 1930s, perhaps a trip down memory lane; amble through portions of Greenwich Village around Washington Square and you're in the late 1700s; visit the new steel apartment buildings along the East River by North Williamsburg and you're catapulted into the twenty-first century. There's something for every taste.

A site doesn't have to be big to jog one's memory. In the midst of the street's humming activity, I spot a small bronze plaque in front of an old six-story limestone and brick tenement at 225 East Ninth Street in Manhattan, one of many scattered throughout the city, commemorating historical sites and events. The plaque announces that the building once housed a branch of the Hebrew Technical Institute, founded in 1884. German Jewish leaders at the time felt that training Eastern European immigrants to be productive manual workers would counter the stereotype that Jews were parasites and unscrupulous moneylenders. One of its founders was the great poetess Emma Lazarus. This building served as the Lucas A. Steinam School of Metal Working. Indicative of its prestige, those supporting the institution included some of the biggest names in New York City—Joseph Bloomingdale, Jacob Schiff, and Henry Seligman.

Statues are yet another physical space worth mentioning. There are thousands of them in the city, the majority of them in parks. Plaques usually tell of their significance, but save for famous ones, like the Soldiers and Sailors Monument on Riverside Drive, they are unappreciated by the average user of these spaces. Since the statues are often old and preceded the arrival of more recent groups to the area, people using the park often give the plaques little notice or fail to understand the importance or relevance of what is inscribed on them.

Walking on Hillside Avenue in Jamaica, Queens, I come across Major Mark Park, which sits on the south side of Hillside from 175th to 173rd Streets and is surrounded by tall apartment buildings. It's a rainy day and few people are there, other than some homeless types, laborers, and a guy in a blue T-shirt frolicking with his cute dachshund. My attention is drawn to the elegant bronze statue in the middle of the small park, an angel with a palm frond in her right hand and a laurel wreath in the left. There's no commemoration plaque, nor even the name of the monument's creator. The only indication of what it stands for is a span of dates, "1861–1865," the period of the Civil War, etched into the granite pedestal. But if you were a recent immigrant, foreign tourist, or otherwise unaware of what those years meant, you wouldn't have a clue.

A quick search reveals the statue's history and purpose. It was built by the French-trained sculptor Frederic Wellington Ruckstull to remember Union Army soldiers and sailors of Queens who were killed in the Civil War. The statue has been conserved through the efforts of the Adopt-A-Monument Program, created by the Municipal Art Society and the New York City Art Commission. And Ruckstull was apparently an equal opportunity employee, having designed such monuments for Northern and Southern U.S. communities. It was a specialty of his. When all is said and done, the statue is another example of how these organizations maintain the city's history. A visit to the art commission's website reveals the following question: "Do you know an interesting tidbit about Major Mark Park that you'd like to share? Please send it to us." I wonder how many people have responded.

Last, but certainly not least, space isn't simply the space in your community. It's what you can see—a skyline, a park, skyscrapers, and so on. A longtime resident of gentrifying Washington/Hudson Heights extols the virtues of his community, saying, "Rockefeller didn't allow development of the palisades across the river. He owned them. So the New Jersey view on Chittenden Avenue is pristine north of the George Washington Bridge. This is one of the most secret spots in New York, the openness here. People just don't know about it." This anonymity gives the area a special status, a certain cachet.

"Would it be the same view south of the bridge?" I ask.

"I don't think so," he responds. But only in a sense, it turns out. The fact is that those people also have a great view of both the bridge in front of them and the river. It's just a different, yet still very nice, view.

In line with this concern about views, the Trivium, a small green space in the city, was built in newly resurgent Washington Heights.

"Trivium" is an old Latin word for the space created when three roads come together. It's located at the confluence of Pinehurst Avenue, Cabrini Boulevard, and 187th Street. When people sit on the benches there, they have a view of the Hudson River, a prized feature for nearby apartment dwellers. Fittingly, the Trivium is named after Charles Paterno, who built Castle Village Apartments, where almost all of the apartments have river views. Its user-friendliness is enhanced by the U-shaped bench that encourages eye contact and conversation.[40] These special little touches engender community pride and solidarity, especially when their unique features are made known to the residents.

1. *Centro de La Paz* (Center for Peace); motivating ghetto youth. 124th Street between Second and Third Avenues. Photo by Jesse Liss.

2. They made it; a home in Mill Basin, Brooklyn. Photo by Jesse Liss.

3. African eatery; home away from home. 116th Street near Malcolm X Boulevard. Photo by Jesse Liss.

4. Muslims and Jews side by side. Photo by Jesse Liss.

5. Harlem bike shop; a visit to the "doctor." 124th Street, east of Fifth Avenue. Photo by Jesse Liss.

6. Edgewater Park; a white enclave by the water. Photo by Jesse Liss.

7. Harding Park; a taste of Puerto Rico in the Bronx. Photo by Jesse Liss.

פסק הלכה
מהרבנים דעיר ליקוואד יצ״ו

**Stockings whose
color closely
resembles the
skin are not to
be worn.**

פסק הלכה
מגדולי הרבנים שליט״א

8. "You're in my country now"; Hasidic dress code. Photo by Jesse Liss.

9. Looks like a border, but it isn't. Flushing Avenue between Lee and Marcy Avenues. Photo by Jesse Liss.

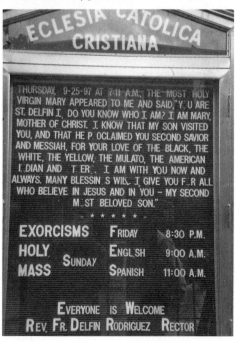

ECLESIA CATOLICA CRISTIANA

THURSDAY, 9-25-97 AT 7:11 A.M., THE MOST HOLY VIRGIN MARY APPEARED TO ME AND SAID," Y U ARE ST. DELFIN I DO YOU KNOW WHO I AM? I AM MARY, MOTHER OF CHRIST. I KNOW THAT MY SON VISITED YOU, AND THAT HE P OCLAIMED YOU SECOND SAVIOR AND MESSIAH, FOR YOUR LOVE OF THE BLACK, THE WHITE, THE YELLOW, THE MULATO, THE AMERICAN I DIAN AND T ER . I AM WITH YOU NOW AND ALWAYS. MANY BLESSIN S WIL J GIVE YOU F R ALL WHO BELIEVE IN JESUS AND IN YOU — MY SECOND M ST BELOVED SON."

* * * * *

EXORCISMS   FRIDAY   8:30 P.M.
HOLY   ENGLSH   9:00 A.M.
            SUNDAY
MASS   SPANISH   11:00 A.M.

EVERYONE IS WELCOME
REV. FR. DELFIN RODRIGUEZ RECTOR

10. Exorcisms and saints; Eclesia Catolica Cristiana. Grand Avenue between 180th and 181st Streets. Photo by Jesse Liss.

11. El Flamboyan Garden; the greening of the city. Tinton Avenue at 150th Street. Photo by Jesse Liss.

12. Edgar's Cafe; the poet as manager. Between Ninety-first and Ninety-second Streets, Amsterdam Avenue. Photo by Jesse Liss.

13. Justice Sonia Sotomayor Houses; uplifting the community. Corner of Watson and Rosedale Avenues. Photo by Jesse Liss.

14. Waterfall in the park; drowning out the city. Fifty-first Street between Second and Third Avenues. Photo by Jesse Liss.

15. Hidden beauties of New York; Chinese Scholars Garden in Snug Harbor. Photo by Jesse Liss.

16. Beach boardwalk in Staten Island; in view of the Verrazano Bridge. Photo by Jesse Liss.

17. Delicate floral design; original sidewalk art. Wadsworth Avenue and 192nd Street. Photo by Jesse Liss.

18. Le Veau D'or Restaurant; a unique selection of books. Sixtieth Street, just west of Lexington Avenue. Photo by Jesse Liss.

19. Lucky Fish store. Who's lucky? The fish? Forsyth Street, between Rivington and Stanton Streets. Photo by Jesse Liss.

20. The letter *M* with engraved garland. 59 West Seventy-first Street. Photo by Jesse Liss.

21 a and b. Trompe l'oeil and other graffiti art in Brooklyn. Meserole Street and Waterbury Street. Photo by Jesse Liss.

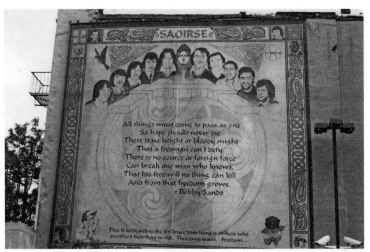

22. IRA freedom mural painted on woven canvas. 124th Street, between Second and Third Avenues. Photo by Bob Marcus.

23. Icons of history in Brooklyn at Steve's Place. 2056 Eighty-fifth Street. Photo by Jesse Liss.

24. P. De Rosa Grocery; a shrine to values and respect for family. 180 1/2 Eighth Street, between Fourth and Third Avenues, Gowanus. Photo by Jesse Liss.

25. The Kissinger Steps; climbing the immigrant dream. Overlook Terrace at 184th Street. Photo by Jesse Liss.

26. Gentrification comes to Harlem; the Sutton, hard by the Polo Grounds projects. Bradhurst Avenue, 145th to 155th Streets. Photo by Jesse Liss.

27. Trade Fair Supermarket; appealing to a mixed consumer cohort. 130-10 Metropolitan Avenue. Photo by Jesse Liss.

28. Hallelujah Praise the Lord Auto Sales. 131–32 Sanford Avenue. Photo by Jesse Liss.

6

FROM WASHINGTON HEIGHTS TO HUDSON HEIGHTS, FROM SOHO TO SOHA
Gentrification

One recent Mother's Day, while driving on the Long Island Expressway around 7:00 pm, I noticed that the heavy traffic was coming from the island toward the city. Why? Because the urban gentrifiers were coming back from visiting their mothers. These mothers represent the earlier generations that, from the 1950s to the early 1970s, left the apartment buildings in the city for a piece of heaven in suburbia. During those decades, every Mother's Day they made the reverse trek to see *their* elderly moms in the city. Now, in 2011, they were old and their children had moved to the city while they stayed behind in the suburbs, empty nesters in places that they no longer considered dream houses and communities, waiting for their next major migration. This time they were going to what is called by them, in bittersweet terms, "God's Waiting Room"—Florida, or perhaps Arizona or California.

Therein lies the major story of gentrification in New York City. We begin this chapter with a discussion of who moves into gentrifying communities. The past twenty-five years have seen a large population shift as hundreds of thousands of young people have streamed back to the city that their parents abandoned. In this they have been augmented by large numbers of gentrifiers from all over the country. Both groups have been attracted by the opportunities in the Big Apple as it has shifted from an industrial economy to a service economy. Coming at first as single, unattached adults, in recent years young people have been putting down roots, deciding more often than not that they want those roots to be in the inner city. From living spaces, to restaurants, to services provided by municipal government, these demographic changes have transformed the city in many ways. And although low-income residents can be found in all five boroughs of New York City, this drift toward city living is part of a larger trend in which the poor are increasingly found in the city's outskirts and suburbs.

The places where people put down stakes differ greatly. East Harlem isn't Park Slope, and Brooklyn Heights isn't Ditmas Park. The areas themselves are part of a hierarchy of preference, where people who can't afford one community grudgingly accept living elsewhere, using cognitive dissonance to rationalize their decisions.

The reasons why people move into these changing neighborhoods—their own arrival is, in fact, the major change—are varied. Amenities vary from one locale to another, both in kind and in degree. There are the usual considerations: transportation, schools, shopping, noise, air quality. Most of the newcomers also look for a certain level of cachet, of "coolness," that will give them the feeling that they have moved into someplace different, cutting-edge, and special. Sometimes it's the wine bars, chic restaurants, and funky shops, but it can also be places that remain from the old days that suggest an effort to preserve the neighborhood's original character. And then there are those in search of diversity, a community where they can meet and mingle with others whose backgrounds differ from their own.

The gentrified area one chooses to live in could be an existing residential neighborhood that is improving or an industrial section of the city that is becoming more residential. It could even be a stable community where the homes or location appeal to those who are looking for a quiet, centrally located, and affordable place to live. Being near the water, parks, or a beach may also play a role in how such decisions are made.

The places to which the gentrifiers move are by no means empty. Large numbers of poor people reside there, many of them in public

housing projects or tenements that they have called home for generations. These areas are often in the process of gentrifying—still
somewhat dangerous and run down but beginning to improve. The
young professionals must make a decision. Are they willing to live
cheek to jowl with people who will not exactly welcome them—
indeed, who may resent them as better-off interlopers? Are they
willing to risk being mugged and robbed? Are they ready to put
down a million dollars for a condo a block away from tenements
that are home not only to those less well off but also to drug dealers and other unsavory characters? It turns out that most people
who choose gentrified neighborhoods feel the benefits of living in
these communities outweigh the risks.

In this chapter we deal with a number of core issues. First,
what is the impact of the poor on gentrifying communities and
vice versa? Have the gentrifiers really displaced the poor? When
is it displacement and when is it not? The areas that gentrifiers
move into often have poor residents. Some leave, others don't, but
why and the extent to which this happens are often unclear. And
when the poor vacate apartments, it's difficult to know if they have
stayed in the area or moved elsewhere, and whether or not where
they have moved to is better than what they left behind. The research on these questions is often inconclusive.

Next we tackle how, when, and why neighborhoods change.
Change, as we will see, doesn't happen all at once. It's a gradual
and uneven process, depending on economic and social factors. It
also depends on which neighborhood you're looking at. Here we
look at different parts of the city and the degree to which they've
changed. How do we know a neighborhood has changed? Can
any neighborhood change? Are there parts of the city that cannot
change, or is everything on the table? Are there certain factors that
make gentrification almost impossible? A look at recent history
in the city will confirm that many areas that seemed unlikely to
gentrify have done so or are in the process of doing so. Harlem,
Bedford-Stuyvesant, and Washington Heights are good examples.
But this has not been the case with other neighborhoods.

City government plays a huge role in how change is effected,
through tax abatements, support for a plethora of nonprofit

organizations, and through the work of many city agencies like the Landmarks Preservation Commission; the Housing Development Corporation; and the Department of Housing, Preservation, and Development. The presence of nearby colleges and universities is also a factor in the equation.

In addition to the poor, the other major element living in gentrifying communities is the entrenched population of working- and middle-class people who have lived in these areas for generations. Do they oppose the newcomers, and are the gentrifiers able to establish relationships with them? On what basis? Where do their interests come together, and where do they diverge? Listen to what representatives of both groups have to say when they express how they feel about where they live.

> This is a great neighborhood, East Harlem. Here I am, living in a beautiful condo building where a one-bedroom apartment goes for $480,000. We've got people from California, Seattle, everywhere. It's young professionals. Up the block there's a Creole restaurant and a nightclub with good eats and music, mostly jazz. The waitresses are mostly young women from Poland and Russia who don't have green cards and want to earn good money off the books. And while it's not perfectly safe, they have shuttle buses that will take you to the subway at night. I love it. I'm in Manhattan for half the going rate.
>
> —*A twenty-nine-year-old hedge fund manager from Chicago*

> The young people who live here today, they're not that friendly, a little arrogant. If someone moved in here today, I'd invite him over. "What are you cookin'?" the guy would say. And I'd shoot back, "Spaghetti." "That's great, I'll be there," he'd say. What bothers me most is these people put all sorts a stuff in the trash cans on the street that they should throw away in their own cans—newspapers, bottles, and their household garbage. And then they're the first ones to complain that there are rats around. But I stayed here because it was my mother's house and so the rent was reasonable. I like it here. It's still home.
>
> —*An eighty-five-year-old lifelong, Italian American resident of*
> *Carroll Gardens, Brooklyn*

These two views reflect the wide gap between those who share space in many of the city's neighborhoods. Nowhere is the distance more evident than in the gentrifying parts of the city. In most cases neither party wants to leave, even if they have little in common. The people who are moving in are often urban pioneers armed with optimism, hope, and more than a little moxie. When their welcome is mixed, they at least have each other to lean on. Those who view them skeptically nevertheless appreciate the benefits that accompany their arrival—safer streets and better services. The question, which we'll explore, is how and to what extent these groups relate to each other.

This chapter doesn't deal with areas like the Upper East Side, Tribeca, or Forest Hills, Queens, because these locations are long established. People move there all the time, but their doing so does not give us the best chance to better understand the city. It's only when various aspects of a neighborhood are changing that issues, problems, and innovations develop. Since most of the options under discussion involve communities in flux, how a neighborhood is changing is of great interest.

And now let's take a closer look at all the questions raised here and see how they play out. When we do so, it will become clear that gentrification is one of the most critical issues facing New York City.

Who Moves In?

New York's gentrifiers come in many guises and forms. The most common are people looking for a nice, safe, convenient place with some pizzazz and, naturally, in their price range. In short, they want to live in a modern or refurbished apartment or house that also retains, if possible, some elements of the way the city used to look. They are often pleased with the idea that they're making the city a viable and vibrant place. Most are looking for upscale restaurants, nice bars, theaters, boutiques, good schools for their children, and other amenities. Economics generally determines where they end up. And that can occasionally lead to some pretty strange decisions.

On September 19, 2010, an article appeared in the Real Estate section of the *New York Times* offering praise about a neighborhood.[1] A couple, both teachers, described their block as "beautiful." They admitted it wasn't their first choice, but rather a fallback option after house purchases in Brooklyn and Queens had fallen through. They had rejected Bedford-Stuyvesant and Bushwick as not safe enough for the money. However, their "beautiful" block was none other than Undercliff Avenue in the West Bronx, where, as discussed earlier, a particularly violent gang had taken over the street, terrorizing the inhabitants until just five months earlier. Moreover, the River Park Towers—a Mitchell-Lama- and HUD-assisted apartment complex right around the corner—is possibly one of the worst of its size in the city, one that requires a constant police presence, often in the form of an NYPD cherry picker with lookouts peering out from it.

A second group of gentrifiers is similar to the first but places emphasis upon the history and character of the neighborhood. These "historic preservationists" have views similar to those of intellectuals like Jane Jacobs and Sharon Zukin.[2] Bedford-Stuyvesant is a changing area and is home to numerous cafés, like one on Nostrand Avenue. "In the place that we built," says one of the female owners, "me and this African American woman who's my partner in the café discovered that this location may have been a station for the Underground Railroad." This young white woman is clearly a gentrifier with a sense of place, culture, and history who likes the area because it makes her and her partner a part of history and gives them a feeling that they're in a community with deep and meaningful roots. It may even make her believe that in moving to Bed-Stuy she's accomplishing something important.

And where does this desire emanate from? Perhaps her own knowledge or experiences. For this woman, the interest was a basic part of her persona. "I was a Harlem Renaissance major at the University of Maine, a weird place to study this topic, but I did." She isn't really interested in complete gentrification, because when that happens the community loses its character. She's into the "blackness" of the place and wants to preserve that. And so she's on the side of the preservationist blacks and whites who live there.

Incidentally one sometimes sees connections between one neighborhood and others. Farther up Nostrand Avenue, near Lafayette Street, I pass the Sugarhill Supper Club/Restaurant and Disco, a reference to the famous Sugar Hill area of Harlem.

As Zukin demonstrated in her book *Loft Living,* artists have often preceded wealthier gentrifiers. This is still the case. One new area for artists' studios is Bushwick, especially near the Ridgewood border, referred to by locals as "Bushwood." One artist with whom I chatted explained, "Bushwick, unlike Ridgewood and North Williamsburg, has more open space for studios. There aren't many artists here yet, and sometimes I miss not having a coffeehouse on Myrtle, but it's worth it price-wise. Besides, I can still go to a great German bakery." At first you might say that for some people it's difficult to accept that they've "settled," that they're not living in the place of their dreams, the "in place." And then, when the artist goes on to talk about the lack of amenities—Starbucks, bookstores, clothing stores, art-movie houses, you realize that there's substance to the complaint, that in order to be satisfying, a neighborhood must have many attributes. Outliers like this artist hope these features are imminent.

While a recession may slow down gentrification in terms of major projects undertaken by developers and government, there are other factors that work in different directions—to wit, a willingness to move into less desirable digs. Young people starting out on their own are often strapped for cash in the best of times. Abe Cavin Quezada, a twenty-two-year-old music producer, lives in a five-hundred-dollar-a-month apartment in Bedford-Stuyvesant near Marcus Garvey Boulevard. As he put it, "Before this I was living in a loft in Bushwick. . . . This apartment is nicer and has more amenities, but the neighborhood is noticeably fishier. In Bushwick, I never really felt threatened. Now, the sounds around here are more aggressive. I'll see 20 guys ride by on a motorcycle, or hear gunshots outside my window. . . . And one day, in the middle of a Sunday afternoon, I saw a guy on a motorcycle with a handgun. It was not a reassuring sight."[3]

And more and more people, according to figures compiled by the New York City Planning Department, are doubling, tripling, and even quintupling up. Let's remember, these are often young people who are not picky. Ben Craw lives in a tiny bedroom on Lorimer Street in North Williamsburg. "I have a bed, a desk wedged between the bed and the wall, a folding chair, a window with a great view of the skyline. That's really all I need," he observes. Craw, a Connecticut native, earns about forty thousand dollars a year as a video editor with the *Huffington Post* and gives the following rationale for putting up with this, one that has motivated millions of New Yorkers through the past: "I always loved New York. I couldn't wait to get out of my house. In terms of the jobs I wanted, the social life I wanted, I didn't care where I lived as long as it was in the city. I wasn't sure what I wanted to do, but I knew that whatever it was, it would be most possible here."[4]

This almost mystical belief represents the energy that fires up New York's inhabitants, that enables them to endure challenges and hardships. One can just imagine the thoughts going through Craw's mind as he looks at the city's silhouetted buildings and its twinkling lights across the river and dreams about what his future may be in this city of magic, mystery, and opportunity.

In the eyes of many people, gentrification equals whites moving in, but that's not always the case, certainly not in Clinton Hill, Fort Greene, and Harlem, where many middle-class blacks have made a go of it. What makes these communities attractive to them is that they don't have to feel self-conscious about being black, that they can express—even celebrate—their black identity and transmit that to their own children.

Where Do They Go?

In every borough of the city there's a hierarchy of areas, with some in greater demand than others. Gentrifiers are keenly aware of this system and know that their address can communicate a message about themselves—such as how much money they have as well as their tastes and preferences. Let's look at Brooklyn, for example, where there are two broad tiers of desirability. The top tier would be Brooklyn Heights, Cobble Hill, Carroll Gardens, North Williamsburg, Dumbo, Greenpoint, and Park Slope. The next would be East Williamsburg, Fort Greene, Clinton Hill, Prospect Heights, parts of Bedford-Stuyvesant, Greenwood Heights, portions of Gowanus, Boerum Hill, the "Back" part of Red Hook, Ditmas Park, Windsor Terrace, Prospect-Lefferts Gardens, and Prospect Park South. Within the second group there are differences in racial composition and types of housing, convenience to transportation, and the like. Overall, however, all of these areas are part of a mass movement of mostly whites, interracial couples, and black middle-class families who are reshaping the demographics of North and Central Brooklyn.[5]

These areas are distinctive in various ways. Prospect Park South is made to order for those who prefer large, rambling homes that have charm and grace. Dumbo is definitely for the avant-garde. Some people will look at the converted industrial buildings and ask, "What's the big deal?" about one of Brooklyn's most coveted neighborhoods. If you want a miniature version of the UN go to Ditmas Park, where residents point with pride to the number of ethnic groups living side by side in apparent harmony.[6] If you want a place that's heavily Catholic with a still sizeable, if aging, Irish population, you should consider Windsor Terrace. Want Manhattan-brownstone chic? Brooklyn Heights and Cobble Hill are likely to do it for you. And on and on.

Some of New York's gentrified sections are distinct but not easily defined. Red Hook has fairly cheap rents. A one-bedroom in a renovated building is about fifteen hundred dollars a month. But you have to bike or take a bus to Carroll Gardens for a subway. In a way it's like a cheaper Dumbo. There's industrial authenticity by dint of the buildings, and there's grittiness, the water, cobbled streets, quaint townhouses, and great views of the Manhattan skyline. Red Hook has character, bars, plus a huge Fairway grocery and an IKEA. It's a really interesting area. Van Brunt Street is the main thoroughfare, where the stores are. And there's a lot of working-class history here. It's about a third gentrified, a third industrial, and a third really poor housing projects. It's a work in progress, and one day it will *really* be discovered. Yet even now Red Hook has a vibrant spirit, as many people here feel they're pioneers on the verge of something.[7]

Reasons for Moving

The intellectual debate on why and where gentrifiers move falls between two broad groups: the production or supply-side hypothesis, and the consumption or demand-side hypothesis. The former, led by human geographer Neil Smith, focuses on his rent-gap hypothesis. This concept asserts that gentrifiers are drawn to neighborhoods by the lower rents that result when developers can rehabilitate or build at a cost low enough to allow them to make a profit. The latter group, following the lead of David Ley and others, argues that gentrifiers are attracted more by the cultural appeal of the big city—the arts, the mix of people, and living with others who value such things as diversity and cultural activities. Richard Florida, while agreeing that economic factors like firms located in urban areas matter, believes that the driving force toward cities is creative people in search of diverse and tolerant communities.[8] As we'll soon see, that force actually involves many of the factors noted here. Let's look at them in detail:

Amenities

Once housing is taken care of, other amenities become relevant to new residents of a neighborhood. One of the most important of these is the availability of nearby restaurants, cafés, and wine bars. Most of the gentrifiers are young, and nightlife is the hub of their activities. These people love to gather in eateries, especially those that have outdoor seating, just like they do in, say, Paris. The fact that so many people flock to them underscores the safety of the neighborhood, and indeed the presence of such places outside reduces the likelihood of crime. In the morning hours the Internet cafés both reflect and enhance the area. For many, doing their work in these spaces is much more attractive than being holed up in a cramped studio apartment. That's why they're sometimes called "coffices" by patrons.

But the locals don't always see it that way at all, even if such establishments do make the neighborhood less dangerous. For them these places emphasize the class divide. As one Harlemite who has lived in a public housing project for his entire life said about a new café, "We don't eat there. I went in there for a piece of cake and it was like four bucks! I can get a whole cake for four bucks. Obviously they don't want too many of us in there. We don't get down like that spending four dollars for a piece of cake, know what I'm saying?"[9] The resentment in his statement is visceral. He cannot ever feel comfortable with such people. He's disapproving and disdainful.

In her book *Harlem Is Nowhere*, Sharifa Rhodes-Pitts describes this feeling well: "I couldn't help but wince when noticing my elderly neighbor Mr. Edward standing outside the door of that new café, but never going in. He hovered next to the entrance, drinking a seventy-five-cent cup of bodega coffee." As a black person the author is sensitive to how the gentrifiers see the situation. She reports on a conversation she overheard between two white men, one of whom was visiting his friend's new neighborhood, Harlem: "*'This is fabulous,'* he exclaimed. . . . *'Really, you have to do something to get the word out. There need to be more* people *up here.'*"[10] More people? Harlem has lots of people. Obviously, the man meant people like himself.

Boutiques are another important feature, whether they're art galleries or clothing stores. The rapidly evolving Lower East Side is practically awash in such establishments. According to one study, in December 2010 there were sixty-four art galleries in that area, with more in the planning stages. The main reason art galleries pick up and move to the Lower East Side is because they are priced out of Soho and Chelsea. Some complain that these areas are "too commercial." But can one really say that with a straight face when the galleries charge thousands of dollars for paintings and a menswear boutique charges the reduced price of $210 (down from $299) for a "chambray button-down shirt"?

Sometimes artists on the Lower East Side combine their art with depictions of the local population, which is heavily Chinese. Mark

Miller, owner of an art gallery and whose family has, interestingly, owned a uniform store next door since 1903, had an exhibition of art that emphasized aspects of the Chinese community. It featured such objects as Chinese and American currency, fake luxury-brand bags, and empty Chinese-brand cigarette packs. Mark asserts that he's reaching out to the Chinese community, but Fang Xu, a sociology graduate student who has researched the area, suggests that these images of fake bags and smoking are hardly flattering to the Chinese. Mark happens to be a local influential, serving as president of the current Lower East Side Business Improvement District.[11] In any event this is a revealing example of how syncretism occurs as the Chinese, Jews, and hipsters all come together in one setting. Xu also observes that the cultural clash usually associated with residents occurs in rather similar ways on the commercial streets as hipsters vie for space and zoning benefits with the old-time stores.[12]

For the gentrifiers, shopping isn't only about boutiques. After all, many can't afford these crazy prices, maybe not even the new age restaurants, where high prices and minuscule portions often unite. They need major shopping centers, not Payless, but something affordable and of reasonable quality. Enter the 117th Street shopping mall in East Harlem, near FDR Drive. Called East River Plaza, it's a brand-new beautiful shopping area with a nice view of the river, a key factor in making an area attractive. The mall offers a Costco, Bob's Furniture, Target, Best Buy, Marshall's, Old Navy, Pet Smart, Starbucks, and other well-known stores. It also offers more than enough indoor parking. Customers come from the Upper East and West Sides, but the shopping center is a particular boon to those living in East Harlem, including the gentrifiers. People usually take the subway, a bus, or a cab to get there. If shoppers don't want to carry their purchases home, for twenty-two dollars they can have them delivered to their home or office anywhere in Manhattan.

Easy transportation is very important for anyone who lives in New York City. That's why in North Brooklyn neighborhoods near the L line are quite gentrified. The same is true of certain parts of western Queens, like Sunnyside and Astoria, where various subways run. But now, increasingly, there's another option. People who live in North Williamsburg can take a ferry to Manhattan for a quiet, scenic fifteen-minute ride and dock at Thirty-fourth Street and First Avenue or on Wall Street. The ferry is cleaner and often quicker than the subway, and it comes every twenty minutes at a cost of only four dollars. Walt Whitman, author of the elegiac nineteenth-century poem "Crossing Brooklyn Ferry," would be shocked at the view of the Brooklyn and Manhattan skylines of today.

The New Yorkers I spoke with said they feel completely connected to Manhattan, in large part because it's so easy to get there. The ferries stop in various locations, including Atlantic Avenue, Brooklyn Bridge, Hunters Point, and Greenpoint, and this method of transportation will undoubtedly increase in importance as time goes on. In fact it's already happening, as current demand far exceeds availability. Almost 350,000 riders have paid to travel on the ferry since it began service in June 2011, far more than the 134,000 users originally predicted.[13]

While the gentrifiers are not an especially religious group, for those who care about religion, nearby churches of their own faith are yet another amenity some people seek. One of the new ministers in the city is actually the son of televangelist Jim Bakker. The churches typically have both old-timers and newcomers, many of whom often find common ground in social activism. They are also aware of the possibilities of connecting spiritually. At the Chabad/Lubavitch Center in North Williamsburg, "every Friday evening, a black coated and bearded rebbe stands on crowded Bedford Avenue inviting young, inactive Jews to the Sabbath meal. . . . During the meal, humor and generous amounts of alcohol are punctuated with impromptu blessings and prayers and serious questions posed to the rebbe about Judaism and religious observance."[14] Of course, there's no way to tell from this description how many of the visitors return, how many become more deeply interested, and how many are just looking for a free meal and an interesting experience.

Similarly, according to longtime real estate agent Stu Rubinfeld, there's a rabbi at the Max Raiskin Center in the East Village on Sixth Street who uses jazz concerts to attract the young and hip, with the goal of showing them how Judaism is relevant even if they're secular. There are also mixers and singles events for this crowd. And their buzzword is often *tikkun olam,* Hebrew for "repairing the world," or, if you will, social activism. "These people will identify with Judaism, but not in the traditional sense. They'll be hipster Jews," Rubinfeld told me. If so, it'll be yet another form of Judaism, one whose dimensions are not yet known.

Serving as a bridge between the locals of long standing and the new arrivals is not that easy. As the pastor of Ascension Episcopal Church in Greenpoint observed, "I hear from old-timers, 'You're just trying to appeal to Yuppies.' There's real resentment underlying their attitude to new people. You have a lawyer who just moved in and then you have a construction worker who grew up in the neighborhood. The [result] could be explosive. I think there will be some confrontation. But older members will lose in numbers. You have to run two congregations and hope they get along."[15] Regardless of the difficulties, the church provides a unique opportunity for exposure and learning, because these two types would not ordinarily meet and interact anywhere else.

Research that has been conducted on this topic found that the gentrifying areas of New York have not, on the whole, become more secular. Rather, a number of congregations revitalized and other new ones were created. Clearly, those that are more capable of adapting to what the newcomers want or need will do better. Besides social activism, a key element is that as these people marry and start families, they will see the church as a possible option for providing their children with day-care centers, religious training, and values that may reflect their own upbringing.[16]

There are no statistics on it, but many young professionals throughout the city do identify religiously. A visit to any number of churches or temples will verify that. For example, increasing numbers of young Modern Orthodox Jews are moving to Park Slope, Prospect Heights, as well as Carroll Gardens and Cobble Hill. Many of them hail from the Upper West Side and were looking for less expensive apartments. One new synagogue, the Prospect Heights Shul, has programs that typify what younger people are looking for—social action, joint activities with non-Orthodox congregations, emphasis on women's participation, and the like.[17] And the churches on the Upper West Side and in Hudson Heights are attended by many young professional worshipers, with multiple services available to their congregations.

Cachet

What gives a neighborhood cachet? What makes it "cool," "in," or "hip"? It's an elusive, almost will-o'-the-wisp and intangible quality that defies easy categorization. Yet you know it, or at least think you know it, when you see it. Whatever it is, cachet can mightily influence gentrifiers' decisions about where to move. And once a location acquires that status, it can lead people to lose all perspective about what the area has to offer, even to the point of irrationality. "We absolutely have to find a place in Park Slope," one says to the other, "no matter what it costs." As such, the subject of cachet is worth looking at.

A study of Boerum Hill, Brooklyn, by sociologist Philip Kasinitz demonstrates the complexity of how neighborhoods earn cachet. You need a catchy name that you can tie into a history, an organization of people determined to raise the neighborhood's image through house tours, boundary adjustments to make the neighborhood attractive, residents who are politically involved on the local level, and landmark status to protect the neighborhood from overdevelopment and changes to its character. After doing all of this, Kasinitz notes, the residential blocks in Boerum Hill were a perfect Jane Jacobs–type fit. They were short, with buildings that were "unified and consistent," and small enough to encourage cohesiveness. Black residents did not approve of these efforts and perspectives, detecting racist overtones in the linking of the area with Anglo-Saxon roots in the nineteenth century and with separating the area from the nearby projects.[18]

One area of New York City that is gentrifying is the part of Washington Heights west of Broadway, from 181st Street to the Cloisters, where Inwood begins. The neighborhood was first established in the 1920s and 1930s and was renamed Hudson Heights by a local community group, the Hudson Heights Owners

Coalition. By renaming the area the organization has done something that is usually initiated by real estate agents, who always appreciate the cachet a catchy name can bring. Name a place after a beautiful and famous river and—bingo!—it becomes a great sales pitch. Why? Because people love to tell others they live in a place that sounds upscale, that has gorgeous views (even if their own apartment doesn't), and that, even if relatively few have ever heard of it, is in Manhattan.[19] Another good example is the designation of Southern Harlem as "Soha." If it conjures up the image of Soho, that's because it's meant to, so that the neighborhood can acquire cachet.

Dumbo/Vinegar Hill is a neighborhood that treasures and promotes authenticity. It is its cachet. And despite the fact that there are other areas like Red Hook that also have authenticity by way of factories, very old houses, and cobblestone streets, Dumbo has become a much "hotter" place. Why? It's far easier to get to (using the F or A trains) than Red Hook, which has no subway. Plus, the shiny skyscrapers across the river and the projects and remaining tenements along the waterfront make for a fascinating juxtaposition between the old and the new—you can see all of Gotham's history with one glance. Dumbo has projects, but they are much safer and smaller than those in Red Hook. The area still has factory buildings, some of which have been converted into luxury or middle-class apartments while retaining the outer factory-structure look. And in the subsection of Vinegar Hill there are many row houses dating back more than a century. A Con Ed power plant, complete with smokestacks reminiscent of earlier days, overlooks the waterfront. Brand-new buildings pop up from time to time as demand soars. Finally, people judge the area to be safe. One late afternoon I'm walking by a brick apartment building a block from the Farragut Houses when I stop to talk with a forty-something woman dressed in black jeans and a beige acrylic sweater. "I've lived here for ten years and it's fine," she tells me. "I've also got two kids. There's a boundary here that isn't crossed."[20]

In her book *Naked City*, Sharon Zukin describes how North Williamsburg, Brooklyn, became "hip" in the 1990s. Private, illegal, music parties like the underground Rubulad were held in deserted lofts, warehouses, and even Polish bars. They were advertised on the Internet and through email and were open to the public, provided, of course, you looked cool enough to be approved by the burly bouncers standing guard at the door. Then, after the place was seen as "in," commercial establishments and upscale living spaces followed. In becoming cool, North Williamsburg followed the path of 1970s Soho and the 1980s East Village.[21]

Artists, writers, and artisans looking for space in Brooklyn went to North Williamsburg and took over abandoned lofts there, because the older areas like Cobble Hill and Park Slope were too expensive. At first the authorities chased them out, saying manufacturing, with its jobs, was what mattered. But the jobs were gone, and, besides, many artists were living there legally, in both lofts and apartments. According to Zukin about 2,000 of them were living there out of a total population of 115,000.[22]

North Williamsburg's combination of artists; boutiques; and entertainment scenes, both large and small, located in an area with decaying industrial buildings, small apartment houses, and dwindling or slowly growing populations of natives and immigrants—Mexicans, Poles, blacks, some Italians—plus the danger of adjacent Bushwick, all combined to give the area a feeling of what Zukin calls "nouveau grit." It was gritty and hip, two types of authenticity. It had the look and feel of the old, but it also had new artistic spaces and hangouts, as well as music venues run by musicians, often difficult to find, which added to their cachet.[23]

While there's no question that people are in search of, and value, cachet, there's a danger to actually finding it. Once change of this sort happens in too many neighborhoods, it's no longer a phenomenon; rather, it's a trend that shapes a city. Thus, when people look at North Williamsburg, they're looking at a type of cachet created earlier in Soho and the East Village. In this way what was once a one-of-a-kind phenomenon loses its uniqueness and its feeling of specialness. It's sort of a glut of culture. On the other hand, developing cachet in many areas is a good problem for a city to have.

There's also commercial cachet, when areas capitalize on a community's national reputation. Harlem is world famous, and as it gentrifies, real estate agents and residents alike seize on that status.

As I am standing outside Harlem's largest multiplex theater, on 124th Street, I spot some camera crews setting up. "What's going on here?" I ask a tall man dressed in black and wearing dreads.

"It's a premiere for an *Indiana Jones* flick. Harrison Ford and, I heard, Fergy are coming here tonight."

"Really," I say.

Clearly interpreting that as skepticism, he shoots back, "Yeah, this is like the seventh premiere we've had here recently. What you think? Harlem is local? We're *international*. Tom Cruise has been here."

We see here that as much as some Harlemites resent the newcomers, there's pride in the fact that the ultimate trendsetters, famous movie stars, are actually coming here.

Today some fifty thousand people a year visit the Apollo Theater in Harlem. However, the awakening is more "bricks and mortar" than the cultural explosion that marked the famed Harlem Renaissance of the 1920s and 1930s. Certainly the theater's once-a-week amateur night has nothing to do with the Apollo's storied past. Other places in the neighborhood also piggyback on history and culture to create a connection with the old that was gold, one that serves the area's economic goals. Take, for example, the creation of the Strivers Gardens complex located from 134th to 135th Streets and Frederick Douglass Boulevard (Eighth Avenue). It features new condominiums named after Duke Ellington and Ella Fitzgerald. The real, original Strivers Row section was on 138th and 139th Streets, between Douglass and Adam Clayton Powell Boulevards. And why not? It sounds good and there's nothing illegal or wrong with it. The area around 125th Street, Harlem's commercial nerve center, now features underground parking, upscale shops, two new high schools, a Harlem Walk of Fame, and an IHOP restaurant nearby.

Preserving History

A good number of gentrifiers like the idea that in their midst lie restaurants, bars, and private clubs that have been there a long time. But even if they don't like it, such relics remain, stubbornly resistant to rent increases and the newcomers' different tastes. Each neighborhood has community institutions that have been around forever. In Prospect Heights it's Tom's Restaurant, a joint that's been there since 1936. In a way it grounds the neighborhood, giving it some semblance of a past. Greenpoint has Polish restaurants, like the tiny place Łomzynianka on Manhattan Avenue owned by natives of Łomza, Poland. It's filled with young people who enjoy the traditional food at rock-bottom prices. The Emerald Inn, an Irish bar on Columbus Avenue near Sixty-ninth Street, is another relic. But these are exceptions. Most simply close or follow the pattern of the Second Avenue Deli, forced out of the Lower East Side and into another area by steep rent increases.

Often overlooked in discussions about preservation are the aging residents, oral historians who literally embody the past. A senior citizen living in a three-bedroom apartment on Fifth Avenue near 109th Street reports that his landlord offered him $500,000 if he would move out. The landlord could then rent the apartment for $6,000 a month instead of the $880 the man is now paying as a rent-control tenant. He could also sell it for over $1 million. The man wouldn't consider moving out, because he likes it there and would only have to pay more elsewhere. If this group, as a class of people—namely, elderly lifelong New Yorkers—left the city, something essential to its nature would be lost.

I speak with a middle-age German Jewish man in Washington (now Hudson) Heights, who shares with me some of his neighborhood's history as we walk through it.

> This is a post–World War Two building, and it was first populated mostly by German Jews. There are still some of them, along with young singles, many of them Orthodox. It's called the "Adenauer Building," after the German chancellor who did the *Wiedergutmachen* [Holocaust survivor reparations] deal. Running from Overlook Terrace up to Fort Washington Avenue is a long stone staircase—132 steps to be precise—called the "Kissinger Steps," because Henry's parents lived in a building near the top of the staircase. Henry used to take these steps as he went to George Washington High School over on Amsterdam Avenue. He started at City College

of New York and then transferred to Harvard after being discovered in the army intelligence unit.

Without such knowledgeable individuals, preserving history becomes much more difficult. We also see here that gentrifiers aren't the only ones for whom cachet matters. The identification with a world-famous political figure makes this man feel special. The community where he grew up also produced a world-famous figure. (See figure 25.)

These tidbits remind us that so many areas have a distinct and even distinguished history that sometimes sets the stage for gentrification. For those gentrifiers inclined to think this way, like the preservationists mentioned earlier, it means they are now a part of it and that in its rebirth they are its latest incarnation, usually after an intermediate period of decay. Part of the narrative almost always is "This place used to be so terrible." In that way it's an ego-satisfying tale. "They," the gentrifiers, turned it around; they did it. "And now look how much an apartment here costs," they crow, especially if they arrived in the early stages and got a bargain.

Another remnant of the past is the *Catholic Worker,* a newspaper co-founded by Dorothy Day and Peter Maurin, and active in the political struggles of the 1960s. The paper still exists, with offices located on Third Street just east of Second Avenue. An employee tells me they now have about twenty thousand subscribers "and the list is growing." The paper costs a mere one cent. Antiwar activist Father Daniel Berrigan, now in his early nineties, lives not far away in a church on Houston Street. These institutions anchor the East Village historically and give it a certain cachet that may or may not be appreciated by the newcomers, depending on their perspective and knowledge of history.[24]

Just a bit farther down the block, at 77 East Third Street, is the historic headquarters of the New York chapter of the Hells Angels Motorcycle Club, established in 1969. "No Parking Except Authorized Hells Angels," the sign outside reads. Seven gleaming motorcycles are parked out in front, and there is a plaque dedicated to "Vinnie: 1948–1979." His motto was "When in Doubt Knock 'em Out!" I catch up to a young man wearing a navy blue blazer and rep tie, who is leaving his apartment next door. A plate on the building says, "New York Law School," and the owner rents it out to students from other law schools as well. An odd juxtaposition, I think, since the Hells Angels weren't exactly considered model, law-abiding citizens. The students' take on them is quite egalitarian. "They're pretty good people," one tells me as his friends nod in agreement. "I have no problem with them. They keep the neighborhood safe, because nobody messes with them." Once again, especially in the current era of terrorism and a safety-first mentality, whatever works seems to be fine.[25]

Sometimes historic districts are not gentrified but exist in a "gentrified state" amid neighborhoods that are considered to be undesirable, or are even in a pre-gentrified state. One good example is the Belmont/Arthur Avenue section of the Bronx, also known as the Little Italy of the Bronx, which is surrounded by a poor, overwhelmingly black and Hispanic area. After the Italians began to leave, Albanians and Puerto Ricans moved in. Today the neighborhood is a vibrant tourist destination bearing no resemblance to the surrounding areas—that is, the Bathgate Industrial Park and the Crotona Park area. The presence of students from nearby Fordham University, who rent apartments in Little Italy, also helps. And there are gentrifiers too, looking for inexpensive homes. When an area has a combination of business interests, populations who don't move so quickly, and students, it can maintain itself.

The area is so successful that, in the words of Ivine Galarza, district manager of Bronx Community Board #6, "On any Saturday or holiday, any given weekend, you cannot walk because it's so congested. People come from all over—Jersey, Connecticut—to get their meats, breads, and cheeses." I can attest to the accuracy of these statements from personal experience. There are many delicatessens, Italian and Albanian restaurants, including the Zagat-approved, top-rated Roberto's, along with an assortment of bakeries and cafés. The Feast of Saint Anthony at Our Lady of Mount Carmel Church is held in Little Italy every June, featuring games, rides, amusements, and singing groups like the Wanderers.[26]

The area also has peculiar historical continuities. The community was built up by the cigarette-manufacturing Lorillard family in the mid-nineteenth century. Today Dominican workers make a wide array of fine cigars right in front of you in an indoor mini-mall while you wait. A cigar-chomping friend of mine claims they're among the best he's ever had.

One somewhat bizarre example of preserving history is an old flophouse at 220 Bowery that was formerly known as the Prince Hotel. The two entrepreneurs who spruced up the place retained the building's narrow cubicles topped with chicken wire on one floor and now rent them to down-and-out people for less than ten dollars a night. Renaming the hotel the Bowery House, the owners' purpose was to create "living history," with the above-mentioned residents described as "an asset to the property." What is striking here is that the owners do not seem to consider the embarrass-ment they may be causing the impoverished people to whom they rent. Sure, those people are happy to have a place to stay, but one wonders if they don't resent being showcased as if they were on display in a zoo.

On the two floors above these inexpensive rooms, the hotel's cubicles (or, as the owners call them, cabins) are more upscale, featuring custom-made mattresses and shared bathrooms with heated floors and marbled sinks. The idea is to give a clientele made up mostly of European and American visitors to the area a taste of the flophouse days of yore, when the Bowery was "drunk heaven," but in a more attractive way. The cost? Anywhere from $62.00 to $129.00 a night, including a free guided tour of the en-tire building.[27]

The Quest for Diversity

Ethnic and racial diversity is definitely a positive when gentrifi-ers mull over their residential options. This notion was a com-mon one, but it was often stated as an advantage of where they were *already* living rather than as a reason for choosing to move there in the first place. Sometimes I had the feeling that the pluses of encountering new groups were a surprise to them, that these were groups of people they might have been hesitant to meet, but once they did so, in their building or local PTA, they found them to be interesting, pleasant, and even exciting. The following comments by a woman living in diverse Ditmas Park, were fairly typical: "There's a real sense of community here, lots of young people, especially artists. A three-bedroom in a modest prewar building is $1,390, and it's only three blocks from the train. And the diversity is incredible. There are, like, forty languages in the public schools here. I prefer more progressive, and here it's more 'old-style.' I can't believe how expensive Dumbo is. I mean, how can you work with the hum of the trains? It's a little chichi [in this sense, affectedly trendy]." Further evidence of Ditmas Park's diversity, albeit in another way, may be discerned from the eclectic range of books in the windows of the Internet cafés that dot the streets—Virginia Wolfe, Dickens, Doris Lessing, the *Norton Anthology of American Literature,* but also the not-so-highbrow Steve Martin, James Michener, and Sue Grafton.

Prospect Heights is another fount of diversity. Along Washington Avenue, which borders Bedford-Stuyvesant, you'll find the usual coffeehouses, wine bars, and trendy Thai restaurants but also West Indian and Southern-style eateries. I pass by the Underhill Playground. It's a model of racial integration, with a roughly equal number of black and white parents supervising their children as they play in the sandbox, climb various types of equipment, or just race around. I wonder if the integration also extends to play dates at each others' homes.

Brooklyn Bridge Park in Dumbo, close to Brooklyn Heights, offers further evidence of diversity of all sorts. Yuppies and teenagers vie for space on benches and in the grass as bicyclists and roller-bladers speed past babies in strollers. An occasional Hasidic or traditional Muslim family enjoys a family outing as a Czech documentary film crew points its cameras at the space across the water where the World Trade Center once stood. Carnival music accompanies a brightly lit carousel whose riders include Asian couples seemingly in love and small Hispanic children accompanied by adults. There's even a wedding party having itself filmed against the Lower Manhattan skyline. On a nearby street, posters are mounted on a faded, multicolored brick wall in preparation for the upcoming Dumbo Arts Festival.

In West Harlem, the Dinosaur Bar-B-Que at Twelfth Avenue and 125th Street offers up some interesting food. Zagat gives it a 22 rating, describing the fare as "mouthwatering, swoon-worthy sides, chased with buckets of beer are yours at this rockin' West Harlem barbecue joint set up like a biker bar, complete with picnic tables and sticky floors. Middle America pricing." And the customers are a mix of white and black families—some sharing tables—locals, working-class types, college students from the nearby universities, no doubt, and tourists. Barbecue is soul food too, though this is no Sylvia's (the iconic soul food Harlem restaurant). Dinosaur Bar-B-Que's offerings are more Southwestern style—Texas Brisket Plate, Big-Ass Pork Plate, ribs, beans, mac 'n' cheese. It also serves Mexican-type Churrasco chicken. The brick interior has exposed pipes along the ceiling. The mirrored bar is lined with high-backed chairs and is done up like a saloon. Everybody is here and everybody is welcome.

Dinosaur Bar-B-Que is but one example of such mixing. What's happening in New York is a fusion of culture at all levels of social life, both in the workplace and in the city's restaurants. At the intersection of Ryerson Street and Myrtle Avenue on the north side of the avenue is the Sapolo Spanish and Chinese Restaurant. And directly across the street you have La Stalla, featuring Italian and Mexican cuisine, and right next to that you have the Sushi Okdol Korean and Japanese Restaurant. So in one small area are three totally separate eateries, seemingly unconnected, representing six different cultures. That's New York!

One community that has a mix of many cultures is Roosevelt Island, formerly called Welfare Island (the insane, criminals, and the poor actually lived there at various times). It was built up in the early 1970s and is a bit less than two miles long, running from roughly Eighty-fifth to Forty-sixth Streets. In 1989 a subway stop was created for Roosevelt Island. Fears that this planned, moderate- to middle-income community would lose its safe, small-town flavor did not materialize. The island has about ten thousand residents and is known as a quiet place with few cars and easy access from Manhattan (tram and subway) and Queens (bridge and subway). Its population is about 45 percent white, 27 percent black, 14 percent Hispanic, and 11 percent Asian, with 3 percent defined as "other." As I walk through it, I get the sense that it's part of the city—indeed the island is surrounded by the city—but that it's in another place, a category by itself.

Not to be omitted from this discussion is that the gentrifiers' very presence adds to the diversity of New York, because they themselves come from a variety of cultures. I frequently looked through the names inside apartment buildings in these areas and was amazed at the number of ethnic groups that appeared to be represented. The Upper West Side, for instance, was once very Jewish, then very Hispanic, then both. Today these groups are augmented by the gentrifiers. A look at the names of some of the residents in an apartment building on West Seventy-eighth Street tells the story: Jabido, Hagstrom, Balphy, Evans, Burney, Abrams, Flanders, Taylor, Park, Matarazzo, Gillespie, Blackshire, Ahearn, Lee, Martin, Leman, Gorman, Chan, Maartens, Ruocco. The building is a veritable UN, and it's a five-story walk-up. Almost no Jewish or Hispanic names, but plenty of Irish, Italians, and probably WASPS.

Gentrifiers and the Poor

They stand there, the tenements, brick, usually reddish-colored structures, both separate from and within the neighborhoods of New York. Sometimes they run for ten or more blocks, two avenues wide, and in other locations they comprise just a few short streets. People tend to avoid them and exercise caution if they need to pass by the buildings. Even the residents of the area, who know more about where and when it's safe to walk, keep a watchful eye out, especially after night falls. The tenements have been part of the city's urban landscape for decades, but today there's a difference.

The good housing is pushing out or rendering irrelevant the bad housing, and that includes both the tenements and the projects in these areas too. Perhaps because space is at such a premium, perhaps even because Section 8 people live in well-appointed buildings, or simply perhaps because crime is lower, people don't care that much if they live near a project or run-down tenements. Or maybe they've just made a decision that this is the price of living cheaply near their place of work.

Warren Street in Boerum Hill has townhouses in a one-block section that dead-ends into low-income projects at both ends of the block. One is the 1,134-unit Gowanus Houses; the other, the 528-unit Wyckoff Gardens. Yet prices remain high for available condos in the area. One four-bedroom unit went to contract for $1.15 million. A real estate agent noted the connection between professionals moving in and a stronger police presence that encouraged buyers, adding, "Also, when the market is down, the projects are a factor. When it is up, the projects aren't a factor." People do complain about the failure of the police to crack down on crack users and dealers who hang out by the projects and the violence their presence encourages.[28] The strong market may in fact be a self-fulfilling prophecy, because when demand is high, people are less choosy. Plus, high demand leads to a belief that the area is going to get even better.

Studies by New York University's Furman Center for Real Estate and Urban Policy have concluded that people moving into an area are not deterred by the projects or low-income residents in general.[29] And it is an irony that the new arrivals reportedly look at the incumbent poor as though *they* are the outsiders. As one longtime resident complained, "They look at you like you don't belong here."[30] Still, brutal crimes occasionally occur in gentrifying neighborhoods, serving as a rude awakening to residents that this is still New York City, not Scarsdale or Old Brookville. Those who had reservations to begin with may leave as a result, but the majority are apt to rationalize their decision by characterizing such events as aberrations.[31]

People with whom I spoke were voluble in expressing their satisfaction with the shift. One of these people, who for decades has lived near the poor, run-down, and massive Red Hook housing project in a small clapboard house on Luquer Street, two blocks from the Battery Tunnel entrance, told me, "In the eighties we had shootings, crack-heads, you know. My brother called the cops all the time. He exaggerated so they should come, and they did. But after Giuliani took over, things changed. They began paying attention and things got better. Now it's amazingly gentrified. Nobody cares what's around the house, just that it's ten minutes from Manhattan." In 2001 this person's family bought another house right next to the projects for $150,000. Today it's worth eight times that.

Savvy gentrifiers do take into account the fact that a nearby public housing project could be a crime problem, but that fact is weighed against the positive aspects of the neighborhood. Everywhere in the city there are gentrifying areas that have public housing projects in the neighborhood or just beyond its borders, a block or two away. Sometimes the project is part of the border. But good housing near places of work is in short supply. As more and more gentrifiers move in, their numbers create safety and the police step up their efforts to patrol and protect.

I ask residents of Dumbo/Vinegar Hill about the low-income Farragut Houses situated at the edge of the neighborhood. "I've lived here seven years, and it's not a problem," a man who works out of his home told me as he walked his dog. "There are some muggings, but that's New York. The police have said this is a better project as these projects go. More likely you'll have a domestic dispute, but that's about it. I walk alone sometimes at night, and nothing's ever happened to me." (To be fair, he does have a fairly large dog, though it's a Labrador, not a Rottweiler.) Some projects are, in fact, a lot better than others. Contrast Farragut with, say, the Ingersoll/Whitman projects on Myrtle Avenue in Fort Greene, where drug dealers, gangs, and squatters have taken over more than a few of these dwellings.

That said, no one should be fooled into believing that nothing ever happens to those who live near the projects or other areas where the poor reside. Crime may be down, but if you're a victim statistics mean nothing. I ask a cop in downtown Brooklyn about why people don't mind living in fancy buildings along Flatbush Avenue near the projects. There's annoyance in her eyes, and she actually grimaces as she answers the question.

The area's all right. But they don't understand when they get mugged. They say somebody snatched their pocketbook. Well, what do you expect if you gonna live across the street from a project? And they be lookin' at their laptops in their cars, handling their portable GPS. They gonna have problems because they don't know what the hell they're doing. They shouldn't be moving here. They complain, but we can't be everywhere at once. You're a New Yorker. You wouldn't do that. What are you supposed to do when somebody sticks a million dollars in your face? I grew up in Brooklyn. I understand the neighborhoods.

The police do feel the political pressure from the newcomers, people who complain vociferously when these things happen, and they're not used to it in this precinct. In a way the police justify the actions of the locals when they say, "Well, what do you expect if you gonna live here?" They also reveal their own resentment about the new arrivals when they say "somebody sticks a million dollars in your face." In other words, it's being stuck in their faces too, since they see it as well. The degree to which the police are less than enthusiastic about protecting the gentrifiers can also affect and even slow down the process of change in an area.

Do Gentrifiers Displace the Poor?

Have the gentrifiers really displaced the poor, or have they, for the most part, simply entered their communities? This is a major and greatly debated issue in the field of urban studies. It cannot be resolved in this book, but it must be addressed.

Logically, visually, and anecdotally it would seem that the poor have been displaced. When you compare communities like Fort Greene, Clinton Hill, Boerum Hill, Harlem, Washington Heights, Astoria, and elsewhere, you'll find that there are tens of thousands more middle-class people residing in these places than was the case twenty or thirty years ago. In other words, gentrification has occurred on a massive scale in many areas that were once predominantly home to the poor. Blocks that formerly housed the poor now contain many well-off people. Community advocates insist that rapacious, profit-hungry landlords are doing everything in their power to oust the remaining poor so that they can reap the profits occasioned by their departure. For instance, there's the case of a property in Harlem that housed poor women and children and was run by the nonprofit Queen Mother Dr. Delois Blakely organization. With the mortgage in arrears, the property's owners are fighting off foreclosure. Plans are under way to turn it into a Starbucks. The residents will be displaced, and there are other situations like this in the area.[32] In his book *Selling the Lower East Side*, sociologist Christopher Mele describes a similar process that occurred in the East Village over a number of years.[33]

On the other side of the debate you have people like Lance Freeman, who studied Fort Greene and Harlem and concluded that, contrary to popular opinion, gentrification did not force out most of the poor. Most of them stayed where they were.[34] This is supported by a national statistical study of the American Housing Survey by researchers at the Furman Center led by Ingrid Gould Ellen, a professor of public policy and planning. It found that across the nation there was virtually no displacement of the poor as a result of gentrification. In fact, gentrifying or gaining neighborhoods showed slightly *lower* exit rates than non-gaining areas, and a number of the original residents actually gained in income. Rents rose too, and even though their incomes didn't rise enough to offset the higher rents, poor people remained. This may be because they were willing to pay more for better services in an improved neighborhood.[35] On the other hand, an investigation of both quantitative and qualitative data by political scientist Kathe Newman and geographer Kelvin Wyly challenged the view that displacement of the poor is minimal.[36]

Thus we see that the evidence on this question is contradictory and therefore inconclusive. One problem is that the quantitative data may not be close enough to the ground to tell us what's really going on. Sheer numbers don't always tell the story that well. People often base decisions on a variety of factors, and only in-depth interviews can uncover the process that led to those decisions— namely, the weight given to each factor. For example, the landlord may never have provided enough heat. He may never have dealt adequately with roaches and rats in the building. People complained bitterly but remained where they were. Then, when there was a shooting down the block, that was the last straw. Is this displacement? Yes and no. A couple is planning to retire to North Carolina in a year. The building's maintenance has never been good, but they've lived with it. Suddenly the wife's sister, who lives in North Carolina, has a stroke and needs her sister to come down from New York and help her. The couple moves, and when asked why, they say it was because of the sister *and* the fact that the building was in bad shape.

Changes in a gentrifying neighborhood can have a strong impact on longtime poor residents. For instance, an area is becoming gentrified and a man living there can no longer get coffee for seventy-five cents, because the grocery store has been replaced by a far more expensive Starbucks. When he hangs out in front of the building, the police threaten to arrest him for loitering. The new white and black population is wealthier than he'll ever be, and they make him uncomfortable. He cites all of the above as reasons for leaving, but which of them are most important?

Ultimately, what constitutes displacement? Technically, it's when people are forced to leave against their will. But how is that to be determined? When a neighborhood changes economically, the remaining poor no longer feel welcome. They are not being literally forced out, but they feel they are and their new living conditions make it difficult for them to feel comfortable and survive. In the larger sense, they have been displaced by gentrification.

I've spoken with many landlords, tenants, and community organization leaders in my travels through New York City, and each group's arguments have some merit, though their perspectives may be biased by self-interest. The tenants always want better services and will not easily admit to having damaged their apartments, if, indeed, they have. Community organizations receive funding from various sources in amounts that are dependent on how much their services are needed, though one must add that such organizations do a great deal to help tenants who are ignorant of their rights and of how the system can work against them. The landlords want to maximize their profits and argue that because rent control and rent stabilization mean that people cannot simply be thrown out, they must foot the bill for tenants who do not maintain their apartments. Yet landlords are prone, for reasons of self-interest to exaggerate tenants' failure to keep their dwellings in good order.

An off-the-record discussion I had with one landlord was particularly revealing regarding how tenants are convinced or pressured to move out. I asked him, "How do you persuade a person to leave?"

"It all depends on what they want," he responded. "I had a building with one tenant left that I wanted to convert. So I said to him, 'What would you like? Is it a girlfriend? I can get you one.' 'No,' he said. 'I want an apartment.' I said, 'Fine. Would you like to move to Florida or stay here?' 'I want to be in the city.' 'Okay. I'll give you a nice place in one of my other buildings at fifty percent of the rent here.' 'Great,' he said. And that was it. We made a deal and both parties were happy. The new place was even bigger than where he was and in a neighborhood nearby."

This conversation sheds light on what goes on behind the scenes. There's a give and take. It's not like some people imagine—namely, that harassing letters go out and heat is turned off. Today these tactics are not as easy to use as in the past. If a landlord fails to provide heat in a timely fashion and the tenant complains, an oil truck is sent by the city to the location to fill the tank and the building owner is charged for it.

Statistically, this and other cases look like displacement on paper, but are they really? That's why one must ask, did those who were replaced remain in the neighborhood? If the building exists and was improved, were the tenants offered any deals? Does a person who leaves a tenement and moves into Section 8 housing qualify as displaced in the same way as a tenement resident who moves into another substandard dwelling? Until there is more extensive research on the subject analyzing what happened and where, we can't possibly know the full story.

National studies are often unable to distinguish between people who have left their building because it was torn down or because of a fire. More important, if new housing is built on vacant land five years after the residents have departed, how are we to know what happened? Did they leave because the landlords stopped providing services, or was it a voluntary decision, perhaps because their own fortunes improved? The first case is much closer to displacement than the second.[37]

There's one major piece of the puzzle that's missing here: we know almost nothing about where the poor who left went. I know of no study that has examined this very important issue. They were not interviewed at the time they departed, and no one has tried to track them down. Did they go to Long Island's Suffolk County? To other states? Or did they just move to other neighborhoods? How many are there in each category? How can we talk about what happened to the displaced if we don't know where they went? Without that information, we can't find out *why* they left and are left in the dark as to perhaps the most crucial part of the process.

This discussion intersects with a heated policy debate that rages alongside it. Much in that debate turns on whether New York City allowed whole segments of its poor to be displaced against their will. Critics of gentrification concede that attracting people of means to the city is obviously very important if it is to thrive. Cities all over America, like St. Louis and Detroit, went downhill because they became the province, mostly, of the poor, which greatly eroded their tax bases. But New York has been a different story. It has become a place that attracts those with money and the upwardly mobile. The change began when the Koch administration, through a variety of economic incentives, encouraged real estate interests and the private sector in general to invest in a broad range of economic projects that provided goods and services. The Dinkins administration was also friendly to such interests, especially that of the United States Tennis Association and the Disney/Times Square initiative, which began in earnest under Carl Weisbrod, then executive director of the 42nd Street Development Project. So was the Giuliani administration, which supported business interests and played a major role in making the city feel safe and prosperous. Once that happened, the process accelerated during the Bloomberg administration, and many more people with money came and started raising their kids here.

Michael Bloomberg, in particular, has endeared himself to many gentrifiers, because he represents what they feel a mayor of the twenty-first century should be. Politically liberal, he champions business and real estate development; is unabashedly in love with Manhattan; cares about making the city user-friendly to cyclists, joggers, and park enthusiasts; and makes healthy living a priority, banning smoking or unhealthy soft drinks wherever he can. One of his pet endeavors, reflecting his enthusiasm for out-of-the-box ideas, is financing a project at his alma mater, Johns Hopkins University, to genetically engineer mosquitoes in a way that would prevent the spread of malaria.

In a March 2013 interview I asked Mayor Bloomberg what achievements had given him the greatest satisfaction. Among many factors, he cited areas revolving around health issues, supporting cultural institutions, climate-change measures, and the like. But he also took credit for broader accomplishments such as "driving down crime to record lows; extending life expectancy by three years; outpacing the nation in job growth; transforming a broken public school system and turning it into one that the Obama administration has hailed as a national model; creating the nation's largest affordable housing programs. None of it would have happened without the incredibly talented people who we were able to attract to our administration." Doubtless, others who came before him and people today, outside his own circle, also deserve credit for both initiating and carrying out these programs. Regardless, these comments demonstrate that the mayor is very cognizant of the big picture.

Nevertheless, when I asked Bloomberg what he felt are the greatest challenges facing the city, his answer and his focus on the economy made clear what his priorities are—namely, those that most concern the middle and upper class, because, as he sees it, they are the ones who will contribute the most to the city's success as a world center.

> The challenge for any city is not just to keep up with the changing times, but to help lead the change. That's what we're trying to do in every area of the city's life. Think about the economy. We've invested a great deal of time, energy, and resources to make our city more attractive to industries that are growing—from bioscience and technology, to film and fashion, to tourism and arts and

culture. Part of that work is making our city a more attractive place for people to live and work in—safe streets, good schools, beautiful parks, exciting cultural opportunities. If a city is a magnet for people, then investors will follow. I've always believed that talent attracts capital far more effectively than capital attracts talent. That's why I think that New York City is better positioned to lead the tech revolution than Silicon Valley. We're already catching up, and we're working to accelerate that by producing more homegrown tech talent through computer science in middle and high school. And we're also collaborating with world-class universities to increase investment in applied sciences here in the city—to attract the best and brightest scientists and engineers. The new Cornell/Technion Applied Science School is a decades-long project, and it's a great example of how we're working to ensure tomorrow's innovators are using New York City as their campus.

This is not a man who agonizes over his decisions. Sure, he cares about his legacy, as anyone in his position would. But it's not a preoccupation by any means, at least not now. He's definitely visionary, self-confident, even brash, as the following exchange, vintage Bloomberg, makes clear.

"As you look back, are there any decisions you made that you regret?" I ask.

The mayor replies: "We're focused on making the most of every day we have left. As the countdown clock at city hall says, 'Make Every Day Count.' We're not going to spend our last months in office gazing at our navels. We're going to stay focused on our goals and doing the job the people of New York City expect us to do."

Beautiful as formerly poorer parts of New York City like Harlem or Bedford-Stuyvesant might look today, there is a concern that a world-class progressive city worthy of the name cannot consider itself a success if it fails to attend to the needs of its less fortunate residents. There are still plenty of poor people in this city, clustered in various areas like South Jamaica, Melrose, Brownsville, Manhattan's Alphabet City section of the Lower East Side, and portions of Staten Island's northern area. They need to be helped, according to this line of thinking, and both government and the private sector must do more to provide a safety net for the poor by creating more affordable housing, jobs programs, and better municipal services. Precisely how those things are to be accomplished is beyond the scope of this book, but the first step is to make such plans part of the municipal agenda.[38]

The Changing City

The Unevenness of Change

Most gentrifying, or even gentrified, neighborhoods cannot be considered completely gentrified, because it's a generally uneven process, depending on what the neighborhood was like originally. Huge housing projects can slow down the process of gentrification; so can groups of people who simply refuse to move, no matter how much pressure they get or how enticed they are. Commercial zones where store owners refuse to vacate despite receiving good offers are another factor. This means that some of the areas people move into are a mixture of gentrified and non-gentrified within the same neighborhood.

Take, for instance, East Harlem. Large areas between 110th and 125th Streets along Third Avenue and Lexington and on the side streets have been gentrified. But 125th Street itself, eastward from Lexington Avenue all the way to Second Avenue, where it is funneled into the Robert F. Kennedy Bridge—or, as it is still popularly referred to, the Triborough Bridge—has not. The intersection at Lexington and 125th is beautifully described in a photo essay that appeared on *Slate* by the world-famous street photographer Camilo José Vergara. If you stand at that interesection, you will see the ghetto and much of its ugliness and liveliness all rolled into one. Along with plain old shoppers, there are "down-and-out canners bringing their cans and bottles to the recycling center on East 124th Street. Some are recently released hospital patients, plastic I.D. bracelets still on their wrists . . . . a few carry on intense conversations with themselves. This corner of New York is particularly attractive to street evangelists, who readily find people in need of salvation." There's a flourishing drug trade; "loosies," or single cigarettes, are available; men wearing sandwich boards advertise for nearby stores; and prostitutes advertise for themselves.

It also makes for great free theater of a sort. Vergara explains: "Corner regulars tell me about the hustles they've witnessed, such as the wheelchair-bound man who suddenly stood up and started running from the police, wheelchair under his arm. Once I saw a street preacher instantly change his sermon when a recycling truck pulled up next to him. He began telling those around him that their souls were garbage and needed recycling—otherwise they were going to hell. The driver of the truck heard this and laughed loudly."[39]

I also find myself questioning how many other wheelchair frauds are plying their trade around the city or whether such suspicions are uncharitable to the genuinely disabled. It's a tough call. I recall a story my friend from Brooklyn told me. She had always given money to a crippled woman on crutches who regularly rang her bell. She'd even invited her in for tea and cookies sometimes. The woman was not always appreciative. "You used to give me rainbow cookies," she complained once, not liking that day's offering. Perhaps my friend should have known never to trust an ingrate. And then one day my friend was shocked when she saw the same lady walking in another neighborhood—but without crutches!

Gentrification doesn't happen all at once. It's a process with many twists and turns.[40] Park Slope today looks beautiful, with block after block of brownstones in excellent condition. But it wasn't always like that. Here's one person's recollection of her experiences when she and her husband moved there in 1979.

> Eleventh Street was bad then. It was still a slum. Our neighbor across the street referred to his rundown brownstone as "Jaws." The center of Park Slope was very good, from the name streets to Eighth Street. Flatbush to Seventh Avenue was good. But from 1979 to about 1983, Fifth Avenue was a hell-hole. It was working-class, though, not a really dangerous place. We were robbed several times during the years we lived there. We moved there because we wanted a house with a convenient commute. But it took too long to get to

work, and the trains were not reliable then. And I had to stand forty minutes every day on the subway. And we believed Park Slope was going up. We were definitely part of the early gentrification process. But the brownstone we got was in bad shape. Every time it rained water would cascade down our walls. We had to put in a floor.

It was actually homesteading, not exactly gentrification. Everyone had the same crappy brownstones. We were very proud of the gas lamp outside our house and of our little garden. And the fact was you could get a three-story house and a basement rental for a grand total of $90,000. We sold it a few years later for $180,000, so we made money on it. Carroll Gardens was also a mess then, and so was Boerum Hill, and if you walked into Prospect Park at night, you had a very good chance of getting mugged.

Today prices for brownstones in Park Slope begin at $1.5 million and go much higher. The comment that Park Slope was "not really a dangerous place" followed by "We were robbed several times" over four years reminds us that the 1980s were a time of far lower expectations. A few robberies didn't qualify as "dangerous."

My Hudson Heights informant tells me about the beef longtime locals and new age arrivals have with the Hispanic teenagers who ride their bikes down the steep hill from where Overlook Terrace begins, reaching terrifying speeds estimated at eighty miles per hour. "They're a terror known as the 'bike boys.' This is their sport, and there is a lack of playgrounds. But sometimes they injure street crossers. Werner Gruenebaum was hit and laid up for months. There've been community meetings, with the police coming, but nothing is ever done." Hudson Heights, however, has a large population of low-income Hispanics, and it appears they don't plan to leave the neighborhood anytime soon. In such cases the old-timers and the gentrifiers simply have to get used to the status quo—in this case the "bike boys."

Greenpoint is yet another example of the segmented way change occurs. Most of the stores on Manhattan Avenue and Nassau Street are Polish-owned and operated. But on nearby Franklin Street it's a different story. Franklin has almost no Polish presence, dominated instead by bars, cafés, an English-language bookstore called Word, and newly constructed apartment buildings. As one researcher describes it, "Walking down Manhattan Avenue and up Franklin Street is akin to walking in two separate neighborhoods."[41]

Today's gentrifiers were in many cases preceded by an earlier generation. In a study of the Lower East Side, sociologist Richard Ocejo describes how these pioneers, who often moved there because the rents were cheap, can become upset by later, well-heeled arrivals who introduce elements like bars and clubs that are not in any way representative of what the neighborhood once was. Although the earlier gentrfiers may deny it, they are in many ways similar to the more recent gentrifiers. Yet they are also more likely to know about and be sensitive to what the neighborhood once was.

In this way the earlier gentrifiers are a bridge between the old and the new. Why do they care about the area's "true" character? Because nostalgia and its preservation give people a sense of identity, belonging, and community, all of which help to justify and validate their decision to move there. This quest is frequently shared by the newest residents too, even if they don't care as much about preservation of the local institutions, customs, and "look" of the neighborhood. Moreover, the new gentrifiers are not nearly as likely to relate to the poorer incumbent residents. This is in contrast to, say, the 1970s. In his classic work *Streetwise,* Elijah Anderson cites a resident's description of the newcomers during that era: "People were unpretentious. They would dress in a laid-back way and act down to earth. Such a person could be spotted on the streets as a countercultural person. . . . They would dialogue about anything."[42]

Today's Lower East Side has sleek new apartment buildings, chic restaurants and nightclubs, a Whole Foods store, and much more. One interesting attraction is the Bowery Hotel, a beautifully appointed place with uniformed doormen where rooms go for more than three hundred dollars a night, right around the corner from a shelter for the homeless called Renewal on the Bowery. In the mid-1960s, flophouses on the Bowery charged ten cents a night for a bed in a cubicle. I know because my first sociology project was interviewing derelicts on the Bowery for a study called

"The Homelessness Project." Directed by Columbia sociologist Theodore Caplow, its goal was to better understand the causes and nature of homelessness. My primary assignment was to interview those who previously had refused to talk to interviewers, a daunting but fascinating challenge. History is never completely erased from changing neighborhoods; if you look hard enough you'll find it. One reminder here is the Grand Hotel, a flophouse that's not grand at all and charges only twelve bucks a night for a room.

There are all sorts of signs that foretell and even hasten change in a neighborhood. At the Williamsburg border of Bushwick, one can see notices posted outside a café for French lessons, yoga classes, and new age eateries. At this point 90 percent of the community is Hispanic, and the most frequently displayed sign, actually a billboard, seems to be, "Divorce—99 Dollars," and it's in Spanish.

In Washington/Hudson Heights gentrification is traveling south of 181st Street and west of Broadway, all the way to streets numbered in the lower 160s. How do you know? When you see a young Chinese American woman with two kids walking her dogs, accompanied by a Hispanic-looking man who might be her husband or boyfriend. Then another white guy comes by with his dog and is joined by a black woman and her dog, and they all have a fifteen-minute conversation on 163rd Street and Riverside Drive.[43]

I turn around and walk up a grassy knoll toward the streets, passing a small area with park benches set up against a concrete slab table with black and white squares. Suddenly I recall a day from my teenage years. I am playing chess at precisely this location with a white-haired elderly man and winning. And he is cursing me out for doing so. It is one of the aspects of this voyage that repeats itself over and over. So many of the places I have visited in the last few years bring back childhood memories decades later: Times Square, where I was pick-pocketed when I went there at age fourteen, on New Year's Eve. Fortunately my wallet had nothing in it. Borough Park, Brooklyn, an area I once walked to from Washington Heights, just to see if I could do it. The trip took five hours. And then Coney Island, where my older brother, Mark, rode the Cyclone roller coaster. He had bought two tickets, for two consecutive rides, but the first one so sickened him—I remember his greenish complexion after he stumbled off the car—that he declined a repeat performance. It's a reality; I have a nostalgic bias toward this city that makes this effort deeply personal.

I had a discussion with an Asian medical student who, with his girlfriend, rents a three-bedroom apartment on 162nd Street near Fort Washington Avenue for about twenty-seven hundred dollars a month. This compares with about forty-five hundred dollars a month on Ninetieth Street and Columbus Avenue. He explained that the apartment is lovely because whenever someone moves out, the landlord guts and rehabs the apartment. Everything's brand-new. "It's safe, though I keep my eyes open. There's loud Spanish music at night, but it's not so bad." He says others like him are moving in.

"But the names by the buzzers are mostly Spanish," I say.

"They're old," he responds. "They haven't removed them yet." Thus the area is even more gentrified than appears to be the case.

Quantitative information can also be helpful in determining the degree of change. An analysis of U.S. Census data shows that between 2000 and 2010 the population of non-Hispanic whites increased by about 17 percent along the Grand Concourse in the South Bronx, especially between 153rd and 167th Streets, which is now a historic district. People can buy spacious apartments there for less than three hundred thousand dollars. Crime has dropped sharply in recent years, and the commute to Manhattan is a little more than a half hour. Most of the buyers are savvy New Yorkers looking for a good deal, but some are Europeans unaware of the Bronx's unsavory past—namely, the 1970s and 1980s.[44] Other features are nearby Yankee Stadium, the courthouses, and the Grand Concourse itself. Many people feel safer living on a very wide street with lots of traffic.

Houses of worship also tell a tale. Walk into services and see who's there, or ask reliable informants. Hudson Heights is almost completely gentrified, and that is corroborated by a visit to a formerly dying synagogue, Mount Sinai Congregation, which attracts about four hundred people to its weekly services, most of them young Modern Orthodox singles. They took over the synagogue from the remaining old-timers and are now the major force there.

But there's a catch: these people are often transients. They're not necessarily going to put down roots in the Heights. Most are fresh out of college. They're working at their first job. For the moment, though, they're content to be in an Orthodox community where the rents are lower than they are in the mecca for Orthodox singles, the Upper West Side.[45] Plus, those who leave Hudson Heights might return at a later point.

Can Any Neighborhood Change?

On Shakespeare Avenue in the Morris Heights section of the Bronx, there's a beautiful new residential building dubbed the Shakespeare. It offers a gym, a learning center, and a washing machine and dryer on every floor. The problem is that there's no infrastructure in this community except for convenient transportation. There are no upscale restaurants, boutiques, or cafés, all of them essential to discerning gentrifiers. If you want to understand what gentrification looks like in its embryonic state, go to the Shakespeare's listing at Urban Edge (http://www.urbanedgeny.com/property/shakespeare -apartments-0). There are photos of treadmills, Nautilus weights, and stationary bikes, plus a roof deck with a great skyline view, albeit the Bronx skyline rather than that of Manhattan. Another Shakespeare website proclaims, "A great lifestyle is more attainable than you think." Vision, imagination, and guts will one day pay off, no doubt, but not until there's an infrastructure in the rest of the neighborhood to support it.

The description of the apartments is technically correct. For example, the "effortless commute" means there's great transportation to Manhattan, but you must walk for five to ten minutes through a still-rough-around-the-edges neighborhood to get to the subway on Jerome Avenue. You can also walk across a nearby bridge and be in Washington Heights in twenty minutes. The drive would be a mere three minutes from your building to the FDR Drive. And you can walk to Yankee Stadium in fifteen minutes. All of this was made possible through a cooperative effort by the Atlantic Development Group, the New York City Department of Housing

Preservation and Development, and the New York City Housing Development Corporation.

Most people are totally unaware of nice, inexpensive housing possibilities like the Shakespeare. I took one of my departmental colleagues from the CUNY Graduate Center there for a little tour. She grew up on Shakespeare Avenue right across the street from the Shakespeare, and she could not believe what she saw. "This has changed everything for me. I came here expecting to be totally depressed about what had become of my old neighborhood. Instead, I'm thrilled beyond belief. This is amazing—all these new buildings. And my old elementary school is still there, looking beautiful, just as it was. I can't get over it."

There are also anomalies in non-gentrifying neighborhoods of this sort. Several miles east of the Shakespeare you'll discover Crotona Park, which has a lake, swimming pool, tennis courts, and playing fields. All of these amenities speak to the park's potential. There are poor neighborhoods around Crotona Park, a ten-minute drive away, and the park used to be a notoriously dangerous place. On the other hand, unknown to most people, high-level tennis matches featuring players from all over the world are sometimes played at the park in August, and the seating opportunities are great, owing to the remote location. A fair number of these players compete in the U.S. Open, and you can watch them play at Crotona Park for a fraction of the price—that is, for free. During the week in the late afternoon, high school students from some of the exclusive private schools of the Upper East Side play their tennis matches in the park. You go where there's room to play. Nearby are the Bronx Botanical Gardens and the world-famous Bronx Zoo. And five minutes from Crotona Park is the Arthur Avenue Italian shopping and dining area, totally safe and gentrified. In sum, the area has real potential, though again, it's a ways off.

Now let's turn our attention to Hunters Point in Queens. The neighborhood runs along the East River, next to Long Island City, and it's not one-tenth as dangerous as the Bronx. There are gleaming new high-rise condos and co-ops, either for rent or sale, depending on what the market will bear, from about Forty-seventh to Fiftieth Avenues. Aside from the 1996 CityLights Building, these high-rises were built in the mid-2000s, and more are going up to join the five already there. They sport magnificent views of the eastern Manhattan Midtown skyline. In the spring of 2009 you could have rented a two-bedroom apartment with a nice river view for three thousand dollars a month or even less, compared to four thousand dollars for the same on the Upper East Side, a difference of about 25 percent. Another difference is that you can't get the same panoramic view of Manhattan living in Manhattan as you can in Hunters Point. And it's one stop away from Times Square on the 7 line. Amenities in these buildings typically include an indoor, sky-lit, glass-enclosed, heated pool; a gym; a spacious fitness center with saunas, steam rooms, dressing rooms, and showers; activities ranging from card games to bocci, to yoga classes; and a tennis bubble nearby.

Sitting on a bench one cloudless, sun-drenched afternoon, gazing at the UN Building across the water and the Fifty-ninth Street Bridge, I find myself wondering why more people don't live in Hunters Point. Do they simply not know about it? Are they Queens-phobic? Or is this just the dawn of the soon-to-come eastward migration? Certainly the amenities are already here. Restaurants, coffeehouses, and boutiques have sprouted along Vernon Avenue like the blossoms on the trees that line the nearby shore. A gleaming, spotless Whole Foods supermarket, serving gourmet foods as well as oven-fresh pizza, heightens the appeal. A large Duane Reade pharmacy is next door too. Indeed, demographically, the area seems to be attracting mostly families and young couples just starting out, and the stores' customers reflect that. Perhaps 75 percent of the high-rise population falls into this category.

There are also numerous new and smaller six- or seven-story buildings that lack the amenities of their more glamorous, taller counterparts, but their lower asking prices attract those looking for a cheaper and roomier alternative to a Manhattan studio apartment on a noisy street in the East Village or in Hell's Kitchen on the Far West Side. These share the street with salt-box-shaped three-story clapboard houses, with their peeling paint suggesting that less-than-affluent residents live within them. There are also numerous tiny, two-story, yellow-brick, semi-attached houses that appear to be more than one hundred years old.[46] Can Hunters

Point become a Cobble Hill, Dumbo, or Chelsea? It may not have enough to offer. But it can certainly be a community that's a big notch below them yet still quite attractive.

To discover dramatic change one need go no farther than Harlem's Bradhurst Avenue, now called W.E.B. DuBois Avenue, which extends from 145th Street to the Polo Grounds projects by 155th Street. Until the mid-1990s Bradhurst Avenue was one of Harlem's most notorious locations for drug dealing and crime in general. Jackie Robinson Park, which runs along the avenue, was considered unsafe at any time of day or night. Today it's a new world. On the corner of 145th and Bradhurst you have the luxury condominium called the Langston, after Langston Hughes. This is followed by the Sutton, named for the Harlem political leader and former Manhattan borough president Percy Sutton. (See figure 26.) Next to it sits the Ellington, in memory of jazz icon Duke Ellington. You can now walk the length of Bradhurst Avenue in complete safety, even at night, though somewhat less so because of the projects at the north end, whose residents must look upon the street with envy—so close, yet so far away in terms of what they can afford.

Here are the words of Don, a maintenance worker at one of these buildings. Balding and dressed in a red-and-gray-checked flannel shirt, with owlish gold-rimmed glasses, he greeted me with a firm handshake. I had found him in the boiler room after someone in the building told me that he was the "neighborhood expert." When I told him I was trying to understand the Bradhurst area now as compared to the past, he stared at me intently, like a man with something on his mind. He's a bouncy sort of guy, and he frequently punctuated his responses by jumping off the bench where he was sitting and describing, with windmill-like motions, how things had changed over time. I soon learned graphically what Bradhurst used to be like in the "bad old days."

> Let me tell you somethin'. These apartments are worth $100,000. But if I gotta pay $100,000 to live somewhere, I wanna be where there's grass around me. These are just glorified tenements. You still gotta fix the leaks in the bathroom and the stove when it breaks. Any apartment where I can hear somebody burpin' next door is not an apartment that *I* want. Actually, these apartments go from

$300,000 to more than $400,000. They got condos and co-ops. They got all sorts of stuff here. One time, dammit, in June of 2010, they told me there's maggots here; you know, they feed on human flesh. I went to look at them and there must have been a half million maggots comin' up out of the ground, through cracks in the sidewalk. I don't know where the fuck they came from. When they came here to build and knocked down them old buildings—I swear to you I am not exaggeratin'—they knocked some of these walls down in the tenements here, and they discovered bodies in the walls. People had been buried here for years.

And some of them was there because of Preacher [Clarence Heatly], the drug dealer, who ran this place. He'd say, 'I like this car,' and you'd have to give it to him. If not, you could end up dead. That was when crack was big. Then he went upstate. He died there, killed by a prisoner. Can you imagine? What a way to go. He controlled this state. All the drug dealers were afraid of him. He'd say, 'Give me money.' They'd have to give him money."

"So how did crack die here?" I ask.

"People just got tired of the crack. The crack epidemic started in Los Angeles in South Central and it came back east. That started all the wars. So many people got strung out. And then they just got tired of being drugged out and not havin' any money."

"Is Harlem becoming more white?"

White? I call this area above 145th Street West Village! You got white people, yuppies moving in here. All the prejudiced people, they died out. These yuppies don't give a shit. They just wanna get to their jobs. People get tired of having to have two-fare zones and everythin' else. Nobody wants that shit. So that's how the neighborhood completely changed. This is now a very interestin' neighborhood. And it's a lot safer now than it was before. Actually, in the early seventies Bradhurst was a very nice area. Then came the crack epidemic and it all changed. Now it's back to where it was before.

Gentrification is even more apparent when it is not news, and never more so than when it is *in* the news, but not *news itself.* This is what I took away from a December 21, 2010, *New York Times* article about New York City doormen and the range of tips they received from Manhattanites. Vignettes were presented about six buildings, the amounts they received, mostly in the one-hundred- to two-hundred-dollar range, and some weird gifts like a collection of expensive cufflinks, a 1991 burgundy Honda Accord, and a velvet smoking jacket. And there, among all these posh addresses, was the Langston! It was described simply as "a 186-unit condo in Harlem with four doormen." What's more, the *only* photo accompanying the article was that of doorman James Greene, standing in front of the very same Langston, his gloved hand resting on the very same Honda Accord.[47] The casual yet prominent description of the building speaks volumes about how far gentrification has come in Harlem. It's just like all the other doorman-staffed buildings in New York City. And you can't call the newspaper article an indirect sales pitch, because the street location for the Langston isn't even given.

Emblematic of the changes that have taken place over time is the Starbucks at 145th Street and Bradhurst. Even the older buildings on Bradhurst are gentrifying. What's interesting is that one block away from the still unsafe Polo Grounds projects, white people are walking their dogs. They're not afraid. Rucker Park, a world-famous basketball venue, is across the street from the projects. They have exhibitions here, and many NBA players have played in the park.

"Is this a safe area?" I ask a graduate student at CUNY who lives in a five-story walk-up on Bradhurst one block away. She's from Slovenia, has a trace of an accent, but has lived in the United States for many years. Her apartment was renovated when she moved into this older five-story building. She walks around the area at night and is not fearful.

"Who cares?" she says with bravado. "I can't worry about that. Nothing has happened to me yet, and it's what I can afford. So I take my chances."

Areas Resistant to Change

The areas that have experienced the least gentrification in New York City are East New York, Brownsville, and various parts of the West and South Bronx. In a *New York Times* article about

Brownsville titled "Where Optimism Seems Out of Reach," Ginia Bellafante writes how the murder rate there has not fallen at all since 1998. And the infant mortality rate is the highest in the city, about the same as that of Malaysia.[48] Decades of neglect, lack of private investment, distance from the city center, and large numbers of low-income people have all contributed to this unfortunate state of affairs. There are, and always will be, adventurous souls willing to take a chance on an area and build there, but if it happens in Brownsville, it is likely to be a long and difficult road.

I walk toward Roberto Clemente State Park in the Morris Heights section. The park sits on the Harlem River, just to the right of River Park Towers. It's deserted and doesn't look like much, but there is a police car parked nearby. I ask a white officer about safety in the neighborhood, and he comes back with, "Why do you wanna know?"

"Because my kids may be moving back from Los Angeles and I'm trying to find a cheap apartment for them. I realize the Bronx isn't Long Island, but still. . . . " I leave the question hanging.

"Well, there's a lot of crime," he says. "Listen, this is a really high crime area. And the warmer it gets outside, the more crime activity you have. I'm sure there's other places you could find. Last night there was a car outside. They just took it. A guy got stabbed up the street too. You see this cherry picker? My partner's up there right now. They only put these things in bad areas, and it's broad daylight right now. I'd go Hoboken, over in Jersey, or Long Island."

He clearly thinks it's ludicrous for someone to want to move here when there are nice, peaceful suburbs beckoning. He has not considered issues like commuting and the very idea of living in the city, not to mention the fact that to gentrifiers New York's suburbs are often viewed as dull places.

I decide to test his dour assessment and talk to a black superintendent about renting an apartment a block away in a building on Sedgwick Avenue. The building has twenty-four-hour security and market-rate apartments available for about twelve hundred dollars a month for a one-bedroom. It looks good—a decent, tall, redbrick structure about fifteen stories high facing the Harlem

River. It's a two-minute drive from Upper Manhattan, with public transportation nearby.

Giving me a quick once-over, the super says, "It's all right, but for a guy of your ethnicity, I don't know."

I inquire about a building across the road. "What about this big building across the street from you, River Park Towers?"

He smiles. "I call that Vietnam. It looks fancy, but it's Vietnam. It used to be good, but over the years they let everything, every *thing* in there. And now you could get killed in there." True enough, but his own building is only relatively safe, considering its location.

Can gentrification ever happen here in an area where more than one-third of residents lived below the poverty line in 2000? New housing construction for those whose income restrictions make them eligible, improved public schools, and a $20 million renovation of Roberto Clemente State Park offer some hope. The pattern is one that is being repeated elsewhere. Real estate agents in East and Northern Harlem, places like Beacon Mews on 139th Street, east of Malcolm X Boulevard, direct their appeals to potential buyers priced out of Harlem's better areas. Realtors in Fort Greene look to people unable to afford Prospect Heights, while those in Bed-Stuy seek to attract buyers unable to get what they want in Fort Greene. And real estate agents in the Bronx hope that people looking for homes in Washington Heights will consider other communities, perhaps even the long-established middle-income Executive Towers over on the Grand Concourse.

Will a community that is minutes away from Manhattan by car but separated by the Harlem River and in another borough be seen as geographically off-limits in a way that cannot be overcome? Or will people say, "The hell with it. Let's take the plunge," once they see the price and what they'll get for it? Are the few urban pioneers who've already taken that plunge in places like the brand-new Shakespeare and other new buildings just the first wave? And when will the rest of the gentrifiers come, creating the shopping, restaurants, and coffeehouses that will really transform the area? The people will decide.

The Role of Government in Change

Throughout the poorer parts of the city—South Bronx, East New York, Corona, Queens—are buildings ranging from two to as many as fifteen or so stories funded by government money. They are generally rented and sometimes purchased by working- or lower middle-class people whose limited incomes qualify them for generous mortgages at low interest rates.[49] In some cases they are existing renovated structures. These are not gentrifiers, but indigenous residents who are simply improving their situation. However, they can stimulate gentrification by outsiders because their homes are new and attractive-looking and because their inhabitants take pride in their homes and maintain them. As a result, the look of the entire neighborhood changes.[50]

Section 8 programs distribute vouchers that help low-income families across the country pay rent and utilities. The governmental agencies pay a "fair market rent" (FMR), which may not relate to the true market rents in an area; the tenant pays 30 percent of his or her income, and the Section 8 program pays the difference between the tenant contribution and the rent, capped at the FMR. Since 2008 in apartments where landlords participate in the program, those who pay less can live in the same building as full payers. They have the same amenities, nice views, and appliances. Depending on their financial situation, they could end up paying only 25 percent of what market-rate people pay. Does this make the full payers reluctant to move into such buildings? Are they jealous, and do they show it? And just how do these two groups interact with each other on a daily and long-term basis? Some interesting research could be done on these questions, to say the least. Anecdotally, the difference in rents doesn't seem to be a major problem, according to the thirty or so people I asked. And are there crime issues? With regard to that question, remember that low earners must meet strict credit requirements, supply references, and agree to home visits. Plus, they don't want to lose these good apartments.[51]

One good example of how these government programs are intertwined with gentrification is the Atlantic Yards development

project in downtown Brooklyn, designed by famed architect
Frank Gehry, and under construction by developer Bruce Ratner.
Bloomberg approved the project, and it has accelerated gentrification in the surrounding areas. The yards are owned by the New
York Metropolitan Transportation Authority, but the developer
can also take nearby properties by the laws of eminent domain.
There's a brand-new sports arena for the Brooklyn Nets, and plans
are under way to develop 4.5 million square feet of office space.
To overcome community opposition, Ratner consented to what's
known as a Community Benefit Agreement in which he agreed to
give the community various housing benefits.

Future plans for the Atlantic Yards project call for fourteen residential towers with 6,430 apartments plus two commercial buildings. Some will be completed in the next few years, but the whole
project may take twenty years to finish. Not surprisingly, there has
been a flood of boutiques, upscale eateries, and the like, opening
at the rate of one a week on Flatbush Avenue. As usual, we know
who's moving in but very little about who's leaving.[52]

Since its creation in 1965, the New York City Landmarks Preservation Commission (LPC) has landmarked thousands of buildings.
Owners of buildings who seek such a designation must provide
documentation to legitimate the claim that the building deserves
such status. You need a special permit to make exterior renova-
tions, and demolition is restricted as well. The effect of being des-
ignated a city landmark is often to drive out the poor, because they
can't afford to restore it but are also not allowed to destroy and
replace it with a new building. Most applications are approved. A
lesser but still important designation is for a building or area of a
building to be placed on the National Register of Historic Places.

The LPC also approves the designation of historic districts
within the city, whether it's the Upper East Side or the Longwood
District in the Bronx.[53] The commission has approved at least two
hundred historic districts in the last decade, and probably many
more will be approved by the time this book is published. The
movement to restore and preserve in recent years has perhaps
been as strong as the trend toward development and construction. These designations can affect gentrifiers in either direction

depending on their opinions about these matters. Some want to live in historic districts for the cachet and because they believe in historical preservation. Others don't care and are hungry for available space even if it means knocking down the old.

An important question is how to decide when a building is worth preserving. How do we determine what's beautiful—a low-rise building that's part of St. Vincent's Hospital, which is seen as an example of 1950s Modernism? Usually it's experts who make these decisions. No matter how one feels, the buildings, parks, and streets of New York City embody its history, culture, and values as expressed by all of those who came before us and created them. You can't discard these places without at least evaluating their importance. That's what was behind the creation of the LPC. History in New York City is as important as it is in London or Paris, or at least it should be.

Universities and Change

Universities can be, and sometimes are, change agents in the gentrification process. Students attending universities welcome the chance to live in reasonably priced dwellings near their campuses and are therefore willing to take chances regarding safety. While most of these students successfully avoid being victims of crime, some are mugged and occasionally seriously injured or even killed, though the latter is rare. The risk is particularly problematic when it's a private university that has a more affluent student population unfamiliar with an urban and unsafe environment.

Nevertheless, schools like Columbia, NYU, Pratt, and Fordham push on despite frequent community opposition, taking over and renovating buildings for both campus housing and apartments. One benefit is that by increasing the number of students in the area, it becomes safer for everyone. Some schools employ shuttle buses and post security guards on streets considered dangerous.[54] Columbia is near some unsafe low-income projects in West Harlem, NYU's area is basically safe, and Pratt and Fordham's Bronx campus are fairly safe. Regardless, the presence of these universities in the community does enhance the gentrification process. The same is true, of course, of hospitals in the city when their employees elect to live near work despite the risks involved.

The newest addition to this pattern is the City University of New York, which has built an apartment building in already gentrifying East Harlem for graduate students and faculty at 165 East 118th Street near Third Avenue, which opened in the fall of 2011. Though some criminal incidents have been reported in the area, the residence is highly popular, and why not? Rents range from two thousand dollars a month for a one-bedroom to twenty-seven hundred dollars for a two-bedroom with a terrace. Amenities include a doorman, fitness center, and a rooftop garden. The apartments were fully occupied soon after the place opened.

For the most part, crime around the CUNY residence hasn't been a problem, but there are some issues. For example, there had been drug dealing across the street before it was built, and it took a concerted effort by Victor, the building's streetwise and feisty Hispanic superintendent, to drive the dealers away. With his frequent calls to the local police precinct, he's a latter-day example of Jane Jacobs's "eyes on the street." But Victor also spoke hopefully of the cameras with a zoom function that are being installed in his building. "You would be able to see Park Avenue [two blocks away] from here!" he boasts. The widespread use and acceptance of cameras, of course, is something that Jacobs did not anticipate.

The imagery embodied in the moniker for Myrtle Avenue during the 1980s, "Murder Avenue," lives on for those in the know. Yet an article in the *New York Times* on February 15, 2011, by Fred Bernstein, told about an eleven-year effort to revitalize the area. It began with the formation of the Myrtle Avenue Revitalization Project, headed by Thomas F. Schutte, president of Pratt Institute. He had a real stake in the project, because Myrtle Avenue was the closest shopping area to the campus. Its initial efforts included sweeping streets, removing graffiti, and finding retailers to take over empty space. And in January 2011 Pratt opened the doors to Myrtle Hall, a $54 million, six-story building containing offices, classrooms, and galleries.

Arrangements of this sort often require the involvement of other parties, and this project was no exception. The owner of the property, real estate developer Michael Orbach, had no desire to sell it to Pratt, but he and Schutte became acquainted and an unusual deal was struck. Orbach would control the first floor and basement as retail space, and Pratt would control the building's upper floors. This highlights the reality that gentrification works best when different parties partner, which requires that everyone's interests be served.

Opposition to Gentrification

Black opposition to whites moving into areas like Bed-Stuy and Fort Greene is unusual, though this attitude may partly be due to the fact that despite gentrification these two neighborhoods have so far remained mostly black. When such resistance is expressed, it frequently has to do with differences in lifestyle, cultural and class issues, or an increase in harassment because of a greater police presence, like not being able to drink alcohol in public. Architecture professor Lance Freeman argues that creating mixed-income communities in inner-city gentrifying neighborhoods might be easier than in the suburbs, because those who move into gentrifying areas are generally more liberal and hence more receptive to subsidized housing for the poor than are suburban residents. Otherwise they wouldn't have been willing to move in the first place.[55] But if it becomes too "mixed," then gentrifiers might not find where they live so attractive. Notwithstanding their presumed greater tolerance for the poor than suburbanites, research, as yet not done, might reveal that the real dream of many of these gentrifiers is that the poor will leave.

In her witty and, at times, scathing novel of the mores of life in Park Slope, Amy Sohn describes some of the criteria and prejudices of those living there. They reveal that tolerance has its limits.

> Karen had read in *New York* magazine that houses in the [P.S.] 321 zone cost an average of $100,000 more than similarly sized apartments in 107 but felt that was a small price to pay if it meant your kid went to a school that was 62 percent white instead of only

43. . . . The apartment was not only on a name street, which meant the northernmost, priciest area of Park Slope, but a park block. Better, it was in short walking distance of the Prospect Park Food Coop. . . . The North Slope was also closer to the central branch of the Brooklyn Public Library and the Montauk Club, where Karen already schlepped twice a week for her Weight Watchers meetings.[56]

As a Brooklyn resident and a *New York* magazine columnist, Sohn knows what she's talking about. Because the book uses real place-names and streets, it is a valuable document for the researcher. Her comments can be taken in several ways. Is Karen expressing racism in her comments about the school, or simply a desire to be in a better academic environment? Perhaps a little of each? Is she interested only in status, or is it real estate resale value that she's concerned with when she explains why she wants to live on a name street? It's obvious that for many people a good library plays a role in their purchase decision, but it's not so clear that being near a weight-loss location matters enough to mention, unless, of course, you're very concerned about your weight. Regardless, Sohn's book is quite accurate in many respects. No one would disagree with her up-to-date anthropological description of the streets, as in the following: "Down on Fourth Avenue, a gritty strip of tire repair shops, gas stations, and glass cutters, new modernist buildings, featuring million-dollar lofts, were going up each day."[57]

On occasion, opposition to gentrifiers can make for strange bedfellows. Crown Heights has seen a 15 percent increase in the white population over the past fifteen years. The Hasidic Jews don't like the lifestyles of some of the incoming whites, especially what they see as immodest dress, and the black community is worried about being priced out of the neighborhood. When some real estate agents tried to rebrand the neighborhood by renaming it ProCro (combining Prospect Heights and Crown Heights), Assemblyman Hakim Jeffries was vocal in his opposition to what he saw as catering to the gentrifiers, saying, "I was offended. The collective efforts of the black and Jewish neighbors are what made Crown Heights the destination and the attractive neighborhood it is today."[58]

I asked former mayor Dinkins about the Crown Heights riots that occurred during his tenure and rocked both the Jewish and black communities. His response revealed how much the events still bother him, a man who frequently describes New York City as a "gorgeous mosaic."

> It was very unfortunate, a tragedy. But I feel the police were not fully prepared for that. I used to say the New York City Police Department is the best in the world at controlling riot situations, but they should have done a better job. What really annoyed me was that I had been a friend of the Jewish community and Israel for many years. When Ronald Reagan went to Bitburg to honor the German war dead, I went with the American Jewish Congress to Munich and was one of a very few privileged to speak at the grave site of the White Rose organization—young Germans who were executed simply for handing out leaflets against the Nazis. But those who chose to do so chose to forget all that. They also neglected to consider that, following the Rodney King verdict in 1992, there were riots all over the country but not in New York. You'll find maybe three or four people who will remember that. We had something called Increase the Peace Corps. They were volunteers who took to the streets and it worked.

An unintentional consequence of gentrification is that the new urban pioneers make those who are there already—that is, blacks—in communities like Crown Heights or Harlem, more aware of what they might lose in this process and prouder of what they do have: brownstones, parks, stores, and the by now indigenous culture. This can also lead people to strengthen their own group identity and attachment to a community they have long taken for granted.

This phenomenon is an ironic downside to gentrification. People in poor neighborhoods fight to bring down the crime rate. Then, as a result of the lower crime rate, gentrifiers move in, rents go up, and the poor may then be displaced by those with greater wealth. The organizers of these efforts can end up feeling guilty about having caused their own local allies and friends to be replaced.[59]

Relating to New Neighbors

How well do the gentrifiers get along with those whom they meet in their new communities? Can the cultural and class differences be bridged? The answers to these questions appear to be mixed. Gentrifying neighborhoods provide venues, or spaces, if you will, where people can meet. One example is the Red Room Lounge at 181st Street and Bennett Avenue in Hudson Heights, which offers open mike nights. You'll have a singer-songwriter from Tennessee, Nick Swan, playing on the same program as a local rapper, Chunk Rodríguez. And there'll be poetry and hip-hop on the same night.[60] The neighborhood—once heavily German Jewish, mostly Orthodox; Greek; Cuban; and Irish—became heavily Dominican and now attracts increasing numbers of yuppies, penurious assistant professors and teachers, as well as hopeful actors and screenwriters. Some people think the higher rents and a corresponding lack of development have created friction between the poorer, mostly Hispanic locals and whites, who are driving prices upward. Bringing people together through music, drinks, and food is one way of relieving the tensions.

The pattern appears elsewhere too, in places like Paradise Alley in Flushing, where Koreans occasionally stop by for a drink, and at the Blarney Bar in Jamaica, Queens. Speaking of his changed clientele, a mélange of blacks and Ecuadorians, the owner of the Blarney Bar, Peter O'Hanlon, says, "If an Irishman comes in now, we treat them with kid gloves because we don't see them very often." But, regardless, he notes, "As long as a man comes in and sits down and acts like a gentleman, I don't care where he comes from."[61]

Speaking with an African American in his forties who lives on Macon Street in Bed-Stuy, I heard this positive assessment of the gentrifiers:

> Gentrification *is* the issue. I was born in this house and have lived here my whole life. I'm an art collector. We went through the bad sixties, the riots, and then we realized by the eighties that we can't let this neighborhood get run down, and we have to get involved. So

we did. If you look at me you can see that even though one of my parents was white, I look black and that's how I identify. But I don't care about color. Beneath we're all human beings and we have to live together. I'm happy that whites are moving in. I have German tenants across the street and they're fine.

Thus we see that self-interest is a factor in people's attitudes about gentrifiers. The Bed-Stuy resident pragmatically believes that not being friendly is counterproductive and that "we have to live together." Similarly, a sports area in Hunters Point for handball and basketball has Hispanic, black, and Asian kids and yuppies playing together. They too spoke of a need to "get along." The youths attend Information Technology High School. In New York City disparate groups often have to share space.

Some people, however, are not so charitable in their evaluations of gentrification, displaying negative views that seem based on both perceived and real class differences. A longtime Hispanic resident of Park Slope who works as a teacher's aide in nearby Sunset Park expresses her feelings about the yuppies in her neighborhood: "They even complain that the birds make too much noise. They don't want Whole Foods to come in, because they buy everything from farmers. And they want to ban cars in all of Park Slope. They should go back to the Midwest, or wherever they came from. You know how I know this? I go on the Park Slope blog." Is she stereotyping? Quite possibly, since she acknowledges having no friends from this group. Clearly, outreach by community leaders could be helpful in such cases.

There appears to be a feeling, even by people who are middle and working class, that the gentrifier types look down on them. In explaining why she moved to Parkchester, a middle-class community in the Bronx, Evelyn Liston, a consultant to musical composers and organizations, put it as follows: "It [Parkchester] was a green oasis and the people were so nice. They're not yuppies or whatever. They're just really good people with solid income who want to invest and have a nice place to live."[62]

On the south side of Williamsburg I discover a development, Schaefer Landing, in which both Hasidim and gentrifiers reside. I wonder to myself how the two groups get along. A young, German-born resident explains it to me: "They allocated a percentage for the poor—namely, Hasids—in order to get the tax breaks. But the Hasids only use the street entrance on Kent Avenue, whereas the yuppies get the back with the river views, and so they're really segregated." He likes the arrangement because, as he put it, "I don't like or dislike these people. I just don't have anything in common with them." I ask an Orthodox Jewish resident about this set-up and he confirms this, telling me that the Hasidim live on all the floors on the Kent Avenue side.

"How do they deal with the Sabbath restriction against using an elevator if they live above, say, the ninth floor?" I ask.

"They walk," he responds. "The men take the stairs. They could use the exercise. And the women don't go to *shul* [synagogue] on Shabbos, so they stay upstairs, eat, take care of the kids, and visit each other. And during the week there's an area where they can walk to the water and the children can play in the grass."

This is an example of side-by-side gentrification. The Hasidim and the gentrifiers live adjacent to each other but have almost no contact. Members of both groups told me they prefer it that way. In the nearby Roberto Clemente projects, Hasidim and Hispanics have been living in the same buildings for many years with little or no friction, although they interact very little beyond saying hello. And in most Section 8 buildings in the city, the norm is for the poor and the well-off to live together in the same building.

Sometimes getting along doesn't have to do with the group to which you belong, but with your own persona. The following conversation with a college student who lives in Washington Heights in the low 150s below Broadway was quite revealing in many respects. He has longish, dark brown hair and is wearing blue-tinted sunglasses even though it's a cloudy day.

"About twenty percent of the people on my block are white. You can tell which block is like that because the supers spend more time on the streets hosing down the area in front of the building. I live in a basement apartment. When I was scouting out this area for livability, I saw this nice wine store and wondered how they can make any money in this part of town. But when you see it and who's coming in to buy, you realize the neighborhood is changing. I moved here from Ninety-third and Amsterdam because it's cheaper. The rent here is fifteen hundred dollars a month for three bedrooms. On Ninety-third it would be about forty-five hundred."

"Do you have contact with the Dominicans here? Can you develop relationships with the people here?"

"I'd say yeah, in my case anyway, because I smoke pot and so do the young locals here. Sometimes I even buy it from them. You kid around with them and they hang around with you. In general you don't associate with people like these in the area. But I'm different from my friends. I'll go out and look for it. They don't have the guts to do it."

"Is it safe when you come home at night?"

"For me, yes."

"And for whom would it not be safe?"

"Those who aren't cool. I had a friend who walked around here safely because he did the 'I'm a cop' routine. But you have to be careful with that, because you're on their block. It's *always* their block."

"Is the place gentrifying?"

"Slowly, and a lot of the white people are poor. Or they're students."

What I learned from this exchange is, first, that blocks that have more gentrifiers get better attention, as in the super hosing down the sidewalk. Second, that the wine store was a sign for this student indicating that there were others here like him. Third, that the rent differential for him is huge—one-third the price of the Upper West Side—and it helps if you live in a basement apartment. Fourth, that pot is an ice-breaker, especially if you're a customer. Fifth, that there's variation within the same category—students— namely, that some are shy, even afraid to do this. Finally, that walking around is safer if you have a relationship with the locals. In sum, you can't generalize; there are lots of factors that determine the social relationships that develop in these communities.

For comparative purposes, look at the following account of living in the same area by a married man named Jim with a young son who resides a bit farther down from the college student, on

136th Street between Broadway and Amsterdam Avenue, and who hails from upstate New York. I catch him as he's entering his three-year-old apartment building around 7:00 PM. With his charcoal gray suit, matching tie, and leather briefcase, he looks like a typical executive, which, in fact, he is. He's "white-bread," but his wife is Puerto Rican.

"Everyone's friendly. They're not my buddies, but they all know me." Jim feels comfortable in the neighborhood, but only up to a point.

"Would you send your kid to the local public school?" I ask.

"Hell, no!" he exclaims. "When we get to that point we'll look around for a private school. You have to remember that Columbia has bought a lot of stuff around here on the basis of its rights to eminent domain. So the whole area's going to improve, and I can't imagine we won't have options."

And maybe, given that the IRT subway is only two blocks away and that new age restaurants are springing up in the vicinity, it's likely that Jim will have options. I also notice in my walks that quite a few whites, mostly students, already live in the old tenements. And on the blocks between Broadway and Riverside Drive, like 138th Street, there are many decent brownstones with whites living there too.

"But how did you feel," I persist, "about living here where you're in the only new apartment building on the block, as, say, compared to Brooklyn Heights?"

"Things are very different now. Today people live all over. And don't forget, I couldn't get this type of place for this price in the other areas."

Like it or not, Jim's comments suggest he would live elsewhere if he could, but he can't get what he wants there. Today, as opposed to fifteen years ago, these rough areas are a real option, made possible by reduced crime rates and an acceptance of the presence of professionals by the locals. And yet that's still not true everywhere. In many parts of the Central and South Bronx, for instance, you can still walk miles without seeing a white face.

Jim is a perfect example of a practical gentrifier. He wouldn't consider living here if he had more money. Unlike the student I spoke with, he's not interested in becoming friends with the locals. They're not his type and he knows it.[63] Obviously the kids on the block are not going to be the after-school playmates of choice, if at all. Jim just wants to be superficially friendly so that he can get along with his neighbors. Maybe his Spanish-speaking wife helps with the language barrier too. Let's keep in mind that because of his status as a responsible family man, he can't play the pot-smoking student who's cool. He justifies his decision by making himself part of a larger body of like-minded souls. "Today people live all over," Jim opines. Because of nearby Columbia University, the subway, and the eateries, he thinks he might be coming in on the bottom floor of a new community of gentrifiers that will grow. Parenthetically, one of the things that gentrifiers must get used to is that at night the teenagers, and the men, hang out. The Dominicans here have a loud street culture. They may even make remarks, but it's not taken seriously by those in the know. They're just acting out and you have to get used to it.

Here's a third situation involving a different sort of person. He's actually not a gentrifier, but he's part of the scene because he's one of those who were left behind, and they're all over the city living with gentrifiers, immigrants, and just regular folks. The community is South Ozone Park, and it's predominantly Guyanese these days, but it was once white and Catholic. Near 133rd Avenue, standing outside his immaculate split-level home, with a large American flag proudly flying in the yard, I meet John, a brown-eyed, stocky white man with close-cropped hair, sporting a dark gray North Face sweatshirt and holding a straw broom in his hand. He is wearing a cap that says, "Duck-Hunting," though I learn later that although he owns a rifle, he does not hunt.

"Your place looks beautiful and everything's swept clean," I say.

"Always, always."

"What kind of style is that gleaming silver railing?"

"That's stainless steel. The main ones who do it are the Chinese. They have the market for it. Just type in 'stainless steel.'"[64]

"Is this is a safe neighborhood?"

"Safe? It's safer than it ever was. I'm here fifty-three years. I was born here. It went through its times. It was once Irish, Italian.

There was robberies later on. Now it's mostly Indians from Guyana. They're building mansions all over. I mean, there are still some whites here—my friends, Lenny and Larry. But nobody bothers nobody here."

"But can you be friends with the Guyanese? I mean, do you have enough in common with them?"

"Yeah, they're all workin' people here."

"You have 'em over to your house for a beer?"

"Naw, I don't get too friendly with anybody like that. More 'Hi.'"

"How do you feel about all the people moving away?"

"What am I gonna do? I mean the houses' value went up."

"How come you didn't sell?"

"Because I'm still working for Con Ed. I got thirty-five years. I got two more years and then I go up to Greene County, upstate. I got twenty-five acres. Nice house.

"You got a nice flag."

"That's the only flag I fly. [This may be an indirect reference to the Hindu prayer flags found in many yards here.] Here's where you're good, not near Rockaway Boulevard," he adds.

"What about Ozone Park?"

"Ozone Park. Yeah. At one time it was all mob. From here on to Aqueduct Racetrack it's all white. Check out the house around the corner. It's got stained-glass windows, brand-new, huge camera, sculptured bushes, digital signs. They're Indians. Beautiful."

John's a holdover with one foot out the door. He claims that it's possible to be friends with the Guyanese, but his definition of friendship is a bit narrow. He will not have them over for a beer, stating plainly, "I don't get friendly with anybody like that." He's clearly not into diversity, and the comfort level of sameness just isn't there. But he does appreciate the way his Guyanese neighbors have done their houses up. I also ponder, briefly, how he perceives me. In an earlier time in the area's history, when it was mostly white, he might not have spoken so freely. I would be an outsider, despite my white skin. Today, however, with so few whites left, I'm in *his* group, even though he's just met me.

But such limited interactions with others are not always the case. There are those who sometimes seize the opportunities for social interaction that this metropolis provides. Take the surprising case of David, an Orthodox Jew who lives in Holliswood, Queens, and whose wife follows the tradition of covering her hair. His upstairs neighbors are a lesbian couple, hardly an approved-of lifestyle among the Orthodox. Yet David and his wife are good friends with the couple and trust them enough to use them as regular babysitters for their children. In fact, the lesbians even take the kids to their own summer home for mini-vacations and on one occasion told the mother, "We love your kids as much as you do, if not more." The degree of trust David and his wife have in their neighbors is quite amazing, considering the different values of the two communities.

One final case demonstrates that within groups class can trump race. A middle-class, stylishly dressed black woman in Bed-Stuy who owns a home and business in the community related her tale of woe to me. "I've been here many years and we made strenuous efforts to keep it in the community, so to speak. I bought up the block on Lewis Avenue around the corner, and we rented out space to restaurants, bookstores, and other upscale places. One condition was that they [the business owners] had to live within walking distance of their place of business. That way it would be run by people from the community." This is the kind of thing black gentrifiers are sensitive to.

"Now we're involved with efforts to get permission for a wine bar on Nostrand Avenue," she continued. "And we're facing opposition from the old-timers, who say, 'We don't want it. We worked so hard to get these winos out of the area and you want to bring them back in.' "

"But isn't a wine bar different from a liquor store?" I ask. "Can't they see what you've done here?"

"They can and we told them the young people need a place to hang out in, but they're the old-timers and we're the new people. They see us as more successful, more educated, and different. When I first applied for permission to build a place here, they said to me, 'Who are your parents?' meaning, 'you're not one of us.' You see, it's a class thing, not a race thing."

"What if you patronized some of the old corner stores?"

Her voice rises an octave as she glares at the very thought of it. "I'm not going into some place with a bullet-proof window and some little holes to talk through or a joint that serves food but isn't clean!"

I suggest ways of making the old-timers feel included, of talking to the ministers of the churches they attend and making donations. She agrees but isn't too hopeful. This struggle develops along class lines and is going on elsewhere in the city too, wherever areas are gentrifying. The point is that it has almost nothing to do with race and points to why even cultural similarities and a common history do not always mean a lot.[65]

After four years of walking the neighborhoods of New York and conversing with many people, as well as from personal observation, I've concluded that most gentrifiers do not really mix with the natives, often preferring people who, like them, are new to an area instead. And why not? After all, they have more in common with other gentrifiers. The truth is that authenticity, eating in local ethnic restaurants, and having conversations with people whose origins, values, and lifestyles are quite different from their own can be fun. But these places are often more something they want to dabble in or experience, not a community they wish to permanently join. In the end they're too comfortable in their own skin. That's why they are who they are. What this means is that they are *in* the neighborhood but not *of* the neighborhood, even after having lived there awhile. Perhaps this phenomenon will change somewhat over time as they get used to the idea of living with others who are different from them. Besides, some of the gentrifiers may themselves have grown up in less privileged environments than those to which they currently belong. More likely, however, the neighborhood they have moved to will become more homogeneous as the overall cost of living makes it possible for only the well-off to remain there.

When all is said and done, gentrification is a complex issue. It has swept through many parts of the city and has been helped

along by many interests. It is changing the face of New York and
will shape its future for decades. By observing it on the ground, it
becomes possible to see these complexities from different angles,
many of them positive, some not necessarily so. We now turn our
attention to an equally complicated question: the future of ethnic
identity in this city. Interestingly the issue has some striking paral-
lels with the gentrification process with respect to class and residential patterns.

7

ASSIMILATION, IDENTITY, OR SOMETHING ELSE?

The Future of Ethnic New York

The following snapshot of a Queens neighborhood highlights the importance of ethnicity in New York City, as well as the United States in general. Ethnicity can mean race, religion, or national origin, or a combination of them, and it is affected by both culture and class, though which of the two is most important has long been debated. Richmond Hill, Queens, is a true amalgam of ethnic groups and includes Peruvians, Mexicans, Sikhs, Indians, and Pakistanis, with Guyanese (Hindus, Muslims, and Christians) possibly the largest group among them. The northern part, between Eighty-fifth Avenue and Jamaica Avenue, also has clusters of Irish, Italians, and Jews.

The stores along Jamaica Avenue are of all types—groceries, real estate offices, beauty salons, restaurants, and fast-food places. A local favorite near 110th Street, Armando's Pollo Rico, is a Peruvian eatery where you can get a quarter of a chicken, French fries or rice, soup or salad, and soda, all for $5.75. Specialties include *papa rellenas,* a deep-fried potato stuffed with ground meat, and *choclo con queso,* boiled Peruvian corn with white cheese. One supermarket on Hillside Avenue clearly tries to appeal to a mixed consumer cohort: "Trade Fair Supermarkets: We Carry Full Line of Spanish, Guyanese, Indian, & Bangladesh Ethnic Products." (See figure 27.) On 112th Street near Jamaica Avenue is a religiously observant Bukharian Jew who owns a jewelry and watch shop, selling and repairing. He gets along with everyone, he tells me.

Indeed, in such a polyglot area, why shouldn't he? I wonder, though, how he would interact with members of a nearby church on Jamaica, whose storefront sign reads, "Iglesia De Dios Israelita," and is adorned with drawings of a Star of David, a menorah, and stone tablets, inscribed with Hebrew letters. There is no cross in sight, but it is an *iglesia*, or church, as opposed to a *synagoga*. Farther down Jamaica is a storefront church that bills itself as the Temple of the Rivers of Living Waters. Pastor David Magallenes's phone number is listed outside.

This microcosm of peoples is replicated in other city neighborhoods like Elmhurst, Queens; Ditmas Park, Brooklyn; and Washington Heights, Manhattan. And although they have their disagreements, they all get along remarkably well. Their efforts to maintain their identity do not occasion any anxiety, or much concern, by city government or anyone else. Their differences are simply a fact of life in this incredibly varied metropolis. But this fact of life has major ramifications. The proximity almost forces people to learn about and get to know each other. They learn from one another that dealing with one's ethnicity in the American context is a complex issue but one that all incoming groups must face. Moreover, as noted in a personal observation by my colleague Philip Kasinitz, the fact that New York is a mass-transit city forces encounters, at least visually, with a multitude of different groups.

But even as ethnicity remains a powerful force in New York, assimilation into American life and culture has become an equally strong phenomenon among the city's residents, including many of its newest arrivals. In 2010, nationally, there were more than twice as many interracial or interethnic marriages than was the case in 1980, and a large number of these marriages were in trend-setting New York City. The rate, 15 percent, reflects greater general tolerance of such marriages. According to studies by the Pew Research Center, interracial and interethnic marriages were viewed more favorably than same-sex marriages or the rising rate of single motherhood. And more than a third of Americans say that an immediate family member or close relative has married someone of a different race. In short, these mixed marriages are becoming more and more common with each passing year. In other findings, more black men than women marry outside of their race, but far more Asian women than men do so. Asian-white couples earn more than white-white or Asian-Asian couples. Also, Hispanics and blacks who marry outside their race are more likely to have college degrees.[1]

Of New York's estimated 8.3 million people in 2010, non-Hispanic whites made up about 33 percent, Hispanics 28 percent, blacks 26 percent, and Asians 13 percent.[2] Some 36 percent of New Yorkers are foreign-born, and more foreigners legally enter New York than any other city. It also has the largest gay population of any U.S. city. With same-sex marriage now legal in the state, the number of marriages between gays will surely rise. While not an ethnic group, they are certainly a distinct one.

This chapter focuses on the future of ethnic identity. Will the dominant pattern be assimilation, identification, or a hybrid version of the two? To answer this question, it's important to understand the contact that different groups have with one another. How they are viewed by outsiders is another critical issue. Are they accepted? Has prejudice lessened over the years? And, most significantly, how do ethnic groups identify nationally, religiously, racially, and in other ways? The answers to these questions are important because they can tell us what kind of society we will become in the next fifty years. Will it be one where tolerance and respect are the hallmarks, or will it be marked by mistrust and conflict? Let's start by looking at the astonishing variety of contacts that New Yorkers have with other groups.

Daygration

A form of contact exists in society that I've dubbed "daygration." It's never been categorized as such, yet I believe it deserves further study. Daygration refers to the contact that takes place when the group that lives in an area interacts with people of other groups who are there only during the day. And although the people from outside the area return to their homes in the evening, they are in contact with the resident groups either for most of their waking hours or for special events that can have a meaningful impact on participants' perceptions of each other. What relationships develop in these circumstances? How meaningful are they? Do any real friendships emerge that include socializing, or are they merely superficial exchanges with no deeper meaning? How do they shape and affect perceptions between groups? Are these individuals seen as representative of the group or as exceptions to the rule? What are the larger implications for group relations?

Examples of daygration abound in New York City. A few of them, like Korean delis and their minority customers, have been studied. The newer groups, like Yemeni deli owners and Pakistani gas station proprietors, who work but don't live in Hispanic or black areas, have not. These are important cases because their presence means that the dominant group does not live in isolation from others and that defining a neighborhood purely by present residence misses an important part of the story. I say "present" because I've discovered that a number of those who work in these areas once lived there. In such cases relationships may also be influenced by one side's memories of a time when those now residing there were seen as outsiders or newcomers.

Sometimes institutions with white members remain in, say, a once-white neighborhood, and blacks work there during the day and service them. A good example is the Sunrise Center, a large senior citizens complex with exercise activities, dental screenings, Alzheimer's and dementia programs, nutritional counseling, games, movies, meals, a beauty salon, and lots more. The center is located in Canarsie, Brooklyn, on East Ninety-sixth Street and Avenue J. Hundreds of elderly whites are regularly bused into Canarsie from Brighton Beach, Sheepshead Bay, and elsewhere to spend their entire day in a beautiful facility. The staff is mostly minority, and relationships develop there as well. The elderly take note of how the minority members treat them. Are they friendly and helpful, or are they cold and unresponsive? Whatever the case, they talk about it to friends and younger family members from other communities. In this way perceptions about groups develop and spread.

Another fascinating example is the federally subsidized Yeled V'Yaldah preschool program, located in an otherwise unused synagogue on Farragut Road that flourished in the old days. The security guards and other staff are local blacks, one from the nearby Glenwood public housing project. In addition, some of the preschoolers are black and are in the same classes as the predominantly Jewish kids, who are bused in from all over Brooklyn. The draw for both groups is that as long as the program is open to all, it's funded by the government and free. Preschool being children's most formative years, such close contacts are likely to make a lasting impression on both sides. After all, the children will play together, form class friendships, and develop likes and dislikes for one another.

Some communities work harder at maintaining their culture than do others. The Ukrainian community of the East Village was once quite large. When drugs and violence began to plague the community, many Ukranians moved out to Queens, Brooklyn, and New Jersey. Yet they traverse long distances today so that their children will maintain a strong sense of identification with their culture. As one Ukrainian put it, "Ukrainian parents, who are very family-oriented, began to worry about their children. They didn't raise their children as street kids." When in the 1990s the area was gentrified, they couldn't afford to return. And yet "their children come to this school [the Catholic St. George School] to learn Ukrainian language and culture." They're only there during the day, but as a result they become exposed to other ethnicities. The school itself has adapted and now accepts students from the black and Hispanic communities as well as Muslims and Jews. These new groups are obviously studying and playing together. Research by sociologists Mario Luis Small, Monica McDermott, and Robert Sampson further demonstrates the important role played by schools, day-care centers, and other nonprofit groups in the life of neighborhoods.[3]

Contacts can occur even when members of a group are simply passing through. I was walking in a predominantly Orthodox Jewish area, Kew Gardens Hills, with four graduate students and entered a kosher takeout place called Meal Mart. "These are students from my New York City class," I explained casually to those behind the counter as I told the students about the food items in a glass display case. It was the holiday of Succoth, when Jews eat in *succahs* (booths) for eight days.

"Have they ever been to a succah?" asked a black-hatted, bearded young man with two small children in tow.

"No," I replied, "but we're hoping to."

"Why don't you come to mine?" he offered. "I live around here."

"That's great. Thank you so much. When should we come?"

"I'll call my wife. Come in about half an hour. Call me on my cell when you're almost there."

And so it was. We came and were ushered into his succah, which necessitated walking through the living room and entering the temporary habitat that had been constructed on his porch. The man, an assistant principal at a nearby all-boys yeshiva, had prepared some cookies, called *rugelach,* and fruit juice. He patiently explained the meaning of the holiday to us. "It's considered very important to invite guests into your succah. I actually sleep here at night, weather permitting." His four small children came in and said hello, followed shortly by his wife, a young woman who had grown up on Manhattan's Upper West Side.

What made the encounter so noteworthy was that, first of all, it was a very busy time for them—Friday morning—and they were getting ready for the festive last two days of the holiday, cooking, cleaning, and so on. Second, my students weren't Jewish, so there was no incentive of bringing Jews closer to Judaism. One was from Germany, the other German Irish, the third generic American from Massachusetts, and the fourth Korean. By inviting them into his home, this man significantly affected the view the students have of Orthodox Jews, and they said so. Years later, at least two of the students still have fond memories of the encounter and how they were treated.

Meeting on the Same Turf

Even when different groups live in the same neighborhood, appearances can sometimes be deceiving. You can walk through an Asian area and think of it as belonging to one Asian group, but closer examination reveals that it's not. One study of the Japanese enclave in the East Village found that quite a few Koreans work in Japanese-run restaurants. Moreover, the area is becoming more Pan-Asian, with Koreans, Taiwanese, Thais, and Chinese moving in. Members of these groups tend to shop in stores owned by the others.[4]

Most areas of the city have a mix of peoples living in them who have daily contact with one another and who share the space. This isn't a question of outreach. Rather, it just makes sense to have good relations with neighbors. Typical is the response by a middle-age, strictly Orthodox Jewish woman in Flatbush, Brooklyn, who reports that she is very friendly with her next-door Italian American neighbor. She is wearing a long, navy blue skirt down to her feet (referred to within the community as a "floor-sweeper"), with a loose-fitting white blouse, and, covering her hair, a dark kerchief. "Her [the woman's neighbor] and her friends are just amazing. When I had to go regularly to the hospital for outpatient treatments, her son took me there every day over two weeks. My husband's working three jobs, so it was a godsend."

"But these are not people you would have over for dinner, are they?" I ask.

"Only because my husband objects, because he feels we can't return the invitation and come to them, because we're kosher. But I wonder about that. I mean, why can't we come with a kosher pizza and eat it on paper plates? Or couldn't we take them to a kosher restaurant?"

"Are the Italians different than other non-Jews?" I ask.

"I think they're a lot like Jews. You know, the family structure and how food is important to them."

The sense you get here is that of a person who wants to be more open and friendly, but whose husband is resistant because he fears it will threaten their identity as Jews. Regardless, I heard dozens of stories from people who talked of the friendships they had developed with neighbors whose backgrounds were completely dissimilar.

In an exploratory study of relations between Chinese and Jews on the Lower East Side that included interviews at a senior citizens' center, one of my graduate students, Fang Xu, came up with some interesting findings. Like the Jews and Italians, the two groups share similar cultural values—namely, respect for the family, veneration for the elderly, interest in education, and concentration in business. Most of the Jews living on the Lower East Side in the last fifty years have been Orthodox. The Chinese have also been there for a long time, first arriving in the 1870s, even before mass Jewish immigration made it a prime neighborhood starting in the 1880s.

Elderly Jewish respondents interviewed by Xu expressed positive views of the Chinese, noting their respect for the elderly, family values, and quiet nature. Both Jews and Chinese do play mahjong a lot, but they play it with completely different rules. And, of course, there is a language barrier. One Jewish respondent spoke of playing ball together with Chinese neighbors and going over to visit each other. It appears as though there's very little conflict between the two communities. Because the Jews are more Americanized, one suspects they will have greater rapport with the artsy and yuppie types who have been moving there recently. In fact, some of their own children may be, and indeed are, sometimes in the same communities. Nonetheless, there are a few second-generation Chinese who have become part of the art scene, though this is probably less the case with the Chinese than among the Jews.[5]

When groups have more in common, it's easier to have meaningful contact. Bishop Nicholas DiMarzio observed, "We can work with the Orthodox on various issues—school vouchers, respect for religious practices, family values. The Orthodox often prefer to work with us rather than with non-Orthodox Jews."

If one wants to see ethnic contact, social progress, and true turf sharing in New York City, the experience of a Hebrew charter school in Brooklyn is a perfect case in point. The Hebrew Language Academy, housed in a yeshiva, has children attending from many nationalities. The school's program emphasizes Israeli culture and Hebrew, but the students are also taught about Christmas and Ramadan. The student body is one-third black, with a sprinkling of Hispanics. With regard to religion, it is made up of Jews, Muslims, and Christians.

Aalim and Aalima, twins who are students at the school, delight in speaking Hebrew with each other. It's sort of like their secret code, one their father does not comprehend. Aalim is happy to sing his favorite song in Hebrew: "My land of Israel is beautiful and blossoming. / Who built it and who cultivated it? / All of us together! / I built a house in the land of Israel. / So now I have a land and I have a house in the land of Israel!" What's remarkable is that Aalim and Aalima are Muslims. And the school they attend not only teaches songs about Israel, but it also displays the Israeli flag throughout the building and celebrates Israel Independence Day as part of its cultural program.[6] That's a lot more than your usual musical and culinary outreach programs with groups that have ethnic or racial tensions.

Strange and Unusual Contacts

Right-wing Orthodox Jews are very careful about contact with the opposite sex. I well recall the response of a Hasidic man in South Williamsburg when asked by one of my students why their buses were segregated by sex. "No mingling, no mingling," was his retort. "And we follow it very strictly in other ways too. Women can't walk in our community unless they are modestly dressed," he added.

Thus it was surprising for me to be greeted by an outgoing, pretty, flaxen-haired, blue-eyed woman of about thirty, dressed in a tight, form-fitting sweater as I walked into a large, upscale kosher supermarket in a very religious Jewish neighborhood. In fact, the store was owned by ultra-Orthodox Jews. This is not symbolic contact. It's real.

"Hi!" the woman exclaimed. "Try some of this cheese. It's delicious. You'd never believe kosher cheese could taste this good." Her comments were an obvious nod to the belief of many Jews that the nonkosher version of steak, pizza, or wine is always going to be better because there are no restrictions in how to make it, and also because those who keep kosher are a captive audience, thereby reducing the incentive by manufacturers and retailers to improve the product.

But in this case the claim had additional validity because the woman is a convert from Colorado who ought to know the differences in taste. She has a captive audience too. But it's not only those who want kosher food. It's devoutly Orthodox men who seemed to be getting a kick out of talking to and flirting with this woman from another planet. When I entered the store I saw two of them speaking with her, and when I left forty minutes later, they were still there, ostensibly sampling the toothpick-stabbed pieces of cheese, but actually engaged in animated conversation, punctuated by laughter, even giggles.

There are issues here that ought to concern the fervently Orthodox. The woman is attractive by any reasonable standard. Opportunities for physical contact—including handshakes, for starters—all forbidden, abound. And the Western accent, so different from that of New Yorkers, most probably conveys a sense of the exotic, of forbidden fruit, to those unaccustomed to its sound. The owners and the customers were obviously practicing cognitive dissonance, recreating the existing reality to suit their economic and perhaps voyeuristic goals.

I strike up a conversation with her, saying, "Where are you from?"

"Colorado. This rabbi I met offered me a job here last year. I was going through a divorce and I needed something to do. I've been in the cheese business for about six years. And I'm learning about all the holidays and customs and which cheeses are kosher."

"Are you Jewish?" I ask.

"Yes, but I converted. My mom's not happy about it, even though she's got Jewish blood, which she won't admit to, but we're mixed in with a lot of Catholics. So legally I wasn't Jewish. And my mom says, 'But you were baptized.' 'Great,' I say. 'Whatever.' I go to shul every week. I eat kosher. I go to a Conservative temple and sometimes I go to Orthodox. But I have a Jewish boyfriend now. A rabbi and his *rebbetzin* helped me get to this point, though I would say they kept me captive in their basement."

"How did you end up in New York?" I ask.

"I was here by accident, on a cheese marketing project, and I got laid off, so I decided to stay."

Strange, to say the least, but the lessons learned are not. First we see that even in the most insular society people crave contact, a craving augmented here by the fact that it's a pretty woman. What's even more interesting is that the woman was knowingly hired by her ultra-Orthodox bosses. In joking around and engaging in extended conversation with her in a public place, the devout men who do so are risking criticism and even censure by their communities. This situation reminds us that even the ultra-Orthodox cannot avoid contact with the outside world in an urban environment, notwithstanding their efforts to do so. Many less obvious contacts happen in all sorts of businesses in the city, where the Orthodox must have contact with others. Most important, the story demonstrates that anyone can meet anyone in a densely populated area. Because of that reality, the city facilitates contact among different communities simply by its existence.

The next unusual case is of a totally different sort, even though the man is also a devout Orthodox Jew. He belongs to the Lubavitcher, also known as Chabad, community. Although Jews in the Lubavitch movement are very observant, they are quite liberal in their relationships with the nonobservant Jewish community and are generally more open in their attitudes toward the larger society. Moreover, the entire experience was a stereotype-defying one.

I'm walking up East 167th Street around Grant Avenue in the South Bronx on a Friday afternoon in late May 2010 when suddenly I see a Hasidic-looking man leaving a school building. Of medium height, he is wearing a large black skullcap and has a pretty substantial, graying beard. And his *tzitzis,* the strings from the fringed religious garment he wears under his shirt, are hanging out on each side of the shirt at hip level. I catch up to him and quite spontaneously ask, "What's a religious Jew like you doing here?"

"Me? I work at the school up the block, Middle School 22."

"What do you do there?" I ask.

"I'm a dean," he tells me. "As a matter of fact, I'm the dean of discipline."

"Really," I say, thinking to myself that he doesn't look too big or tough, and as an Orthodox Jew, in this rough part of town, in a middle school, the kids must run all over him. How can he understand their life and culture, so different from his own?

"How are you able to control them?" I ask. It turns out I'm wrong on most counts.

"Why not?" he answers, smiling. "I treat them like human beings. I've never had any trouble."

"Do they ever say anything about how you look?"

"Not really." He gives a quick laugh. "Given the way people dress around here—I mean, the African Muslims with their skullcaps, beards, and robes—I actually fit in pretty well. I'm just another weird dresser. Up here anything goes. In fact, very often they don't even realize I'm Jewish."

"But what about the parents, particularly those who are Muslim?" I persist.

"I've never had a problem with them. They're very respectful. They just want their kids to get a good education. The problems for the kids are often their difficult home situations, but personally I get along great with them. I deal with behavior, not religion. I love the kids and I love watching how they progress. I never take lunch, because I'm so busy resolving problems and I'm here from eight to five. The only issue for me is the traveling. I have to come here all the way from Crown Heights by subway."

And then, almost as if on cue, two black kids, perhaps eleven or twelve years old, a boy and a girl, emerge from a Kennedy Fried Chicken joint. Seeing their dean, they greet him joyously, giving him a high five and saying, "Hello, Mr. T." and "How y'all doin'?"

"That's my nickname," he explains, with a chuckle. "My last name begins with a 'T.' I'm Tuvia Tatik."

"Was it an adjustment for you to be here, at first?"

Not really. You see, I didn't grow up *frum* [religiously observant]. I was raised as a nonreligious Jew in the Bronx and went to DeWitt Clinton High School. And I used to play basketball at the Jewish community center in this neighborhood. So I knew about the outside world and about public school. I also live in Crown Heights, which has a large black population. And you know who hired me? Another frum Jew who has a doctorate from Harvard, Shimon Waronker. He's the principal and he was written up on the front page of the *New York Times*. Google it; you'll get a beautiful seven-minute video. Before he came this was one of the twelve worst junior high schools in the city. And when he came to this country from Chile, he didn't know a word of English. So when he took this job, they laughed.

"But at least he knew Spanish, and that's very important here," I counter. Tuvia agrees with me. Indeed, I do remember the article.

"There's even another Orthodox Jew in the school," he tells me, "but he's 'Modern,'" he adds. "He doesn't wear a *kippa* [skullcap] in the building."

The discussion demonstrates that there's often more to a situation than meets the eye. Tuvia has certain informal credentials that make him particularly qualified, more so than the typical observant Jew. First, he wasn't brought up Orthodox. Second, he grew up in the Bronx and played basketball there as a kid. Third, he's a public school product. Fourth, he belongs to the Lubavitch sect, which is the most outgoing of the Hasidic groups. Fifth, as I learn, he's a trained psychologist who studied at Touro College. Finally, he lives in a mixed black-white community. These characteristics stand him in good stead as he faces daily challenges.

"Why do you think there's so little anti-Semitism in your school?" I continue.

"I'll be honest. It's because we're a predominantly Hispanic school, about seventy percent. And the Hispanics have more respect for religion in general. And even with the Muslims, we talk about religion. Some are actually from the Middle East, from Yemen."

When we part at the subway entrance, I say, "I'm so glad I met you. It was really interesting. And I wouldn't have met you if you hadn't come out of the building at that moment."

Tuvia's response highlights his faith-based approach to things. "One of the foundation stones of Hasidic philosophy is that everything is preordained. God doesn't let a leaf fall from a tree without some purpose to it, even if we don't know what it is. God willed that we should meet. I was supposed to leave at three o'clock because it's *erev shabbos* [shortly before the Sabbath], but I was schmoozing with the other dean—we schmooze together. You can call me at any time."

"What misconceptions do your friends in Crown Heights have about the kids you work with? Do they think they're wild kids?"

"That's the thing," he answers. "We have kids in this school—they're like diamonds. They ask me about my *tzitzis*. I explain it to them. Mostly they don't even ask."

To be sure, most fervently Orthodox Jews are not as tolerant as Tuvia, just as they are not as welcoming to outsiders as was the man who invited my students into his succah. But that is what makes these examples so interesting. Because New Yorkers have constant contact with other groups, the possibility for such unusual and productive encounters is greatly enhanced.

This case is a great example of ethnic learning. Think of how Tuvia shapes the views of students and colleagues by virtue of the fact that the group he represents is such a stereotyped group. Hasidim (and Jews) are often viewed by blacks and Hispanics as cheap and unethical in the sense that they worship the almighty dollar. Most have no real contact with Jews, and if they do it's as landlords, merchants, or as TV caricatures. For Muslims the stereotypes are even worse, shaped as they are by Middle East politics. On the other side of the equation, think of how Tuvia changes the narrow view many members of his own community have about minorities. "They're wonderful, my kids," he tells his neighbors. He's a walking ambassador for his people. And the children, who are at an impressionable age, are likely to carry their experiences with him for a lifetime.

Prejudice

In the 1970s and 1980s, Canarsie, Brooklyn, was contested territory, with more and more African Americans moving in as Italians and Jews left. Writing about the neighborhood, urban studies researcher Keith McClean argues that white residents displayed racism and xenophobia in their fears of blacks who moved in. As late as

1980 Canarsie was almost 90 percent white. The blacks were mostly middle-class newcomers, with income and education levels that were often higher than those of the whites living there. Today the neighborhood is virtually 100 percent black. It's a middle- to lower middle-class community and many residents are of Caribbean origin.[7] Perhaps the fears by whites were exacerbated because many had felt forced out by poor blacks in earlier years from the crumbling areas of East New York and Brownsville. Thus the real question is, did racism prevent whites from being able to distinguish between poor, unemployed ghetto dwellers and the largely successful middle-class blacks who were frequently overpaying for their homes in Canarsie?

Thirty years ago in Queens, blacks lived in Laurelton and whites in Beechhurst. They still do, but something is very different now. In the earlier period, blacks couldn't easily move to Beechhurst or other white areas. They would have faced raw prejudice, outright hostility. Today people can live wherever they want, and that is a right blacks fought hard to achieve.

Yet it does not necessarily mean that this right, once attained, will be exercised. Blacks can live in Beechhurst or Douglaston, Queens, yet hardly any choose to do so. Why? The truth is that many blacks feel more at home in their own communities, where they will not be judged or stereotyped by whites. These neighborhoods are also places with restaurants, clubs, shopping, and religious institutions that cater to their needs and preferences. In addition, it cannot be ignored that there is sometimes a residual dislike for whites because of past history.

Writing perceptively in *The Cosmopolitan Canopy,* sociologist Elijah Anderson reports, "When I pass by a black man alone among his white colleagues, he gives me a knowing look, or even greets me; the others are unaware that we've just had a privileged communication." He goes on to note that black professionals learn that even nice and seemingly open whites may not be fully trustworthy, at least from the black person's perspective. They become disillusioned as they see that such whites might be friends with the white racists whom they themselves see as the enemy.[8]

Conversely, whites can live in a very safe middle-class, Queens neighborhood called Cambria Heights, yet almost none do. It is a black community, but it is so by choice. Many whites just feel more comfortable living with other whites. They're not pioneers in race relations, and they aren't particularly interested in expanding their social horizons. That is their prerogative.

Paradoxically, other neighborhoods, like Woodside and Forest Hills in Queens, as well as Ditmas Park and Sunset Park in Brooklyn, are models, if you will, of integration. In these areas residents of all backgrounds have made an affirmative decision that they like the diversity. Then again, is how and where they're living really integration, or is it simply parallel coexistence? Based on my own observations, I believe it's both. The trick lies in knowing where it is, where it isn't, and the attendant consequences of each.

In areas like Chelsea, Greenwich Village, Prospect Heights, Clinton Hill, Williamsburg, Forest Hills, Co-op City, and Lefferts Gardens, one can see many more interracial couples than was the case twenty years ago. A good deal of mixing occurs among residents of communities who share common borders and whose members go back and forth between the neighborhoods, eating and hanging out in the same places or attending school together. Good examples of this phenomenon are Brooklyn's Washington Avenue, which demarcates the Bed-Stuy and Prospect Heights border, or Vanderbilt Avenue, which marks off Fort Greene from Clinton Hill. But you must walk through these parts to see the cross-racial contacts. Look at them on a map and they appear more segregated. And it is a fact that Harlem and Bed-Stuy now have many more white residents than they did in earlier years. Similarly, a visit to the city's college campuses, especially those that make up CUNY, confirm that there's far more social mixing of the races today than was thought possible back in the 1960s and '70s. The bottom line is that it's much more complex than it appears.

Attitudes have been changing gradually through the years. In Jackson Heights the transition in the 1970s from white to diverse was fairly smooth, without the panic selling that usually accompanies such major shifts. It is a sign of how attitudes toward minorities have changed in recent years that in the 1990s white residents of Jackson Heights vigorously resisted attempts to have their children bused to nearby white schools in Astoria because of overcrowded schools in Jackson Heights. Besides wanting to stay local, people wanted their children to benefit from the more diverse experience of attending the Hispanic- and Asian-dominated schools in their own communities. In earlier times most people in Jackson Heights would have been delighted at the chance to have their children attend a mostly white school.[9]

Former mayor Ed Koch gave the position's current occupant, Michael Bloomberg, a good deal of credit for the change in attitude. In my interview with Koch, he said of Bloomberg, "He changed the racial climate in this city. There is absolutely *no* racial animosity that I can discern. Obviously there are individuals, but in terms of racial anger, it doesn't exist anymore. How did he do it? His personality just fits the need. It's bland, not controversial. *I* was a little controversial," he said, laughing.

Prejudice has declined not only racially but also among similar groups. I asked Marie Adam-Ovide, district manager of Queens Community Board #8, if she fears that the Haitians and West Indians in general will adopt poor cultural values in the second generation as they try to gain acceptance from their American-born peers. She says no.

> These were mostly my parents' concerns. They put certain people in a box—"Don't get into trouble with the Jamaicans because of 'this,' nor with African Americans because of 'that.'" But then you go to school, where you meet kids and find that some of them are *not* getting into trouble. And I find that *they* get the same stuff from their parents for similar reasons. "Don't hang out with the Haitians, because they're stuck up"; and they called them "Frenchie" because they went to school and they dressed a certain way. In Haiti you went to school in uniforms. So here I had slacks and skirts but not jeans, and that did not go over well in school. Pretty soon I convinced my parents to let me wear the jeans, because I told them if I didn't I was going to get beat up.

Clearly, Adam-Ovide feels that she has more in common with the younger generation. She is also conforming to her peers, because her ethnic dress didn't go over well with them.

At the same time, no one should be naive about this issue. There is still prejudice, as was made crystal clear to me in an interesting conversation I had with a white man who had retooled his business, located in Canarsie, to serve the needs of the changing community. It is a textbook case of a person who harbors strong prejudicial views but conceals them because he gains from serving the needs of the very people he dislikes. He sells products that cater to the black community. The neighborhood itself is quiet, relatively safe, and the residents are mostly working- and middle-class blacks.

While his views were shared by other whites in the area with whom I also spoke, many, including both Jews and Italians, the predominant groups formerly in Canarsie, sharply disagreed with them.

We changed, so we thrived. All the Italians are gone, gone, gone. We had protests here, in front of my place. One thing I can say. I don't have my own people asking me for favors because they know me, or because they're my cousins. The blacks? I say to them, "Pay me or you don't get." And you know what? They pay. I saw the change coming as early as 1993 and I adapted. Most didn't. The rib guy closed, the pizzeria, they went under, the catering place closed. The Jewish temple does well because they rent it to the Hasids from Crown Heights. They come here to worship on the Sabbath.

"But how do they do that? They can't drive on the Sabbath," I say.

"They come by bus. You gotta see it. The beards too. They go to classes there."

"On Saturday?"

"No, you're right. Not on Saturday; on weekdays. The temple did a smart move."

"Why do people run?"

"I dunno, but the people who held out got big money. The first wave, they panicked and they got nuthin'. The prices here today are crazy, six hundred grand for a two-family."

"Why so much?"

"You gotta understand, you gotta get into the mind-set. You take a two-family house. They live on the first floor. First thing they do is they Sheetrock the basement. So now they got an income in the basement. Now they Sheetrock the garage and insulate it. Now they got a garage they rent to people. Where you had four people—Italian, Irish, German, or Jewish—livin', now you got forty people livin' there. They get subsidized by the government. They get mortgages you and I couldn't get."

Frank sees the changes in his old neighborhood as part of a trend in Brooklyn. "It's only a matter of time. Look at Bensonhurst. That's becoming Chinese. There's no neighborhoods left for us that we could afford. There's Dyker Heights and Bay Ridge. Who'd wanna live there? You gotta buy a parked car there to sleep in. And you got them, the whaddya call it, the Lebanon people over there."

"You mean Muslims?"

"Yeah."

Frank is a bitter man who feels as though the world he once lived in was destroyed by an alien black invasion. His prejudiced views are apparent, and he makes no bones about it. Paradoxically, he praises African Americans as people who, unlike his own people, pay for what they get. He gives himself credit for adapting his business to their needs, but, ultimately, without them he wouldn't have a business. His prejudices extend to others, as can be seen when he refers dismissively to Muslims in Bay Ridge as "the Lebanon people." Hasidic Jews are called "the beards." Implied is the idea that nicknames will do just fine for people he doesn't know and probably doesn't want to know. Frank doesn't see those people the same way as he sees Jews in general, whom he described to me as "excellent people." He resents blacks for getting mortgages he could not obtain and denigrates them for supposedly putting forty people into a space that whites would allocate to only four people. What is clear here is that there are certain individuals who will be unaffected by changing times and attitudes. They are yet another part of the city's population, though they are clearly in the minority and their numbers are dwindling.

Sometimes one incident speaks volumes. The following story indicates the latter, in my opinion. My wife and I attended a gospel concert in Newark, New Jersey, on September 13, 2012. Many in the audience were from New York City. It took place in a cavern-ous auditorium and featured a contest between six choirs. Of the perhaps fifteen hundred people there, we and possibly three oth-ers were the only whites present. The crowd seemed to be mostly working class. Each group was voted on by both the judges and the audience. Only one of the six groups had whites singing; the others were all black. The integrated group, which brought the as-sembled to their feet, won hands down. I doubt that would have been the outcome fifteen years ago. For me, the incident was a sign of how far the black community had traveled from the open racial hostility that typified the '80s and early '90s. The congregation's votes demonstrated that merit, not race, was what mattered, that the term "post-racial society" might become a broader reality in the not-too-distant future.

The Complexity of Identity

In our search to understand what makes New York City really tick, perhaps nothing is as complex as ethnic identity. Individual and group motives for identifying converge and diverge in myriad directions. It's only by examining the individual components of identification that we can begin to understand their appeal. These include country of origin, religious beliefs and practices, physical appearance, language, residence, economic motives, emotions, per-sonal experiences, personal crises, cultural synthesis, sexual orien-tation, education—the list is endless.

It's important to remember when breaking down the reasons for identifying that it's often a *combination* of elements that makes a group so attractive. A person's identity can include, say, religion, community, race, language, and economic considerations all at once. Human beings are naturally free to pick and choose from these. They also have the option of adhering to one all-encompassing framework of identity. Further complicating mat-ters is the role of perceptions and prejudices of the outside world as factors in the process of identification. That said, without an attempt to decipher all of this, our understanding of New York

City's many peoples would be woefully inadequate. The goal here is not to give a comprehensive presentation. That would require a separate book. Rather, it's to explain, through an examination of what's happening in various neighborhoods, the range of possibilities and permutations. There is evidence that in an era when people feel freer to strike out in new directions, they, especially the young, are exercising their options. The number of areas explored in this discussion alone demonstrates that.

National and Ethnic Identity

We can begin with some observations regarding the Hispanic/Latino community, which in 2010 numbered some fifty million people. Hispanic identity is especially complex, encompassing terms like "African," "Indian," "Caribbean," "white," "black," "New Yorican," "Latin," or "Hispanic." While most Hispanics check off "White" on the race question, "some other race" (one of fifteen choices) has become an increasingly popular choice for Hispanics who see culture—ethnic group, nationality, religion, customs, and language—as much more important than merely color.

In the 2010 U.S. Census, of the more than 50 million Hispanics, over 18 million chose this category, up from 14.9 million in 2000. Because of uncertainty over how to respond, many, like Erika Lubliner, whose father is Jewish and mother is Mexican, left the answer blank. A physician raised in California, Erika grew up in the cultural milieu of her mother. "Believe me, I am not a confused person," she said. "I know who I am, but I don't necessarily fit the categories well." The decisions that are made by the U.S. Census Bureau in such cases have important implications for voting districts, evaluating discrimination in employment, and other areas.[10]

Smaller ethnic or national groups in America similarly display great variety but tend to be lumped together by most Americans. As sociologist Madhulika Khandelwal shows, Indians, for example, are a particularly variegated group—Jains, Hindus, Moslems, Christians; South and North Indians; Gujaratis, Bengalis, Sikhs, Parsis, Jews, and others. Does the perception itself affect their assimilation? Certainly Indians themselves are often puzzled when Americans combine their groups into one racial or ethnic or national category. Also, for Indians, religion and secularism are more intertwined than in the West, which tries to separate them. In India, secularism represents tolerance for all religions, both beliefs and practices.[11]

Like the Indians, Russian Jews are another group of people who have a strong sense of ethnic identity, though they do not identify much religiously. They feel strongly about their Russian heritage and have a high rate of inmarriage. However, the most recent study by the UJA-Federation of New York, in 2011, found that, unlike the Indians, most Russian Jews avoid Jewish educational and religious organizations because of fears that these groups will try to pressure them into greater observance.

Clearly, as we saw in chapter 2, on immigration, one's country of origin is a critical identity marker. People are in constant contact with their homelands and maintain friendships with those who come from their country. It is an important component of their identity. As time goes on the bonds loosen. Less understood is how people from different lands in the same area relate to one another—Cambodians, Vietnamese, and Laotians; Dutch, Belgians, and French; or Nigerians, Ghanaians, and Senegalese. All this remains to be evaluated, and much will depend on what happens in the larger society.

While much less dominant in the city today than thirty years ago, there are still sizeable numbers of white ethnics. They are largely of middle or working class, predominantly Catholic, and of European origin. Their rough-edged white ethnic culture is still present in New York City and can be best appreciated in the Irish and Italian enclaves of Brooklyn, Queens, and the Bronx. Areas like Gerritsen Beach, Edgewater Park, Breezy Point, Howard Beach, and Woodlawn are good examples. Industries like the building trades, the unions, the police and fire departments, and even the Fulton Fish Market (now relocated to Hunts Point) allow for its expression and are their strongholds. White ethnic culture involves a certain sense of humor that is challenging, feisty, and almost self-deprecating at times. In his introduction to Barbara Mensch's excellent photographic volume, *South Street,* Philip Lopate writes

that one reason the fish market lasted for so long was because
working-class New Yorkers don't expect comfort and are resilient.
The paradox and uniqueness, perhaps, of New York City is that in
many ways it is both ultramodern and traditional.[12]

Religious Beliefs and Practices

One form of ethnicity that is particularly strong in New York is
religion. Muslims have become more observant since 9/11, turning
inward, perhaps in part, as a response to discrimination.[13] Tens
of thousands of Hasidic Jews remain in their communities, with
only small numbers defecting. Many young people are choosing
to affiliate with one religion or another, a good number of them
with evangelical groups. Significant numbers of non-affiliated Jews
are becoming observant. More recent immigrants, like Colombians, Haitians, Ghanaians, and Chinese, share churches in formerly
all-white neighborhoods. Analysts who focus on class, an important trait, need to also face the reality of religion and ethnicity's
persistence.[14]

Another indication of religion's strength is the existence of thousands of tiny storefront churches that dot New York's urban landscape. Their appeal is certainly not their physical structure. It's the
spirituality, the soul that lies within their confines, that brings the
people in. These little churches use broad slogans to attract adherents, like the Christian Faith Cathedral (a misnomer if there ever
was one) on Ogden Avenue in the Bronx, where a wooden sign
outside features a biblical quotation: "Where there is no vision the
people perish: Proverbs 29:128." And what did they do with that
quote? Underneath it are the words, "The church of vision, with
you in mind."[15] Now let's look more closely at the many features
of religious identity.

Pyong Gap Min's carefully researched work on religion and
ethnicity, *Preserving Ethnicity through Religion in America,* demonstrates that religious rituals, which are based on beliefs, play a
critical role in ethnic survival. Hindus don't attend services that
frequently, but their temples serve as symbolic unifiers for the community. The real preservation of ethnic identity, however, occurs

at the local level—daily prayers, dietary rules, and regular rituals. Because these practices are an essential part of Indian culture, the children of immigrants from India also maintain their identity and reinforce it by identifying with Hinduism. Israeli Jews are also highly involved ritually with the Jewish community, more so than the average Jew, according to the UJA-Federation study done in 2011. They are more apt to belong to synagogues, give to Jewish charities, and send their children to Jewish day schools than other Jews.

Muslims must observe dietary restrictions, and city residents have grown accustomed to seeing signs advertising halal meat. But the dilemmas exist in smaller arenas as well. For example, during Ramadan observant Muslims refrain from eating during the daytime. Because the Ramadan holiday often falls during the hot summer days, Muslim teenagers who play basketball outside sometimes do so at a more leisurely pace, and without food, players lack energy. To send a message to others that the game isn't serious and to slow themselves down, they play in slippers and flip-flops rather than sneakers. Nor can they go to the beach, where they could dehydrate. Some of these Muslim teens might chafe at such restrictions, but others find a silver lining. As one youth said, "I feel like God is liking me even more since I started fasting."[16]

Iglesia Ni Cristo, located at 45-33 Twenty-first Street in Hunters Point, Queens, is a Filipino Protestant evangelical church. It's part of a worldwide movement founded in 1916 by Felix Manalo in the Philippines and today has several million adherents. Five thousand congregations of Filipino Protestants can be found in the Philippines, and more than six hundred exist elsewhere in the world. The religion rivals the Jehovah's Witnesses in size.

There are an estimated two hundred Filipinos residing in the area around Iglesia Ni Cristo.[17] One spring Sunday I attended services there. The redbrick building with an impressive tin roof is neo-Gothic, a style typical of this movement's houses of worship, favoring tall, narrow spires. The pastor, a serious, intense man, repeatedly exhorted those in the filled room to never miss services, saying that God is most present in a community of believers. He cited verses from the scripture to support virtually every point he made but always returned to the theme of attendance, even asking those there to verbally agree with him on this score. Speaking in a singsong cadence, he further admonished them to avoid romantic involvements with nonmembers and to eschew any illegal activities.

Later on I met with the pastor, a rather humorless, intense man, who nevertheless greeted me cordially inside his small, neat office in the basement, where Sunday School was in progress. When I asked why men and women sat separately, he smiled thinly and said, "Because it's forbidden according to the scriptures, and distracting, to have mixed seating." There was, however, a twenty-five-member mixed choir that sang beautifully. Ministers are rotated and he will soon be taking over a much larger congregation on Seventy-second Road and 112th Street in Forest Hills. In general the congregants were quite friendly and welcoming. Everything is very military and precise, with people filing out row by row after services, starting with the front-row pew. No deviation from the rituals is permitted, according to the pastor. "The rules are a central part of our tradition and must be followed to the letter," he declared.

On a sunny Sunday afternoon in the fall of 2010, I took several graduate students to South Williamsburg to see how the Hasidim there lived. We engaged an elderly Hasid in a conversation. He looked at me when answering but never once made eye contact with the four female students who were with me. He then spoke about how they maintain their culture by their dress, religious practices, speaking in Yiddish, and not pursuing a higher education. When I spoke to him alone he elaborated, saying,

> You know why we don't mingle, why I don't even look at your women students? I'll explain it like this. I'm an electrical contractor. Maybe twenty years ago I was in a Young Israel synagogue, where the *moderneh* [Modern Orthodox] go. I started a conversation with a young woman, and I discovered that she actually knew *gemorah* [Talmud]. She could tell how to *schecht* [slaughter] a chicken so it should be kosher. And she was beautiful. And I realized I could easily go for such a woman. But this would mean losing my whole

chassidus [Hasidic culture], leaving my community. So this is why we don't mingle. It's too dangerous. You could let your whole way of life go.

People who practice this way of life will not easily disappear. The Hasid's words make clear how important a set of rituals are to a community's survival. He admits that exposure to other lifestyles could cause him to leave his own. He enjoys interacting with the more modern Orthodox women, but doing so is not worth it if it means giving up any part of his religious identity.

One of my German students was absolutely shocked to see Hasidim. "I am amazed," she said. "I thought this way of life was completely destroyed by the Nazis when they killed millions of Jews in Poland and Hungary. I mean, I knew there were millions of Jews in America, but not Jews who looked like this." I explained to her that these were the descendants of the small remnant of Hasidic Jews who immigrated to the United States after the war and rebuilt their lives on American soil.[18] "Would they start screaming if they heard me speaking aloud to my friend in German?" another German student asked. "Hard to say," I replied. "Some might, but most probably won't even recognize German from Dutch, or Flemish. Their Yiddish is quite different. And they might not care."

In a study of another ultra-Orthodox Brooklyn community, Borough Park, a student of mine, Cynthia Magnus, describes a humorous incident that highlights both the community's ethnicity and its insularity. "Boro Park [this is the usual spelling by residents] is one of the few places that I have ever seen anyone trying to hitchhike. Driving through the neighborhood I noticed a young man in conservative black garb trying to thumb a ride down Fourteenth Avenue. I thought the unfortunate teenager must be very late for *shul* to resort to hitchhiking, so I slowed to offer him a ride. As I did, he looked perplexed and waved me away."[19]

It appears that the hitchhiker had three expectations here: first, that it's safe to thumb a ride; second, that there's a good chance he'll get a ride; and, third, that only a fellow Hasid would pick him up. Magnus violated the third norm: she's a woman. That she's not observant and not even Jewish is irrelevant, because even

Orthodox women would not stop for a man, knowing he won't ride with a woman except in an emergency, Orthodox or not. In the larger sense, hitchhiking is today a rarity, but not among people here, who expect help from their coreligionists.

Even the more outward-looking Chabad Hasidim follow rituals and customs very punctiliously, which greatly enhances the solidarity of their movement. The young are especially fervent. Three times a year, on the major Jewish holidays of Passover, Shavuot, and Simchat Torah, they have an outreach program. They walk, several thousand strong, in the late afternoon, along and way beyond the streets of Crown Heights, their center, to the far reaches of the city, even the Bronx and Queens. They visit synagogues on these holidays and try to engage the local congregants in wild song and dance in order to raise the levels of spirituality in their temples. The event is called *tahaluchah,* meaning, literally, a walk.

Bystanders stare at them as they pass by, wondering what the young celebrants are doing but not asking, because they feel a bit intimidated and because the Lubavitcher, with their distinctive dress, do not seem very approachable. As they stride along, they frequently burst into the songs and melodies that characterize the Chabad movement. It is an impressive display of ethnic solidarity, with participants from all over the United States, Europe, Latin America, and Israel. What makes it even more remarkable is that their leader, Rabbi Menachem Mendel Shneerson, the last Lubavitcher rebbe, has been dead for many years. As they say, "But his spirit lives on!"[20]

Why do rituals and customs matter so much? Because they ground the community and give it the unity that occurs when many people are doing the same thing, one that sets them apart from others, thereby making its followers feel special. Because the traditions are not generally known to outsiders, those who adhere to them feel somewhat unique. These perceptions are enriched when, as is often the case, the traditions go back hundreds, if not thousands, of years. Members feel they are the latest link in a long chain of history that they are duty-bound not to break.

What about the nonobservant Jews living everywhere in the city? There are still plenty of them, at least half a million. Often

they reject formal affiliation. When that happens, those wanting
to identify as Jews must find other ways to connect. And they do.
Here's one account by Steve Sachs, a forty-five-year-old magazine
executive who lives with his wife in Fort Greene.

> There aren't Jewish institutions in Fort Greene or very close by. We
> joined a synagogue in Park Slope, but we wanted to find other fami-
> lies and just create some kind of community here. And we created,
> about a year and a half ago, a monthly potluck dinner. We thought
> we'd get maybe two or three families, and the first time we did it
> we had about 40 people here between kids and adults, and we were
> stunned! At the end of the evening we said, "Would people like to
> get together again?" People said yes. So now we meet the second
> Friday of every month. It rotates; people just volunteer and say, "I'll
> do the next one." Some people come every time, and some people
> kind of pop in and out, and there's always new people coming.[21]

This is typical of how young people, turned off by organized
religion, find ways to express themselves. What's interesting is that
they too center it on a ritual, the potluck dinner. This can't compare to the hundreds of practices followed by the Orthodox, but
one ritual tends to give birth to others related to it; for example,
there might be (and perhaps is by now) a discussion of Jewish
culture while eating. In a sense this example demonstrates how
religion isn't necessarily dying among the young; rather, it's changing and evolving into new forms. In Ditmas Park I see an ad for a
"Ditmas Acoustic," referring to a secular music program at Temple
Beth Emet at 83 Marlboro Road in Flatbush, Brooklyn. It's a way
to get people into the temple without being "too Jewish."

The clergy is aware of the need to respond to this segment of the
population. According to Rabbi Joseph Potasnik:

> We are reaching some young people, but not enough. What that
> says to us as clergy is that we have to respond to their needs and
> views. For many young people the word is "spiritual." It's a catch-
> all. "I can be part of a community in the clouds." Many don't want
> commitment with rules, and they want to feel flexible and free to
> disengage if they so choose. "I want to feel religion in the heart,"

they say. "I don't have to do anything with my feet, with my hands."
If we don't reach the young, we're finished. How do we do it? We
can't just be a bunch of grumpy guys who are angry when we talk.
If we criticize people for not coming or participating, they'll turn
off. They'll say, "I have enough problems at work or at home, and
now I walk into a place where I'm seeking solace or support and
this person here is castigating me." Guilt may inspire some people
temporarily, but it has a negative long-term effect. We also have to
emphasize the social justice issues that resonate with our younger
generation. Being religious isn't just measured by what we say inside the sanctuary but by what we do outside the house of worship.

Religious Identity among the Young

There is an interesting development among younger professionals
in the city. Evangelical Christian religion, it seems, is increasingly
attractive to urban professionals and is establishing a foothold
in areas like the East Village, the Upper East Side, Chelsea, Park
Slope, and elsewhere in the city. There are now more than one hundred English-speaking Evangelical churches in Manhattan, south
of Harlem.[22] They're in a difficult position in liberal New York
City on certain issues, like gays and abortion. As one pastor put it,
"It's prudent for us as an East Village church to know where we
stand and what the Bible teaches, but not to lead with positions
that polarize people. I want our church story to be so much more
than where it stands on one hot topic issue." In this sense the new
evangelicalism is a "generational break" from people like Jerry Fal-
well and Pat Robertson, looking for emotional and spiritual meaning and emphasizing love for all. While evangelicals don't approve
of gay lifestyles, they nevertheless welcome gays as human beings.

The attraction is often emotional. Evangelicals are looking for
meaning, but why? Perhaps it's because in a fast-moving world
where technology has sometimes stifled personal interaction, these
people seek something that's missing in their lives—stability and
warmth, and a larger vision. Youth group leader Sara Frazier
explains the East Village church's vision: "Me and all my white,

well-educated friends from N.Y.U. are in my house with all these kids and Bloods and ex-cons and mothers. . . . The vision is that the cool hipsters and all the people in the projects, this will be their home."[23]

Young Jews are also becoming interested in religion, but not necessarily the established denominations. A sign outside the Kabbala Centre at 155 East Forty-eighth Street declares, "You Deserve Great Things." I walk into a modernistic welcome center. Off to the side are several shelves of books for sale. I glance at a display of bottles of "Kabbalah Water" for sale. Beneath the display is a book by a Japanese author, Masaru Emoto, detailing how his research found that water that has positive thoughts directed at it changes in its composition. It's called *The Hidden Messages in Water* and has sold over four hundred thousand copies, it is claimed.

A young worker with a slight Russian accent tells me, "We have a meditation on the water, and it becomes infused with holiness. Actually, if you drink Poland Spring water and have the right consciousness, it can change also."

"So there's no difference between Poland Spring and Kabbalah Water?" I ask, sounding a bit skeptical about the whole thing.

She eyes me warily and says, "I don't say it's gonna be exactly the same, but it can work either way."

Yet even the Kabbalah enthusiasts vary demographically. If you had to take a guess as to where there might be a Kabbalah center in Brooklyn, you could easily think of ten communities with new age Jews—places like Park Slope, Cobble Hill, Brooklyn Heights—but Bensonhurst, with its Asian, Italian, and Russian groups wouldn't be among them. The Christian and Jewish Russians are among the city's most secular groups, and their Jewish population has strongly resisted attempts to involve them. In part, this is due to the anti-religious atmosphere that dates back to communist times. And yet there is a Kabbalah center located on Eighty-fifth Street near Twentieth Avenue inside an apartment building, the Bnei Baruch Kabbalah Center. It started three years ago. I ask an elderly Russian woman passing by about the place. She replies, "I fully support the Kabbalah Center and I'm a Protestant. I also support the Lubavitcher rebbe. I've visited his grave in Queens."

I enter the Kabbalah Center through a side door of the apartment building and meet one of the staff members. "Whom do you attract?" I ask him.

"Everyone is interested. I don't want to talk bad about other places, like the one in Manhattan. But we are not commercial. We teach straight Kabbalah. We have about eighty people who come here, off and on. It's a very diverse group of mostly younger men, women, Americans, Russians, Israelis, you name it. We are nondenominational."

As I discovered when walking the five boroughs of New York, this type of outreach is very much what churches of all types do. Most religious groups try to build a sense of community. True, they're selling something, but they're at least doing it with warmth and kindness. One Sunday afternoon I found myself in the Church of the Restoration Temple, at Forty-sixth Street and Church Avenue in East Flatbush, Brooklyn. I couldn't help but be impressed by the members' love for others and their avoidance of strident statements about how nonbelievers are going to burn in hell. Hundreds of paper bags containing home-cooked turkey or ham dinners were being prepared for distribution to those in need. Although I was the only white person there, it made no difference whatsoever in how I was treated by the blacks who were there. To them I was just a guy taking a walk. When I returned two hours later, almost all of the dinners had been given out. These events are an essential part of church activities everywhere in the city, and they make a huge difference to those on the receiving end. But what was most striking to me that day was that almost all of the volunteers were young teenagers or people in their twenties.

It was no different at East Harlem's Holy Tabernacle Church on 114th Street near First Avenue. It's a down-home gospel church with lots of enthusiastic singing and dancing. I take my PhD students there every year to show them what a non-tourist-oriented Harlem church looks like. The crowd consists mainly of children ranging in age from toddlers to teenagers and adults, who are usually their parents or older siblings and friends. Most are dressed to the nines because it's an important day for them. If that's the case generally—and I observed the trend of youth participation at many other churches—then these institutions have a bright future indeed.

There's another significant trend among the young that needs to be emphasized, and that is that the religio-ethnic identities chosen by them are seen as personal options that are irrelevant to how they relate to one another. For most young people today, religion, color, or ethnic background have little impact on friendships, social patterns, and, increasingly, in marriage or cohabitation choices. Differences are openly discussed, explored, and even joked about, though rarely in a seriously denigrating way. That is a sea change from the past. It plays out in both the workplace and in social lives that are increasingly multiracial.

It's too soon to say what's happening with the children of the immigrants, a young but very different group of people. However, preliminary findings suggest that they reflect the general patterns of Americans. They are Americanizing, and although they belong ethnically to various groups, they do not identify religiously with a specific group. In other words, when they identify as Catholics or Protestants, it's more with the religion than with the religion's ethnic makeup, say, Hispanic or Korean Catholics.[24]

Appearances Count

Color and other physical traits are critical markers and determinants of identity. They have been carefully studied by researchers for decades. Similarly, for quite a few groups, ways of dressing are important markers of identity. Sikhs, Muslims, Hasidim, Indians, and Africans all have unique clothing that can set them apart. Sometimes dress is a matter of custom, and other times it's part of a person's religious laws.

In general, ethnic groups today have far less desire to hide their ethnic identity than their predecessors. In the past, Jews frequently had nose jobs. They claimed it was because of a deviated septum, but Jews themselves knew better. The Irish, wanting to look "more American," had their ears pinned back. Today immigrants and the children of immigrants also have medical procedures to change their appearance, but it's just as likely to be out of a desire to look *more* ethnic, and this is a new trend that reflects pride in who they are.

In Washington Heights, Latinos ask to have their buttocks rounded and enlarged. In the words of one Dominican woman, they want "the silhouette of a woman. We Latinas define ourselves with our bodies," she said. "We always have curves." In Flushing, Chinese may well request larger earlobes. "The bigger the earlobes, the more prosperous you are," according to plastic surgeon Dr. Jerry W. Chang. They also ask for an upturned nose to be turned "all the way down" because of a belief that prominent nostrils "permit fortune to spill out." Still, there are many Asians who ask for the opposite, demonstrating that the perceived standards of the dominant culture still prevail. Among the most popular procedures is double eyelid surgery, which makes eyes look rounder. Similarly, Russian immigrants ask for breast implants because large breasts are valued in American culture.[25] If nothing else, these varied trends demonstrate the push-and-pull forces that exist and the fact that ethnic group members cannot be easily stereotyped in how they view such matters.

Dress and physical appearance can be treated only in tandem with other factors. A closer look at the Sikh religion makes this abundantly clear. I visited a Sikh temple at 101st Avenue and 114th Street in Richmond Hill, Queens, a number of times and had firsthand opportunities to observe their behavior. Many of the men wear the traditional turbans and refrain from cutting their hair. It's one of the key tenets of their faith. Hair is considered holy, and the Sikhs have many stories of people who were tortured and even lost their lives because they refused demands to cut their hair. In their view the more they suffer for their beliefs, the more they can prove the strength of their devotion.

The younger generation is more liberal, but many younger Sikhs still attend services on a regular basis. In the temple, seating for men and women is separate, though they sit in the same large, open room without a partition, in full view of each other. Men sometimes go to the women's side to chat informally. To gain entry you just have to take off your shoes and cover your head with a bright orange kerchief. Often there is singing and music along with the prayers. A religious figure sits in a separate room and will offer specific prayers for you. Food is served in another room 24/7 and is offered to all who come, residents or visitors. This consists of tea, rice, pita bread, and vegetarian soup (everything is vegetarian). Thus we see that it's dress and long hair *together* with other important elements—the prayers, the ceremonies, and vegetarianism—that shape their identity. Although I have been to the Sikh temple many times, alone or with my students, no one has ever asked for a donation or other assistance. Each time, they have invited me in, offered food, and let me know they were available to answer any questions about their faith.

Language

Many immigrant groups do their best to retain their language even as they acclimate to America and the English language. Keeping their native language is not only a question of what they're comfortable with but also a reluctance to part with what they left behind. Plus, certain concepts, feelings, and emotions cannot be easily translated, if at all, to another language. Dominicans are most likely to retain their native language, and Russians are least likely to do so. But overall almost all children of immigrants are fluent in English, and most of their immigrant parents make an effort to speak English in the home. The children of immigrants are often proud of their bilingual capabilities. But, as is always the case, other factors are at work too when it comes to cultural retention. Videos, visits back home, and communicating with foreign nationals via the Internet also play important roles.

Sometimes the accent, and not the language, can be a marker of identity. West Indians believe that an awareness by others that they're from the West Indies gives them a higher status—and they may be right, depending on who's listening. Other accents, however, may have negative connotations. For example, the accent and argot of old Brooklyn, a staple of many films and comedy routines about the borough before the 1980s, is almost—but, as I discovered, not quite—dead.

Hanging around candy stores and delis in Bensonhurst, I watched and listened as groups of teenagers from nearby public schools came in, chattering and primping during recess, buying snacks such as Devil Dogs or Wise potato chips and cans of soda. They were oblivious to my presence, and I discovered that words like "dem" and "dose" rolled easily off their tongues, as did questions like, "Is you'se goin'?" or "Is you'se buyin' this?" These remarks were not made in any kind of mocking or joking tone, and there was no reaction by the listeners, who usually responded in kind. They were a mix of whites, possibly Italian Americans, and Asians. I wondered how these vestiges of what I thought was a vanished past survived. Were they transmitted through families? Clearly second-generation children from Russia or China learned these pronunciations, not from their immigrant parents, but from their American-born classmates.

A week later, as I was talking with a middle-age plumber in the neighborhood, I noticed that he spoke the same way as the teenagers in Bensonhurst when he asked me, "Where did you'se get this dog from?" (I use my dog sometimes as an ice-breaker. Most people talk easily to dog owners, so long as the dogs aren't pit bulls.) Clearly it would be awkward to ask the speakers whether or not they're aware of how they speak without destroying rapport. But I have found that using poor grammar when conversing with those who do so themselves makes them feel you're one of them; in that sense it's a marker of identity. Given that most of these people have moved out of areas where such forms of speech are typically heard, words like "dem" and "dose" will soon be extinct. For outsiders they serve as a reminder of what once was another world as well as to strengthen group identity.[26]

Neighborhoods

There are areas that have remained quite ethnic for a long time. One of them is the mostly Irish Woodlawn area in the Bronx. It's a little enclave, beginning at 233rd Street and extending to the city line with Westchester County. It also borders Van Cortlandt Park on the northwestern border. The eastern boundary is the Bronx River Parkway. It's an area of well-kept homes throughout, along with well-maintained apartment buildings. Katonah Avenue, the commercial hub, features more than a few pubs, and the fare in the restaurants is very Irish: Irish breakfast, shepherd's pie, corned beef and cabbage, Dublin-style fish and chips, Irish sausages, Gaelic steak, and much more.

The Woodlawn area has been augmented in recent years by a steady stream of Irish immigrants who are comfortable with the familiar. Signs in the travel agencies advertise cheap fares, jobs for nannies, and help in obtaining a green card. People are invited to drop in at the Emerald Isle Immigration Center to talk about feeling lonely, combating a DWI ("driving while intoxicated," sometimes referred to as "a diwi"), and anything else on their mind. Irish concerts are also announced through flyers distributed and pasted on the walls and windows of local shops. Immigration to the area ebbs and flows in accordance with the Irish economy. In 2010 there was a downturn and immigration increased once again, after declining for some time.[27]

Similar observations could be made about other neighborhoods like West Indians in East Flatbush, Poles in Greenpoint, Guyanese in Richmond Hill, Hasidim in Williamsburg, and Koreans and Chinese in Flushing. In each instance the neighborhood and its stores, churches, playgrounds, and so on allow members to have an A-to-Z life in which their togetherness reinforces their culture.

Each community has different concrete markers of identification. Again, religion is an especially powerful presence in New York's poor communities. As I stand on Morris Avenue and East 151st Street in the Bronx, I spy the usual Chinese takeout place, here known as Mr. Wonton; a health center; and a Jamaican restaurant. But this location is also known as a religious place, almost a shrine, as evidenced by a neat, gold-lettered sign set against a red background. The sign reads, "On this site, on October 2, 1979, His Holiness, Pope John Paul II, blessed the faithful of the community." Thus history has been both made and preserved. For the people of the South Bronx it means that the leader of the world's Catholics cared enough to visit the neighborhood and bless those who live here.

Ethnicity Makes Sense Economically

Sometimes I see people selling items like foods, herbs, pocket-books, or tape recorders, with an African flag nearby waving in the wind. A Washington Heights fast-food eatery on Broadway and 166th Street apparently seeks to capitalize on the iconic appeal of a black hero when it dubs itself the X Café in the shadow of the Malcolm X Museum. There's nothing wrong with this. In fact, it demonstrates the power and appeal of ethnicity itself and is a form of ethnic identity. Such appropriations, however, are clearly for economic gain.

Brooklyn's giant, kosher, and upscale Pomegranate supermarket tries to appeal to buyers by letting it be known that they donate unsold food to the Jewish poor at the end of each day. But people are skeptical, nonetheless. "Doesn't it sound a little implausible that every night they give all the leftovers to the hungry?" says one elderly Orthodox woman. "You're not going to make any money that way."

In Flatlands, Brooklyn, I meet a skullcap-wearing Bukharian barber who appears to be in his late thirties. His name isn't Tony, but on top of the store window a sign reads, "Tony's Barber Shop." There may be some value in using Tony's name for older Italian men who knew the real Tony. But this barber, who travels here every day from Kew Gardens Hills, Queens, has his own come-on sign next to the first one: "Shomer Shabbos" (Sabbath observer). Unlike a kosher food establishment, where the man's level of observance matters to customers, it makes no material difference whether the barber keeps the Sabbath or not. It's just a none-too-subtle appeal to ethnic loyalties. Actually, it's sort of like the old signs that encouraged African Americans to "Buy Black." It seems to be an unwritten rule in the city that you can openly appeal to your own group. Actually, it does matter in a different area—the conversations in the chair. It means you have more in common with the man with whom you are likely to speak for twenty minutes once every month if you're a similarly observant Jew.

Here's another instance. There is an auto repair shop in Flushing, seemingly run, if one can judge from the Chinese writing on the sign outside, by Chinese people. Its name is Hallelujah Praise the Lord Auto Sales, at 131-32 Sanford Avenue. (See figure 28.) The shop sits about two blocks from the far more American-sounding Home Depot a block away. A Cherokee Jeep is parked in front with a personalized New York State license plate that reads, "Isaiah58." On the back window of the Jeep, stick-on letters spell out, "My Father Created Heaven and Earth." Religion is alive and well in this city, at least in one part of Flushing. And one can assume that some of the customers share the proprietor's strong religious feelings.

In a sign of outreach to nonobservant but culturally Jewish Jews, I've come across restaurants that are clearly not kosher making accommodations for such people. It's an example of ethnic tolerance—actually empathy—but also a good financial idea for the restaurant, since it attracts customers. I'm told by the owners that people have had positive reactions because it makes them feel they can have a family Seder at the restaurant without having to do the work. Moreover, they're also not into the religion part, like reciting the Haggadah for hours on end. This interest in celebrating the holiday in some way is not surprising, since Passover is the most widely observed holiday among Jews of all denominations as well as those who belong to no denominations.

In line with this I pass by Tuscan, a fairly high Zagat-rated Carnegie Hill Italian restaurant on Madison Avenue. It has a special Passover menu: Tuscan chicken livers with *haroseth* (a sweet holiday concoction made of fruits and nuts) and matzo, followed by gefilte fish, then chicken soup and matzo balls, with a main course of Tuscan pot roast and chicken with oven-roasted potatoes, spinach, string beans, and Brussels sprouts, and concluding with a dessert: a coconut macaroon with chocolate sauce. The price is sixty-five dollars per person. It was never a big deal when nonkosher restaurants did a "kosher-style" dinner. But these were primarily Jewish-oriented places to begin with, like the Carnegie or Stage delis. This, however, is something new—an Italian restaurant boldly advertising such a menu. It's obviously an important attraction, since they're putting it in the window ten days before the Passover holiday. On a regular day you can have all the shellfish and pork you want. The lesson is that ethnicity matters to Jews even if they're not at all observant, because religion is only one aspect of ethnicity. It's a perfect example of "symbolic ethnicity," a term first coined by the eminent sociologist Herbert Gans. In his view it was often the last stage before assimilation. After all, what staying power could such forms of identity have?

One last example of religious/economic symbiosis: In the northernmost corner of Manhattan, on Ninth Avenue, near 219th Street, there's a car repair place that is festooned from end to end with banners from every country in the world. The owner explains, "My father came here as an immigrant from Greece, and he really appreciated this idea of a country where people could come from any nation and make it. Putting up these banners was his way of giving back to America. We have customers from all over the world." I mention this last because it's not clear that the man gains any customers from this display, though he does believe that it helps. However, he doesn't know for sure. In that sense it's a measure of identity's complexity: there's often more going on than we think.

Synthesizing from Other Cultures

If it strengthens their own group in any way, efforts will be made to connect to others, no matter how tenuous the connections may be. An interesting sidebar is how religious connections can even be made to a distant, seemingly unconnected past. In the summer of 2009, a five-day "consecration ceremony" was held at the Hindu Temple Society of North America's Ganesha Temple, one of the largest in the country. The city is home to about seventy-eight thousand Indian-born residents and their children, most of them Hindus.

This ceremony and its rituals are said to give the various stone deities of the Hindu faith a "divine energy." Among the featured participants in the summer ceremony was thirty-seven-year-old Minnie, an Indian elephant who "wore a gold-studded shield on her forehead and carried a bare-chested Hindu priest with a silver-tasseled parasol." Ganesh is the name given to the elephant-faced deity credited with removing all "problems and obstacles." A cow, holy to Hindus, was also present in the temple. It was "petted and fed unpeeled bananas until it rebelled and had to be led outside." Hindu priests, wearing red and orange *dhotis* (loincloths), stood barefoot atop scaffolding high above the ground and poured water on the deities and temple towers. In a response reminiscent of Hasidim who try to catch pieces of thrown bread from a challah started by their leader, members of the crowd attempted to catch the drops of water as they fell to the ground.[28]

Coincidentally, Flushing, Queens, the site of the temple and of a large Hindu community, is where local colonists in 1657 signed the Flushing Remonstrance, long seen as a precursor to the proclamation of religious freedom found in the Bill of Rights. The signers were protesting the persecution of Quakers, but we can assume that they would have applied their ideas to Hindus too, since they did mention Jews, Egyptians, and Turks in their protest. In point of fact, Bowne Street, named after John Bowne, who let the Quakers meet in his home, now has an eclectic mix of Hindu temples, a synagogue, a Chinese church, and a Sikh *gurdwara* (house of worship).

Like the Quakers, the Hindu founders of the temple faced prejudice when it opened some twenty years ago, and the connection was not lost on them. Eggs were thrown at the temple by people who, it was suspected, viewed the Hindu faith as a cult. The temple is now fully accepted, and its current president, Dr. Uma Mysorekar, was an invited guest in the National Cathedral ceremony at President Obama's first inauguration.[29]

The commonalities between early and later persecution and the similar outcomes emphasize how religious discrimination followed by gradual acceptance is a recurring feature in American history. They also suggest that Hindus will eventually become just as accepted in the United States as Quakers are today. And the accident of geography serves as a wonderful way to highlight it.

African Americans have had a long and ambivalent relationship with Jews. On the one hand, the two groups have had conflict in terms of merchant-customer, landlord-tenant, and principal-teacher conflicts. But such differences between the two cultures have been overshadowed by their alliances against prejudice during the civil rights era and earlier. They also feel a strong connection historically. Blacks identify with the ancient Israelites who were enslaved and wandered in the desert as a people without a land. And black ministers frequently discuss the Jews in quotes and stories about them in the Bible. In fact, certain black sects claim to be the "real Israelites" and identify with the Ten Lost Tribes.[30]

African Americans have also sought to connect themselves with the much larger Muslim world. After breaking with Elijah Muhammad, Malcolm X tried to bring the African American Muslims into closer alignment with that world, moving away from the Nation of Islam's racial rhetoric and toward a universally united Islam. Eventually Malcolm X became convinced that the Koran, as expressed by the Prophet Muhammad, was racially color-blind. And ultimately he opposed prejudice against all religions.[31]

It's no surprise to find some very unusual groups in this city. One religious group that I came across, the School of Kemetic Thought and Spirituality, defied easy definition. Based in Burkina Faso (formerly Upper Volta), the religion began thousands of years ago when a dynasty of kings was established by peoples who migrated from Egypt in the days of the pharaohs. It practices the traditions of the Gourmanche/Dogon peoples, which include polytheism, spiritualism, speaking the Medu (hieroglyphic) language, meditation, chanting, forms of breathing, and more. I speak to one of their representatives who has just opened what is called an Earth Center at 405 Lefferts Avenue on the corner of New York Avenue in Lefferts Gardens, Brooklyn, a predominantly black area. There are various food and liquid products for sale, as well as tapes of lectures; the center offers classes too. The neighborhood is mostly black, but people from other backgrounds are there as well. In a way it seems more like an Eastern religion, like Buddhist or Hindu, but historically it's from Africa.

The earnest young white man who runs it is quite American, having grown up in Montclair, New Jersey. A slight, bearded fellow, he is serious and knowledgeable, a former student at Wesleyan University. He gives me his business card, which identifies him as "Nekhitem Kamenthu, 1st Generation Secretary, Treasurer and Instructor." There are hieroglyphic-like inscriptions on the card that look fascinating, but I can't understand them. The card's other side has a photograph of a turbaned African man dressed in a white robe with interesting-looking designs, standing beneath a tree, and addressing a group of young black children. The inscription, set between the photo and the center's website address, reads, "The sun never sets, it is man who moves away from the light."

Nekhitem explains to me, "This is a pre-Greco-Roman religion that is still being maintained, with kinship relations, medicines, government, philosophy, spirituality—everything. The pharaoh was the main king in this three-tiered system. Then you had regional kings and small kings. And a number of them moved west from the Nile Valley and settled in the Niger Valley. And it's that Nile Valley culture which is being preserved here."

It strikes me that New York City is the perfect place for this religion, because it is cosmopolitan and home to so many large and small groups. It's an "anything goes" type of place. It is also a city that seems to be in the midst of a religious revival of sorts. An African-based ancient religion answers so much of the yearning by peoples, especially blacks, for discovering and learning about their roots and origins. On top of that, the new age elements—meditation, exercises, and healthy living, also appeal to the young. And the worship of many deities gives it an exotic air as well.

Gays

Homosexuals are not an ethnic group in the usual sense of the word, but they're certainly a distinct one with its own set of cultural norms and values. They are defined by sexual orientation, include both males and females, and have suffered tremendously from discrimination in the past. They have made great strides as a community in the last thirty-five years. One of the high points for gay culture has been New York State's passage of the same-sex marriage bill on June 24, 2011, signed by Governor Andrew Cuomo just five minutes before midnight. In a way this bill symbolizes how far the gay community has come.[32] To see how much progress has been made, contrast this with the situation during the 1970s, when gays engaged in furtive sex along the Lower West Side's semi-abandoned piers or in private clubs like Plato's Retreat.[33]

Speaking with several gays in a bar along Eighth Avenue in Chelsea, I sought to learn how they viewed the bill's passage. Their answers were revealing. One, a graphic artist, said, "Sure, we're happy, though it's a little late. The bill gives us legal status and that will affect our self-image. We will feel respected." Another man, an attorney, spoke about the long-range impact. "Look, the Civil Rights Bill in 1964 didn't change things right away. The negative attitudes were still there, but *over time* attitudes do change." "Right," said a third, who declined to discuss the work he does. "There's still lots of homophobia, though it's more and more in the closet." He laughed.

Overall, gays have benefited from a sea change in public opinion as more and more New Yorkers have come around to the idea that gay people are entitled to the same rights as anyone else. Many people today feel that gays have a right to their lifestyles, even if it's not one they themselves would choose. They have also come to believe that being gay is a personal matter and that, moreover, it's not an illness. Even those who do not believe that being gay is "normal" have become more tolerant of it.

Like many ethnics, this is a group whose sense of identity and group solidarity has grown. They have realized that uniting gives them strength, but they have also benefited from being a highly educated group with a real presence in the media, arts, education, and commerce. This has greatly increased their clout, especially as more and more people have openly declared themselves to be gay. And as more and more heterosexuals in powerful positions learn that their own close friends or relatives are gay, they have become more accepting of gays. All this is radically different from the society of three decades ago.

What changed were shifting values and attitudes generally, the same evolution that resulted in changing views about immigrants, blacks, and women. Increased contact, greater education, and better enforcement of people's rights, all played major roles in this transformation into a more inclusive society, and these efforts paid off as public opinion shifted. Whereas in 2004 a Quinnipiac poll showed 37 percent support for same-sex marriage among New York State residents, that number increased to 58 percent by 2011. The movement had come a long way from its most visible symbol: a riot at the Stonewall Inn in the West Village in June 1969.[34]

Interestingly, most social change appears radical at first, seeking to promote agendas that challenge the social order. In a key sense this effort was the opposite. By asking for the right to marry, gay activists were advocating to become part of a bedrock tradition of the family, similar to the demands of the early civil rights movement for integration rather than separatism. In that sense the identity of gays as outsiders shifted even though their identity as gays did not.

As *New York Times* columnist Frank Bruni wrote in an opinion piece, "Saying 'I do' to 'I do' is much more effective—not to mention more reflective of the way most gay people live—than strutting in leather on a parade float. We're not trying to undermine the institution of marriage, a task ably handled by the likes of Tiger Woods, Arnold Schwarzenegger, John Edwards and too many other onetime role models to mention. We're paying it an enormous compliment."[35] Thus, this massive organized effort symbolizes how "establishment" the movement has become. It also suggests a shrewd calculation that if gays become part of the establishment, they will guarantee their standing and their long-term security in American society.

The thirty-year fight against AIDS has also played a crucial role. As shameful as the disease was in the minds of Americans, AIDS made it necessary for gays to "come out of the closet." It was the only way they could get society to realize how many of its members were affected by the disease, which afflicted them disproportionately.[36]

Nevertheless, opposition to same-sex unions remains. After all, 42 percent of New Yorkers polled in 2011 did not support the idea. That was also made clear by Dennis Poust of the New York State Catholic Conference, who admitted, "In many ways, we were outgunned."[37] Nonetheless, legislators pushed through provisions protecting religious organizations from penalties by the state if they refused to accommodate those wanting same-sex marriage ceremonies performed in their facilities.[38]

But even in conservative circles, attitudes are changing, often fueled by personal experience. No less a conservative icon than Andrea Peyser made that clear when she opened her *New York Post* column on gay marriage with the words, "I give in." Writing about the recent marriage in Massachusetts of her niece to another woman, she observed, "Despite abstract discomfort over normalizing gay unions, I don't know of a soul who would discriminate against the nice guys next door. Nor would I deny my niece happiness that is evident in the size of her smile."[39] Clearly, the greater general tolerance for all sorts of group identification has had an effect on how gays are perceived too. In short, New York City is just a much more open town today than it was thirty years ago.

Which Way, New York?

What will the city look like fifty years from now in terms of ethnicity? Will assimilation be the norm, or will most residents continue to identify primarily with their ethnic groups? In a groundbreaking book, *Blurring the Color Line,* sociologist Richard Alba addresses this question from many angles. Although the discussion is about the United States generally, the Big Apple has often been a bellwether for the country in terms of national trends.[40]

Alba begins by asking whether President Barack Obama's election really means that much in the larger scheme of racial and ethnic progress. He notes that today there are more black than white males in prison. Ethno-racial minorities today constitute 60 percent of those incarcerated. Additional pessimism about residential segregation persists and is even prevalent in many parts of the United States, including New York. One-third of the country's black children remain mired in poverty. Hispanics are also faring poorly, though not as badly as blacks. Given this state of affairs, many scholars believe that assimilation may not occur for another hundred years, if ever.

But things could change, says Alba, and the rest of his book is devoted to a searching and insightful analysis of how and why that could happen. He points to the experiences of white ethnics, who largely came here in the period from the mid-nineteenth century to the early twentieth century, when discriminatory immigration laws reduced their numbers to a trickle. Rejecting the argument that these groups ultimately succeeded because they were white, Alba reminds us that the white ethnics were—like today's blacks, Hispanics, and to a far lesser extent, Asians—also considered "unassimilable." Italians were stereotyped as criminals and primitive; the Irish as drunkards and rapists; and the Jews as communists, Christ killers, and money grubbers. Today these judgments sound ancient.

Alba points out that more and more baby boomers are retiring from the workforce. An estimated fifteen million new jobs will therefore be available by the 2030s. This will open up new opportunities for people in general, including minorities. Using statistical data from many sources, including the 2005 and 2006 American Community Surveys, Alba demonstrates that minorities are already moving into better positions, especially in the public sector. He asserts that governmental agencies and private organizations can play an important role by pushing for equal treatment and expanded opportunities. For those in favor of assimilation, Alba recommends narrowing the gap in education, continuing Affirmative Action for the foreseeable future, and promoting, wherever possible, residential integration.

There is evidence from other sources, too, supporting the movement toward assimilation. Philip Kasinitz found that only 20 percent of the children of immigrants feel it's important to marry within the group.[41] In 2008, 20 percent of black males and about 9 percent of black females in the United States married non-blacks. In addition, 50 percent of American-born Asians have married non-Asians. Furthermore, it appears likely that in thirty years or so, people of mixed-race heritage will constitute a majority of the population in the United States.[42] Among whites, signs of assimilation were already clear twenty years ago. The 1990 U.S. Census shows that 56 percent of whites were married to people with no ethnic group in common, a quarter had some overlap, and 20 percent were identical in ethnicity. Almost 70 percent of Japanese were intermarried in 1990, and that figure is increasing. This shows the degree to which one racial boundary has diminished. In 1950 the intermarriage rate for Japanese was only 5 percent. For Jews the rate jumped from 11 percent in 1965 to about 50 percent of those who have married since 1985.[43] Today the numbers of intermarried couples are significantly higher all around.

Anecdotally, I have learned that many New Yorkers not only support the trend toward marriage between different groups but also view it positively as a way of reducing prejudice. A good case in point is an Irish-Jewish couple living in Staten Island. One of their children married someone who is of Irish, Cuban, and Italian descent. The other child has a spouse they call a "white-bread" from Illinois. This, they believe, is the future and they love it. "He's a wonderful son-in-law," they say. These comments were typical of many I heard in conversations with a broad spectrum of New Yorkers. I well remember asking a waiter in a Harlem restaurant about his national origins. "I'm everything," he responded. "My mother is Gabonese and French, and my father is Polish and Chinese. I guess I'm just an American." Hopefully, society will come to a similar conclusion.

Others say that this perhaps romanticized vision faces considerable obstacles and may not come to pass, at least not for a very long time. There is still plenty of residential segregation in New York, whether it's by choice or not. We can't be sure how much attitudes of whites toward minorities will change over time. The presence of large numbers of undocumented minorities will slow down the assimilation process. Blacks and many Hispanics in particular will continue to face significant hurdles, because color is still a major barrier. That said, it would still seem that the salience of color, and certainly ethnicity, will eventually decrease in significance, especially as intermarriage between different races results in muted hues of gold, olive, beige, and many other skin shades, accompanied by a fading away of other physical traits.

Notwithstanding the questions later raised about fiscal shenanigans, the wave of the future may perhaps be exemplified best by the election of New York City comptroller John Liu. His parents symbolically exemplified the immigrant—and, one might add, political—dream when they named their sons Robert, Edward, and John after the Kennedys. It's not just that Liu is the first Asian elected to citywide office. He is that. But what's more important is that Liu, whose parents came to the United States from Taiwan, was elected by an unlikely coalition of other immigrants besides his own group, including Pakistanis in Brooklyn and Koreans in Queens. And, of course, he also needed to pull in votes from New Yorkers in general, of all backgrounds.

At his swearing in Liu was clearly aware of the significance of his election. In terms that could have been applied to earlier waves of newcomers, he referred to a history of "second-class citizenship" and a voter registration drive that brought about "groundbreaking milestones for a country built by immigrants. I am humbled to be part of that wave of change."[44] And as he stood on the podium, smiling broadly with fists clenched high above his head, to the applause of all those present, you knew history was being made.[45]

Shortly after Liu's status as an Asian American became tarnished amid charges of illegal campaign finances, another role model burst onto the scene—Jeremy Lin, point guard for the New York Knicks. Also a child of Taiwanese immigrants, Lin electrified the city and the country when he scored a whopping 114 points in his first four games as a Knicks starter, a modern NBA record.

Untold numbers of Asians became interested in basketball overnight, thrilling to his accomplishments. "All the Asian-American guys want to be Jeremy Lin, and all the Asian-American girls want to marry him," asserted graphic designer Su Nam.[46] To be sure, it was a stereotype-shattering phenomenon. Asians are thought of as particularly talented in the sciences, especially math, computers, and engineering. They are not known for their sports prowess in basketball. On the other hand, Lin possessed certain traits that are generally associated with being Asian. Academically successful, he was a Harvard graduate and he exhibited a self-effacing attitude, going out of his way to praise his teammates as opposed to emphasizing his own stats.

It's highly doubtful that there will be a wave of Asian American basketball stars, just as there are very few of Jewish or Arab origin. But the idea that this could happen to a Chinese American was enough to engender pride in a group that has experienced considerable prejudice and discrimination since coming to these shores. This was much more a Pan-Asian event than a Chinese one as Koreans, Filipinos, and Thais crowded around televisions in bars and restaurants to watch the phenomenon known as "Linsanity." In taking this bastion of American sports by storm, Lin stood out as a symbol for all Asians that made them more American than almost anything else could have.

Then there was the fact that Lin wears his Christian faith on his sleeve—or at least his jersey. He thanked God for his success and shone the spotlight on the fact that large portions of the Asian community, including the young, are regular churchgoers. This combination again demonstrates the complex interplay between race, religion, and ethnicity. The nuances at work here were aptly described by fellow Asian American Michael Luo, who wrote in the *New York Times*, "Some have predicted that Lin, because of his faith, will become the Taiwanese Tebow, a reference to Denver Broncos quarterback Tim Tebow, whose outspokenness about his evangelical Christian beliefs has made him extraordinarily popular in some circles and venomously disliked in others. . . . From talking to people who knew him through the Harvard-Radcliffe Asian American Christian Fellowship, and watching his interviews, I have the sense that his [Lin's] is a quieter, potentially less polarizing but no less devout style of faith."[47] Now, of course, he's with the Houston Rockets (and doing well there too), but he will not be easily forgotten by New Yorkers of all backgrounds.

The cases of Liu and Lin highlight the web of forces at work when it comes to acceptance. There's a certain duality here that characterizes what's happening in general. The acceptance of Asians by the mainstream is clear. Yet, at the same time, Liu and Lin have advanced in tandem with the maintenance of their Asian identities. In fact their accomplishments are seen as stemming from both individual traits and the fact that they are Asian. Jeremy Lin's religious identification is similarly thought of as an individual decision but also one that's part of a trend among Asian Americans throughout the country.

Reflecting on all of this, it's safe to conclude that New York City has three groups. First there are the identifiers. They are proud of their heritage and actively identify with it. Second, there are the assimilationists, who play down their ethnicity and hope for a future when such differences are irrelevant. And then there's a third group: people who embrace contact with others but also maintain their own identity. It may be that none of these groups will dominate. And in all likelihood there will be many new hybrid groups in the future. Regardless, it is very likely that all of these groups will coexist under a banner of tolerance. If anything has emerged from this exploration of the city, it is that people agree almost universally that there should be freedom of choice in where and how one wants to live and identify.

8

CONCLUSIONS

The conclusions drawn in this book are based largely on the more than six thousand miles I walked through the streets and parks of New York City over a four-year period. During that time I observed the life of the street close up and participated in its daily activities. I hung out on street corners, attended community meetings, sat in parks, went to concerts, danced in nightclubs, and spoke with hundreds of people from every walk of life. In truth I've actually been walking this city since I was a young child, having been raised here. This gave me a valuable perspective in that I was able to assess the changes in New York over a long period of time. My travels were augmented by a careful reading of the books and articles that have been written about the city that pertain to my field of sociology.

This is more of a qualitative work, relying heavily on the results of intensive observation and interviews, of both the spontaneous and planned varieties. But it also integrates findings by others of a more quantitative nature. Since this is the first attempt to evaluate the city sociologically as a whole, using ethnography as a method, it should be seen as an exploratory effort. Hopefully, future researchers of the city will find the information gathered and presented here of value in their own work.

Overall what has emerged with great clarity from this effort is that *New York today is a city that is enjoying a tremendous renaissance.* This is a remarkable contrast with the New York of the 1970s and early '80s. First, its streets are safer—and cleaner—than they ever were, with throngs of people walking the city both day and night. The energy of its people largely emanates from two key population groups, one external and one internal: the immigrants and the gentrifiers. The immigrants, who come from every corner of the world, have reinvigorated the city with their often incredible drive and ambitions, which are, in turn, fueled by the dreams they have of changing the trajectory of their own lives for the better. The gentrifiers are largely young and professional. Because of their own high levels of talent and accomplishments, they have transformed the perception and reality of New York City as a cutting-edge and fashionable place, one suffused with new ideas, incredible energy, commercial growth, and a palpable sense of excitement that make its residents feel proud to call it their permanent home.

The following are some of the most striking conclusions of this book:

1. New York is an exceedingly rich and complex city made up of diverse people and villages. Its residents are, by and large, a highly sophisticated population stemming from both their personal life histories and the fact that they live and function in a highly modern and technologically advanced twenty-first-century, world-famous city.

2. While crime remains a serious problem in the city's poorest areas and must be addressed, most New Yorkers feel that the decrease in crime is the major factor accounting for its rejuvenation. What's surprising is the fervor and frequency with which this view is expressed.

3. Immigration is a key force that gives New York much of its dynamism. The presence of newcomers will continue to shape the city in myriad ways in the future.

4. There is broad sympathy for the undocumented at every level of society. This is of critical importance because their large numbers make a solution for this problem absolutely necessary if the city is to continue to thrive and grow.

5. Gentrification is a hugely important phenomenon in this city, dramatically changing neighborhoods and resulting in major population shifts that have reshaped New York.

6. Contrary to the stereotype of the cold, hard city, most New Yorkers are friendly, outgoing, gregarious, and eager to help.

7. The ambivalence felt by outer borough residents toward Manhattan has greatly diminished.

8. The trauma of 9/11 has become a permanent part of New Yorkers' consciousness. The passage of time has made little difference in how strongly they feel about the events of that day. Most significantly, however, this terrible tragedy has served to unify the city, exemplifying its ability to replace the despair with an almost triumphant belief in the resilience of its inhabitants.

9. Today people of different ethnic and racial groups can live wherever they want, given the tremendous decrease in discrimination over the past thirty-five years. Nonetheless, large numbers still choose to live among their own. However, they do so because they want to, not because they have no choice. Conversely, those people who prefer diversity can and do opt for such communities too.

10. Groups that are traditionally hostile to each other before immigrating get along surprisingly well in New York.

11. The greater emphasis on health and the environment has affected the city in many areas.

12. New Yorkers use public space in many positive and creative ways that express both their outer and inner selves, thereby making clear what's really important to them, especially with regard to leisure-time activities.

13. The long-term trend in the city is toward assimilation. However, significant numbers of people are also moving in the other direction, toward greater identification with their own religions and ethnicities.

14. Another emerging trend is the development of hybrid identities that combine elements of various cultures in ways that are new and unique.

And now, let's take a more in-depth look at the findings. One of the most important findings of this book is that New York City is both a collection of many separate communities and a unified whole. New Yorkers think of their communities as if they were miniature countries with their own histories, rules, customs, and identities. In a way this attitude is an attempt to manage the realities of living in a large anonymous place through creating a space that they can identify with and truly call home.

Paradoxically, New Yorkers are equally proud of living in a world-class city, and they identify strongly with that idea too. Tourist destinations like the Empire State Building, Radio City Music Hall, Central Park, and the Metropolitan Museum of Art have a different meaning for them. Such places are *really* theirs, because they live in the city where these places are located, and therefore they're accessible to New Yorkers all the time. In addition, it's their taxes that support the existence and well-being of these clearly national treasures. This has resulted in the image of a "New York type," a person who is brash, self-confident, a bit of a smart-aleck, someone with "attitude." These characteristics are obviously stereotypes, but as such, they contain a kernel of truth.

There's tremendous variation among the city's neighborhoods. Some are a virtual UN, while others have only one or two ethnic groups residing within their confines. Some are on the water or adjacent to parkland, others in densely populated areas. There are areas with one-family homes and those that contain only apartment buildings.

Regardless of their location, a critical determinant of a neighborhood's attractiveness is whether or not it has a sense of community. For each neighborhood, that sense of community is all about friendliness, warmth, and pride in where they live. This is augmented by the existence of community characters, people who enhance a community's uniqueness and who contribute to its life and viability. Amenities like recreational facilities, good shopping and transportation, restaurants, and entertainment are also linchpins in a community's attractiveness. Conversely, the proliferation of satellite shopping streets and malls in poorer neighborhoods has made them more autonomous and disconnected from the city as a whole, as has the lack of good transportation wherever that's the case.

Community gardens are a particularly important feature of urban life today. They engender pride and purpose among the residents who help create and maintain them, and they make the neighborhood look more like a true community. Some neighborhoods have cachet and others don't. This can depend on the mix of people who move there, especially those who are famous, and how good a job the community does in presenting its own history and image.

New York is now perhaps the safest large city in the country. No one appreciates that more than those who lived through the 1970s and 1980s, when crime reached epidemic proportions. What is striking is how often New Yorkers comment with pride on the city's low crime rate. They see it as one of the most significant accomplishments in terms of changing their daily lives as well as the city's image. And yet nothing is ever perfect. Large pockets remain in the city that are virtually untouched by this trend. In these areas people treat the statistics extolling crime's downward spiral with disdain and disbelief, largely because their own neighborhoods have not become safe by any standard. The homeless and panhandlers, by the way, are still with us. Their overall numbers have been reduced over the years, there is far greater tolerance for them and they are far more visible than ten years ago. City folks have become largely apathetic to their presence, treating them simply as chronic annoyances.

Another development has been the greatly increased use of surveillance cameras, thousands of them, in both public and private locations. This is an outgrowth of past fears of crime and present concerns about terrorism. My conversations with many New Yorkers validated the assumption that most city dwellers have no objection to the cameras, arguing that safety trumps privacy. Criminals and police both agree, telling me that the cameras are very effective.

Immigration to New York has truly changed the city, with more than three million people having arrived in the city since the 1960s. The immigrants' energy and ambition to remake their lives and to achieve their dreams have had a major impact on the city, giving it a certain dynamism that can be felt by anyone who walks the streets, especially the teeming neighborhoods in which they have settled. The lands they come from often differ from the origins of earlier waves of immigrants, and this has resulted in a reshaped cultural map of the Big Apple. Moreover, many immigrants come with economic capital and networks, some of them surprisingly sophisticated. This has the unintended but real consequence of decreasing the opportunities for Puerto Ricans and African Americans who have been mired in poverty here, sometimes for generations, and who are trying to take advantage of the new options created by a more open society.

The immigrants tend to live among their own kind. This is partly because of the comfort level they feel when they do so and partly because of the fact that certain groups have come in waves over a short period of time. This has an isolating effect in certain neighborhoods where one group is especially numerous. There are large areas in the city where very few people speak English. Parts of Flushing, Queens, and Bushwick, Brooklyn, are good examples. Immigrants learn English more slowly as a result and are not forced to make the contacts with others that they need in order to adjust to life here. Most immigrants, however, reside in the midst of larger mixed areas. They meet others in schools, parks, community centers, houses of worship, as neighbors, and in the workplace. This has always been the case, but each new mix has its own, often unique challenges. The adaptation of Muslims has been significantly affected by 9/11, an event that had a tremendous impact on the city. Many Muslims have turned inward to their communities because of prejudice against them.

The volume and rate by which immigrants have entered the boroughs have resulted in a constantly shifting tableau of ethnic groups. A neighborhood that was formerly home to white ethnics changes over in a few short years to one that is Asian or Hispanic. A community that is Hispanic becomes Pakistani. This process means constant flux as the immigrants move, and the stores they patronized and the places of worship they attended must relocate as well. Children of immigrants who attended schools in one area are also uprooted. One benefit of this process of change is that it somewhat counteracts the isolation discussed before, because in moving to new neighborhoods the immigrants are forced, at least initially, to interact with outsiders. These two processes—isolation and contact—occur unevenly. Some areas experience much change while others experience very little of it.

Important demographic changes have occurred in New York City over the past few decades. One is the large increase in the

Asian population, which today numbers over one million people. Hispanics have also increased in number, with Mexicans the fastest-growing group. By contrast, non-Hispanic whites and blacks have diminished in size in the last decade. The Jewish population has grown larger in the past ten years, but its composition has changed, with many more of these Jews, about 40 percent, identifying themselves as Orthodox. Overall what this means is that New York is more white in Manhattan and in the gentrified areas of Brooklyn and Queens, and has a growing population of immigrants in various stages of adaptation.

The immigrants of recent times are far more likely to have strong transnational connections, and they visit their homelands more frequently. A new pattern is for highly educated children of immigrants to move back to their parents' countries. But this may well turn out to be a temporary phenomenon fueled largely by difficult times in the United States.

All immigrants must face the dilemma that has confronted foreigners since the beginnings of this land: how to integrate into a new culture and society without losing the elements of the old way of life that they often miss and of which they were once an integral part. The current climate of tolerance for differences has enabled the newcomers to maintain their identity more than previous generations were able to. One major outcome of the research was in documenting the great importance of religion in the immigrants' lives. For them their faith is a source of much comfort and fellowship with like-minded believers. Religious institutions also provide many essential services: they help people network and find jobs, provide counseling, and give them the friendship that helps sustain them in difficult times. And ultimately religious institutions give meaning to people's lives.

A closer look at New York's immigrant population reveals differences within groups as well, especially in terms of class, religion, culture, geography, and language. The various agencies and organizations that engage the newcomers need to be sensitive to these distinctions if they are to help them. Another interesting finding was that groups who have been hostile to one another in the homeland have dramatically different relationships here. The conflicts back home seem irrelevant in the American context. Many see their move to America as an opportunity to develop friendships that they had once considered unthinkable.

Undocumented immigrants make up a large part of New York's population, and not much is known about them. They are an estimated six hundred thousand in size and growing each year. Their future is uncertain, since much depends on the degree to which the government will allow them to legalize their status, in line with the beginning steps taken by President Obama. One somewhat surprising conclusion is the overwhelming sympathy that citizens of every socioeconomic level feel toward the undocumented, despite high unemployment among their ranks. They are generally perceived as hardworking individuals who are also willing to take jobs others don't want. The undocumented people I spoke with were perfectly happy to converse and did not exhibit anxiety about being deported. The feeling seems to be that as long as they do not get into trouble with the law, they will not be bothered. They make use of public facilities from parks to hospitals, their children attend schools, and they live pretty normal lives.

In the past twenty-five years New York has been part of a seismic demographic shift of young urban professionals moving into the central city from the suburbs and other parts of the country. Attracted by jobs; easier commutes; and amenities like entertainment, upscale restaurants, and safer streets, they have given new life to the city with their presence. And increasingly they are raising families in neighborhoods their parents may have sought to escape from a generation ago.

Gentrifiers fall into two sometimes overlapping categories: those who move into communities because of the available amenities and the convenience of living near work, and preservationists who are attracted by the character and history of certain neighborhoods. These are augmented by a supporting cast of students and artists who move into the least expensive housing available in these neighborhoods, usually industrial pockets, often doubling and tripling up.

A serious examination of New York's neighborhoods made it crystal clear that, generalizations notwithstanding, the city remains very authentic. It has "historical cachet." If you want nostalgia, you just have to look for it in the right places. There are large stretches of Gotham that still retain the flavor of old New York. Traverse Bensonhurst or Bay Ridge, and you'll find that the Brooklyn of *Saturday Night Fever* lives. Go on foot through Northeast Bronx streets like Rowland, St. Peter's, St. Raymond's, Zerega, Paulding, Crosby, Radcliffe, and Bogart, and you'll find one-hundred-year-old homes and apartment buildings the norm, relatively untouched by gentrification. The inhabitants today are a mix of the earlier ones and more recent arrivals. Thus, there are little pizza shops like Crosby Pizza Stop that sell the old-style thick slices with the strong cheese aftertaste. The Bangladeshi places offer halal meat, the Indian restaurants serve up samosas and *aloo gobi,* and the bodegas sell a little bit of everything. You'll have no trouble finding a parking spot, because just about everyone is local and walks to the stores.

The gentrifying locales fall into two broad tiers of desirability that are perceived as such. Each has its advantages and disadvantages. Amenities are a key factor in people's decision to move to a particular neighborhood. Once a certain level of services is reached, a neighborhood can and does acquire cachet, meaning it's seen as an "in" place, a judgment that creates a snowball effect, as it did in Dumbo and North Williamsburg. However, this trend may be approaching a saturation point. And once change takes place in too many neighborhoods, they lose the specialness that made them a drawing card in the first place. Diversity is another consideration for at least some gentrifiers. They often express favorable views regarding diversity, but usually those opinions are formed *after* they've moved into a mixed area. Diversity is not often cited as an initial consideration in their choice of residence. The term means one thing when it's directed at minorities of similar social status who are also gentrifiers, as opposed to those who are indigenous to the area and poor.

Do the gentrifiers actually displace the poor? Yes, but the degree to which this happens is unclear, because the evidence is inconclusive. Both sides of the debate have been discussed in this book. In any case the city must do more to help the poor by continuing to provide services and create programs for them.

Gentrification is an uneven process, and neighborhoods often fall somewhere along the continuum, which means that gentrified parts intermingle with those that have not yet reached that stage. There are also parts of the city, such as East New York and portions of the Bronx, where gentrification will take a long time to become a reality, if ever. It's wise to keep in mind, however, that forty years ago few people could even conceive of places like Bushwick, East Harlem, or the Lower East Side ever becoming gentrified.

Another important conclusion is that in gentrifying parts of the city the good housing is overwhelming the bad housing, or at least making it a nonissue. People are far more willing to move into areas that have tenements or projects nearby than they were twenty years ago. The market is strong, crime is generally down, and demand makes people believe that things will get better soon even if there are occasional serious crimes that jolt the community. People at every income level also attribute this trend to the fact that people in general are more educated and thus relations are better between groups.

The most important agency for change is the government, which provides generous funding, usually through loans or through direct contributions for lower-income families who qualify. With this financial support they can live in new homes that upgrade the surrounding area, giving it greater potential for gentrification. Section 8 housing makes apartments available for the poor in the same buildings that are home to higher-income people who pay market rates. These trends have accelerated in recent years, and so far having poor and well-off in the same buildings has not seemed to be much of a problem.

Universities are also players in the gentrification game. When they purchase buildings adjacent to their campuses and then rehabilitate the buildings and rent them out to students, staff, and faculty, they make the area safer and attract other gentrifiers. In cases where the universities pay for the construction of dormitories, student and program centers, and buildings containing classrooms and offices, they change the look and feel of the entire area. The indigenous don't always put out a welcome mat for them, however, because often it's their own apartments that are being lost, and this takes precedence over the general improvements that occur.

It's worth mentioning that gentrification isn't enthusiastically welcomed by everyone. There is sometimes a strong undertone of resentment against the gentrifiers by locals who feel the neighborhood has become too pricey for them and that it's no longer their neighborhood. These tensions can, at times, turn into open conflict.

A major finding of this exploration of New York is that gentrifiers and the poor with whom they live are neighbors but rarely friends. They live side by side, but other than hello or a quick superficial exchange of pleasantries, there's no real contact except in emergencies, where both parties temporarily rise to the occasion. Each has its own group with whom they have much more in common. And there is a perception by many longtime residents that the gentrifiers are snobby and look down on them.

The outer boroughs continue to have an ambivalent relationship with Manhattan, though this is less true than in the past. Gentrification, which has upgraded many parts of Brooklyn and Queens, may have played a role in this shift. Those living in the outer boroughs feel that they're New Yorkers in every sense of the word even as they remain fiercely partisan about their own communities. Manhattanites are often clueless about the New York beyond the waters of their island, though this is less so than in the pre-gentrification days.

Yet there is one thing that unites all New Yorkers, and that is the memory of 9/11. People from every borough perished in the conflagration, and the monuments to the horror of that day are commemorated in hundreds of locations throughout the metropolis. To this day, people ask each other whenever the topic comes up, "Where were you when it happened?"

One of the enduring features of many neighborhoods in this city is the tremendous differentiation *within* them. One block can be serene and peaceful, the next loud and boisterous. One can have beautiful houses while the next looks like a slum. Block associations are an integral part of city life and they play a major role in the stability of communities, but the "eyes and ears" that Jane Jacobs wrote about—those living and working in the neighborhood who stand watch over it—matter just as much.

One general principle is that neighborhoods often look and feel completely different in the evening than they do in the daytime, in different seasons, and on weekdays as opposed to weekends. The people, the activities, the look, the safety factor, everything, can change. What you come to understand when walking the streets of New York is that the city's communities fairly hum with activity, day and night, and that so much of what is meaningful about life can be found in them. This is truest of the informal life that goes on in the streets, stores, and in people's homes.

Also critical to a community's essence are its organizational networks—youth and senior citizens centers, health organizations, religious clubs, and other groups. When a van sponsored by the Museum of Natural History comes through the neighborhood and the kids get a visual lesson on dinosaurs, that's something they'll remember. When every Wednesday a twenty-five-year-old woman has the children's full attention as she weaves a tale of adventure and suspense to a bunch of four- and five-year-olds sitting on a sidewalk in the still poor South Bronx, making it come alive with lifelike Sesame Street–type figures and capped off with refreshments, it's an experience they'll likely carry with them forever. And the senior citizens centers, community swimming pools, and local sports arenas—these are the soul of the city. This is where friendships are made and cemented and where people feel wanted and even important.

Education is a significant factor in every city neighborhood. One major development has been the charter schools that have sprung up around the city. Funded by private groups, these institutions have forced both the parochial and public schools to improve their offerings and programs. They have also made parents feel they don't have to accept failing schools as part of the price for living in a poor neighborhood. The schools, I've also found, have occasionally become battlegrounds between different populations with varying perspectives on the best way to educate children. This is especially so when an area is gentrifying.

New York's housing projects have been around for decades and are still an important factor in community life. The lack of safety, the stigma associated with them, and their lackluster, even grim, appearance affect whatever communities abut them. On the other hand, the projects are functional, providing adequate living quarters for over four hundred thousand people, and because they are cost-effective, they will remain part of the New York scene in the foreseeable future. One change between now and the 1980s is that their presence and that of deteriorated tenements is no longer the deal-breaker it once was when gentrifiers look for a home. Space convenient to work and transportation is just too hard to come by these days.

Technology, especially transportation and communication, has made a tremendous impact on the city of New York and across the country. It's a huge topic, well beyond the purview of this volume, but we can at least touch on it. Cell phones and other electronic devices allow people to converse with others and take care of their needs while they're heading for a subway or out shopping. They can use such devices to deal with impending danger by calling the police. These gadgets greatly relieve boredom by transporting people to other worlds. In short, they have dramatically changed the way we live our daily lives. Also, ATM machines grease the wheels of commercial exchange at the retail level. Because of them more stores are open all night. And people can buy more easily and more often and in greater amounts because they have access to cash 24/7. Employees can pass the downtime when there are no customers by texting, emailing, and playing online video games.

Another significant finding of this study was the importance of leisure time in the lives of people throughout the city. Precisely because they lead busy lives—even getting to work is often a time-consuming challenge—opportunities to relax are something New Yorkers really need and value. Evaluating the many ways in which this need is met brought into sharp focus other issues worthy of attention.

Choices made regarding the use of spare time are often ones that strengthen or at least reflect the salience of ethnic identity. There are concerts all over the city where the performance is geared to one or another group, whether they are Irish, Jamaican, Polish, Jewish, or Latino. Of course, leisure activities are secondary to primary concerns like health, family, and work, but when they emerge, ethnic identity frequently takes center stage. Besides concerts there are dances, poetry readings, films, museums, religious ceremonies and events, sports, parades, and thousands of informal gatherings on the streets, in restaurants, and in people's homes. What these activities demonstrate is an intense desire to stay connected to one's roots even as one becomes Americanized.

Because these events are generally public and because public space is shared with others, these activities can become lightning rods for conflict. A religious procession that means a great deal to its participants might not be shown proper respect by others living in the area who don't share, or who even reject, its values. A parade might engender hostility from those who disagree with the marchers' sentiments. How to use community funds might become a major dispute as people disagree on what the priorities should be. When people live in crowded conditions, conflicts are often much more confrontational.

At the same time, leisure activities also unify people. This often occurs through the myriad fraternal orders and social clubs where mostly older folks meet to enjoy one another's company and be involved in group activities. These organizations play a critical role in the decisions by senior citizens to remain in changing communities. Sometimes these are located in Ys and in senior citizens centers run by the city.

Although bars are locales for meeting friends in all the boroughs, Manhattan, in particular, doubles as a destination point for those who enter it only on weekends in search of a good time. Here strangers strike up conversations that sometimes blossom into relationships. For friends who travel there together, being in Manhattan and going bar hopping is just another advantage of living within easy reach of the Big Apple.

While members of ethnic groups may play soccer or baseball together, sports are generally seen as neutral ground where everyone, regardless of background, can participate. Time and time again, whether in the East Bronx or Northern Queens, I was struck by how the participants in basketball, baseball, or soccer games represented a veritable UN as they played together. Even bocci, long the domain of Italian Americans, is attracting people from other groups. As to sedentary games, chess has gained significantly in popularity, especially among blacks, and dominoes is ubiquitous in Hispanic communities. Finally, bingo remains popular among the elderly, giving them a reason to gather socially and relieving the isolation they sometimes feel.

Spectator sports also bring people together. As I sat in sports bars, I repeatedly noticed how strangers broke the ice by inquiring about the score, segueing into extended conversations about the teams, and finally giving each other high fives or groaning as their teams scored or failed to do so. Finally, the major sports teams in the city both unify and divide the city, depending on which teams you root for.

New York also serves as a living theater for its inhabitants. I have often felt that in a way it is the world's largest museum, a description that generally applies to other great cities as well. The architecture, the sights, and the masses of people all come together in a way that makes just being in New York a special, exciting event. You turn a corner and come across a film being made. You emerge from a subway to the sound of sirens wailing and the sight of lights flashing. An altercation, perhaps, a police chase in progress, or someone being rescued from a burning building. One gets the feeling that anything can and does happen here.

Perhaps more than any other space, parks of all kinds and sizes are places where people of all backgrounds interact—playing Frisbee, watching their small children frolic, or simply lying in the sun or shade and relaxing, perhaps listening to music or chatting with others. It's in the parks, with their peaceful atmosphere, that the warmth and openness of the city comes into clearer view. Everything seems to be occurring in slow motion in contrast to the speed at which the city normally moves.

The underlying focus of many programs and events is to educate through entertainment. Arts festivals expose people to forms of art and music that broaden their horizons. Nightclubs are geared toward familiarizing outsiders with music, poetry, and dances.

And schools do their share in bringing culture to the communities where they exist through plays, lectures, and other events open to the public. New York has streams, rivers, forests, wildlife refuges, and large greenbelt areas within its boundaries, especially in the outer boroughs. Both the extent of nature's offerings in a city that is often thought of as the quintessence of urbanization and the high level of interest shown in them were revelations to me.

In looking at how New Yorkers spend their free time, it is clear that there is a generally stronger emphasis today on the environment and health. Alliances have been created that focus on conservation of areas used by people who enjoy hiking, fishing, boating, bird-watching, and other activities. Play-street organizers have stated that activities like yoga, jumping rope, and running, while fun, are also healthy. It's worth mentioning that smoking in public has been largely banned, as opposed to thirty-five years ago. This general concern may even have played a role in the new rating system for the city's restaurants that evaluates them for cleanliness.

Walking the city's streets allowed me to see its buildings, sidewalks, walls, monuments, and signs as a patchwork of spaces. Systematic walking of every street led to the realization that people's perceptions of their neighborhood's spatial boundaries (or others they visit) are limited. This is because most us are familiar with only the blocks that we have an interest in—where our school is, where our friends live, houses of worship, hangouts, and so on. Yet we describe it as "Flatbush was a place where . . . ." or "Forest Hills is. . . . "

The city has an equalizing effect in that the wealthiest communities can never totally exclude the outside world, largely because they are on city property and people can simply walk through them. Even gated communities like Seagate in Brooklyn and Breezy Point in Queens can be easily penetrated on one pretext or another by resourceful individuals.

The battles over space in the city show how it is a flashpoint for those with strong feelings. The board of a building makes a rule that residents cannot allow their dogs to defecate in front of it. A far larger principle over sidewalk use is established when a law is passed requiring all dog owners to clean up after their dogs. The right to film movies in the public square is another battleground between competing groups, with the city often weighing in on the matter.

Each borough contains large industrial areas that have never been seriously explored. People come from all over the metropolitan area to buy supplies for their homes and businesses, have their cars repaired, and obtain fresh food at wholesale prices. How these areas affect the residential ones adjacent to them is unknown, as is what goes on there generally.

All of the outer boroughs have motels and hotels catering to tourists who are eager to avoid the high price of staying in Manhattan. Most of those tourists who stay there are visitors from other countries. Though their main focus is on Manhattan, the visitors also walk around the outer borough neighborhoods, eat in the local restaurants, and shop in the stores, thereby learning how the "other half" lives. The effects of this on their perceptions of the city and Americans in general are unknown.

The city's streets have been radically transformed in the last fifteen years or so. Pedestrian walkways have replaced automobile thoroughfares in some of New York's busiest areas. The priorities in the current era are safety, the environment, and aesthetics. And bicycles are now much more appreciated, with lanes reserved for their use on most of the city's largest thoroughfares. The sidewalks are crammed with items for sale. Permits are readily granted for farmer's markets and street fairs selling food and clothing. The result has been to make the city feel more alive and exciting, and, ultimately, more "user friendly" for everyone.

Another characteristic of the city is the frequency with which New Yorkers appropriate public space for themselves. A memorial to someone's mother is created on the sidewalk by a tree. Domino players furnish a small part of the sidewalk with freestanding closets and a bookcase, folding chairs, and a table. They leave it there overnight, paying a homeless man to guard it. No one seems to mind.

Besides advertising their wares, people throughout the city use signs and artistic drawings on stores, billboards, and other areas to convey political, religious, and social messages, many of them exhortations. These range from a five-story mural about Irish hunger strikers, to a yard crammed with fascinating memorabilia about Brooklyn, to a residential brownstone whose first-floor window advertises a grocery store that no longer exists. Why is that? Because that's what the grocer wanted, and his grandchildren still follow his wishes. Some of the statements on the various signs are idiosyncratic, clearly reflecting one person's opinion and the right to express it. Residents also make full use of balconies, front yards, and rooftops in whatever ways they wish, many of which are visible and interesting to passersby. People put clothing, toys, and furniture on the streets, and now they are joined, increasingly, by books.

In the 1970s graffiti was seen as a scourge to be eliminated, especially from subway cars. Today, while not yet mainstream, it's respected as an art form and can be found mostly in industrial sections of the city. From Hunters Point to East Williamsburg, to the South Bronx, world-famous artists and lesser mortals do their thing, employing dazzling colors to produce stunning and sometimes grotesque panoramas of all sorts. Some of these artists have achieved almost mythical status, and visitors in the know come from everywhere to look, photograph, and interpret their works. The change in attitude is a result of shifting perspectives about art and a greater openness in society toward innovativeness.

One of the major questions with which this endeavor began was whether Americans are assimilating or maintaining a strong sense of identity. The answer is multifaceted, because interaction between groups occurs in different ways. As I looked at these interactions, I discovered that there's an umbrella for a certain type of relationship, which I dubbed "daygration," meaning intergroup contact that takes place in ethnically segregated communities only during the daytime. When it happened in an auto repair shop or deli, it didn't amount to much, but in a senior citizens center or school it was significant, because meaningful relationships could, and sometimes did, develop. In such instances people shaped perceptions about others. This is a topic worthy of further investigation.

Because the city is so densely populated and because so many different nationalities share its spaces, it facilitates contact between groups by its very structure and existence. An Asian teacher works in a school with a mostly Hispanic student population. A Hasidic woman works in an office where no one is Jewish. A black police officer is assigned to a mostly white area. When carefully analyzed, such relationships can teach us a great deal about ethnicity as a whole. The likelihood of such pairings in most parts of this country is slim to none, unless it's in Chicago, Los Angeles, Miami, or another big, multiethnic metropolis.

Although it hasn't disappeared completely, prejudice in New York City has declined greatly in the past thirty-five years. This opinion was shared by most New Yorkers with whom I spoke. The election of Barack Obama was frequently cited as evidence of this trend in my conversations with a broad range of informants. People feel they can live wherever they want to and that prejudice in the workplace and socially has significantly declined. However, many people prefer to live and, in many cases, socialize, with their own group even as they take comfort in that knowledge. Others are eager to live in truly integrated communities and are doing so. What's important is the need to respect whatever choices people make.

Literally millions of New Yorkers voluntarily identify with their ethnic, racial, or religious groups. The motives vary greatly, from the psychological to the economic, but it's clear that identity serves many purposes or it wouldn't be so prevalent. And people often identify with a particular group for a combination of reasons, not just one or two. Further complicating matters is that in today's world, people's backgrounds are more mixed than ever before, and they can therefore easily claim to identify with three or four groups. Among the most common ways of identifying are color, nationality, beliefs, rituals and practices, language, and dress. Lately there seems to be increased interest in religion by young professionals, an interest that often stems from a search for deeper meaning in one's life. It's a new development that bears watching.

Yet there are also large numbers of individuals in this same metropolis who have embarked on the road to assimilation with equal fervor. They believe that a world where everyone mixes and assimilates will be a better world for all. Even among those whose own parents are immigrants, only 20 percent feel it's important to marry within the group. And the trend toward assimilation is supported by data from the 2010 U.S. Census. New York City may buck the national trend for a time because of the sheer numbers of foreigners who continue to enter it. But even if this is so, it is unlikely to alter the long-term direction of movement toward assimilation.

Overall there's been a significant rise in the number of interracial couples living in New York, a trend that is also occurring nationally. What I saw time and again on my journey through the city was races and different ethnic groups mixing socially—eight such people having dinner together, three or four walking down a street, another four sitting together in a movie theater. It's a pattern that I've also observed becoming more common in my classes and in the college cafeteria, a pattern that contrasts very sharply with what I experienced in the 1970s and 1980s.

But we need to think about what such assimilation will really mean. It won't necessarily mean what it did in the past—namely, losing one's culture and becoming a bland form of non-identified American. Rather, it will mean people treating their ethnic identity in a matter-of-fact way, describing it as part of their life history and taking pride in the elements of it that have significance to them personally. In other words, assimilation will exist, but it will be far from the only, or even primary, characteristic that determines who people are as individuals, unless they want it to be.

As a consequence of intermarriage, distinct identities will be diluted and the ultimate effect will be a dilution of identity as a whole. How many people will make the choice to remain apart and identify with only one group remains to be seen. The retention of one's identity will depend mostly on the needs it satisfies and the functions it has. Because individuals will feel free to choose, many, perhaps even a majority, will end up identifying somewhat with groups to which they nominally belong. But there will be tremendous variation as to how much or how little they identify. No matter which of the three groups predominates—identified, assimilated, or a hybrid of the two—New York fifty years from now will almost certainly be an even more tolerant city than it is today, just as it is much more progressive today than it was fifty years ago.

If current trends continue, the city as a whole will turn into a place that caters primarily to the middle and upper classes. It will remain a showcase for visitors and a popular public image for urban America. The immigrants will either join the middle classes or move elsewhere. The poor areas are shrinking steadily as developers create new preserves for the privileged. The infrastructure that the poor need to survive—cheap restaurants and grocery stores, low rents, inexpensive clothing stores—will diminish. Only the projects will remain, and they too may vanish one day.

On the other hand, the numbers of poor people here legally and the half-million-plus undocumented are a large group that will not disappear. And the working poor who perform work that is necessary, but that no one else wants to do, must have places to live within easy commuting distance. Large segments of the city's population will continue to advocate for and protect them. Even if such efforts falter, those poor who live in rent-stabilized apartments or still-existing projects will probably not move, because they'll have nowhere to go for the same price.

New York City is today a resounding success story. It has managed to combine the best of both the new and the old into a place that is unique and exciting. But it will require both luck and skill to maintain its standing. A major economic depression could significantly alter the dynamic, with those who sustain its economic base heading for cheaper places in the outlying areas.

Taste itself is fickle and subject to change. Significant numbers may rediscover the more spacious central and outer rings of Brooklyn and Queens and create satellite communities that pleasantly mimic Manhattan and the current nearby outer borough favorites like Greenpoint, Brooklyn Heights, Williamsburg, Astoria, Hunters Point, and Sunnyside. An upward tick in crime could rekindle the perception, never too far from people's minds, that the city is unsafe. And that could bring everything crashing down, especially for those who have made the city home for their children.

Finally, if high-speed transportation expands to new areas, those places could then compete with the city as attractive residential alternatives.

In conclusion, New York has so much to offer on so many levels that it will remain one of the great cities of the world for a long time to come. That is its destiny.

NOTES

CHAPTER ONE. INTRODUCTION

1. Some examples are Gregory 1998; Rieder 1985; Mele 2000; J. L. Jackson 2001; Poll 1962; and Sanjek 1998.

2. There were times when I told people up front that I was writing a book, but even then I often said it in a low-key way, not specifying that I was a professor. I did so when I determined that my questions would be taken more seriously because these people were in positions of authority and wanted to feel that they were not just wasting their time in idle chitchat.

3. Still, the amount that has been written on New York City is vast, and I made a conscious effort not to read much more until I had completed walking the city. I wanted my own ideas to be as fresh and uninfluenced by existing research as possible. I also followed the classic approach of Barney Glaser and Anselm Strauss (1967) to inductively proceed from my observations to general theoretical propositions and conclusions. See also Katz 2010. Most ethnographers do use theory, more likely inductively, but deductively as well (Anderson 1999; Duneier 1999; K. Newman 1999). In their important article on this subject, Wilson and Chaddha (2009) elaborate on these two approaches.

4. Under Commissioner Janette Sadik-Khan, the status of bike riding was greatly elevated as bicycle lanes proliferated throughout the city. But as sociologist Jen Petersen (2011) has pointed out, it's still a car-oriented town, and pedestrians and cyclists often compete with each other for available space.

5. Sam Roberts (2012b) has an insightful article about the benefits of walking in terms of appreciating the city.

6. Sometimes patterns of dress can even become part of the delusional systems of the mentally ill, as in the case of Matthew Colletta, a man who in 2006 went on a shooting spree that killed one person and left five others injured. The reason? The victims were all wearing red or traveling in a red car. Colletta believed the Bloods gang was after him and must have felt he was acting in self-defense (Kilgannon 2009d).

7. That said, unacquainted black people are more likely to engage one another in eye contact than with whites, because they may have a mutual friend in common or might be able to have a future relationship (Anderson 2011, 113). For an important discussion of adolescents' avoidance of violence in their neighborhoods, see Sharkey 2006.

8. The idea of New York as a welcoming city can be gleaned from statistical information too. In May 2010 Mayor Michael Bloomberg celebrated the 311 help line's one hundred millionth call since it began operations in 2003. The program has 306 full-time operators, and the annual tab to run it comes to $46 million. Elissa Gootman (2010), a *New York Times* reporter who spent a week fielding calls, gives some examples of the questions asked: Why is the water in someone's sink brown? How do you file a complaint against a home aide who steals your

aunt's money? How do you find a dermatologist in the Bronx who accepts Medicaid? Why was a certain letter not delivered? How can I stop smoking? Other questions have been about barking dogs, finding out which jail a relative has been taken to, noxious odors wafting through the air somewhere, and so on. Clearly, with so many calls this is a much-needed service. Having people available to help, or at least soothe frayed nerves, improves the city's ability to function. Who knows how many people ended up not doing something reckless or harmful to others because someone listened to and tried to help them? We don't often think about it, at least not until we're in a similar situation, but without these safety nets a city can quickly descend into chaos.

9. Chicago, New Orleans, and working-class parts of Boston are probably exceptions to the rule.

CHAPTER TWO. SELLING HOT DOGS, PLANTING FLOWERS, AND LIVING THE DREAM: THE NEWCOMERS

1. B. Howe 2010, 58.

2. Among the most important works on immigration to New York City are those of Nancy Foner, 2000, 2001 and 2005a; Kasinitz et al. 2008. The combined work of these researchers greatly enhances our understanding of the second generation of immigrants. Besides my own work and specifically cited works, some of the information in this chapter relies on the American Community Survey figures released between 2006 and 2009, the New York City Department of Planning figures, Foner 2005a, Kasinitz et al. 2008, and Fessenden and Roberts 2011. The details are often quite interesting. Dominicans are predominantly poor, have the largest families, and lack formal education; yet 20 percent of them regularly send back money to their homeland. There are more foreign-born Chinese living in Flushing, Queens, than native-born, while American-born exceed the foreign-born in Manhattan's Chinatown. As a whole, the community is heavily working class. In 2006–2007 the Koreans ranked behind only the Indians and Chinese among students coming here from abroad for higher-education studies. Many of the West Indians have come here because they have both high unemployment and high education in their homelands and most of the women work (Foner 2005a). Included in this group are about eight hundred thousand Haitians and their offspring. Ecuadorian arrivals have increased significantly in recent years, passing Colombians.

3. Davletmendova 2011; Turhan 2012. For information on another small community of people, the Nepalese, see Pokharel 2012.

4. Fessenden and Roberts 2011. Some of the discussion on residential changes is from this article and from interactive mapping studies and reports generated from the CUNY Center for Urban Research. I am indebted to Richard Alba for pointing me to this resource. The rest of the information on this issue stems from my own observations walking through these areas.

5. Semple 2011a; Beveridge 2006b.

6. Khandelwal 2002, 6–9, 17.

7. Glazer and Moynihan 1970; Alba, Portes, et al. 2000.

8. Nathan Glazer also admitted that he overestimated the abilities of the African Americans and Puerto Ricans to move up (Alba, Portes, et al. 2000). He seemed

to accept the arguments by Robert Blauner and John Ogbu that these groups are so persecuted, victimized, and embittered that it's hard for them to really advance. Although this point may be true in general, many African Americans and Puerto Ricans have succeeded over time. It's also significant that researchers have found that immigration lowers crime rates (Ousey and Kubrin 2009), as well as poverty levels (Moore 1997). For an excellent overview of the problems that have faced Latinos through the years in New York, see Haslip-Viera and Baver 1996. For more on the Puerto Ricans, see Haslip-Viera, Falcon, and Matos Rodríguez 2005.

9. Some of the discussion in this section relies on Beveridge 2006a; Coplon 2008; Semple 2010d; R. Smith 2006; Stoller 2002; Foner 2005a, 110–20; Kinetz 2002; Kim 2009; D. González 2009a; and the Fiscal Policy Institute. Jeffrey Passel (2007) of the Pew Hispanic Center, estimates that the undocumented come in roughly equal numbers from South and East Asia (23 percent); the Caribbean (22 percent); and Mexico and Central America (27 percent). The rest are from South America, Africa, Europe, and the Middle East.

10. Even in the old days, when immigrants came mostly from Southern and Eastern Europe, this was a primary first-generation path for upward mobility. For more, see Alba, Portes, et al. 2000; Min 2001, 2008; Sassen 1988; Waldinger 1996a; Zukin 2010a; Gold 2010.

11. Kang 2003. For more on how and why these niches develop and their consequences, see Foner 2001.

12. Most groups are seen as favoring their own, but some are viewed as more inclined in this direction than others. In a paper on Astoria, Queens, and its Greek population, Lauren Paradis (2011) cites numerous examples of clannishness and rudeness to outsiders.

13. Berger 2010b.

14. B. Howe 2010, 169–70.

15. Ibid., 6.

16. Min 2008, 52.

17. Sharman and Sharman 2008, 97–110.

18. Cordero-Guzman, Smith, and Grosfoguel 2001; Semple 2012.

19. Foner 2005a; Grasmuck and Grosfoguel 1997.

20. Poros 2011. See also Massey, Alarcón, Durand, and González 1987; Portes 1998; Sanjek 1998; Stoller 2002; R. Smith 2006.

21. Brown 2009; Orleck 2001; Foner 2001.

22. Lehrer and Sloan 2003, 324–25.

23. Santos 2010a.

24. These feelings about politics can last far longer than the immigrant phase. Egyptian Americans have been living in Astoria since the 1960s, but they still reacted very strongly to the recent upheavals in Egypt (Bilefsky 2011a). For a concise and good summation of the role of music, see Foner 2001, 18.

25. Montas owns several such themed establishments. One of them, the Montas Restaurant in Ridgewood, Brooklyn, is a favorite hangout of famous sports stars, including Pedro Martinez, Alex Rodríguez, Carlos Delgado, and Sammy Sosa.

26. Beveridge 2008a. Foner and Alba (2008) highlight this when they contrast the roles played by religion in Europe and in the United States in helping immigrants to adapt. The authors argue persuasively that its role is greater in the

United States, in part because Americans are much more receptive to religion than are Europeans and because of the government's general approach to religion.

27. Lehrer and Sloan 2003, 24–25.

28. Berger 1986. See also Min 2010, 24–26, on the Koreans. In New York City about 59 percent of Koreans are Protestant, 14 percent Catholic, 8 percent Buddhists, with about 19 percent professing no religion. Many Korean immigrants shifted over to Protestantism upon coming here, because the religion gave them social services, organizations, and networking possibilities that helped them acclimate to life in America. The immigrants sometimes have unique practices and emphases. For an interesting discussion of the many roles played by water in the diverse faiths that exist in the city, see Kornblum and Van Hooreweghe 2010. Botanicas, shops selling herbal remedies and charms, also have an important presence in the city. Although their focus is more in the area of magic than religion, the lines are not always clearly drawn. Browsing through a botanica off Myrtle Avenue in Bushwick, I read an ad for a devil's candle to be used in a cemetery, an idea that is possibly influenced by Catholicism.

29. Slotnik 2010. See also Stoller 2002, vii, xi.

30. Kasinitz et al. 2008; Rumbaut and Portes 2001.

31. Remeseira 2010, 4; Zentella 2010, 323. For an interesting discussion of how West Indian teenagers in Brooklyn negotiate their identities, see LaBennett 2011.

32. Semple 2011b.

33. Kwong and Miscevic 2005, 253; Herbst 1988.

34. Coles 2011, 40.

35. There is a small chain of pizza parlors in Queens known as Singa's that caters to the Indian palate. As one such connoisseur observed, "Where else would you get such wonderful hot chili topping, and mango drink, to go with a pizza?" (Khandelwal 2002, 43).

36. Robbins 2011b.

37. Kershaw 2002.

38. There is a long history of conflict between blacks and Puerto Ricans over jobs in the public sector and political influence. Overall, Latinos are often cited by Hispanic scholars as doing worse than blacks, but recent census data might lead one to think otherwise, at least nationally. According to the March 2004 *Current Population Survey*, national annual household income rates were $51,235 for whites; $30,187 for Hispanics; and $26,269 for blacks (with $25,878 for black Hispanics). But New York City is different; there, in the 2000 census, it was $27,757 for Hispanics and $31,058 for blacks (U.S. Census Bureau). Regardless, it's clear that both groups are at the bottom of the income scale and have a long way to go.

39. On the possibilities for ethnic coalitions, see Mollenkopf 1999; W. Helmreich 1973; Novak 1971.

CHAPTER THREE. DINERS, LOVE, EXORCISMS, AND THE YANKEES: LIVING TOGETHER

1. D. Goodman 2009.

2. See Ruderman 2012 and Mahler 2005. Mahler also observes that it wasn't always the landlords who burned down the buildings. Fires were also started

accidentally by residents, and in places like Bushwick arson was committed by criminals who found it easier to remove valuable copper tubing from houses after the building had burned down. And in some instances, families themselves set fires, knowing that Social Services would have to resettle them in quarters that were better than where they were living at the time. Oddly enough, the fact that a neighborhood has a bad reputation reduces the likelihood of certain kinds of violence. Because of that reality, people are far more careful about what they do. They will not jump out of their cars to complain if someone has double-parked and blocked them. They will not easily argue with people. Why? Those people could kill them. In this way an area's bad reputation becomes a form of social control, a kind of law among the lawless. "It keeps irritation in check" (Anderson 1999, 27). Interestingly, the South Bronx today has far more new housing than the West Bronx. This is in large part because so many more sections of the South Bronx went up in flames during the '70s and '80s, thereby allowing developers to start from scratch. Indeed, the West Bronx, which can look deceptively peaceful, has some of the highest crime precincts in the city—for example, the 46th Precinct.

3. Mooney 2011b. For more on safety issues in Bushwick in recent decades, see Ehrenhalt 2012, 80–82.

4. Flegenheimer 2011. It's worth mentioning that one of the most godforsaken and dangerous areas in the city is Mariners Harbor. It is located in Staten Island on the northern side, not far from the Goethals Bridge. Tough youths hang out in front of grim-looking projects, shouting expletives at passersby and occasionally threatening them. For more on gangs, see Venkatesh 2008.

5. At the start of 2011 the official count by the city of homeless persons living in the streets and subways was 2,648, though to those who feel uncomfortable about their presence the number is probably perceived as much higher. Recently, BronxWorks, an organization that works with the poor and homeless, had a party for the hundreds of people it has helped. A formerly homeless man, who had lived on the streets for ten years before accepting an apartment, had this to say about his experiences: "Not every day is my greatest day. But my worst day here is better than my best day on the street" (Secret 2011). For more on the loopholes that allow mentally ill homeless people to avoid necessary treatment, see Hollander and De Avila 2013.

6. Duneier 1999. See also Edwards 2012.

7. For more on panhandlers, subway musicians, and the politics of this sensitive issue, see Tanenbaum 1995, especially p. 165. In the end this situation is no different from owners of nearby bars giving their patrons another community in which to drink and socialize, in addition to the one where they live. Of course, in a sense such establishments are also formed and shaped by their location. A bartender at Fresh Salt, a bar near the now-departed Fulton Fish Market, told me, "When the Fish Market was here, we used to have happy hour at 7:30 AM, because that's when the workers got off their jobs." Today the area is well on the way to gentrification, with average sales prices closer to one million dollars (Satow 2011). For a gripping photographic account of the Fulton Fish Market, see Mensch 2007.

8. Roberts 2011a.

9. Moody 2007, 134–38. See also Karmen 2000; Powell 2012.

10. Dewan 2009. See also Katz 1988 for an interesting discussion of the psychological factors, such as thrills, for committing crime.

11. Sharman and Sharman 2008, 173.

12. Madden 2010. See also Michel Foucault (1975), in which he takes the "Panopticon" approach regarding surveillance in hospitals, schools, and work settings, and how it creates a docile and controlled society.

13. Katyal 2002. While not saying that better parenting, jobs, education, social programs, and law enforcement can't work, Neal Katyal says that better physical design of urban spaces can significantly limit crime and that insufficient attention has been paid to this idea. Typical social solutions focusing on the environment of offenders and their age, race, joblessness, and family situations are expensive and don't always work. Besides, according to statistical research cited by Katyal, almost two-thirds of crimes aren't even reported and only one-fifth of all reported crimes are ever solved. Moreover, as is well known, incarceration and rehabilitation programs are largely ineffective in achieving their goals. In addition to better physical design, Katyal argues that government regulation can also help. Included in his suggestions for such regulations are making funding for projects dependent on crime impact statements and disclosing crime rates in the area to investors and prospective residents; creating zoning requirements and building codes that inhibit crime; and bringing tort suits against landlords who fail to make necessary changes in design and who fail to disclose limitations of design in their buildings.

14. Kate Cordes (2009) asks in her study of the community why Greenpoint, which first welcomed Polish immigrants in the 1880s, has remained so strongly Polish for 130 years. That's a really long time compared to, say, Jews in Brownsville, Italians in Bensonhurst, the Irish in Inwood, and almost every other ethnic group. Among the reasons given are that the lack of easy transportation to Manhattan creates insularity. Additionally, the G train that runs through the area has spotty service, so much so that it is also referred to as the "Ghost Train." Moreover, successive waves of immigration from Poland, especially after World War II and in recent years, have replenished the population. Then there are spatial factors. As Cordes notes, "The residential neighborhood is swaddled in rings of industrial zones and cut off from burgeoning Williamsburg by the slash of the BQE [Brooklyn Queens Expressway]." She also cites the fact that until very recently the area had never been attractive to gentrifiers and also had a low crime rate. Finally, there is the fact that Greenpoint is a full-service community—with ethnic stores of every kind, churches, and cultural organizations—that, given the inherent conservatism of the working-class and strongly identified Poles, makes them content to stay put. In fact, the percentage of Greenpoint residents who can walk to work is 13 percent, more than twice the New York City average of 6 percent. Based on her own observations, Cordes concludes that Greenpoint "feels like a self-contained neighborhood and there is a palpable village feel on the streets," and that it's "a place where people know each other well."

Actually, New York is full of enclaves. An enclave can be made up of distinct ethnic, religious, or racial groups. It can be made up of union workers, gays, the homeless, people of wealth, and so forth. For a complete discussion of this concept, see Abrahamson 2005. For a highly informative discussion of Ditmas Park, see Berger 2007. For an overview of the components that make a community click, see Zhang 2012. Incidentally, the smallest-in-size ethnic community in New York City resides predominantly in one Bronx apartment building on University Avenue. The group, with eight families, comes to forty people, all Bhutanese refugees from Nepal. About 60,000 Bhutanese have been accepted by the United States since 2007, and New York City has about 170 of them. Most of them have never had electricity or indoor plumbing in their homes. It's quite an adjustment, and they rely on each other a lot for help and advice on how to build new lives in America (Semple 2009e). For more on the Bhutanese immigrants, see Lehrer and Sloan 2003.

15. Other examples are Seagate, Brooklyn; Breezy Point, Broad Channel, and Hamilton Beach, Queens; and Silver Beach, Bronx. Research has shown that gated communities lead to greater segregation by reinforcing existing patterns of segregation in the general area where they are situated (Vesselinov, Cassesus, and Falk 2007). See also Low 2000 and Berger 2012f.

16. Writing in the *New York Times,* reporter Lizette Alvarez describes the movement into Harding Park by Hispanics who were intent on improving their lives as "a matter of pride for a group of people tired of being blamed, historically, for degrading entire neighborhoods." The area became Hispanic in the 1980s and '90s. One of the early homesteaders, who steadily improved his bungalow, was Pepe Mena, who recalled shouts of "Spic, get out" when he first came to Harding Park in 1964. Eventually, the city sold the area to a homeowners association for $3,200 a plot (Alvarez 1996).

17. Two other examples of such bonhomie are Edgewater Park and Silver Beach, both in the Bronx. There's a group called the Edgewater Redcoats, which organizes an annual Memorial Day parade, and there are bingo games, Easter egg hunts, and a community newspaper, the *Edgewater Park Gazette.* Both communities have lifeguards and beaches, as well as private security arrangements (Toy 2009b).

18. Berger 2011a. It's clear that different communities have different perceptions of themselves and varying levels of satisfaction with life in them (Santos 2009). This is reported in the Citywide Customer Survey of 2008 (City of New York 2008).

19. Ruderman and Schweber 2012.

20. Collins 1999. See also Whyte 1988, 43–47; Mensch 2007; Barry 2010; and M. Fernandez 2011, for more on these types of people.

21. Feuer 2002.

22. Perhaps this isn't as strange as it sounds. Exorcisms are rare within the Catholic church and are widely frowned upon, to say the least. However, the *New York Times* reported on a two-day conference held in Baltimore on how to deal with it. The reason? There are many people out there who believe they have been possessed by the devil (Goodstein 2010).

23. As Marwell (2004, 231, 352) has noted, more than one-third of the laws passed by the New York City Council, 36 percent, between 1990 and 2000, concerned naming parks, plazas, streets, malls, ball fields, triangles, and the like, after various people—war heroes as well as ethnic, community, financial, and political leaders.

24. P. Goodman 2004. It makes no difference that the barber shop is in Long Island. The point is the same.

25. Kornblum and Van Hooreweghe 2010. What is interesting is that this activity automatically expands the horizons (no pun intended) of its residents. It's different from using a subway or bus, because the boats aren't simply, or even, modes of transportation. Moreover, they're not conveyances shared with strangers. They're part of a lifestyle, one that's mobile, one that gives its users the opportunity to get away from it all by going out to sea, where they can relax on their decks and commune with nature. Yet, at the same time, they can easily return to where they live. This shared sense of freedom binds those who avail themselves of it in a way that transcends ordinary activities, for it means they have a pleasurable secret that can be shared and appreciated only with those who have themselves experienced it.

26. Sanjek 1998, 223. One Orthodox woman moved from Borough Park to the Dahill Road section in Flatbush and now misses the old neighborhood. "I moved here for a bigger apartment," she explains. "But I miss Borough Park because it was the center of the Orthodox community. That's where Eichler's book store is, where they have the Purim parade, and where most of the religious people live." Jane Jacobs (1961) was critical of the Decentrists, people like Lewis Mumford and Ebenezer Howard (whose thinking Jackson Heights developers used as a model), saying the idea of separating commercial, civic, and residential areas, and housing them in low-lying structures isolated the city from its own parts, so to speak, and eroded its vitality. Good examples are St. Louis and Philadelphia, with Atlanta a mixed result. New York works, but partly because of its density of population and a scarcity of housing. See also David Halle (2003), whose book contrasts spread-out Los Angeles with centralized New York City. He identifies a New York School of Thought, which, in his view, includes Jane Jacobs, the architect Robert Stern, Sharon Zukin, Kenneth Jackson, and Richard Sennett.

Communities sometimes create a venue, a "happening place," for art, thinking that such places can be good for business generally. One such case in point is the art galleries on the Lower East Side. Robert James, owner of a vintage boutique menswear establishment on Orchard Street, puts it this way: "I like to keep things in the neighborhood. I shop local for the raw materials for my designs, shops like Zarin's or Belraf's. I get my thread from a girl on Eldridge. I do things very local." And he's friends with locals. "We all know each other. Last night I went to a party with the girl from the Dressing Room [a nearby boutique and bar]." And, in a case of economic cooperation, he sends customers to a local hat store, which, in turn, reciprocates. "I wear his hats, he wears my clothes" (Xu 2010). This may be a good selling point in the neighborhood. Conversely, people may wonder, assuming they know this, if James is really getting the best quality by almost dogmatically buying local. Irrespective of such considerations, what matters most, perhaps, is that such practices greatly heighten the sense of community that makes the neighborhood viable, vital, and prosperous.

27. This is similar to a description of the Hispanic food vendors in Red Hook, who "cook with the soul and with the heart, just as if they were cooking at home. This is how you get what you get over here: *fresh* authenticity" (Zukin 2010a). Another good case in point is Coqui Mexicano, a cramped little eatery

in the South Bronx, by Brook and Third Avenues. Cops, businessmen, and locals regularly go there to eat and gossip. What determines a restaurant's support level in the community? Often it's the quality of the food and the owner's personality. Alfredo Diego has what you'd call style. "The place even has a lending library run by Alfredo's wife, Danisha Nazario. It consists of a small bookshelf." But as blogger Ed Garcia Conde says, "This shelf might not look like much, but we have no bookstores around here. That in itself would be a huge loss" (Dolnick 2010a).

28. Berger 2010d.

29. Under Giuliani many of the lots were auctioned off and protests escalated, including the release of ten thousand crickets at an auction. Bloomberg was more tolerant, agreeing to carry out environmental reviews before turning over the use of the gardens. The gardens aren't always used for gardening. Puerto Ricans, for example, on the Lower East Side, often used them as hangouts. They built casitas, little shacks, and inside the men played dominoes or cards and listened to music (Martinez 2010; Smith and Kurtz, 2003; Zukin 2010a, 193–208; Makris 2008). Perhaps the gardens are a way of using food to reconnect with nature in general, with one's heritage, or even a personal past (Kornblum and Van Hooreweghe 2010, 51). Another interesting aspect of the city is that so many of the gardens are founded by people whose good works often remain known only in the communities they served. The movement dates back to 1973, when Liz Christy of the Council on the Environment in New York City created the first community garden at Bowery and Houston Streets. Every time a Clyde Haberman, or Susan Dominus, or Jim Dwyer writes about one of these gardens, we learn more about them, but they are merely a drop in the bucket, one filled to overflowing with so many others that may have lessons to teach us. Consider the case of Padre Plaza in Mott Haven, erected to honor Father Roger Giglio (1943–1990), founder of St. Benedict the Moor Community Center. He came from Woburn, Massachusetts, and was a chaplain at Lincoln Hospital. He left there in 1985 to focus on the problems of addiction and alcoholism, establishing the St. Benedict Center for homeless people. He died young, at age forty-seven, of cancer, but the center continues. The park is beautiful and has a gazebo, as well as several small gardens and London plane trees that provide ample shade on hot summer days.

30. The whole experience of seeing the memorial feels eerie to me because I was waiting for the number 3 bus on February 21, 1965, on a Sunday afternoon, along 165th Street, just east of Broadway, when I saw two men racing by me with a crowd of perhaps forty or fifty people in hot pursuit. I instinctively stepped back as far as I could inside a doorway as they went by. Malcolm X was eulogized on February 27, and Ossie Davis spoke at his funeral before a crowd of about twenty thousand people. He is buried in Ferncliff Cemetery in Hartsdale, New York. Years later I met one of Malcolm X's daughters on a TV show, and when I told her what I had seen on that fateful day, she questioned me very closely about it. "What did the men look like?" she asked. I answered as best I could. Today it is widely agreed that the perpetrators were supporters of Elijah Muhammad who were angry with Malcolm X for having broken with their leader. For an excellent account of what happened inside the ballroom, see Marable 2011.

31. Barron and Baker 2012.

32. Sorkin 2009, 172–77.

33. Neighborhoods in densely populated urban areas often subdivide into what some have called "microneighborhoods." For example, in Greenwich Village there's an area along Bleecker Street between Tenth and Eleventh Streets that is filled with chic boutiques whose prices rival those found in Paris. Nearby Christopher Street features sex shops, while theaters and artists predominate on West and Bethune Streets. In the old days the Lower East Side had Orchard Street for inexpensive clothing, while East Broadway featured electrical appliance stores (Thompson 2005). There are also informal neighborhood markers that separate one area from another—a park, creek, grocery store, school—all of which are known to residents. Shoes, mostly sneakers, hanging from telephone wires can serve as boundaries, but not necessarily. They are mostly found in poor areas and sometimes they are thrown there by gang members to delineate their territory; but they can also simply be baby shoes or old sneakers that were once worn by neighborhood kids. Occasionally the shoes on the wires memorialize someone who died young, a reminder that tragedy is never very far away in the ghetto.

34. Barnard 2009c. See also Bearman's (2005) interesting book, *Doormen*.

35. At 940 Garrison Avenue in the Bronx, I enter the Point Community Development Corporation, a nonprofit group dedicated to bringing programming, arts, and culture to the residents of Hunts Point and offering classes in music, photography, visual arts, academic tutoring and the like. The group even has a class called "No Beef Thursdays," using a free vegetarian meal as a hook to draw the youth, mostly teenagers. Participants have worked on projects like restoring a natural habitat on North Brother Island and learning how to grow their own food in the local community gardens. Students also take classes in technology, writing resumes, public speaking, computer programming, applying to college, and so on. At 6 Hancock Place in West Harlem is a firehouse built in 1909 in the smooth limestone, terra cotta, Renaissance Revival style typical of that era. It has now been converted into the Faison Firehouse Theater, founded by Tony Award–winner George Faison, near Amsterdam Avenue. Faison has a Harlem vision, and one of the theater's major undertakings is "The Respect Project," a production company that performs at schools, juvenile detention centers, and homeless shelters throughout the city. Its themes revolve around date rape, gang warfare, teenage pregnancy, and illiteracy, and are intended, as one worker there put it, "to heal the victims of violence." One analysis of 2000 census data based on hundreds of zip codes found that organizational resources decreased as the proportion of blacks living in a neighborhood increased. On the other hand, the resources *increased* as the proportion of foreign-born in a neighborhood grew larger (Small and McDermott 2006).

36. The 1950s version of this program was the public library's Bookmobile (Schonfeld 2012).

37. Leland 2011c.

38. Berger 2012d; Ukeles and Grossman, 2004; Englander 2004. The black community has a different structure when it comes to satisfying the social and economic needs of the elderly. Lodges and fraternal orders have long been integral to the black community, serving primarily older folks. They are still there, albeit in diminishing numbers, and those who frequent them are almost all elderly. As you walk thru Bed-Stuy and Harlem you still see banners and signs denoting

the continued existence of these lodges, even 120 years after they were founded. Like the B'nai Brith for the Jews, they were started in part because the mainstream orders—the Masons, the Odd Fellows, and the Rotary often barred blacks from membership. They also provided assistance in times of sickness and death. On 123rd Street between Malcolm X and Adam Clayton Powell Boulevards, you have the Supreme Grand Lodge District Number 1 Independent Order of Mechanics, Preston Unity Friendly Society Inc. It represents the West Indies, United Kingdom, and the Netherlands. It was started in November 1906 and covers North and South America. I also see nearby a Masonic Temple on 122nd Street. On 121st Street at number 160, there's a really overstated organization: "The Consolidated Masonic Jurisdiction National Supreme Headquarters." Many of the lodges here and throughout the city date back to the heady 1920s when these clubs thought they could make a mint from the boom in building construction. But it didn't last and many ended up selling their properties at a loss. Today few remain (C. Gray 2003).

39. For excellent analyses of how community, ethnicity, and politics intersect in New York, see Marwell 2004 and 2007 and Mollenkopf and Emerson 2001. Successfully combining these three elements is a real challenge because, as Mollenkopf (1999) implicitly acknowledges, politicians understand each group's cultural values, economic experiences, and how they interact with and are influenced by the other groups.

40. For more on this issue, see Zukin 2010a.

41. J. Hernandez 2009b. As of 2000, about 1 million children ages 6–18 attended public schools in the city. There were 1,350 schools and 90,000 teachers. Another 245,000 youngsters were in parochial or private schools. In the second generation about one in ten graduated from a parochial high school and 27 percent had attended one for at least a year. An additional 3 percent graduated from a nonsectarian private high school. Kasinitz et al. (2008) point out that most of the students at CUNY are the first in their families to have gone to college.

All second-generation groups performed better than the native minorities in terms of high school and college graduation rates: Dominicans did better than Puerto Ricans (by 10 percent); West Indians did better than African Americans; Chinese and Russians did better than native whites (which may show the drive of immigrants' children) (Kasinitz et al. 2008, 137–38). Dominicans have the hardest time in the second generation of the immigrant groups. More blacks graduated high school than did Puerto Ricans, but more Puerto Ricans graduated college than did blacks. This may be due to family issues (238). Except for native whites, women in all groups are more likely to have graduated college than men.

Kasinitz et al. (142–43) first give the usual reasons for immigrant/second-generation success cited in the research: parental expectations and involvement, maintaining ethnic ties, and so on. Then, using multivariate analysis for their own data, the researchers come up with additional reasons for success. The strongest factor was the educational level of the parents. There was also residential (read school) stability, number of siblings, both parents being in the home, being female, good schools (145–67). They conclude that the second generation has not been significantly affected by the lower performance levels of African Americans and Puerto Ricans.

42. Gabriel and Medina 2010; Herbert 2010a; Lewis-McCoy 2012.

43. A. Newman 2009, 2011; Ronalds-Hannon 2011.

44. For more on crime and the feeling of apartness inside the projects, see Kilgannon 2011; Jacobson 2012.

45. Bloom 2008. For a critique of city housing, see Zipp 2010. A study of four Harlem public housing projects by Terry Williams and William Kornblum, based on 1980 census data, concluded that the projects were relatively safe when compared to the neighborhoods in which they were found. The study examined gainful employment, drug addiction, crime, and children's school performance. While there were problems in the projects, they tended to be more stable and secure than the surrounding neighborhoods. Today, things are different because the areas around many of the projects have improved due to gentrification. For excellent accounts about life in the projects in earlier times, see Ragen 2003 and Schonfeld 2012. The most recent attempt to build low-rise housing is taking place on Staten Island's North Shore, where a private developer is building nine hundred units of low-rent housing, with additional financial investment by the city (Bellafante 2011c).

46. B. Howe 2010, 12–13. See also Viteritti 1992 on the possible secession of Staten Island from the city.

47. Staten Island homes display more flags than anywhere else in the city, and I have a theory about that. It may be because residents of the island don't really feel they are part of the Big Apple. They dislike what they see as the snobby, smug, big-city mentality. By identifying so strongly with the United States, they may feel they have transcended that view. They now belong to something national and much more important—the U.S. of A. Of course, they have all the reasons that others elsewhere have for showing or raising the flag—patriotism, conservative values, and so on. It's just that this animosity toward the rest of the city is an additional factor.

48. Foner 2005b. For an especially moving account by a 9/11 widow about her husband, a firefighter, see *A Widow's Walk* by Marian Fontana (2005).

49. For more on the importance of this issue, see Ehrenhalt 2012, 234–36.

Chapter Four. Dancing the Bachata, Playing Bocci, and the Chinese Scholars' Garden: Enjoying the City

1. Whyte (1988, 140) has an interesting discussion of waterfalls that helps us understand the allure of the one in the Rockefeller park. Though louder than street noises, it is constant, rather than the staccato sounds of blaring horns and jackhammers. It's also visually soothing. A beautiful and little-known waterfall on the Bronx River can be found off Boston Road and East 180th Street.

2. Iverac 2010. Renewed interest in Harlem by tourists was sparked by curiosity in the early 1990s—before the major drop in crime—in jazz, soul, and funk music, as well as images of Harlem in various films (Hoffman 2003).

3. Tanenbaum 1995; Allan 2010.

4. Curcuru 2010. Some people have questioned the degree to which city residents and the city as a whole benefit economically from such seemingly tourist-oriented festivals (Quinn 2005). But in cases like Staten Island, those who attend these events are mostly local. In Manhattan, such programs attract many tourists,

but Manhattanites and others in the city usually take full advantage of them as well. An open question is what I would call the "guilt factor." When New Yorkers see that people come from all over to enjoy an event, they become inclined to attend as well.

5. D. González 2010. Also, Berger 2012c. For an example of how two groups resolved their differences in the context of a parade, see Haberman 1997.

6. Zukin 2010a.

7. Like so much else in New York, the bowling alley is changing. Today there are high-tech ways of keeping score, flashy bars and bands, and, in a nod to the Jewish Orthodox crowd in parts of Brooklyn, vending machines with kosher snacks (Robbins 2011a).

8. Filkins 2001.

9. "Playing Chess in the 'Hood' " 2007.

10. W. Helmreich 1982. It's a popular game in general throughout the city, with over 2,000 public chess and checker tables scattered among 536 parks.

11. Newman and Schweber 2010.

12. Kleinfeld 2010.

13. Carse 2010. This social function was fulfilled by other clubs for other groups in earlier eras. At the end of Soundview Avenue is a gated waterfront community of 256 high-quality condos. That seems ordinary enough, but to those in the know the name, Shorehaven Condominiums, gives away the fact that this was formerly the site of the Shorehaven Beach Club. Jeffrey Wiesenfeld, a former Bronx resident who went there as a child described the Shorehaven Club in Soundview as a mostly Jewish club in the 1940s and '50s for working-class people who couldn't afford to go to the Catskills. But Bronx historian Lloyd Ultan says it was for middle-class people. Regardless, the owner, a Dr. Goodstein, arranged for buses to take people to the club from all over the Bronx. Everything has to have a hook to sell, and the Shorehaven Club's hook was "The largest saltwater pool in the East." People were told that the surrounding waters were those of Long Island Sound, when, in fact, it was the much-less-attractive-sounding East River. And while it may not have been as classy as the Catskills, it had the same amenities—Ping-Pong, shuffleboard, volleyball, tennis, and square dancing, as well as appropriate entertainment, including people like Buddy Hackett, Myron Cohen, and other Jewish comedians. Those who frequented the club still speak fondly of the end-of-summer highlight—the Miss Shorehaven contest. Those who were there then are obviously no longer there today. But for those who are still alive to reminisce, the Shorehaven lives on in their minds as a place that was fun. In this sense today's population carries on the tradition, even if many of the new places have different names and are visited by different ethnic groups.

14. Roberts 2010g.

15. Jerolmack 2009.

16. Stelloh 2011.

17. Sullivan 2010.

18. Stoddard 2007; Feuer 2011c; Kornblum and Van Hooreweghe 2010; Sharman and Sharman 2008.

19. Less pleasant sometimes is the trip home. Trains and subways carry people back to places like Marine Park, Pelham Bay, and Auburndale in various states of

consciousness and disarray. Conductors on the Long Island Railroad love to tell stories of how they were forced to remove rowdy people from the train. As one tells it: "He didn't have a ticket and he didn't want to pay for it. That's what happens when you have a little beer in you. We don't like to throw them off but he wanted to get thrown off" (Sharman and Sharman 2008, 123). Most likely, many of these people also work in the city and therefore know more about its nightlife. See Reitzes 1986. A new phenomenon in this milieu has been the beer garden. By May 2011 there were fifty-four of them in areas like Astoria, Williamsburg, and in Lower Manhattan. Of course, the most famous one of all, Bohemian Hall and Beer Garden in Astoria, has been here for one hundred years (Feuer 2011b).

20. Kimmelman 2011.

21. Appelbaum 2011.

22. Smiley 2012.

CHAPTER FIVE. TAR BEACHES, SIDEWALK CARVINGS, IRISH FREEDOM FIGHTERS, AND SUPERMAN: SPACES

1. New Yorkers' sense of distance is also bounded by their urban environment. They'll say you can take a bus to get to the train, but you can't walk it. And how far is it? Twelve or thirteen blocks, just a little over half a mile—fifteen minutes. In a more rural area that wouldn't be much at all.

2. Eligon 2010.

3. Perceptions of neighborhoods can affect reality in more serious ways, too. Kasinitz (2000), in his article on Red Hook, argues that the reputation of an area has effects on the fortunes of residents that go beyond their own attributes as people. They are viewed in certain ways by others, especially potential employers, who often reject them because of the area's generally bad name.

4. E. Miller 2009.

5. Actually, the pooper-scooper law is a classic case where, with the consent of the public, the needs of the community as a whole triumphed over those of people who were concerned with the rights of individual pet owners. Before the law was enacted in 1978, the Big Apple was drowning in dog feces to the tune of half a million pounds daily! (Brandow 2008). Former mayor Ed Koch richly deserves credit for pushing this issue.

6. Sorkin 2009, 100–101.

7. Zukin 2010a. Much of this is a continuation of the battle between Robert Moses and Jane Jacobs, between the image of the corporate city and that of the friendly urban village. Zukin argues that authenticity can be a useful tool for improving life in our urban spaces, regardless of whether they are "historically old or creatively new." In her conclusion she clearly defines one of authenticity's key attributes: "Though we think authenticity refers to a neighborhood's innate qualities, it really expresses our own anxieties about how places change. The idea of authenticity is important because it connects our individual yearning to root ourselves in a singular time and place to a cosmic grasp of larger social forces that remake our world from many small and often invisible actions" (220). But if that is the case, then whose "singular time and place" should prevail? The young? The old? The middle aged? The rich? The poor? Those in between? Lefebvre (1991)

has written about how government and business interests appropriate and use what he calls "abstract space" to fulfill their profit-oriented vision of how space should be used, as well as for the purposes of social control.

Zukin (1995) builds on this in her insightful analysis of Lefebvre's work. She describes the revitalized Bryant Park, Times Square, and Sony Plaza as "embodying a new kind of space: a template of privatization for the whole society, an attempt at combining democratic access with social controls" (293). Anyone who's been to these places knows exactly what she means. You can go there and have a good time, but the spatial limits are definitely enforced by those in charge of the space. Zukin makes the following, almost prophetic, observation: "All public spaces, however, are influenced by the dominant symbolic economy. And just now, the dominant symbolic economy owes more to Disney World than to the African Market of 125th Street" (294). Indeed it does. When Zukin's book *The Cultures of Cities* appeared in 1995, that market had not yet moved or, if you will, been removed. It now sits forlornly on 116th Street, far from the madding crowd, between Fifth and Malcolm X Avenues, a victim of more powerful commercial interests on 125th Street. In its new location, with few customers, largely Africans, for its dashikis; long, flowing robes; and beaded jewelry of many hues, it looks more like a colorful ghost town than the bustling shopping center it was once part of. For an introduction to how scholars view space, see Orum and Neal 2010; Low and Smith 2006; Harvey 1985; Foucault 1975; and the exchange in *City & Community* between Herbert Gans (2002) and Sharon Zukin (2002). Gans focuses on a use-centered approach, while Zukin emphasizes the need to concentrate more on the role of power in such evaluations.

8. Conversely, previously industrial areas have been put to other uses. The city recognized that warehousing and shipping had declined in importance and that new ways had to be found to maximize the potential of New York's 538 miles of shoreline. The South Street Seaport, Battery Park City, various parks and esplanades, and preserved wetlands were the wave of the future, a new direction in city planning for these areas. These plans were for all the boroughs, not just Manhattan. By 1998 we had Battery Park City, the Chelsea Piers recreational centers, the state park between 135th and 145th Streets, restaurants, tennis courts, water taxis, and lots more. In sum, this meant a greater sensitivity to taking advantage of the waterfront for the benefit of both public and private interests. An important factor in people's greater desire to be near the water was that the water gradually became cleaner, largely in order to comply with the requirements of federal laws. Cleaner water also had the effect of increased interest in recreational fishing in the outer boroughs. Fishing was still banned in Manhattan, along the rivers, although boating, rowing, and kayaking enjoyed a resurgence (Stern, Fishman and Tilove 2006, 95).

9. Kornblum 1983.

10. J. Hernandez 2010. See Brawarsky and Hartman on Central Park.

11. Stern, Fishman and Tilove 2006, 427–31; Kilgannon 2010b; Caro 1974.

12. Whyte 1988, 200.

13. There's also a space that's under, instead of above, the ground. Two young men are proposing to build another park on a three-block-long transit site to be called the Delancey Underground, but wags have already dubbed it the "Lowline."

It certainly won't be an affront to the New York skyline, given its location be-neath Delancey Street, but it will draw from the great outdoors. Using fiber-optic technology that will direct in natural light, developers hope to naturally grow plants, grass, and trees. Will the MTA approve their plans? Will it attract large numbers? It's difficult to say at this juncture, but since it won't have the High Line's great views and mile-plus length, the new subterranean park will have to find creative ways for people to enjoy themselves—perhaps concerts, rides, or interactive exhibits. It's certainly a unique opportunity to walk through a park that's rain and snow free. So far, the planned park hasn't aroused any controversy (Foderaro 2011b; J. Davidson 2011; Morgan 2012).

14. Robert Caro's (1974) magisterial 1,246 page work was the major critique of Moses, especially his chapter on the Cross Bronx Expressway, titled "One Mile." Moses cared more about building parks, giant swimming pools, prom-enades, cultural venues like Lincoln Center, and highways. Much to the dismay of community activists, the needs of people in the affected neighborhoods were secondary. When Caro's book appeared in 1974, New York was at its nadir and such a gloomy assessment fit in with the temper of the times. In recent years, led by people like Columbia University architecture historian Hilary Ballon, Moses is being appreciated for the major projects that he undertook and successfully rammed through to completion. A 2006 exhibition sponsored by the New York Historical Society and the Queens Museum was called "Robert Moses and the Modern City." The curators were Ballon and the preeminent historian Kenneth Jackson. In a PBS series on New York City, the prominent architect Robert A. M. Stern has this to say about Moses's brainchild, the incredibly complex Triborough Bridge: "It's highway building lifted to the art of sculpture in motion. It's fan-tastic. Under his direction we got some of the greatest public works projects the world has ever seen." In his zeal to remake New York and turn it into automobile heaven, Moses often ignored the protests of residents who viewed his efforts as attempts to destroy their neighborhoods in order to achieve his own goals. In the same PBS series, Caro argued that Moses built bridges to relieve highway conges-tion, but that the bridges attracted more traffic, thus necessitating the building of still more bridges, each of which lessened congestion only temporarily. This approach was favored, according to historian Craig Steven Wilder, who appeared in the PBS series, because Moses gave precedence to physical space over people (Burns, Sanders, and Ades 2008).

15. Kaminer 2010.

16. In his 1988 work, *City*, William H. Whyte points out how public spaces can be made undesirable. Among the ways are spikes and other metal objects mounted on sitting ledges, steep steps, and, tellingly, surveillance cameras. Today, when terrorism is a real fear and there is continuing concern about crime, most people don't think twice about surveillance and tend to see it as a distinct benefit.

17. Chen 2009.

18. Grynbaum 2009a. Forty years ago, in 1972, the city experimented with a mall, closing off fifteen blocks of Madison Avenue for two hours of the lunch period. It was a success, with foot traffic more than doubling. But the mall was soon closed, with the taxi industry leading the opposition. Today their voices are largely ignored. New York has become a far more pedestrian-friendly city, and the

city's allure is partly derived from it being seen as a place where people are out in the streets, enjoying the sights, shopping, and just plain relaxing.

19. Ibid.

20. Dominus 2009.

21. Incidentally, Conduit Avenue in Queens is also connected to the reservoir. That name refers to the original water conduits that were part of the reservoir system. But the word "conduit" is far better known to English speakers than "force tube."

22. Actually, I'm told by someone entering the building that some tourists have indeed seen it. Sharifa Rhodes-Pitts (2011) also writes about a person who uses the sidewalk, albeit to share thoughts through colored, chalk-written aphorisms and exhortations. Another, quite different case of sidewalk use is on Madison Avenue between Fifty-fifth and Fifty-sixth Streets. There the SONY Corporation had placed gaily colored decals outside its headquarters declaring this to be "The Era of You." Such advertising efforts have happened before, and each time, as now, the Transportation Department has ordered them removed, because they violate the city code forbidding advertising on sidewalks (Foderaro 2011a).

23. Whyte 1988, 9.

24. B. Howe 2010, 71–73.

25. Ibid., 191.

26. Zukin 2010a.

27. Sanjek 1998. For a discussion of how space is constructed and used in Jackson Heights, see Ortiz 2012.

28. Wines 2011.

29. Burros 2009.

30. R. Goodman 2010, 107.

31. Sorkin's (2009) description offers one explanation for the stoop's ambiguous status as "a fine, filtering, intermediate space, modulating the transition from the public life of the street to the private life of the building" (67). He goes on to say it's both a meeting place and one where you can see what's going on in the street, who's passing by, who's not cleaning up after their dog, who looks suspicious.

32. The best books on New York City buildings, from both a design and historical perspective, are the *AIA Guide to New York City* by Norval White and Elliot Willensky (2000) and the five volumes about New York by Robert A. M. Stern and his associates (1983, 1987, 1997, 1999, 2006). For more on the Turano house, see G. Gray 2012.

33. Intrigued by the story, I looked up the deeds and various sales of property at this location during the 1880s and early 1890s. It appears possible that parts of this parcel may have been owned by Jews and there could have been such an arrangement. But given the fact that all parties are long deceased, there's no way to know for certain. See New York City Department of Finance, Land Records/ City Register, Block 1754, at the aforementioned address.

34. Modern graffiti made its first appearance in Philadelphia in the early sixties, but soon spread to Brooklyn, the Bronx, and Washington Heights (Ehrlich and Ehrlich 2006). To learn more about the 5 Pointz area, see www.5ptz.com.

35. Crow 2001; Mele 2000, 256.

36. Grynbaum 2009b.
37. The Irish hunger strikers mural was on 124th Street. Battery Park City has a park memorial dedicated to the Irish potato famine of the 1840s, which sent millions of Irish to the United States. It's at the Western terminus of Vesey Street. It's Irish but addresses a different part of their history.
38. LeDuff 1997.
39. Kasinitz (2000) cites a case in Red Hook where a shrine was erected on the site where a murdered school principal had fallen. This transformed the place into one where residents of the community could unite in shared grief. Kasinitz argues that the specificity of places is as important in understanding communal problems as are the larger structural forces around them.
40. Bader 2010.

Chapter Six. From Washington Heights to Hudson Heights, from Soho to Soha: Gentrification

1. Bindley 2010.
2. Jacobs died in April 2006. See Zukin 2010a, 11; and Wichmann 2012.
3. Rosenblum 2010d. While some have argued that the actual numbers of gentrifiers moving into America's inner cities is not that significant (see Kotkin 2010; Massey and Rivlin 2002) this is not the case in New York City, based on my own research. See also Ehrenhalt (2012, 65–88) for a discussion of movement into the Wall Street area and Bushwick.
4. Rosenblum 2010d.
5. For more on gentrification as a whole in these communities, see Hymowitz 2011; Gross 2012. Gentrifying neighborhoods have also generated resentment among perfectly safe, middle-class communities that see them as grabbing all of the attention, which generates into better services and more investment by developers. The president of the Marine Park Civic Association noted that local residents "are constantly reminding elected officials we're here, we're a voting area, we take care of our homes and of each other, and we want to make sure you don't forget us" (Berger 2012e). The problem for gentrifiers is that Marine Park, Manhattan Beach, Bay Ridge, Fresh Meadows, Whitestone, and many other nice communities are simply too far away from Manhattan to be considered.
6. For a great description of Ditmas Park, see Berger 2007, 19–31.
7. See Zukin's insightful discussion of Red Hook (2010a, 159–92). For an early article advocating the building of mega-stores in the city, see R. Kramer 1996.
8. The "rent gap" view, as exemplified by Neil Smith (1996), is part of the newer "political economy" approach to urban life, which looks at the classical writings of Marx, Engels, and Weber on capitalism and how it applies to the city. The best example of such work appears in the writings of the French philosopher Henri Lefebvre. See Lefebvre 1991. For more on the demand side of the argument, see Ley 1986; Florida 2003.
9. L. Freeman 2006, 64.
10. Rhodes-Pitts 2011, 31; emphasis in original.
11. Xu 2010.

12. Ibid. Chinatown itself has moved up commercially, well beyond Canal Street, north of Grand Street, and is closing in on Delancey Street, encroaching on formerly Jewish and Italian strongholds. This geographic movement probably increases the likelihood of the syncretism discussed here.

13. McGeehan 2011.

14. Cimino 2011.

15. Ibid.

16. Ibid.

17. Lipman 2012.

18. Kasinitz 1988.

19. Many cite price, convenience, diversity, and a feeling of "dynamism" as reasons for moving there (Harris 2009). For a better understanding of the significance of names given to gentrifying neighborhoods, see Baudrillard 1994; Lefebvre 1991; Gottdiener 1995. Of course, there are always purists who don't like such things. "It's a phony name," says Andrew Dolkart, who directs Columbia University's historic preservation program. "It was Fort Washington—that's the historic name of the neighborhood" (Harris 2009). Perhaps so, but it matters little to the average resident.

20. On the displacement of factories in Brooklyn neighborhoods, see Curran 2007. Although the discussion is about North Williamsburg, it's even more relevant to Dumbo.

21. Zukin 2010a, 36–37; Mahler 2005, 167–72; Mele 2000, 234; M. J. Taylor 2005.

22. Zukin 2010a, 42–43.

23. Ibid., 47–52. Even during the recent recession, North Williamsburg continued to grow. Two condo buildings, combined with a sixty-four-room hotel (Hotel Williamsburg, North Eleventh to North Twelfth Streets, adjacent to McCarren Park), give residents access to hotel facilities. One resident expressed surprise that people would shell out more than three hundred dollars a night to stay in a hotel where they can see "middle-aged softball players like me run around cement courts" (Cardwell 2010b). That's always the case. Those there in the less expensive days can't see why people would pay more now, because it's still the same place. But with the amenities, restaurants, and safer streets, it's really not the same at all.

24. For more on the *Catholic Worker*, see Yukich 2010.

25. The East Village has a long history of motorcycle gangs (Connell-Mettauer 2002, 101–3).

26. Vandam 2010.

27. Barry 2011.

28. Cardwell 2011. For a fascinating and realistic portrayal of poverty and gentrification in Boerum Hill from the 1980s to the early 2000s, see Lethem 2003.

29. Ellen, Schwartz, Voicu, and Schill 2007.

30. Cardwell 2011.

31. Yardley 1999.

32. Tzou 2011.

33. Mele 2000. See also N. Smith 1996 and Moody 2007.

34. L. Freeman 2006.

35. Ellen and O'Regan 2010. The analysis looked at the internal census version of the American Housing Survey. Another study by researchers at Duke University and the Universities of Pittsburgh and Colorado came to similar conclusions (Kiviat 2008). See also Massey and Rivlin 2002; Vigdor 2002; Ehrenhalt 2012, 234.

36. Newman and Wyly 2006. While they don't address how much of the migration was due to displacement because of gentrification, the most recent statistics have reported a growing trend on the part of New York City blacks to leave the city for the South. About 17 percent of those moving there in the last ten years are from New York, the largest representation of any state. Of course, New York has a large black population, but given New York's attractions, it's still a surprising figure. According to a study done by the Queens College Department of Sociology, slightly more than half of the 44,474 blacks who left New York State, 22,508, ended up in the South. Among the reasons are the economy; a more liberal attitude today toward blacks in the South, coupled with disillusionment about race relations in the city (perhaps because of having had higher expectations); and a feeling that the South embodies their "spiritual and emotional roots" (Bilefsky 2011b).

37. A major area of scholarly debate is about who benefits or doesn't benefit from gentrification. Scholars like Lance Freeman (2006) and Richard Florida (2002) argue that benefits like new resources and better services outweigh the loss of housing for the poor (which Freeman believes has been overstated); the disruption of stable social and familial networks; and a loss of churches, schools, and other institutions that have been bulwarks of the neighborhood for decades, as noted by Perez (2004) and Zukin (1987). There's also a question as to the degree to which past allegiances and participation can be transferred to the new and upgraded institutions that often accompany the newcomers (Zukin 1987). And the businesses that close are not uniformly a loss for the poor. For example, a Pathmark grocery replacing a bodega may be a boon, as would be a Costco, but a boutique or Starbucks versus a cheap coffee joint would not.

38. For more on Bloomberg, see Barbaro 2013; Brash 2011. Regarding the city's moral responsibilities and how its policies affect the poor, see Neil Smith's (1996) influential work. While there is insufficient evidence to make a direct connection between specific departures from gentrified areas by the poor and where they have relocated, the larger pattern based on October 2011 U.S. Census figures shows that since 2000 the number of poor people living in the suburbs increased by 53 percent, whereas the increase in the cities was only 26 percent (Ehrenhalt 2012, 12). Whether they came from gentrifying or poor inner-city areas or from other countries is not known.

39. Vergara 2009.

40. For insightful analyses of how government, banking, real estate interests, politics, and changing tastes all interact in the process of change, see Mollenkopf (1983) and Sanjek (1998). The gradual process of gentrification is well described in Anderson (1990, 26–30, 149–52).

41. Cordes 2009.

42. Ocejo 2011; Anderson 1990, 20. See also Davis 1979; Turner 1987; Kasinitz and Hillyard 1995.

43. For information on the progress of gentrification in Bushwick, see Fruhauf 2012. For more on the role of dogs in gentrification, see Tissot 2011.

44. Berger 2012a; Roberts 2012a.

45. Lichtenstein 2010.

46. The city has been very supportive of the new buildings, with zoning abatements, financing, tax breaks, and the like, because they are an important source of taxes in a place where nothing existed once industry departed. Before these projects were developed, the same types of people who have moved here were going to Hoboken and their taxes were lost to the city. The area is perhaps a harder sell than, say, North Williamsburg or Greenpoint, because unlike those communities, Hunters Point isn't embedded inside an established community with a built-up area of restaurants, dry cleaners, clothing stores, and doctors' offices. It's mostly industrial, with a small residential section.

47. Haughney 2010.

48. Bellafante 2012. See also Berger 2012e and A. Davidson 2012. It appears as if the Bronx may be poised for gentrification. Recent data indicate that more people moved there in the period ending July 1, 2012, than left. The actual numbers were small. According to Joseph Salvo, director of the population division of the city's Planning Department, "You've got to go back to the postwar period in the 1940s when we [last] had a surge of people moving into the Bronx" (Roberts 2013).

49. In the 1970s East New York and Brownsville were considered two of New York City's most blighted and dangerous neighborhoods. Even by the early '90s, East New York was still popularly referred to as the "murder capital of New York." But the first major step in the area's rehabilitation came with the creation of the Nehemiah Plan in 1982, which helped in the building of fifteen hundred two- and three-bedroom attached, redbrick, private homes that looked like some neighborhoods in Queens where this type of housing prevailed (Flushing, Woodside, Maspeth, etc.). The Nehemiah houses and other nonprofit groups that rehab or build in partnership with the city have been a great success story. Of more than sixty thousand, less than 1 percent of them have foreclosed, even during the latest recession. Why? Because they screened very carefully and took little risk. As one owner recalled, "If you didn't have good credit, you were out—it was old-fashioned." Not everyone was happy, not least a woman who penned one thousand letters to the mayor complaining. Her problem? She refused to show proof of income (Powell 2010).

Those who see this approach as excessively harsh need to consider what happens when there is a foreclosure. Everyone loses—the owner, the bank, and the community—especially when the house sits abandoned, easy prey for vagrants and drug dealers. For a good description of how people struggle not to fall victim to foreclosure, see Gonnerman 2009. Some criticized the Nehemiah houses as wasteful because of the low population density, and one group in Brooklyn actually tried something else in 1989. It's known as Spring Creek Gardens, located in Brooklyn's East New York section. These were essentially low-rise, five-story (585 units were built) apartment buildings. Combined with small streets and town squares, the buildings gave the project a small village feel (Stern 2006, 1191–1201). With other, similar projects going forward, East New York as a whole has revived, and some homes there can sell for several hundred thousand dollars. Most of the worst-looking buildings are gone, so with that it is becoming harder and harder to find slums worthy of the name in appearance. And there's clearly no nostalgia for them. It's important to note that for-profit groups do projects of this type.

50. Current programs that encourage gentrification are 421a and J-51 initiatives. The 421a program supports multifamily residential construction. It provides a declining property tax exemption depending on the new value created and is sponsored by the NYC Department of Housing, Preservation, and Development and the Department of Finance. To encourage people to build in neglected areas, builders were granted a tax abatement that allowed them to pay a tax rate for ten to twenty-five years that was based on what the property was worth *before* construction. The J-51 program supports the renovation of residential apartment buildings by giving property tax exemptions and abatement benefits. It's also supported by the above-named agencies. There's also the 80–20 program administered by the New York State Housing Finance Agency, the Housing Development Corporation, and the Department of Housing Preservation and Development. It uses tax-exempt bonds for affordable housing, usually in desirable locations, to benefit those with low incomes. The landlord sets aside 20 percent of the building's apartments for applicants who earn no more than 50 percent of the area's median income. For an interesting analysis of community planning and real estate programs in New York City, see Angotti 2008.

51. The Bloomberg administration has created an initiative known as the New Housing Marketplace Plan to produce or preserve 165,000 units of affordable housing in the city.

52. Berger 2012b. For more on how the government interfaces with and supports private investment to move things along, see Harvey 1985. Perhaps the best-known developer in the city is Donald Trump, who in 1976 became the first developer to receive tax abatements. Over the years he has built luxury apartments on the Upper West Side and in other locations on the East Side. While he has not really concentrated his efforts on gentrifying neighborhoods, his flamboyant personality has made him synonymous with the revitalization of the city.

53. In the Longwood Historic District one sees amazing examples of preservation. I walk on Dawson Avenue between Longwood and 156th Street. The block is idyllic, a quiet street, no garbage, no graffiti, just beautiful century-old brownstones, a pleasure to behold in a most unlikely part of the city. Here one can see slate roofs, brick and stone houses, wood frame glass doors, polished to a high gloss, with gold brass door knobs that glint in the sunlight, all topped by spires and gables that would be at home in a Victorian novel. Farther north, on Jackson Avenue, right off of Boston Post Road between Home Street and 166th Street, are some beautifully preserved, landmarked, old semi-attached homes, brick throughout, even along the sides, with bow windows and beautiful terra-cotta. One or two of them are for sale. The area seems quiet, but it's deceptive. Actually, there are gangs in the projects a few blocks away, but you wouldn't know it from standing here. And around the corner is Morris High School, a rough, high-security place with metal detectors and cameras, patrolled by large, beefy security guards. This is one of the enduring paradoxes of the city. One block can look peaceful, bucolic,

and the next will be a hive of busy activity, with bodegas on the corners, people hanging out and talking, along with litter and graffiti. The behavior of the people on each block and their propensity to gather on it, or not, are generally determined and maintained by the common consent and habits of the people who reside there.

54. This is a nationwide problem in inner cities, be it at the University of Chicago (see Venkatesh 2008) or at the University of Southern California. On a recent self-guided tour in June 2012 through South Central Los Angeles, I was struck by the number of private security officers on the blocks near the university. Speaking with some of them, I learned that two Asian students had been killed there two weeks earlier. They added that while killings are rare, break-ins and muggings are not.

55. L. Freeman 2006, 82–86, 206.

56. Sohn 2009, 13–14.

57. Ibid., 2.

58. Robbins 2012. See also Ehrenhalt 2012, 82. For discussions of attempts to resist gentrification in today's East Harlem, see Maeckelbergh 2012; Wichmann 2012.

59. Special thanks to Philip Kasinitz for highlighting this point.

60. E. Abramson 2009.

61. Kilgannon 2010a.

62. Bleyer 2007.

63. For more on the lack of real relationships between gentrifiers and the indigenous poor, see Anderson 1990, 159; Ehrenhalt 2012, 75.

64. I found the fence company in Flushing, west of Main Street, by Forty-first Avenue and Fuller Place. The fences are built with materials imported from China, which is, in fact, a leading manufacturer and exporter of these products.

65. Berger 2011f; Hydra 2006. See also Wichmann 2012. For an interesting discussion of how different perspectives of gentrifiers and locals play out in community gardens, see Martinez 2010.

CHAPTER SEVEN. ASSIMILATION, IDENTITY, OR SOMETHING ELSE? THE FUTURE OF ETHNIC NEW YORK

1. Saulny 2012.

2. In 2011 the population of New York City was 8,244,910 (Roberts 2012a). The ethnic group figures are rounded off.

3. Jang 2010. There's also a Ukrainian museum across the street from the school. There has been conflict of late, between the newer immigrants, who wax nostalgic about the old Communist regime, and the earlier arrivals, who fled Communism (Lehmekh 2010). For more on how nonprofits affect the life of residents and their neighborhoods, see Small and McDermott 2006; Small 2009; and Sampson 2012.

4. Jang 2010.

5. Xu 2010.

6. Medina 2010.

7. Rieder 1985; Mc Lean 2001; Pritchett 2002. Occasionally, stories will surface about how blacks tried to buy in a white neighborhood and were rebuffed.

In February 2010 the *New York Times* carried a story about how blacks who attempted to purchase a home in Edgewater Park, a Bronx community near the Throgs Neck Bridge, were discouraged from doing so. They applied with the help of the Fair Housing Justice Center (Buckley 2010a). It's unclear whether they really wanted to live there or were just using it as a test case. It matters because one could legitimately ask whether a black couple would really want to live in an area with almost no black residents. For more on the history of urban succession, see Sugrue 1996; Massey and Denton 1993.

8. Sleeper 1991; Krysan and Farley 2002; Anderson 2011, 15–16, 178.

9. Kasinitz, Bazzi, and Doane 1998.

10. Navarro 2012. See also Hitlin, Brown, and Elder 2007 for a critique of current classifications based on a national study. The authors recommend using Hispanic as a choice. A study of Dominicans confirms the rejection of race as a defining category, arguing that they employ language to negotiate identity and to resist racial categorizations (Bailey 2000). A study of dating habits found that Latinos are much more apt to prefer dating whites than blacks. However, they are also much more likely to prefer blacks than whites are (Feliciano, Lee, and Robnett 2011).

11. Khandelwal 2002. See also Saran 1985 for a general overview of the Indian community.

12. For more on these groups, see Novak 1971; Gans 1982; Zeitz 2007.

13. For more on responses to 9/11 and changing patterns in religious observance among Muslims, see Bakalian and Bozorgmehr 2009 and Mahon 2013.

14. See Alejandro Portes's comments in Alba, Portes, et al. 2000, 244. Kasinitz, Bazzi, and Doane (1998) have also commented on the parallel lifestyles of different groups sharing spaces in Jackson Heights, Queens. For more on a rightward religious shift within Orthodox Judaism, see Heilman 2006.

15. Tony Carnes, a Texas native, is heading an effort to identify every single house of worship in the city (Oppenheimer 2011).

16. Dominus 2010. In 2009 the New York City Council passed a resolution to add two Muslim holidays to the school calendar as days off. There are at least six hundred thousand Muslims residing in the city, and this was seen as a nod to them, until then only Christian and Jewish holidays being on the calendar (Semple 2009c). Do holidays like Id al-Fitr, which commemorates the end of Ramadan, and Id al-Adha, which signifies the end of the annual pilgrimage to Mecca, rise to the level of Christmas? It doesn't matter. What's being said is that Muslims are becoming more numerous and deserve recognition for their culture too. Muslims pray in the morning and have a feast and exchanges of gifts with family on these days.

17. Frase 2005.

18. Poll 1962; W. Helmreich 1992. For an account of Hasidim who leave the community, see Winston 2006.

19. Magnus 2009.

20. A good deal of research on religious groups indicates that, generally, the smaller the group, the more committed its members. See Olson 2008.

21. S. Abramson 2010.

22. Leland 2011a.

23. Ibid.

24. See Kasinitz et al. 2008.

25. Dolnick 2011a. In the past, success among minorities was often measured by the degree to which they were accepted. Thus, in the Jewish community of an earlier time, the Jewish mother says to her successful son, "Yes, you're a captain by the Jews, but are you also a captain by the *Goyim*?" And while today this view has much receded, it still exists. In Gish Jen's (1996) perceptive novel about Chinese Americans, a young Chinese woman talks about her immigrant parents: "They comb over the fine example of Auntie Theresa, who is such a good doctor many round eyes go to see her, not just Chinese" (233).

26. I'm not referring to foreigners whose English may be poor for that reason, but to native-born whites who lack that excuse for using poor English syntax.

27. Berger 2011b.

28. Barnard 2009b.

29. Ibid.

30. These black/Jewish congregations are mostly found in Brooklyn, Manhattan, and Queens. One such synagogue can be found at 297 Saratoga Avenue, in Ocean Hill–Brownsville. Called the Sh'ma Yisrael Hebrew Israelite Congregation, it is led by Chief Prince Tzippor Ben Zuvulun. Sometimes Christianity and Judaism are combined. A storefront at 1941 Madison Avenue is home to the Israelite Church of God and Jesus Christ and displays a big Star of David in the window. A chart of the twelve tribes of Israel identifies congregants with various current peoples, including the Haitians, Negroes, West Indians, Mexicans, Seminole Indians, Guatemalans, Puerto Ricans, and Cubans. For more on this subject, see A. Helmreich and Marcus 1998; Weisbord and Stein 1972. I asked a Seventh-Day Adventist elder with a church on Louisiana Avenue in East New York that was once a synagogue why he kept the Star of David on his church. He answered, "Because we all believe in the same God. And there are many Jews who accept Jesus too." I inquired as to why the neighborhood improved over the past twenty years. "Because of Jesus" was his succinct reply. "If you are a believer, then everything comes from God, not the police department or Giuliani's policies." Reverend Waterman, with whom I also spoke, added, "The star makes it kosher, and kosher laws are part of our Bible and what we believe in as Seventh-Day Adventists."

31. Marable 2011, especially pp. 301 and 369. Another way groups preserve their identity is by writing down their history. This is especially so when the groups have come from faraway lands. Several Liberian women on Staten Island have embarked on an oral history project in which women write down stories about their homeland and try to have them published so that the second generation will not forget where they came from (Ludwig 2009). A similar project was undertaken by Iranian Jews from Mashad who came to New York after the Iranian Revolution and who settled initially in Kew Gardens, Queens. Forced to convert en masse to Islam in Iran about 180 years ago, they had maintained their faith in secret. Now that they could practice it openly, they decided to record their struggles to remain Jews for the sake of future generations (H. Helmreich 2008).

32. Confessore and Barbaro 2011.

33. Mahler 2005, 126–29.

34. Confessore and Barbaro 2011. See also Armstrong and Crage 2006; Duberman 1993; Gan 2007.

35. Bruni 2011.

36. For an interesting and passionate discussion of how AIDS devastated the gay community, see Schulman 2012.

37. Barbaro 2011; Confessore and Barbaro 2011. Of course, thousands of Catholics do not share this view.

38. Hakim 2011.

39. Peyser 2011.

40. Alba 2009. Alba's earlier book in 2003, *Remaking the American Mainstream,* coauthored with Victor Nee, focused on the same topic, but the 2009 volume greatly expands it.

41. Kasinitz et al. 2008, 229–35.

42. Roberts 2010e.

43. Alba and Nee 2003, 91–94.

44. Fahim and Zraick 2010.

45. As sociologist Peter Kwong has noted, the shift from reliance on organizations like the Chinese Consolidated Benevolent Association and the tongs to government agencies actually began twenty-five years ago (Kwong 1996, 81–123).

46. Dolnick 2012.

47. Luo 2012; Min 2010.

NEIGHBORHOOD GLOSSARY

These are the neighborhoods mentioned or discussed in the book. In this glossary, "community," "section, "area," and "neighborhood" are used interchangeably. As a word of caution, there isn't always universal agreement, even by experts, on the precise borders of these neighborhoods.

The Bronx

Baychester   in the northeast, between the Hutchinson River Parkway and Pelham Bay Park

Belmont   neighborhood east of Fordham and north of East Tremont

Co-op City   Located in the Baychester section, it's the largest co-op community in the world, with over fifty-five thousand residents and still growing.

Crotona Park East   neighborhood south of the Cross Bronx Expressway, west of the Bronx River, and near East Tremont

East Bronx   the entire area of the Bronx that lies east of the Bronx River

East Tremont   neighborhood south of Belmont and west of the Bronx Zoo

Edenwald   neighborhood between Williamsbridge and Co-op City

Edgewater Park   community bounded by the Throgs Neck Peninsula and lying just east of the Throgs Neck Bridge

Fordham   northwestern Bronx community centered on the Grand Concourse and Fordham Road

Harding Park   south-central waterfront neighborhood, part of the Soundview area, north of the East River, and east of the Bronx River

Hunts Point   neighborhood south of the Bronx River that abuts the Bruckner Expressway

Kingsbridge   Bronx community north of the Marble Hill area and west of Broadway

Longwood   southern area between Melrose and Hunts Point

Melrose   southwestern Bronx neighborhood around 149th Street; also known as the "Hub"

Morris Heights   neighborhood in the west-central Bronx along the Harlem River

Morrisania   located south of the Cross Bronx Expressway, east of Claremont Park

Mott Haven   southwestern community east of the Harlem River.

Mount Eden   west-central neighborhood south of the Cross Bronx Expressway

Parkchester   east Bronx community, dominated by the huge housing development of the same name

Pelham Bay   northeastern neighborhood, west of Pelham Bay Park and south of Pelham Parkway

Riverdale   in the northwest by the Hudson River and Van Cortlandt Park, and south of Yonkers

Silver Beach   gated community near the Throgs Neck Bridge

Soundview   southeast neighborhood, north of Soundview Park, and east of the Bronx River

South Bronx   Originally this meant Mott Haven, Hunts Point, and Melrose, but it has come to also include areas along the Cross Bronx Expressway and north to the Fordham area.

Throgs Neck   located on a peninsula south and west of Long Island Sound and north of the East River

West Bronx   the entire area of the Bronx that lies west of the Bronx River

Woodlawn   in the north-central Bronx, south of Yonkers

Brooklyn

Bay Ridge   section of southwestern Brooklyn between Sixty-first and Eighty-sixth streets, and west of the Gowanus Expressway

Bedford-Stuyvesant   north-central neighborhood south of Flushing Avenue and north of Atlantic Avenue; also called Bed-Stuy

Bensonhurst   southwestern neighborhood next to Borough Park, south of Sixty-first Street

Boerum Hill   neighborhood between Fort Greene and Carroll Gardens and near downtown Brooklyn

Borough Park   neighborhood in the central part of the borough on both sides of Thirteenth Avenue, east of Sunset Park and north of Bensonhurst

Brighton Beach   southwestern area between Manhattan Beach and Coney Island

Brooklyn Heights   community at the northern end of the borough and adjacent to Cobble Hill

Brownsville   southeastern community bordering East New York, between Eastern Parkway and Linden Boulevard

Bushwick   east of Bedford-Stuyvesant and bordering Queens County

Canarsie   located along Jamaica Bay and adjacent to Flatlands

Carroll Gardens   neighborhood near the Gowanus Canal and the Brooklyn-Queens Expressway

Clinton Hill   community located between the Brooklyn-Queeens Expressway and Atlantic Avenue

Cobble Hill   neighborhood near Carroll Gardens and Brooklyn Heights

Coney Island   section of southwest Brooklyn near Ocean Parkway and the Atlantic Ocean

Crown Heights   north-central area located between Atlantic Avenue and Empire Boulevard

Cypress Hills   next to East New York and south of the Queens border

Ditmas Park   part of northern Flatbush and east of Ocean Parkway

Dumbo/Vinegar Hill   stands for "Down Under the Manhattan Bridge Overpass," adjacent to Brooklyn Heights and Fort Greene

Dyker Heights   southwestern community adjacent to Bay Ridge and Bensonhurst

East Flatbush   central borough community, next to Flatbush

East New York   community in the eastern portion of Brooklyn bordering Brownsville and Queens

East Williamsburg   area southeast of Greenpoint and north of Bushwick; still heavily industrial, but now beginning to gentrify

Flatbush   central Brooklyn neighborhood running on both sides of Ocean Parkway

Flatlands   southern neighborhood near Mill Basin and Marine Park

Fort Greene   northern community by the Manhattan Bridge, along Flatbush and Atlantic Avenues

Gerritsen Beach   waterfront community east of Knapp Street, adjacent to Sheepshead Bay

Gowanus   northern area near Carroll Gardens running along the Gowanus Canal

Greenpoint   northern community next to Ridgewood, Queens

Greenwood Heights   community located between Park Slope and Sunset Park

Manhattan Beach   southern waterfront community adjacent to Brighton Beach and Sheepshead Bay

Marine Park   southern community to the south of Mill Basin

Midwood   community that is part of Flatbush

Mill Basin   southern community north of Marine Park

North Williamsburg   area south of Greenpoint adjacent to the East River (also known as North Side) that has greatly gentrified in recent years

Ocean Hill   community adjacent to Brownsville

Park Slope   northwestern area near Gowanus, Sunset Park, and Prospect Heights

Prospect Heights   community next to Park Slope and Crown Heights

Prospect-Lefferts Gardens   area bordering Brooklyn Botanic Gardens and Crown Heights, and Prospect Park South
Prospect Park South   area bordering Botanic Gardens and Flatbush
Red Hook   neighborhood next to the Brooklyn Battery Tunnel bordering Carroll Gardens and Gowanus
Seagate   gated community next to Coney Island
Sheepshead Bay   area next to Manhattan Beach and Gerritsen Beach
South Williamsburg   area bordering North Williamsburg that is predominantly Hasidic and Puerto Rican (also known as South Side)
Sunset Park   area south of Greenwood Heights and west of Borough Park
Williamsburg   see North and South Williamsburg
Windsor Terrace   area near Sunset Park and Park Slope

Manhattan

Battery Park City   area west of the Financial District and south of Tribeca, abutting the Hudson River
Carnegie Hill   community in the northern section of the Upper East Side
Chelsea   western area north of the West Village
Chinatown   community near the Lower East Side and Little Italy
Clinton   north of Chelsea, west of Midtown (part of what was once called "Hell's Kitchen")
East Harlem   area east of Harlem, north of the Upper East Side
East Village   community east of Greenwich Village
Greenwich Village   neighborhood west of the East Village and north of Tribeca
Harlem   central commercial/residential core area between East and West Harlem
Inwood   north of Washington Heights
Little Italy   area near Soho and Chinatown
Lower East Side   area south of the East Village and east of Chinatown
Manhattanville   area just north of the West Side, around 125th Street and Broadway
Midtown   the business and theater district of central Manhattan
Morningside Heights   community in the Upper West Side
Mount Morris   historic area in Harlem, near 125th Street
Noho   area north of Houston Street and south of Greenwich Village
Soho   area south of Houston Street near Tribeca and Little Italy
Sugar Hill   neighborhood in West Harlem, north of 125th Street
Tribeca   (Triangle Below Canal Street) area between Greenwich Village and the Financial District

Upper East Side   area on the east side, along the East River on the east, with Central Park on the west, between Fifty-ninth and Ninty-sixth Streets

Upper West Side   western area along the Hudson River on the west, with Central Park on the east between Fifty-ninth and 125th Streets

Washington Heights   area north of West Harlem and south of Inwood (Hudson Heights is the new name for the area North of 181st Street used by real estate developers and many new residents.)

West Village   area adjacent to Greenwich Village, between Sixth Avenue and the Hudson River

Queens

Auburndale   neighborhood between Bayside, Murray Hill, and Queensboro Hill

Arverne   neighborhood next to Edgemere on the Rockaway Peninsula

Astoria   area on the western edge of the borough, bordering Long Island City

Bayside   eastern Queens, between Douglaston and Auburndale

Beechhurst   northern neighborhood adjacent to Whitestone

Belle Harbor   part of the Rockaway Peninsula

Bellerose   eastern area next to Queens Village

Breezy Point   gated community on the western edge of the Rockaway Peninsula

Briarwood   area near Kew Gardens

Broad Channel   area on Jamaica Bay near the Rockaway Peninsula

Cambria Heights   southern area between Queens Village and Laurelton

Corona   area near Elmhurst and Jackson Heights

Douglaston   area bordering Little Neck and Bayside

East Elmhurst   area near La Guardia Airport, bordering Corona and Jackson Heights

Edgemere   area next to Arverne on the Rockaway Peninsula

Elmhurst   area bordering Jackson Heights and Corona

Far Rockaway   on the eastern edge of the Rockaway Peninsula

Flushing   area near Queensboro Hill and Murray Hill

Forest Hills   area between Kew Gardens and Rego Park

Fresh Meadows   community near Hillcrest and Auburndale

Glendale   near Middle Village and Ridgewood

Hamilton Beach   area immediately east of Howard Beach

Hillcrest   area next to Fresh Meadows and Kew Gardens Hills

Holliswood   neighborhood between Jamaica Estates and Queens Village

Howard Beach   located just south of Ozone Park near Kennedy Airport

Hunters Point   western area along the East River next to Sunnyside

Jackson Heights   near Corona and Elmhurst
Jamaica Center   commercial area next to South Jamaica
Jamaica Estates   borders South Jamaica and Holliswood
Kew Gardens   area adjacent to Richmond Hill and Briarwood
Kew Gardens Hills   area between Forest Hills and Hillcrest
Laurelton   section in southeastern Queens bordering Cambria Heights
Little Neck   area bordering Long Island and Douglaston
Long Island City   area between Astoria and Hunters Point
Maspeth   community near Middle Village and Ridgewood
Middle Village   area bordering Maspeth, Glendale, and Ridgewood
Murray Hill   located between Flushing and Bayside
Ozone Park   near Howard Beach and South Ozone Park
Queens Village   area between Bellerose and Cambria Heights
Queensboro Hill   community near Flushing and Murray Hill
Richmond Hill   area between Kew Gardens and South Ozone Park
Ridgewood   borders Glendale and Middle Village as well as Greenpoint, Brooklyn
South Jamaica   section near Jamaica Estates and South Ozone Park
South Ozone Park   southern community near Howard Beach and Kennedy Airport
Sunnyside   western area near Hunters Point and Long Island City
Whitestone   northern area bordering Beechhurst
Woodside   located next to Long Island City in western Queens

Staten Island

Mariners Harbor   northwestern area near the Goethals Bridge
New Brighton   northeastern area between West Brighton and St. George
Randall Manor   neighborhood bordering New Brighton and West Brighton
St. George   extreme northeastern area where the ferry to Manhattan docks
South Beach   waterfront neighborhood along Lower New York Bay near the Verrazano-Narrows Bridge
Todt Hill   hilly area near Grant City and South Beach
Tottenville   southwestern edge of Staten Island
Travis   located in the west-central part of the borough
West Brighton   area next to Randall Manor and New Brighton

BIBLIOGRAPHY

Abrahamson, Mark. 2005. *Urban Enclaves: Identity and Place in the World*. 2nd ed. New York: Worth.

Abramson, Evan. 2009. "Where Boundaries Are Melting, A Place to Celebrate Differences." *New York Times*, March 21.

Abramson, Stacy. 2010. "The Stories of One Brooklyn Block." *New York Times*, Metropolitan Section, July 23.

Abu-Lughod, Janet, ed. 1994. *From Urban Village to East Village: The Battle for New York's Lower East Side*. Oxford: Blackwell.

Akam, Simon. 2009. "With Every Whack of the Cricket Bat, a Bond." *New York Times*, June 29.

Alba, Richard D. 2009. *Blurring the Color Line: The New Chance for a More Integrated America*. Cambridge, MA: Harvard University Press.

Alba, Richard D., John R. Logan, and Kyle Crowder. 1997. "White Ethnic Neighborhoods and Spatial Assimilation: The Greater New York Region, 1980–1990." *Social Forces* 75: 883–912.

Alba, Richard D., John R. Logan, and Brian J. Stults. 2000. "How Segregated Are Middle-Class African Americans?" *Social Problems* 47: 543–58.

Alba, Richard D., and Victor Nee. 2003. *Remaking the American Mainstream: Assimilation and Contemporary Immigration*. Cambridge, MA: Harvard University Press.

Alba, Richard D., Alejandro Portes, Philip Kasinitz, Nancy Foner, Elijah Anderson, and Nathan Glazer. 2000. "Documentation: Beyond the Melting Pot 35 Years Later: On the Relevance of a Sociological Classic for the Immigration Metropolis of Today." *International Migration Review* 34: 243–79.

Alexander, Jeffrey C. 2004. "From the Depths of Despair: Performance, Counterperformance, and 'September 11.'" *Sociological Theory* 22: 88–105.

Allan, David G. 2010. "Music That Rises above the City's Roar." *New York Times*, April 20.

Altman, Barbara M. 1981. "Studies of Attitudes toward the Handicapped: The Need for a New Direction." *Social Problems* 28: 321–37.

Alvarez, Lizette. 1996. "Hispanic Settlers Transform Harding Park in Bronx." *New York Times*, December 31.

Alvarez, Lizette, and Michael Wilson. 2009. "Their Launching Pad." *New York Times*, Metropolitan Section, May 31.

Andersen, Kurt. 2008. "Because We're Resilient." *New York Magazine*, December 14.

Anderson, Elijah. 1976. *A Place on the Corner*. Chicago: University of Chicago Press.

———. 1990. *StreetWise: Race, Class, and Change in an Urban Community*. Chicago: University of Chicago Press.

———. 1999. *Code of the Street*. New York: W.W. Norton.

———, ed. 2009. *Ethnography* (Special Issue), vol. 10, no. 4.

———. 2011. *The Cosmopolitan Canopy: Race and Civility in Everyday Life*. New York: W. W. Norton.

Angelos, James. 2009. "Parkchester: Closing on a Dream." *New York Times*, New York Region, May 3.

Angotti, Tom. 2008. *New York for Sale: Community Planning Confronts Global Real Estate*. Cambridge: MIT Press.

Appelbaum, Alec. 2011. "Presto, Instant Playground." *New York Times*, Sunday Review, August 14.

Arieff, Irwin. 2009. "Momentum in South Harlem." *New York Times*, Real Estate Section, December 27.

Armstrong, Elizabeth A., and Suzanna M. Crage. 2006. "Movements and Memory: The Making of the Stonewall Myth." *American Sociological Review* 71: 724–51.

Bader, Daniel P. 2010. "The Meaning of the Trivium." *Manhattan Times*, September 15.

Bagli, Charles V. 2008. "For Reinvention, Red Hook Follows Its Roots." *New York Times*, November 23.

———. 2009a. "City and Developer Spar over Coney Island Visions." *New York Times*, February 17.

———. 2009b. "After Two Years of Trying, Owners Give Up on Selling Starrett City." *New York Times*, February 18.

———. 2009c. "Beyond Sideshows, the City and a Developer Face Off over Coney Island's Future." *New York Times*, April 11.

———. 2009d. "Seeking Revival, City to Buy Land in Coney Island." *New York Times*, November 12.

———. 2010a. "As a Neighborhood Shifts, the Chain Stores Arrive." *New York Times*, November 13.

———. 2010b. "After 30 Years, a Rebirth Is Complete." *New York Times*, December 4.

Bahr, Howard M. 1973. *Skid Row: An Introduction to Disaffiliation*. New York: Oxford University Press.

Bailey, Benjamin. 2000. "Language and Negotiation of Ethnic/Racial Identity among Dominican Americans." *Language in Society* 29: 555–82.

Bakalian, Anny, and Mehdi Bozorgmehr. 2009. *Backlash 9/11: Middle Eastern and Muslim Americans Respond*. Berkeley: University of California Press.

Ballon, Hilary, and Kenneth T. Jackson, eds. 2007. *Robert Moses and the Modern City: The Transformation of New York*. New York: W. W. Norton.

Barbanel, Josh. 1991. "Fiscal Reality: Bumpy Streets, Library Cuts and Tuition Rise." *New York Times*, February 4.

Barbaro, Michael. 2010. "Debate Heats Up about Mosque near Ground Zero." *New York Times*, July 30.

———. 2011. "Behind Gay Marriage, an Unlikely Mix of Forces." *New York Times*, June 26.

———. 2013. "Bloomberg to Johns Hopkins: Thanks a Billion (Well, $1.1 Billion)." *New York Times*, January 27.

Barnard, Anne. 2009a. "A Working-Class Neighborhood Seeks Its Place in History." *New York Times*, March 28.

———. 2009b. "Reconsecration, with Bells, Saffron, and Elephant." *New York Times*, July 14.

———. 2009c. "Doormen and Residents: Under One Roof, Yet Far Apart." *New York Times*, November 27.

Barnard, Anne, Adam Nossiter, and Kirk Semple. 2011. "From Hut in Africa to the Glare of a High-Profile Assault Case." *New York Times*, June 15.

Barron, James. 2009. "Subway Killing's Chilling Scenes, Captured by a Photography Student." *New York Times*, November 27.

———. 2010a. "A New York Bloc on the Supreme Court." *New York Times*, May 12.

———. 2010b. "The Floating Lady Surfaces for the Summer." *New York Times*, June 16.

Barron, James, and Peter Baker. 2012. "In Brooklyn Brownstone, Future President Found a Home on the Top Floor." *New York Times*, May 2.

Barry, Dan. 1997. "Darkest Blue Brutality." *New York Times*, August 14.

———. 2010. "Death of a Fulton Fish Market Fixture." *New York Times*, Metropolitan Section, October 15.

———. 2011. "On Bowery, Cultures Clash as the Shabby Meet the Shabby Chic." *New York Times*, October 13.

Baudrillard, Jean. 1994. *Simulacra and Simulation: The Body in Theory: Histories of Cultural Materialism*. Translated by Sheila Faria Glaser. Ann Arbor: University of Michigan Press.

Bearman, Peter S. 2005. *Doormen*. Chicago: University of Chicago Press.

Bellafante, Ginia. 2011a. "Steps Away but Worlds Apart in New York." *New York Times*, Metropolitan Section, September 18.

———. 2011b. "A Diverse City? In Some Ways, Anything But." *New York Times*, Metropolitan Section, October 23.

———. 2011c. "Economic Revival, without the Fancy Cheese?" *New York Times*, Metropolitan Section, December 4.

———. 2012. "Where Optimism Feels Out of Reach." *New York Times*, Metropolitan Section, January 15.

Beller, Thomas, ed. 2002. *Mr. Beller's Neighborhood: Before & After: Stories from New York*, Vols. 1 and 2. New York: W. W. Norton.

Bender, Thomas. 2002. *The Unfinished City: New York and the Metropolitan Idea*. New York: New Press.

Berger, Joseph. 1984. "Study Reports Exodus of Affluent and Educated New Yorkers in Late 70s." *New York Times*, September 19.

———. 1985. "Reagan's Tax Plan: Reductions for Most and Local Effects: New York Leaders Oppose Plan Vehemently." *New York Times*, May 29.

———. 1986. "Koreans Breathe New Life into Queens Church." *New York Times*, July 30.

Berger, Joseph. 2001. *Displaced Persons: Growing Up American after the Holocaust*. New York: Washington Square Press.

———. 2002a. "A Time of Flux for City's Core of Greek Life: Others Discover Astoria as Longtime Citizens Exit." *New York Times*, August 5.

———. 2002b. "Well, the Ices Are Still Italian." *New York Times*, September 17.

———. 2005. "Vegemite Toast and Other Slices of Home." *New York Times*, July 7.

———. 2007. *The World in a City: Traveling the Globe through the Neighborhoods of the New New York*. New York: Ballantine Books.

———. 2009. "West Farms Journal: When Yoo-Hooing Was Big in the Bronx." *New York Times*, July 11.

———. 2010a. "Sunnyside Journal: An Old Synagogue Downsizes in a Desperate Bid to Keep Itself Alive." *New York Times*, January 9.

———. 2010b. "Hunts Point Journal: Foot Soldiers of the Automotive Repair Trade." *New York Times*, April 30.

———. 2010c. "As Russians Move In and Flourish, Resentment Follows." *New York Times*, August 21.

———. 2010d. "A Diner That Was the Special of Every Day." *New York Times*, December 4.

———. 2011a. "There Stays the Neighborhood." *New York Times*, January 8.

———. 2011b. " 'It Keeps the Neighborhood Irish.' " *New York Times*, March 12.

———. 2011c. "Killing Rattles a Jewish Community's Long-Held Trust of Its Own." *New York Times*, July 15.

———. 2011d. "In an Early 1900s Neighborhood, a Glimpse of '2001.' " *New York Times*, July 30.

———. 2011e. "Staving Off Change to the Grit of the Bowery." *New York Times*, October 10.

———. 2011f. "As Tastes Change in Harlem, Old-Look Liquor Store Stirs a Fight." *New York Times*, December 2.

———. 2012a. "No Longer Burning, the South Bronx Gentrifies." *New York Times*, March 26.

———. 2012b. "Impact of Atlantic Yards for Good or Ill, Is Already Felt." *New York Times*, April 16.

———. 2012c. "As Greenpoint Gentrifies, Sunday Rituals Clash: Outdoor Cafes vs. Churchgoers." *New York Times*, May 11.

———. 2012d. "With Orthodox Growth, City's Jewish Population Is Climbing Again." *New York Times*, June 12.

———. 2012e. "As Brooklyn Gentrifies, Some Neighborhoods Are Being Left Behind." *New York Times*, July 9.

———. 2012f. "Enclaves, Long Gated, Seek to Let in Storm Aid." *New York Times*, November 27.

Berman, Marshall. 1982. *All That Is Solid Melts into Air: The Experience of Modernity*. New York: Simon and Schuster.

Bernstein, Fred A. 2011. "Pratt Institute Takes an Interest in Making a Neighborhood Nicer." *New York Times*, Real Estate Section, February 16.

Beveridge, Andrew A. 2006a. "Undocumented Immigrants." GothamGazette.com. April.

———. 2006b. "New York's Asians." GothamGazette.com. May.

———. 2008a. "A Religious City." Gotham Gazette.com. February.

———. 2008b. "A Century of Harlem in New York City: Some Notes on Migration, Consolidation, Segregation, and Recent Developments." *City & Community* 7: 358–65.

Beyer, Gregory. 2009a. "Prosperous Area Seeks Shops to Match." *New York Times*, Real Estate Section, April 26.

———. 2009b. "A Beach Shared by a Tight-Knit Clan." *New York Times*, Real Estate Section, September 6.

Bianco, Anthony. 2005. *Ghosts of 42nd Street: A History of America's Most Infamous Block*. New York: Harper Perennial.

Bilefsky, Dan. 2011a. "Converging on Little Egypt, with Anger and Hope." *New York Times*, January 31.

———. 2011b. "For New Life, Blacks in City Head to South." *New York Times*, June 22.

Bindley, Katherine. 2010. "Living In/Morris Heights, the Bronx." *New York Times*, Real Estate Section, September 17.

Biney, Moses O. 2011. *From Africa to America: Religion and Adaptation among Ghanaian Immigrants in New York*. New York: New York University Press.

Bleyer, Jennifer. 2007. "Living In/Parkchester, the Bronx: 129 Acres, Renewed Yet Affordable." *New York Times*, Real Estate Section, October 7.

Bloom, Nicholas Dagen. 2008. *Public Housing That Worked: New York in the Twentieth Century*. Philadelphia: University of Pennsylvania Press.

Blumenthal, Ralph. 1989. "Black Youth Is Killed by Whites: Brooklyn Attack Is Called Racial." *New York Times*, August 25.

Bobb, Vilna Bashi. 2001. "Neither Ignorance Nor Bliss: Race, Racism, and the West Indian Immigrant Experience." In *Migration, Transnationalization, and Race in a Changing New York*, edited by Hector R. Cordero-Guzman, Robert C. Smith, and Ramon Grosfoguel, 212–38. Philadelphia: Temple University Press.

Boggs, Vernon, Gerald Handel, and Sylvia F. Fava, eds. 1984. *The Apple Sliced: Sociological Studies of New York City*. New York: Praeger.

Borden, Anthony. 1987. "AIDS Crisis: The Sorrow of the City." *Dissent* (Fall): 561–64.

Bowley, Graham. 2008. "The Battle of Washington Square." *New York Times*, November 21.

Bozorgmehr, Mehdi, and Anny Bakalian. 2005. "September 11, 2001, Terrorism, Discriminatory Reactions to . . ." In *Encyclopedia of Racism in the United States*, edited by Pyong Gap Min, 557–64. Westport, CT: Greenwood Press.

Brandow, Michael. 2008. *New York's Poop Scoop Law: Dogs, the Dirt, and Due Process*. West Lafayette, IN: Purdue University Press.

Brash, Julian. 2011. *Bloomberg's New York: Class and Governance in the Luxury City*. Athens: University of Georgia Press.

Brawarsky, Sandee, and David Hartman. 2002. *2002 Views of Central Park: Experiencing New York City's Jewel from Every Angle*. New York: Stewart, Tabori, and Chang.

Breasted, Mary. 1977. "Three-Year Inquiry Threads Together Evidence on F.A.L.N. Terrorists." *New York Times*, April 17.

Brenner, Elsa. 2008. "Living In/Co-op City, the Bronx: Everything You Need in One Giant Package." *New York Times*, Real Estate Section, April 6.

Briggs, Xavier De Souza. 2007. "Some of My Best Friends Are . . .": Interracial Friendships, Class, and Segregation in America." *City & Community* 6: 263–90.

"Brooklyn Principal Cleared of Charges." 2011. *New York Times*, April 15.

Brotherton, David C., and Luis Barrios. 2004. *The Almighty Latin King and Queen Nation: Street Politics and the Transformation of a New York City Gang*. New York: Columbia University Press.

Brown, Patricia Leigh. 2009. "Invisible Immigrants, Old and Left with 'Nobody to Talk To.'" *New York Times*, August 31.

Brown-Saracino, Japonica, ed. 2010. *The Gentrification Debates*. New York: Routledge.

Bruch, Elizabeth E., and Robert D. Mare. 2006. "Neighborhood Choice and Neighborhood Change." *American Journal of Sociology* 112: 667–709.

Bruni, Frank. 2011. "To Know Us Is to Let Us Love." *New York Times*, Sunday Review Section, June 26.

Bryk, William. 2003. "From Jew to Jew-Hater: The Curious Life (and Death) of Daniel Burros." *New York Press*, February 25.

Buckley, Cara. 2006. "Brooklyn Community Is on Edge and in Spotlight after Hate-Crime Arrests." *New York Times*, August 12.

———. 2009. "One Artist Is Hurt, and 200 Others Are Feeling the Pain." *New York Times*, April 19.

———. 2010a. "2 Bronx Communities Are Accused of Preventing Blacks from Buying Homes." *New York Times*, February 6.

———. 2010b. "Agencies Lack Money to Mend Public Housing." *New York Times*, October 25.

Burgess, Ernest W. 1923. "The Growth of the City: An Introduction to a Research Project." *Proceedings of the American Sociological Society* 18: 85–89.

Burgess, Matt. 2010. *Dogfight: A Love Story*. New York: Doubleday.

Burke, Edward C. 1978. "House, 247–155 Supports New York with $2 Billion Bond Guarantee; Koch Calls Vote 'Overwhelming.'" *New York Times*, June 9.

Burns, Ric, James Sanders, with Lisa Ades. 2008. *New York: An Illustrated History*. New York: Alfred A. Knopf.

Burros, Marian. 2009. "Urban Farming, a Bit Closer to the Sun." *New York Times*, Dining Section, June 17.

Burrows, Edwin, and Mike Wallace. 1999. *Gotham: A History of New York City to 1898*. New York: Oxford University Press.

Byrne, David. 2009. *Bicycle Diaries*. New York: Viking.

Calder, Rich. 2011. "Coney Island Revival Creates Brighter Beach." *New York Post*, July 26.

Campbell, Karen E., and Barrett A. Lee. 1992. "Sources of Personal Neighbor Networks: Social Integration, Need, or Time?" *Social Forces* 70: 1077–1100.

Cardwell, Diane. 2009. "For High Line Visitors, Park Is a Railway out of Manhattan." *New York Times*, July 22.

———. 2010a. "When Parks Must Rely on Private Money." *New York Times*, Metropolitan Section, February 7.

———. 2010b. "With Luxury Hotel-Apartment Complex, Williamsburg Continues Its Evolution." *New York Times*, August 17.

———. 2011. "In Brooklyn, A Quaint Block and a Symbol of Blight." *New York Times*, October 25.

Carmody, Deirdre. 1984. "The City Sees No Solution for Homeless." *New York Times*, October 10.

Caro, Robert A. 1974. *The Power Broker: Robert Moses and the Fall of New York*. New York: Alfred A. Knopf.

Carse, Kathryn. 2010. "Bats and Balls at Walker Park." *Staten Island Advance*, August 5.

Castells, Manuel, and John H. Mollenkopf. 1992. *The Dual City: The Restructuring of New York*. New York: Russell Sage Foundation.

Chen, David W. 2009. "In the Future, the City's Streets Are to Behave." *New York Times*, May 20.

Chivers, C. J., and William K. Rashbaum. 2000. "Inquiry Focuses on Officers' Responses to Violence in Park after Parade." *New York Times*, June 14.

Cimino, Richard. 2011. "Neighborhoods, Niches, and Networks: The Religious Ecology of Gentrification." *City & Community* 10: 157–81.

City-Data.com.City-data.com/forum/new-york-city/319770-williamsbridge-section -bronx.html.

City of New York. 2008. *NYC Feedback: Citywide Customer Survey: Report of Survey Results*, December. http://www.nyc.gov/html/ops/downloads/pdf /feedback/nyc_feedback_web_final.pdf.

Cohen, Joyce. 2009. "The Hunt: Space for Friends, Outdoors and In." *New York Times*, Real Estate Section, December 24.

Cohen, Steven M., Jacob B. Ukeles, and Ron Miller. 2012. *Jewish Community Study of New York: 2011 Comprehensive Report*. New York: UJA-Federation of New York.

Cole, Teju. 2011. *Open City: A Novel*. New York: Random House.

Collins, Glenn. 1999. "Louis (Moondog) Hardin, 83, Musician, Dies." *New York Times*, September 12.

———. 2009. "Rent Reprieve for a Fixture on the Upper West Side." *New York Times*, January 5.

Confessore, Nicholas, and Michael Barbaro. 2011. "New York Allows Same-Sex Marriage, Becoming Largest State to Pass Law: Cuomo Signs Bill, Recharging Gay-Rights Movement." *New York Times*, June 25.

Conley, Dalton. 2000. *Honky*. Berkeley: University of California Press.

Connell-Mettauer, Susan. 2002. "Speed Freaks." In *Mr. Beller's Neighborhood: Before & After: Stories from New York*, edited by Thomas Beller, 101–3. New York: W. W. Norton.

Cooper, Michael. 1999. "Officers in Bronx Fire 41 Shots, and an Unarmed Man Is Killed." *New York Times*, February 5.

Coplon, Jeff. 2008. "Hiding in Plain Sight." *New York Magazine*, November 30.

Copquin, Claudia Gryvatz. 2007. *The Neighborhoods of Queens*. New Haven, CT: Yale University Press.

Cordero-Guzman, Hector R., Robert C. Smith, and Ramon Grosfoguel, eds. 2001. *Migration, Transnationalization, and Race in a Changing New York*. Philadelphia: Temple University Press.

Cordes, Kate. 2009. "Striking a Balance: Greenpoint, Brooklyn." Research paper. Department of Sociology, City University of New York Graduate Center.

Corman, Avery. 1980. *The Old Neighborhood*. New York: Linden Press.

Cotto, Andrew. 2011. "Pet Supplies? Yarn? Patter? 'I Got That.'" *New York Times*, Metropolitan Section, December 11.

Coughlin, Brenda C., and Sudhir Alladi Venkatesh. 2003. "The Urban Street Gang after 1970." *Annual Review of Sociology* 29: 41–64.

Cowan, Coleman. 2007. "Sweeping Him off His Street." *New York Times*, March 18. Online Edition.

Cristillo, Louis Abdellatif, and Lorraine C. Minnite. 2002. "The Changing Arab New York Community." In *A Community of Many Worlds: Arab Americans in New York City*, edited by Kathleen Benson and Philip M. Kayal, 124–39. New York: Museum of the City of New York (Syracuse University Press).

Crow, Kelly. 2001. "Citypeople; Preserving the Work of the Artful Tagger." *New York Times*, February 18.

Crowe, Timothy D. 2000. *Crime Prevention through Environmental Design Applications of Architectural Design and Space Management Concepts*. Woburn, MA: Butterworth-Heinemann.

Curcuru, Christina. 2010. "Island Inspiration: Art by the Ferry Gives Our Creative Community Street Cred." *Industry.com*. (July–August): 54.

Curran, Winifred. 2007. "'From the Frying Pan to the Oven': Gentrification and the Experience of Industrial Displacement in Williamsburg, Brooklyn." *Urban Studies* 44: 1427–40.

Currid, Elizabeth. 2007. *The Warhol Economy: How Fashion, Art, and Music Drive New York City*. Princeton, NJ: Princeton University Press.

Dao, James. 1992. "Asian Street Gangs Emerging as New Underworld." *New York Times*, April 1.

Davidson, Adam. 2012. "The Bronx Is Yearning: Why One Borough Seems Gentrification-Proof." *New York Times Magazine*, July 15.

Davidson, Justin. 2009. "Low Income? You're Kidding: Two Architects Offer Far More Than Lip Service to Affordable Housing." *New York Magazine*, March 2.

———. 2011. "The Low Line." *New York Magazine*, September 16.

Dávila, Arlene. 2004. *Barrio Dreams: Puerto Ricans, Latinos, and the Neoliberal City*. Berkeley: University of California Press.

Davis, Fred. 1979. *Yearning for Yesterday: A Sociology of Nostalgia*. New York: Free Press.

Davletmendova, Nargis. 2011. "New Ingredients in the Melting Pot: Kazakhs, Kyrgyz, and Uzbeks." MA thesis. Department of Sociology, City College of New York.

DeParle, Jason. 2009. "Struggling to Rise in Suburbs Where Failing Means Fitting In." *New York Times*, April 19.

Dewan, Shaila. 2009. "The Real Murder Mystery? It's the Low Crime Rate." *New York Times*, Week in Review, August 2.

"A Divorce for Governors Island." 2009. *New York Times*, Editorial, March 27.

Dolnick, Sam. 2010a. "Bronx Neighborhood Fights to Save Its Living Room." *New York Times*, May 12.

———. 2010b. "Report Shows Plight of Puerto Rican Youth." *New York Times*, October 29.

———. 2011a. "Ethnic Differences Emerge in Plastic Surgery." *New York Times*, February 18.

———. 2011b. "Staying Put in a City of Change." *New York Times*, Metropolitan Section, September 18.

———. 2012. "At SoHo Bar, a New Star's Fans Share His Heritage." *New York Times*, February 11.

Dominus, Susan. 2009. "A Times Square for Our Time, Pedestrian in More Ways Than One." *New York Times*, July 1.

———. 2010. "Teenage Summer, the Fasting Version." *New York Times*, August 21.

Dordick, Gwendolyn A. 1997. *Something Left to Lose: Personal Relations and Survival among New York's Homeless*. Philadelphia: Temple University Press.

Duberman, Martin B. 1993. *Stonewall*. New York: Dutton.

Duck, Waverly. 2009. " 'Senseless' Violence: Making Sense of Murder." *Ethnography* 10: 417–34.

Dunbar, Ernest, ed. 1970. *The Black Expatriates*. New York: Pocket Books.

Duneier, Mitchell. 1992. *Slim's Table: Race, Respectability, and Masculinity*. Chicago: University of Chicago Press.

———. 1999. *Sidewalk*. New York: Farrar, Straus, and Giroux.

Dunlap, David W. 2004. *From Abyssinian to Zion: A Guide to Manhattan's Houses of Worship*. New York: Columbia University Press.

Dwyer, Jim. 2009. "What to Make of a Big Deal Gone Sour." *New York Times*, November 4.

———. 2011. "Hauling Cans and Bottles through Brooklyn, for a Hard-Earned Extra Penny." *New York Times*, July 27.

Ebaugh, Helen Rose, and Mary Curry. 2000. "Fictive Kin as Social Capital in New Immigrant Communities." *Sociological Perspectives* 43: 189–209.

Edwards, Aaron. 2012. "As Vendors Hustle for Space, Tempers Flare." *New York Times*, September 3.

Ehrenhalt, Alan. 2012. *The Great Inversion and the Future of the American City*. New York: Alfred A. Knopf.

Ehrlich, Dimitri, and Gregor Ehrlich. 2006. "Graffiti in Its Own Words." *New York Magazine*, June 25.

Eligon, John. 2010. "The Police Say They Smashed a Major Bronx Drug Ring." *New York Times*, May 13.

Ellen, Ingrid Gould. 2000. *Sharing America's Neighborhoods: The Prospects for Stable Racial Integration*. Cambridge, MA: Harvard University Press.

Ellen, Ingrid Gould, Keren Mertens Horn, and Katherine O'Regan. 2011. "Urban 'Pioneers': Why Do Higher Income Households Choose Lower Income Neighborhoods?" Furman Center for Real Estate and Urban Policy. March 8.

Ellen, Ingrid Gould, Michael C. Lens, and Katherine O'Regan. 2011. "American Murder Mystery Revisited: Do Housing Voucher Households Cause Crime?" Furman Center for Real Estate and Urban Policy. October.

Ellen, Ingrid Gould, and Katherine M. O'Regan. 2010. "How Low-Income Neighborhoods Change: Entry, Exit, and Enhancement." U.S. Census Bureau, Center for Economic Studies. September.

Ellen, Ingrid Gould, Amy Ellen Schwartz, Ioan Voicu, and Michael H. Schill. 2007. "Does Federally Subsidized Rental Housing Depress Neighborhood Property Values?" *Journal of Policy Analysis and Management* 26: 257–80.

Emerson, Robert M. 2009. "Ethnography, Interaction, and Ordinary Trouble." *Ethnography* 10: 535–48.

Emoto, Masaru. 2004. *The Hidden Messages in Water.* Hillsboro, OR: Beyond Words.

Englander, Caryl. 2004. *Acts of Charity—Deeds of Kindness: New York's Met Council at Thirty.* New York: Metropolitan Council on Jewish Poverty.

Espinoza, Martin. 2008. "A Neighborhood in Transition, Sometimes Uneasily." *New York Times,* December 6.

Evelly, Jeanmarie. 2010. "White House 'Drug Czar' Visits the Bronx." *Norwood News,* June 17–30.

Fahim, Kareem. 2010. "Energy of Haitian Sound Pulses after a Difficult Year." *New York Times,* September 7.

Fahim, Kareem, and Karen Zraick. 2008. "Killing Haunts Ecuadoreans' Rise in New York." *New York Times,* December 15.

———. 2010. "A New Comptroller, Cheered by Asian-Americans Declaring a New Era." *New York Times,* January 2.

Fálcon, Angelo. 2005. "De'tras Pa'lante: Explorations on the Future History of Puerto Ricans in New York City." In *Boricuas in Gotham: Puerto Ricans in the Making of Modern New York City,* edited by Gabriel Haslip-Viera, Angelo Fálcon, and Félix Matos Rodríguez, 147–92. Princeton, NJ: Markus Wiener.

Fava, Sylvia F., and Judith DeSena. 1984. "The Chosen Apple: Young Suburban Migrants." In *The Apple Sliced: Sociological Studies of New York City,* edited by Vernon Boggs, Gerald Handel, and Sylvia F. Fava, 305–22. New York: Praeger.

Feliciano, Cynthia, Rennie Lee, and Belinda Robnett. 2011. "Racial Boundaries among Latinos: Evidence from Internet Daters' Racial Preferences." *Social Problems* 58: 189–212.

Fernández, Georgina. 2010. "A Brighter Future for the Lower Grand Concourse?" *Bronx Youth Heard* 3: 4.

Fernández, Manny. 2008. "Brawl Involving Firefighters Invites Unwanted Reputation for East Side Bar." *New York Times,* December 15.

———. 2009a. "New York Housing Plan Is Delayed." *New York Times,* January 6.

———. 2009b. "City's Beach Clubs Catch Government Scrutiny." *New York Times,* September 1.

———. 2009c. "2 Brooklyn Complexes with a Ghost-Town Feel." *New York Times,* December 8.

———. 2010. "Public Housing Project to Come Tumbling Down." *New York Times,* February 6.

———. 2011. "Growing Up and Old in the Same Neighborhood." *New York Times*, January 12.

Fessenden, Ford, and Sam Roberts. 2011. "Then as Now: New York's Shifting Ethnic Mosaic." *New York Times*, Week in Review Section, January 23.

Feuer, Alan. 2002. "Secrets of the Dean of the Pie Men: Hints from 59 Years in Pizza: Crust Is Thin, and No Avocados." *New York Times*, Metropolitan Section, April 2.

———. 2011a. "The Wilderness below Your Feet." *New York Times*, Metropolitan Section, January 2.

———. 2011b. "Beer Gardens Everywhere." *New York Times*, May 27.

———. 2011c. "Jamaica Bay: Wilderness on the Edge." *New York Times*, Metropolitan Section, July 31.

———. 2012. "The Hidden Homeless." *New York Times*, Metropolitan Section, February 5.

Filkins, Dexter. 2001. "Connecting Dots, Linking to Roots; In Caribbean Enclaves, Dominoes Are a Summer Fixture." *New York Times*, July 2.

Firey, Walter. 1945. "Sentiment and Symbolism as Ecological Variables." *American Sociological Review* 10: 140–48.

Fischler, Marcelle S. 2009. "The Island's Changing Face." *New York Times*, Long Island Section, September 27.

Fisher, Ian. 1996. "The Human Face of New York's World Wide Web." *New York Times*, August 8.

Flegenheimer, Matt. 2011. "Window Fixtures of Rougher Days Come Down." *New York Times*, December 13.

Florida, Richard L. 2002. *The Rise of the Creative Class and How It's Transforming Work, Leisure, Community, and Everyday Life.* New York: Basic Books.

———. 2003. "Cities and the Creative Class." *City & Community* 2: 3–19.

Foderaro, Lisa W. 1987. "Harlem's Hedge against Gentrification." *New York Times*, Real Estate Section, August 16.

———. 2011a. "O.K., Keep Looking Down: Sidewalks Will Stay Ad-Free." *New York Times*, July 15.

———. 2011b. "From High Line to Low, and Behold: Two Men Have Ideas for Park in Old Terminal under Delancey St." *New York Times*, November 22.

Foner, Nancy. 2000. *From Ellis Island to JFK: New York's Two Great Waves of Immigration.* New Haven, CT: Yale University Press.

———, ed. 2001. *New Immigrants in New York.* Rev. ed. New York: Columbia University Press.

———. 2005a. *In a New Land: A Comparative View of Immigration.* New York: New York University Press.

———, ed. 2005b. *Wounded City: The Social Impact of 9/11.* New York: Russell Sage Foundation.

———. 2006. "Immigrants at Home." *New York Times*, Op Ed Page, November 26.

Foner, Nancy, and Richard D. Alba. 2008. "Immigrant Religion in the U.S. and Western Europe: Bridge or Barrier to Inclusion?" *International Migration Review* 42: 360–92.

Fontana, Marian. 2005. *A Widow's Walk: A Memoir of 9/11.* New York: Simon and Schuster.

Fordyce E. J., T. P. Singh, F. M. Vazquez, J. McFarland, P. Thomas, S. Forlenza, and M. A. Chiasson. 1999. "Evolution of an Urban Epidemic: The First 100,000 AIDS Cases in New York City." *Population Research and Policy Review* 18: 523–44.

Foucault, Michel. 1975. *Discipline and Punish: The Birth of the Prison*. New York: Vintage.

Frase, Peter. 2005. "The Next Neighborhood: Hunter's Point/Long Island City." Research paper. Department of Sociology, City University of New York Graduate Center.

Frazier, E. Franklin. 1957. *Black Bourgeoisie*. New York: Free Press.

Freedman, Samuel G. 1985. "The New New Yorkers." *New York Times*, Sunday Magazine, November 3.

———. 1994. *Upon This Rock: The Miracles of a Black Church*. New York: Harper Perennial.

———. 1998. "From the Ground Up in East New York." *New York Times*, April 4.

Freeman, Joshua B. 2000. *Working-Class New York: Life and Labor since World War II*. New York: New Press.

Freeman, Lance. 2006. *There Goes the 'Hood: Views of Gentrification from the Ground Up*. Philadelphia: Temple University Press.

Freidenberg, Judith, ed. 1995. *The Anthropology of Low-Income Urban Enclaves: The Case of East Harlem*. New York: New York Academy of Sciences.

Freund, Helen. 2011. "Slain over a Glance." *New York Post*, July 26.

Frey, James H., and D. Stanley Eitzen. 1991. "Sport and Society." *Annual Review of Sociology* 17: 503–22.

Fruhauf, Hannah. 2012. "Bushwick: A Forgotten Neighborhood Revitalized." Research paper. Department of Sociology, City University of New York Graduate Center.

Gabriel, Trip, and Jennifer Medina. 2010. "Charter Schools' New Cheerleaders: Financiers." *New York Times*, May 10.

Gamm, Gerald. 1999. *Urban Exodus: Why the Jews Left Boston and the Catholics Stayed*. Cambridge, MA: Harvard University Press.

Gan, Jessi. 2007. "'Still at the Back of the Bus': Sylvia Rivera's Struggle." *Centro Journal* 19: 124–39.

Gans, Herbert J. 1982. *The Urban Villagers: Group and Class in the Life of Italian Americans*. New York: Free Press.

———. 2002. "The Sociology of Space: A Use-Centered View." *City & Community* 1: 329–39.

Gentry, Kendra. 2009. "Then and Now: An Exploration of Manhattan Valley." Research paper. Department of Sociology, City University of New York Graduate Center.

Genzlinger, Neil. 2011. "Invasion of the Pop-Ups: Time for a Smackdown." *New York Times*, Metropolitan Section, August 14.

Gerstle, Gary, and John H. Mollenkopf, eds. 2001. *E Pluribus Unum?: Contemporary and Historical Perspectives on Immigrant Political Incorporation*. New York: Russell Sage Foundation.

Gill, John Freeman. 2005. ""Wonder Years," by Way of Bed-Stuy." *New York Times*, December 4. Online Edition.

———. 2010a. "Living In/Prince's Bay, Staten Island: Horses, Beaches, Boats, and New Houses." *New York Times*, Real Estate Section, September 26.

———. 2010b. "Living In/Hunts Point–Longwood: A Place That Redefines Resilience." *New York Times*, Real Estate Section, November 14.

Gladwell, Malcolm. 2000. *The Tipping Point: How Little Things Can Make a Big Difference*. Boston: Little-Brown.

Glaser, Barney G., and Anselm L. Strauss. 1967. *The Discovery of Grounded Theory: Strategies for Qualitative Research*. Chicago: Aldine.

Glassman, Carl. 2008. "Martinis to Displace Tribeca Pushcarts?" *Tribeca Tribune*, October.

Glazer, Nathan, and Daniel Patrick Moynihan. 1970 (1963). *Beyond the Melting Pot: The Negroes, Puerto Ricans, Jews, Italians, and Irish of New York City*. Cambridge: MIT Press.

Goering, John M., Maynard Robison, and Knight Hoover. 1977. *The Best Eight Blocks in Harlem: The Last Decade of Urban Reform*. Washington, DC: University Press of America.

Gold, Steven J. 2002. *The Israeli Diaspora*. Seattle: University of Washington Press.

———. 2009. "Immigration Benefits America." *Society* 46: 408–11.

———. 2010. *The Store in the Hood: A Century of Ethnic Business and Conflict*. Lanham, MD: Rowman and Littlefield.

Goldberger, Paul. 1979. "Midtown Construction: Problem of Prosperity." *New York Times*, July 30.

———. 1984. "Utopia in the Outer Boroughs." *New York Times*, Sunday Magazine, November 4.

Goldblum, Robert. 2011. "Chewing on Jewish Decline." *Jewish Week*, July 5.

Goldstein, Joseph. 2012. "43 in Two Warring Groups Are Indicted in Brooklyn." *New York Times*, January 20.

Gonnerman, Jennifer. 2009. "Last Home Standing." *New York Magazine*, September 6.

González, David. 1997. "After 12 Steps, One Prayer: To Die Sober." *New York Times*, September 3.

———. 2009a. "A Family Divided by 2 Words, Legal and Illegal." *New York Times*, April 26.

———. 2009b. "Play Street Becomes a Sanctuary." *New York Times*, August 2.

———. 2009c. "Faces in the Rubble." *New York Times*, Metropolitan Section, August 23.

———. 2010. "Still Taking to the Streets to Honor Their Saints." *New York Times*, June 6.

González, Evelyn. 2004. *The Bronx*. New York: Columbia University Press.

Gooch, Brad. 1992. "The New Bohemia: Over the Bridge to Williamsburg." *New York Magazine*, June 22.

Goodman, David. 2009. "A Harlem Tradition: Risking Scraped Skin for Cycling Glory." *New York Times*, June 22.

Goodman, Peter. 2004. "Immigrants Bring Dreams and Combs to N.Y. Shop." *Newsday*, July 24.

Goodman, Richard. 2010. *A New York Memoir*. New Brunswick, NJ: Transaction Books.

Goodstein, Laurie. 2010. "For Catholics, Interest in Exorcism Is Revived." *New York Times*, November 13.

Goodyear, Sarah. 2010. "This Commissioner Takes No Prisoners: Taming the Mean Streets: A Talk with NYC Transportation Chief Janette Sadik-Khan." *Grist: A Beacon in the Smog*, December 21. Online publication.

Gootman, Elissa. 2010. "Insights from a Week as a 311 Operator in New York." *New York Times*, Metropolitan Section, May 16.

Gordinier, Jeff. 2011. "Restaurateur's 'Japantown' Helps Victims." *New York Times*, March 30.

Gotham, Kevin Fox, and Miriam Greenberg. 2008. "From 9/11 to 8/29: Post-Disaster Recovery and Rebuilding New York and in New Orleans." *Social Forces* 87: 1039–62.

Gottdiener, Mark. 1995. *Postmodern Semiotics: Material Culture and the Forms of Postmodern Life*. New York: John Wiley and Sons.

Gottlieb, Jeff. "Change and Revelation: The Movement of Jews in Queens." Unpublished. n.d. Internet, 3 pps.

Grasmuck, Sherri, and Ramon Grosfoguel. 1997. "Geopolitics, Economic Niches, and Gendered Social Capital among Recent Caribbean Immigrants to New York City." *Sociological Perspectives* 40: 339–63.

Gratz, Roberta Grandes. 1978. "How Westway Will Destroy New York: An Interview with Jane Jacobs." *New York Magazine*, February 6.

Gray, Christopher. 2003. "Recalling the Days of Knights and Elks." *New York Times*, August 24.

———. 2009. "In Audubon Park, a Few Surviving Oriels." *New York Times*, Real Estate Section, April 19.

Gray, Geoffrey. 2012. "King Carl of Canarsie." *New York Magazine*, January 8.

Greenberg, Miriam. 2008. *Branding New York: How a City in Crisis Was Sold to the World*. New York: Routledge.

Gregor, Alison. 2010. "Protecting an Array of Gems in the Bronx." *New York Times*, Real Estate Section, March 26.

———. 2012. "All It Needs Is a Name." *New York Times*, Real Estate Section, February 26.

Gregory, Steven. 1998. *Black Corona: Race and the Politics of Place in an Urban Community*. Princeton, NJ: Princeton University Press.

Gross, Max. 2012. "Gowanus Is Upon Us!" *New York Post*, August 11.

Grynbaum, Michael M. 2009a. "Tourists and New Yorkers Take a Rubber Seat in Times Square." *New York Times*, June 11.

———. 2009b. "A Calming Presence amid the Groans and Screeches." *New York Times*, July 6.

———. 2010. "Plan Gives Pedestrians a Plaza at Union Square." *New York Times*, April 24.

Gubernat, Tamara. 2008. "Ridgewood, New York, and Its Borders." Research paper. Department of Sociology, City University of New York Graduate Center.

Haberman, Clyde. 1997. "Two Parades, Same Route? It Can Be Done." *New York Times*, November 28.

———. 2009. "Welcome, Archbishop Dolan! Now Show Us What Ya Got." *New York Times*, April 17.

———. 2011. "Bloomberg Seeks to Show That He Cares." *New York Times*, January 20.

Hakim, Danny. 2011. "Exemptions Were Key to Vote on Gay Marriage." *New York Times*, June 26.

Haley, Alex. 1976. *Roots: The Saga of an American Family*. New York: Doubleday.

Hall, Trish. 1999. "A South Bronx Very Different from the Cliché: Renovated Homes, New Apartments, and Antique Stores." *New York Times*, Real Estate Section, February 14.

Halle, David, ed. 2003. *New York and Los Angeles: Politics, Society, and Culture: A Comparative View*. Chicago: University of Chicago Press.

———. 2006. "Who Wears Jane Jacob's Mantle in Today's New York City?" *City & Community* 5: 237–41.

Hallman, Howard H. 1984. *Neighborhoods: Their Place in Urban Life*. Beverly Hills, CA: Sage Publications.

"Harlem Is Booming." 2010. Advertising insert in *New York Times*, Z: 1–8, October 7.

Harris, Elizabeth A. 2009. "Living In/Hudson Heights: An Aerie Straight Out of the Deco Era." *New York Times*, Real Estate Section, October 18.

Harris, Elizabeth A., and Adriane Quinlan. 2011. "Where the Fight Began, Cries of Joy and Talk of Weddings." *New York Times*, June 25.

Harvey, David. 1976. "Labor, Capital, and Class Struggle around the Built Environment in Advanced Capitalist Societies." *Politics and Society* 6: 265–95.

———. 1985. *Consciousness and the Urban Experience*. Baltimore, MD: Johns Hopkins University Press.

Haslip-Viera, Gabriel, and Sherrie L. Baver, eds. 1996. *Latinos in New York: Communities in Transition*. Notre Dame, IN: University of Notre Dame Press.

Haslip Viera, Gabriel, Angelo Fálcon, and Félix Matos Rodríguez, eds. 2005. *Boricuas in Gotham: Puerto Ricans in the Making of Modern New York City*. Princeton, NJ: Markus Wiener.

Hassell, Malve Von. 1996. *Homesteading in New York City, 1978–1993: The Divided Heart of Loisaida*. Westport, CT: Bergin and Garvey.

Haughney, Christine. 2008. "Old Europe and New Brooklyn in Williamsburg." *New York Times*, November 22.

———. 2009. "Harlem's Real Estate Boom Becomes a Bust." *New York Times*, July 8.

———. 2010. "Tipping the Doorman? Keep the Smoking Jacket." *New York Times*, December 21.

Heilman, Samuel C. 1986. *A Walker in Jerusalem*. New York: Summit Books.

———. 2006. *Sliding to the Right: The Contest for the Future of American Jewish Orthodoxy*. Berkeley: University of California Press.

Helmreich, Alan, and Paul Marcus, eds. 1998. *Blacks and Jews on the Couch: Psychoanalytic Reflections on Black-Jewish Conflict*. Westport, CT: Praeger.

Helmreich, Helaine. 2008. *Rachel's Diary*. Brooklyn, NY: Franklin Printing.

Helmreich, William B. 1973. *The Black Crusaders: A Case Study of a Black Militant Organization*. New York: Harper and Row.

———. 1977. *Afro-Americans and Africa: Black Nationalism at the Crossroads*. Westport, CT: Greenwood Press.

Helmreich, William B. 1982. *The Things They Say behind Your Back: Stereotypes and the Myths behind Them*. New York: Doubleday.

———. 1992. *Against All Odds: Holocaust Survivors and the Successful Lives They Made in America*. New York: Simon and Schuster.

———. 2011. *What Was I Thinking?: The Dumb Things We Do and How to Avoid Them*. Lanham, MD: Rowman and Littlefield.

Herbert, Bob. 1993. "In America: Violence in the State of Denial." *New York Times*, Op Ed, October 27.

———. 2010a. "Where the Bar Ought to Be." *New York Times*, February 22.

———. 2010b. "This Raging Fire." *New York Times*, Op Ed, November 16.

Herbst, Laura. 1988. "The Hidden Lives of the 'Downtown Chinese.' " *New York Times*, Long Island Section, May 29.

Hernández, Javier C. 2009a. "In the Future, the City's Streets Are to Behave." *New York Times*, May 20.

———. 2009b. "City Students Gain in Math; Racial Gap Shrinks." *New York Times*, June 2.

———. 2010. "Hearing on Limits for Vendors Gets Creative Response." *New York Times*, April 24.

———. 2011. "Just Look at This Place. What's Not to Love?" *New York Times*, March 31.

Hernández, Ramona, and Silvio Torres-Saillant. 1996. "Dominicans in New York: Men, Women, and Prospects." In *Latinos in New York: Communities in Transition*, edited by Gabriel Haslip-Viera and Sherrie L. Baver, 30–56. Notre Dame, IN: University of Notre Dame Press.

Herring, Cedric, Verna Keth, and Hayward Horton. 2004. *Skin Deep: How Race and Complexion Matter in the "Color-Blind" Era*. Chicago: University of Illinois Press.

Herszenhorn, David M. 1999. "Protesters Fight Auctioning of Community Gardens." *New York Times*, May 6.

Hinds, Michael deCourcy. 1985. "New Housing Lags in Outer Boroughs." *New York Times*, Real Estate Section, April 14.

Hitlin, Steven, J. Scott Brown, and Glen H. Elder Jr. 2007. "Measuring Latinos: Racial vs. Ethnic Classification and Self-Understandings." *Social Forces* 86: 587–611.

Hochschild, Jennifer, and Vesla Weaver. 2007. "The Skin Color Paradox and the American Racial Order." *Social Forces* 86: 643–70.

Hoffman, Lily M. 2003. "Revalorizing the Inner City: Tourism and Regulation in Harlem." In *Cities and Visitors: Regulating People, Markets, and City Space*, edited by Lily M. Hoffman, Susan S. Fainstein, and Denis R. Judd, 91–112. Malden, MA: Blackwell.

Hollander, Sophia, and Joseph De Avila. 2013. " 'Holes' Are Seen in Kendra's Law." *Wall Street Journal*, January 9.

Holloway, Lynette. 1997. "Shorties and Scholars Agree, the Word Is Rap." *New York Times*, January 5.

Hosler, Akiko S. 1998. *Japanese Immigrant Entrepreneurs in New York City: A New Wave of Ethnic Business*. New York: Garland.

House, Laura. 2008. "Amid Downturn, an Uptick in Doing Good." *New York Magazine*, December 14.

Howe, Ben Ryder. 2010. *My Korean Deli: Risking It All for a Convenience Store.* New York: Henry Holt.

Howe, Marvine. 1985. "Ukrainian Resurgence in East Village." *New York Times,* June 9.

Hoyt, Homer. 1939. *The Structure and Growth of Residential Neighborhoods in American Cities.* Washington, DC: Federal Housing Administration.

Hu, Winnie. 2012. "For an Old Italian Game, a Crescendo of Sorts." *New York Times,* April 24.

Hughes, C. J. 2010. "Living In/Sea Gate, Brooklyn: The Beach Is Never Far Away." *New York Times,* Real Estate Section, September 5.

———. 2011. "26.2 Miles of Change." *New York Times,* November 5.

Hydra, Derek. 2006. "Racial Uplift?: Intra-Racial Class Conflict and the Economic Revitalization of Harlem and Bronzeville." *City & Community* 5: 71–92.

Hymowitz, Kay S. 2011. "How Brooklyn Got Its Groove Back." *City Journal* (Autumn):76–88.

Iverac, Mirela. 2010. "A Tokyo Start, but Most at Home on 125th Street." *New York Times,* April 24.

Jackson, Jennifer V., and Mary E. Cothran. 2003. "Black Versus Black: The Relationships among African, African American, and African American Caribbean Persons." *Journal of Black Studies* 33: 576–604.

Jackson, John L., Jr. 2001. *Harlem World: Doing Race and Class in Contemporary Black America.* Chicago: University of Chicago Press

Jackson, Kenneth T. 1985. *Crabgrass Frontier: The Suburbanization of the United States.* New York: Oxford University Press.

———, ed. 1995. *The Encyclopedia of New York City.* New Haven, CT: Yale University Press.

———, ed. 2010. *The Encyclopedia of New York City.* Rev. ed. New Haven, CT: Yale University Press.

Jackson, Kenneth T., and John B. Manbeck, eds. 2004. *The Neighborhoods of Brooklyn.* New Haven, CT: Yale University Press.

Jackson, Nancy Beth. 2002. "Fort Greene: Diversity, Culture, and Brownstones, Too." *New York Times,* Real Estate Section, September 1.

Jacobs, Jane. 1961. *The Death and Life of Great American Cities.* New York: Vintage Books.

Jacobson, Mark. 2012. "The Land That Time and Money Forgot." *New York Magazine.* September 9.

Jang, Sou Hyun. 2010. "East Village in New York City." Research paper. Department of Sociology, City University of New York Graduate Center.

Jen, Gish. 1996. *Mona in the Promised Land.* New York: Alfred A. Knopf.

Jerolmack, Colin. 2008. "How Pigeons Became Rats: The Cultural-Spatial Logic of Problem Animals." *Social Problems* 55: 72–94.

———. 2009. "Primary Groups and Cosmopolitan Ties: The Rooftop Pigeon Flyers of New York City." *Ethnography* 10: 435–57.

Johnson, Kirk. 1985. "Suddenly, the Barrio Is Drawing Buyers." *New York Times,* June 2.

Jonnes, Jill. 1986. *We're Still Here: The Rise, Fall, and Resurrection of the South Bronx*. Boston: Atlantic Monthly Press.

Kadushin, Charles, Matthew Lindholm, Dan Ryan, Archie Brodsky, and Leonard Saxe. 2005. "Why It Is So Difficult to Form Effective Community Coalitions?" *City & Community* 4: 255–75.

Kaminer, Ariel. 2010. "Has the Big Apple Become the Big Eyeball?" *New York Times*, Metropolitan Section, May 9.

Kang, Miliann. 2003. "The Managed Hand: The Commercialization of Bodies and Emotions in Korean Immigrant-Owned Nail Salons." *Gender and Society* 17: 820–39.

Kappstatter, Bob. 1996. "South Bronx Area on the Way Back." *New York Daily News*, September 29.

Karmen, Andrew. 2000. *New York Murder Mystery: The True Story behind the New York Crime Crash of the 1990s*. New York: New York University Press.

Kasinitz, Philip. 1992. *Caribbean New York: Black Immigrants and the Politics of Race*. Ithaca, NY: Cornell University Press.

———. 1998. "The Gentrification of 'Boerum Hill': Neighborhood Change and Conflicts over Definitions." *Qualitative Sociology* 11: 163–82.

———. 2000. "Red Hook: The Paradoxes of Poverty and Place in Brooklyn." *Research in Urban Sociology* 5: 253–74.

Kasinitz, Philip, Mohamad Bazzi, and Randal Doane. 1998. "Jackson Heights, New York." *Cityscape: A Journal of Policy Development and Research* 4: 161–77.

Kasinitz, Philip, and Bruce Haynes. 1996. "The Fire at Freddy's." *Common Quest* (Fall): 25–34.

Kasinitz, Philip, and David Hillyard. 1995. "The Old-Timer's Tale: The Politics of Nostalgia on the Waterfront." *Journal of Contemporary Ethnography* 24: 139–64.

Kasinitz, Philip, John H. Mollenkopf, and Mary C. Waters, eds. 2004. *Becoming New Yorkers: Ethnographies of the New Second Generation*. New York: Russell Sage Foundation.

Kasinitz, Philip, John H. Mollenkopf, Mary C. Waters, and Jennifer Holdaway. 2008. *Inheriting the City: The Children of Immigrants Come of Age*. New York: Russell Sage Foundation.

Katyal, Neal Kumar. 2002. "Architecture as Crime Control." *Yale Law Journal* 111: 1039–1139.

Katz, Jack. 1988. *Seductions of Crime: Moral and Sensual Attractions in Doing Evil*. New York: Basic Books.

———. 2010. "Time for New Urban Ethnographies." *Ethnography* 11: 25–44.

Kennedy, Randy. 2004. *Subwayland: Adventures in the World beneath New York*. New York: St. Martin's.

Kennedy, Shawn G. 1985. "Fort Greene Integrates as It Gentrifies." *New York Times*, Real Estate Section, June 23.

Keogan, Kevin. 2010. *Immigrants and the Cultural Politics of Place: A Comparative Study of New York and Los Angeles*. El Paso, TX: LFB Scholarly Publishing.

Kershaw, Sarah. 2002. "The Distant Drums of War: In Queens, Indians and Pakistanis Live in Harmony." *New York Times*, June 1.

Khandelwal, Madhulika S. 2002. *Becoming American, Being Indian: An Immigrant Community in New York City*. Ithaca, NY: Cornell University Press.

Kidder, Tracy. 2009. *Strength in What Remains*. New York: Random House.

Kilgannon, Corey. 2009a. "Putting Together a Hamburger, a Neighborhood, and Hip-Hop." *New York Times*, February 20.

———. 2009b. "Local Stop/Little Guyana: India in Queens, with a Caribbean Accent." *New York Times*, Metropolitan Section, May 24.

———. 2009c. "Where Blue-Collar Boys Hoist a Sail, and a Beer." *New York Times*, Metropolitan Section, June 14.

———. 2009d. "Why Was He Shot while Walking the Dog? It Was the Red Shirt." *New York Times*, December 8.

———. 2009e. "Night and Day." *New York Times*, Metro Section, December 13.

———. 2010a. "In Old Irish Sections, Seeing Shifts through a Pint Glass." *New York Times*, March 17.

———. 2010b. "High Line's Next Phase: Less Glitz, More Intimacy." *New York Times*, December 20.

———. 2011. "Feud between Projects Cited in Basketball Star's Killing." *New York Times*, September 15.

Kim, Esther Chihye. 2009. "'Mama's Family': Fictive Kinship and Undocumented Immigrant Restaurant Workers." *Ethnography* 10: 497–513.

Kimmelman, Michael. 2005. "A Billowy Gift to the City." *New York Times*, February 13. Online Edition.

———. 2011. "In a Bronx Complex, Doing Good Mixes with Looking Good." *New York Times*, September 26.

———. 2012. "Towers of Dreams: One Ended in Nightmare." *New York Times*, Arts Section, January 26.

Kinetz, Erika. 2002. "Love's Journey." *New York Times*, February 10.

Kiviat, Barbara. 2008. "Gentrification: Not Ousting the Poor." *Time*, June 29.

Kleinfield, N. R. 2009. "Big Pulpit." *New York Times*, Metropolitan Section, May 24.

———. 2010. "Bingo in the Blood." *New York Times*, Metropolitan Section, November 28.

Koolhaas, Rem. 1994. *Delirious New York: A Retroactive Manifesto for Manhattan*. New York: Monacelli Press.

Kornblum, William. 1983. "Racial and Cultural Groups on the Beach." *Ethnic Groups* 5: 109–24.

———. 2002. *At Sea in the City: New York from the Water's Edge*. Chapel Hill, NC: Algonquin Books.

Kornblum, William, and Kristen Van Hooreweghe. 2010. *Jamaica Bay Ethnographic Overview and Assessment*. Graduate Center, City University of New York. Report. Northeast Region Ethnography Program, National Park Service, Boston, MA, December.

Kotkin, Joel. 2010. *The Next Hundred Million: America in 2050*. New York: Penguin.

Kramer, Rita. 1996. "New York's Missing Megastores." *City Journal* (Autumn): 68–73.

Kramer, Sarah, and Maggie Nesciur. 2009. "One in 8 Million: The Walker." *New York Times*, Metropolitan Section, November 8.

Krysan, Maria, and Reynolds Farley. 2002. "The Residential Preferences of Blacks: Do They Explain Persistent Segregation?" *Social Forces* 80: 937–80.

Kwong, Peter. 1996. *The New Chinatown.* Rev. ed. New York: Hill and Wang.

Kwong, Peter, and Dusanka Miscevic. 2005. *Chinese America: The Untold Story of America's Oldest New Community.* New York: New Press.

LaBennett, Oneka. 2011. *She's Mad Real: Popular Culture and West Indian Girls in Brooklyn.* New York: New York University Press.

LeDuff, Charlie. 1997. "Custodian of a Doomed Ship." *New York Times*, Section 13, April 27.

Lee, Denny. 2002. "A Once Evocative Name Falls Victim to the Bursting of the High-Tech Bubble." *New York Times*, March 24.

Lee, Jennifer. 2002. *Civility in the City: Blacks, Jews, and Koreans in Urban America.* Cambridge, MA: Harvard University Press.

Lee, Trymaine. 2010. "In Changing Harlem, Rift between Old and New Business Owners." *New York Times*, December 20.

Lees, Loretta. 2003. "Super-gentrification: The Case of Brooklyn Heights, New York City." *Urban Studies* 40: 2487–2509.

Lefevbre, Henri. 1991. *The Production of Space.* Translated by Donald Nicholson-Smith. Oxford: Basil Blackwell.

Lehmekh, Halyna. 2010. *Ukrainian Immigrants in New York: Collision of Two Worlds.* El Paso, TX: LFB Scholarly Publishing.

Lehrer, Jonah. 2010. "A Physicist Solves the City." *New York Times*, Sunday Magazine, December 19.

Lehrer, Warren, and Judith Sloan. 2003. *Crossing the BLVD: Strangers, Neighbors, Aliens in a New America.* New York: W. W. Norton.

Leland, John. 2000. "East Ninth Street: Cool Stuff for the Intrepid Sleuth." *New York Times*, Home and Garden Section, November 30.

———. 2011a. "The God Squad." *New York Times*, Metropolitan Section, April 24.

———. 2011b. "Rocked Hard: The Battle of Williamsburg." *New York Times*, Metropolitan Section, May 29.

———. 2011c. "I Have No Neighbors Here." *New York Times*, Metropolitan Section, November 27.

Lessinger, Johanna. 2001. "Class, Race, and Success: Two Generations of Indian Americans Confront the American Dream." In *Migration, Transnationalization, and Race in a Changing New York*, edited by Hector R. Cordero-Guzman, Robert C. Smith, and Ramon Grosfoguel, 167–90. Philadelphia: Temple University Press.

Lethem, Jonathan. 2003. *The Fortress of Solitude.* New York: Doubleday.

Levere, Jane L. 2009. "Retailers Take a Chance on a Mall in the Bronx." *New York Times*, September 2.

Levine, Hillel, and Lawrence Harmon. *The Death of an American Jewish Community: A Tragedy of Good Intentions.* New York: Free Press.

Levitt, Ellen. 2009. *The Lost Synagogues of Brooklyn*. Bergenfield, NJ: Avotaynu Books.

———. 2011. *The Lost Synagogues of the Bronx and Queens*. Bergenfield, NJ: Avotaynu Books.

Lewis-McCoy, R. L'Heureux. 2012. "School's Out: What Happens When Public Schools Shut Down?" Ebony.com. May 2.

Ley, David. 1986. "Alternative Explanations of Inner-city Gentrification: A Canadian Assessment." *Annals of the American Association of Geographers* 76: 521–35.

Liang, Zai, and Naomi Ito. 1999. "Intermarriage of Asian Americans in the New York City Region: Contemporary Patterns and Future Prospects." *International Migration Review* 33: 876–900.

Lichtenstein, Matty. 2010. "Fractured Identities: Community, Identity, and the Transformation of a Congregation." Research paper. Department of Sociology, City College of New York.

Lipinsky, Jed. 2012. "Leaving His Footprints on the City." *New York Times*, Metropolitan Section, March 25.

Lipman, Steve. 2012. "Prospect Park Frum." *Jewish Week*, January 6.

Lockwood, Charles. 2003. *Bricks and Brownstone: The New York City Row House, 1783–1929*. New York: Rizzoli.

Lopate, Phillip. 2004. *Waterfront: A Walk around Manhattan*. New York: Anchor Books.

Low, Setha M. 2000. *On the Plaza: The Politics of Public Space and Culture*. Austin: University of Texas Press.

Low, Setha, and Neil Smith, eds. 2006. *The Politics of Public Space*. New York: Routledge.

Ludwig, Bernadette. 2009. "Little Liberia: aka Park Hill in Staten Island, N.Y." Research paper. Department of Sociology, City University of New York Graduate Center. Expanded version presented at the Annual Meeting of the American Sociological Association, Atlanta, Georgia, 2010.

Lueck, Thomas J. 1996. "A Rise in Visitors, a Shortage of Rooms." *New York Times*, October 21.

Luo, Michael. 2005. "Billy Graham Returns, to Find Evangelical Force in New York." *New York Times*, June 21.

———. 2012. "Lin's Appeal: Faith, Pride, and Points." *New York Times*, Sports Sunday, February 12.

Lyall, Sarah. 1989. "Where Isolation Is Both Curse and Charm." *New York Times*, July 24.

Madden, David J. 2010. "Revisiting the End of Public Space." *City & Community* 9: 187–207.

Maeckelbergh, Marianne. 2012. "Mobilizing to Stay Put: Housing Struggles in New York. *International Journal of Urban and Regional Research* 36: 655–73.

Magnus, Cynthia. 2009. "A Sociology Field Study of the Jews of Boro Park in 2010." Research paper. Department of Sociology, City University of New York Graduate Center.

Mahler, Jonathan. 2005. *Ladies and Gentlemen, the Bronx Is Burning: 1977, Baseball, Politics, and the Battle for the Soul of a City*. New York: Picador.

Mahon, Emily. 2013. "Paradoxes of Piety in Young Muslim American Women: Public Perceptions and Individual Realities." PhD dissertation. Department of Sociology, City University of New York Graduate Center.

Makris, Molly. 2008. "El Barrio: Enclave on the Eve of Transformation." Research paper. Department of Sociology, City University of New York Graduate Center.

Malanga, Steven. 2006. "Silicon Alley 2.0." *City Journal* (Autumn): 35–41.

———. 2008. "The Death and Life of Bushwick." *City Journal* (Spring): 64–73.

Maly, Michael T. 2005. *Beyond Segregation: Multiracial and Multiethnic Neighborhoods in the United States.* Philadelphia: Temple University Press.

Marable, Manning. 2011. *Malcolm X: A Life of Reinvention.* New York: Viking.

Margolis, Maxine L. 1994. *Little Brazil: An Ethnography of Brazilian Immigrants in New York City.* Princeton, NJ: Princeton University Press.

Martin, Douglas. 1994a. "Districts to Improve Business Proliferate." *New York Times,* March 25.

———. 1994b. "A Thoroughfare for Wildlife." *New York Times,* May 16.

Martínez, Miranda J. 2010. *Power at the Roots: Gentrification, Community Gardens, and the Puerto Ricans of the Lower East Side.* Lanham, MD: Lexington Books.

Marwell, Nicole P. 2004. "Ethnic and Post-Ethnic Politics in New York City: The Dominican Second Generation." In *Becoming New Yorkers: Ethnographies of the New Second Generation,* edited by Philip Kasinitz, John H. Mollenkopf, and Mary C. Waters, 227–56. New York: Russell Sage Foundation.

———. 2007. *Bargaining for Brooklyn: Community Organizations in the Entrepreneurial City.* Chicago: University of Chicago Press.

Massey, Douglas S., Rafael Alarcón, Jorge Durand, and Humberto González. 1987. *Return to Aztlan: The Social Process of International Migration from Western Mexico.* Berkeley: University of California Press.

Massey, Douglas S., and Nancy Denton. 1993. *American Apartheid: Segregation and the Making of the Under-Class.* Cambridge, MA: Harvard University Press.

Massey, Douglas S., and Alice M. Rivlin. 2002. "Comments on 'Does Gentrification Harm the Poor?'" *Brookings-Wharton Papers on Urban Affairs.* 174–79.

McFadden, Robert D. 1986. "Black Man Dies after Beating by Whites in Queens." *New York Times,* December 21.

McGeehan, Patrick. 2011. "Pleasant Surprise for East River Ferries: Crowds." *New York Times,* October 17.

McGeehan, Patrick, and Matthew R. Warren. 2009. "Black-White Gap in Jobless Rate Widens in City." *New York Times,* July 13.

Mc Lean, Keith Radcliffe. 2001. "Ethnic Succession: A Study of Racial and Ethnic Transformation in Canarsie, Brooklyn, New York." MA thesis, Department of Urban Affairs, Queens College, CUNY.

Medina, Jennifer. 2009. "Why Is This Christmas Different from All Others?" *New York Times,* December 26.

———. 2010. "Success and Scrutiny at Hebrew Charter School." *New York Times,* June 24.

Meisel, Abigail. 2013. "40 Miles to Work on a Bike." *New York Times,* Metropolitan Section, January 27.

Mele, Christopher. 2000. *Selling the Lower East Side: Culture, Real Estate, and Resistance in New York City*. Minneapolis: University of Minnesota Press.

Mensch, Barbara G. 2007. *South Street*. New York: Columbia University Press.

Merlis, Jim. 2002. "Sal the Barber and the Make-Believe Ballroom." In *Mr. Beller's Neighborhood: Before & After: Stories from New York*, edited by Thomas Beller, 1: 28–32. New York: W. W. Norton.

Mesch, Gustavo S., and Kent P. Schwirian. 1996. "The Effectiveness of Neighborhood Collective Action." *Social Problems* 43: 467–83.

Miller, Elizabeth. 2009. "The Other Tribeca: Diversity amid Affluence." Research paper. Department of Sociology, City University of New York Graduate Center.

Miller, Stuart. 2007. "Turn Left at [Your Name Here]." *New York Times*, Op Ed Page, April 22.

Min, Pyong Gap. 2001. "Koreans: An Institutionally Complete Community in New York." In *New Immigrants in New York*, edited by Nancy Foner, 173–99. New York: Columbia University Press.

———. 2008. *Ethnic Solidarity for Economic Survival: Korean Greengrocers in New York City*. New York: Russell Sage Foundation.

———. 2010. *Preserving Ethnicity through Religion in America: Korean Protestants and Indian Hindus across Generations*. New York: New York University Press.

Minsky, Pearl. 2010. "Your Soap Box: Helen Granatelli, Dongan Hills." *Staten Island Advance*, August 5.

Mitchell, Joseph. 1992. *Up in the Old Hotel*. New York: Random House Digital.

Model, Suzanne. 2008a. "The Secret of West Indian Success." *Society* 45: 44–48.

———. 2008b. *West Indian Immigrants: A Black Success Story?* New York: Russell Sage Foundation.

Molina, Antonio Muñoz. 2010. "Spanish in New York: A Moving Landscape." In *Hispanic New York: A Sourcebook*, edited by Claudio Iván Remeseira, 355–58. New York: Columbia University Press.

Mollenkopf, John H. 1983. *The Contested City*. Princeton, NJ: Princeton University Press.

———. 1999. "Urban Political Conflicts and Alliances: New York and Los Angeles Compared." In *The Handbook of International Migration*, edited by Charles Hirschman, Philip Kasinitz, and Josh DeWind, 412–22. New York: Russell Sage Foundation.

Mollenkopf, John H., and Ken Emerson, eds. 2001. *Rethinking the Urban Agenda: Reinvigorating the Liberal Tradition in New York City and Urban America*. New York: Century Foundation Press.

Mollenkopf, John H., John Pereira, and Steven Romalewski. 2010. "First Reactions to the Combined American Community Survey Data for 2005–2009." CUNY Graduate Center Presentation, December 17.

Moody, Kim. 2007. *From Welfare State to Real Estate: Regime Change in New York City, 1974 to the Present*. New York: New Press.

Mooney, Jake. 2007. "Crime Is Low, but Fear Knows No Numbers." *New York Times*, December 16.

———. 2011a. "Bringing Up Dumbo." *New York Times*, May 8.

Mooney, Jake. 2011b. "Living In/Bushwick, Brooklyn: The Vanguard Alights." *New York Times*, Real Estate Section, July 17.

———. 2011c. "Living In/Prospect Park South, Brooklyn: Houses Are Few but Not Far Between." *New York Times*, Real Estate Section, October 9.

Moore, Stephen. 1997. "The Immigrant Burden." *City Journal* (Spring): 12. Online version.

Morales, Ed. 2003. "Spanish Harlem on His Mind: Puerto Ricans Remember When El Barrio Was Theirs Alone." *New York Times*, Section 14, February 23.

Morgan, Richard. 2012. "Neighborhood Boost Seen from the Lowline." *Wall Street Journal*, December 26.

Moskos, Charles. 1989. *Greek Americans: Struggle and Success*. New Brunswick, NJ: Transaction Books.

Moskos, Peter. 2008. *Cop in the Hood: My Year Policing Baltimore's Eastern District*. New York: Princeton University Press.

Nagourney, Adam. 1997. "Giuliani Sweeps to Second Term as Mayor." *New York Times*, November 5.

Nanos, Janelle. 2005. "Entering This Hall of Fame Takes Heart (and One Spaldeen)." *New York Times*, July 4.

Navarro, Mireya. 2012. "For Many Latinos, Racial Identity Is More Culture Than Color." *New York Times*, January 14.

Newfield, Jack, and Wayne Barrett. 1988. *City for Sale: Ed Koch and the Betrayal of New York*. New York: Harper and Row.

Newman, Andy. 2009. "As Cultures Clash, Brooklyn Principal Faces Assault Charges." *New York Times*, June 27.

———. 2011. "Principal Cleared of Charges in Confrontation with Teacher." *New York Times*, April 14.

Newman, Andy, and Nate Schweber, with Dylan Loeb McClain. 2010. "Police! Drop the Pawn! Step Away from the Table!" *New York Times*, November 18.

Newman, Katherine S. 1999. *No Shame in My Game: The Working Poor in the Inner City*. New York: Russell Sage Foundation.

Newman, Kathe, and Elvin K. Wyly. 2006. "The Right to Stay Put, Revisited: Gentrification and Resistance to Displacement in New York City." *Urban Studies* 43: 23–57.

Nossiter, Adam. 2010. "A Winner Is Announced and Disputed in Ivory Coast." *New York Times*, December 3.

Novak, Michael. 1971. *The Rise of the Unmeltable Ethnics*. New York: Macmillan.

Ocejo, Richard E. 2011. "The Early Gentrifiers: Weaving a Nostalgia Narrative on the Lower East Side." *City & Community* 10: 285–310.

Okeowo, Alexis. 2011. "An African Pageant Reflects the Changing Face of Staten Island: Maintaining Connections to Homelands." *New York Times*, August 5.

Okie, Susan. 2009. "The Epidemic That Wasn't." *New York Times*, Science Times, January 27.

Olson, Daniel V. A. 2008. "Why Do Small Religious Groups Have More Committed Members?" *Review of Religious Research* 49: 353–78.

O'Neill, Joseph. 2009. *Netherland*. New York: Vintage.

Onishi, Norimitzu. 1996. "Merging Identity—A Special Report: New Sense of Race Arises among Asian-Americans." *New York Times*, May 30.

Oppenheimer, Mark. 2011. "Mapping Religious Life in the Five Boroughs, with Shoe Leather and a Web Site." *New York Times*, March 19.

Orleck, Annelise. 2001. "Soviet Jews: The City's Newest Immigrants Transform New York Jewish Life." In *New Immigrants in New York*, edited by Nancy Foner, 111–40. New York: Columbia University Press.

Ortiz, Pilar. 2012. "The Informal Economies of Roosevelt Avenue." Research paper. Department of Sociology, City University of New York Graduate Center.

Orum, Anthony, and Zachary P. Neal, eds. 2010. *Common Ground?: Readings and Reflections on Public Space*. New York: Routledge.

Ousey, Graham C., and Charis E. Kubrin. 2009. "Exploring the Connection between Immigration and Violent Crime Rates in U.S. Cities, 1980–2000." *Social Problems* 56: 447–73.

Paik, Leslie. 2011. *Discretionary Justice: Looking Inside a Juvenile Drug Court*. New Brunswick, NJ: Rutgers University Press.

Paradis, Lauren. 2011. "Astoria: Not 'All Greek to' Residents." Research paper. Department of Sociology, City University of New York Graduate Center.

Passel, Jeffrey S. 2007. "Unauthorized Migrants in the United States: Estimates, Methods, and Characteristics." *OECD Social, Employment, and Migration Working Papers*, No. 57.

Pattillo-McCoy, Mary. 1999. *Black Picket Fences: Privilege and Peril among the Black Middle Class*. Chicago: University of Chicago Press, 1999.

Pérez, Gina M. 2004. *The Near Northwest Side Story: Migration, Displacement, and Puerto Rican Families*. Berkeley: University of California Press.

Perry, Donna L. 1997. "Rural Ideologies and Urban Imaginings: Wolof Immigrants in New York City." *Africa Today* 44: 229–60.

Petersen, Jen. 2011. "Whose Streets?: Paving the Right to the City." PhD dissertation. Department of Sociology, New York University.

Peyser, Andrea. 2011. "Gay Nuptials—This Time, It's Personal." *New York Post*, June 20.

Phillips, McCandlish. 1965. "State Klan Leader Hides Secret of Jewish Origin." *New York Times*, October 31.

"A Plan for Coney Island." 2009. *New York Times*, Editorial, July 13.

"Playing Chess in the 'Hood.'" 2007. MSNBC.com, March 19.

Podhoretz, John. 2010. "The Upper West Side—Then and Now." *Commentary*, May.

Pogrebin, Robin. 2008a. "An Opaque and Lengthy Road to Landmark Status." *New York Times*, November 26.

———. 2008b. "Preservationists See Bulldozers Charging through a Loophole." *New York Times*, November 29.

———. 2008c. "Houses of Worship Choosing to Avoid Landmark Status." *New York Times*, December 1.

———. 2008d. "Preservation and Development in a Dynamic Give and Take." *New York Times*, December 2.

———. 2011. "High Line: The Sequel: Coming Soon: More Room to Roam." *New York Times*, Metropolitan Section, May 29.

Pokharel, Sunita. 2012. "Nepali Living in New York." Research paper. Department of Sociology, City College of New York.

Poll, Solomon. 1962. *The Hasidic Community of Williamsburg: A Study in the Sociology of Religion.* New York: Free Press.

Poros, Maritsa V. 2011. *Modern Migrations: Gujarati Indian Networks in New York and London.* Stanford, CA: Stanford University Press.

Portes, Alejandro. 1998. "'Social Capital': Its Origins and Applications in Modern Sociology." *Annual Review of Sociology* 24: 1–24.

Powell, Michael. 2010. "Old-Fashioned Bulwark in a Tide of Foreclosures." *New York Times*, Metropolitan Section, March 7.

———. 2012. "No Room for Dissent in a Police Department Consumed by the Numbers." *New York Times*, May 8.

Press, Eyal. 2006. "Do Immigrants Really Make Us Safer?" *New York Times*, Sunday Magazine, December 3.

Preston, Julia. 2009. "Mexico Data Say Migration to U.S. Has Plummeted." *New York Times*, May 15.

Pritchett, Wendell. 2002. *Brownsville, Brooklyn: Blacks, Jews, and the Changing Face of the Ghetto.* Chicago: University of Chicago Press.

Prochnik, George. 2009. "City of Earthly Delights." *New York Times*, Week in Review Section, Op Ed, December 13.

Purnick, Joyce. 1980. "Koch Warns Unions on Hopes for Raises." *New York Times*, April 13.

Putnam, Robert D. 2000. *Bowling Alone: The Collapse and Revival of American Community.* New York: Simon and Schuster.

Quinn, Bernadette. 2005. "Art Festivals and the City." *Urban Studies* 42: 927–43.

Ragen, Naomi. 2003. *Chains around the Grass.* New Milford, CT: Toby Press.

Raver, Anne. 1997. "Houses before Gardens: The City Decides." *New York Times*, January 9.

Reitzes, Donald C. 1986. "Downtown Vitality: Factors Influencing the Use of Dining and Entertainment Facilities." *Sociological Perspectives* 29: 121–43.

Remeseira, Claudio Iván, ed. 2010. *Hispanic New York: A Sourcebook.* New York: Columbia University Press.

Rhode, David. 1997. "Crime and Politics Make Most Gangs Come and Go." *New York Times*, October 12.

Rhodes-Pitts, Sharifa. 2011. *Harlem Is Nowhere: A Journey to the Mecca of Black America.* Boston: Little, Brown.

Rich, Wilbur C. 2006. *David Dinkins and New York City Politics: Race, Images, and the Media.* Albany: SUNY Press.

Ricourt, Milagros, and Ruby Danta. 2010. "The Emergence of Latino Panethnicity." In *Hispanic New York: A Sourcebook*, edited by Claudio Iván Remseseira, 201–15. New York: Columbia University Press.

Rieder, Jonathan. 1985. *Canarsie: The Jews and Italians of Brooklyn against Liberalism.* Cambridge, MA: Harvard University Press.

Rimer, Sara. 1985. "Pool and Pride in the Bronx." *New York Times*, August 11.

Rivera, Ray, and Al Baker. 2010. "A Rise in Violent Crime Evokes City's Unruly Past." *New York Times*, April 12.

Robbins, Liz. 2008. *A Race Like No Other: 26.2 Miles through the Streets of New York*. New York: HarperCollins.

———. 2011a. "Bowlers in Brooklyn Enjoy a Haven While It's Still Around." *New York Times*, April 23.

———. 2011b. "After Coming Together for a Frantic Search, a Community Is Left Reeling." *New York Times*, July 14.

———. 2012. "Unease Lingers amid a Rebirth in Crown Heights." *New York Times*, February 1.

Roberts, Sam. 1991. "The Region: The Outer Boroughs Come Closer to the Inner Circle." *New York Times*, Week in Review, June 9.

———. 1993. "New York Hit by Increases in Migration." *New York Times*, March 10.

———. 1994. "In Middle-Class Queens, Blacks Pass Whites in Household Income." *New York Times*, June 6.

———. 2005. "More Africans Enter U.S. Than in Days of Slavery." *New York Times*, February 21.

———. 2008a. "Census Shows Growing Diversity in New York City." *New York Times*, December 9.

———. 2008b. "In Biggest U.S. Cities, Minorities Are at 50%." *New York Times*, December 9.

———. 2009a. "City Nears 8.4 Million as Fewer Leave the State." *New York Times*, March 19.

———. 2009b. "New York, a City Unspoiled. Wait, New York?" *New York Times*, March 23.

———. 2009c. "Hispanic Population's Growth Propelled City to a Census Record." *New York Times*, May 14.

———. 2009d. "What's in a Name? For Hispanics, a Generational Shift." *New York Times*, May 29.

———. 2010a. "No Longer Majority Black, Harlem Is in Transition." *New York Times*, January 6.

———. 2010b. "New York's Haitian Diaspora." *New York Times*, Metropolitan Section, January 17.

———. 2010c. "Census Figures Challenge Views of Race and Ethnicity." *New York Times*, January 22.

———. 2010d. "In a Switch, Manhattan Lost People, Census Says." *New York Times*, March 24.

———. 2010e. "Black Women See Shrinking Pool of Black Men at the Marriage Altar." *New York Times*, June 4.

———. 2010f. "White Population Rises in Manhattan." *New York Times*, July 4.

———. 2010g. "Staten Island, Where Tennis in America Began." *New York Times*, City Room Column, August 21.

———. 2010h. "In New York, Black and Hispanic Strongholds Become More White." *New York Times*, December 15.

———. 2011a. "In Time of Declining Crime, a Survey Finds Fewer Broken Windows." *New York Times*, February 24.

———. 2011b. "Survey Hints at a Census Undercount in New York City." *New York Times*, May 24.

Roberts, Sam. 2011c. "A Striking Evolution in Bedford-Stuyvesant as the White Population Soars." *New York Times*, August 5.

———. 2011d. "Happy to Call the City Home, More Now Move In Than Out." *New York Times*, November 12.

———. 2012a. "Population Growth in New York City Is Outpacing 2010 Census, 2011 Estimates Show." *New York Times*, April 5.

———. 2012b. "Touring the City with Fresh Eyes." *New York Times*, May 4.

———. 2013. "Fewer People Are Abandoning the Bronx, Census Data Show." *New York Times*, March 14.

Rodríguez, Clara. 2005. "Forging a New New York: The Puerto Rican Community, Post-1945." In *Boricuas in Gotham: Puerto Ricans in the Making of Modern New York City*, edited by Gabriel Haslip-Viera, Angelo Falcón, and Felíx Matos Rodríguez, 195–218. Princeton, NJ: Markus Wiener.

Ronalds-Hannon, Eliza. 2011. "Parents React to Sean Keaton's Acquittal." *New York Times*, April 15.

Rooney, Jim. 1995. *Organizing the South Bronx*. Albany: State University of New York Press.

Rosenberg, Noah. 2011. "Ice Cold, 42 Flavors of Nostalgia." *New York Times*, Metropolitan Section, August 7.

Rosenblum, Constance. 2009. "The Grand Cornice and Pediment Tour." *New York Times*, City Section, April 19.

———. 2010a. "Gods, Goddesses, and Elephants for Luck." *New York Times*, Real Estate Section, August 15.

———. 2010b. "An Island Perch with Postcard Views." *New York Times*, Real Estate Section, August 29.

———. 2010c. "A Magnetic Field, with Walls and Roof." *New York Times*, Real Estate Section, October 24.

———. 2010d. "The Big Squeeze." *New York Times*, Real Estate Section, November 14.

Rosenthal, A. M., and Arthur Gelb. 1967. *One More Victim: The Life and Death of an American-Jewish Nazi*. New York: New American Library.

Rovzar, Chris. 2010. "Our Town." *New York Magazine*, January 31.

Ruderman, Wendy. 2012. "414 Homicides a Record Low for New York." *New York Times*, December 29.

Ruderman, Wendy, and Nate Schweber. 2012. "Central Park Rape Victim Says She Reported Earlier Confrontation." *New York Times*, September 15.

Rumbaut, Rubén G., and Alejandro Portes, eds. 2001. *Ethnicities: Children of Immigrants in America*. Berkeley: University of California Press.

Sachs, Susan. 2001. "The Census: New York." *New York Times*, March 16.

Sagalyn, Lynne B. 2001. *Times Square Roulette: Remaking the City Icon*. Cambridge: MIT Press.

Salkin, Allen. 2009. "Anybody Here from Astoria?" *New York Times*, Sunday Styles, October 11.

Sampson, Robert J. 2012. *Great American City: Chicago and the Enduring Neighborhood Effect*. Chicago: University of Chicago Press.

Samtur, Stephen M., and Martin A. Jackson. 2003. *The Bronx: Then and Now*. Scarsdale, NY: Back in the Bronx Publishing.

Samuels, David. 2008. "Assimilation and Its Discontents: How Success Ruined the New York Jew." *New York Magazine*, September 28.

Sandoval, Edgar, and Rocco Parascandola. 2010. "Harlem Neighborhood Lives with Fear and Tears as Deadly Gang War Rages on." *New York Daily News*, October 28.

Sanjek, Roger. 1998. *The Future of Us All: Race and Neighborhood Politics in New York City*. Ithaca, NY: Cornell University Press.

Sante, Luc. 2002. "The Tompkins Square Park Riot, 1988." In *Mr. Beller's Neighborhood: Before & After: Stories from New York*, edited by Thomas Beller, 1: 45–51. New York: W. W. Norton.

———. 2003. *Low Life: Lures and Snares of Old New York*. New York: Farrar, Straus, and Giroux.

Santora, Marc. 2011a. "Gowanus: Big Development Can Wait." *New York Times*, Real Estate Section, July 31.

———. 2011b. "Across the Hall, Diversity of Incomes." *New York Times*, Real Estate Section, September 2.

Santos, Fernanda. 2009. "Are New Yorkers Satisfied? That Depends." *New York Times*, March 8.

———. 2010a. "Here to Aid His Family, Left to Die on the Street." *New York Times*, April 27.

———. 2010b. "A Queens Development Raises Ethnic Tensions." *New York Times*, July 14.

Saran, Parmatma. 1985. *The Asian Indian Experience in the United States*. Cambridge, MA: Schenkman.

Sassen, Saskia. 1988. *The Mobility of Capital and Labor: A Study in International Investment and Labor Flow*. New York: Cambridge University Press.

———. 2001. *The Global City: New York, London, Tokyo*. Princeton, NJ: Princeton University Press.

Satow, Julie. 2011. "The Fish Market Cleans up Good." *New York Times*, Real Estate Section, September 18.

Saul, Michael. 2002. "500 Gardens Saved in City Housing Deal." *New York Daily News*, September 19.

Saulny, Susan. 2009. "Voices Reflect Rising Sense of Racial Optimism." *New York Times*, May 3.

———. 2011. "Black? White? Asian? More Young Americans Choose All of the Above." *New York Times*, January 30.

———. 2012. "Interracial Marriage Seen Gaining Wide Acceptance." *New York Times*, February 16.

Schanberg, Sydney H. 1982. "Gentrifiers: The Lawyers." *New York Times*, May 11.

Schoeneman, Deborah. 2005. "The Waiting Is the Hardest Part." *New York Magazine*, May 21.

Schonfeld, Irvin Sam. 2012. "Not Quite Paradise: Growing Up in a New York City Housing Project." Unpublished manuscript.

Schulman, Sarah. 2012. *The Gentrification of the Mind: Witness to a Lost Imagination*. Berkeley: University of California Press.

Secret, Mosi. 2011. "Smaller Shelters and Persuasion Coax Homeless off Bronx Streets." *New York Times*, October 18.

Secret, Mosi. 2012. "Charges Tell of Iron Grip of a Gang." *New York Times*, February 1.

Semple, Kirk. 2008. "Political Dissension Troubles Liberian Groups on Staten Island." *New York Times*, New York Regional Section, July 28.

———. 2009a. "A Heated Campaign for a Ceremonial Post." *New York Times*, March 28.

———. 2009b. "Korean New Yorkers Hope for Council Seat in Queens, Their First." *New York Times*, May 6.

Semple, Kirk. 2009c. "Council Votes for Muslim Holidays." *New York Times*, July 1.

———. 2009d. "As Ireland's Boom Ends, Job Seekers Revive a Well-Worn Path to New York." *New York Times*, July 10.

———. 2009e. "Bhutan Refugees Find a Toehold in the Bronx." *New York Times*, September 25.

———. 2010a. "New York Haitians See a Chance to Cohere into a Lasting Force." *New York Times*, February 4.

———. 2010b. "In an Italian Enclave in the Bronx, Signs of Mexico Begin to Show." *New York Times*, July 8.

———. 2010c. "Staten Island Neighborhood Reels after Wave of Attacks on Mexicans." *New York Times*, July 30.

———. 2010d. "Long Island Study Rebuts Perceptions on Immigrant Workers." *New York Times*, November 18.

———. 2011a. "Passing the One Million Mark, Asian New Yorkers Join Forces." *New York Times*, June 24.

———. 2011b. "In New York, Mexicans Lag in Education." *New York Times*, November 25.

———. 2012. "Many U.S. Immigrants' Children Seek American Dream Abroad." *New York Times*, April 16.

Senior, Jennifer. 2008. "Alone Together." *New York Magazine*, November 23.

Sennett, Richard. 1990. *The Conscience of the Eye: The Design and Social Life of Cities*. New York: Alfred Knopf.

Severson, Kim. 2009. "Brooklyn's Flavor Route to the South." *New York Times*, December 30.

Shaer, Matthew. 2011. "Not Quite Copenhagen." *New York Magazine*, March 20.

Sharkey, Patrick. 2006. "Navigating Dangerous Streets: The Sources and Consequences of Street Efficacy." *American Sociological Review* 71: 826–46.

———. 2013. *Stuck in Place: Urban Neighborhoods and the End of Progress toward Racial Equality*. Chicago: University of Chicago Press.

Sharman, Russell Leigh. 2006. *The Tenants of East Harlem*. Berkeley: University of California Press.

Sharman, Russell Leigh, and Cheryl Harris Sharman. 2008. *Nightshift NYC*. Berkeley: University of California Press.

Sheftell, Jason. 2011. "Life on the Oval: Parkchester Can Save You Green While Surrounding You with Greenery." *New York Daily News*, Real Estate Section, July 8.

Shokeid, Moshe. 1988. *Children of Circumstances: Israeli Immigrants in New York*. Ithaca, NY: Cornell University Press.

Shulman, Robin. 2005. "A Neighborhood Fixture Too Gruff to Not Love." *New York Times*, June 21.

Siegel, Fred. 2000. "The Prince of New York: Rudy Giuliani's Legacy." *Weekly Standard*, August 21.

Sleeper, Jim. 1991. *The Closest of Strangers: Liberalism and the Politics of Race in New York*. New York: W. W. Norton.

Slotnik, Daniel E. 2010. "Muslim Deli Owners Must Choose Koran or Customers." *New York Times*, January 4.

Small, Mario Luis. 2009. *Unanticipated Gains: Origins of Network Inequality in Everyday Life*. New York: Oxford University Press.

Small, Mario Luis, and Monica McDermott. 2006. "The Presence of Organizational Resources in Poor Urban Neighborhoods: An Analysis of Average and Contextual Effects." *Social Forces* 84: 1697–1724.

Smiley, Brett. 2012. "City Council to Hold Hearing on Controversial Restaurant Grading System." *New York Magazine*, March 7.

Smith, Christopher M., and Hilda E. Kurtz. 2003. "Community Gardens and Politics of Scale in New York City." *Geographical Review* 93: 193–212.

Smith, Neil. 1979. "Toward a Theory of Gentrification: A Back to the City Movement by Capital, not People." *Journal of the American Planning Association* 45: 538–48.

———. 1996. *The New Urban Frontier: Gentrification and the Revanchist City*. New York: Routledge.

Smith, Patricia K. 2005. "The Economics of Anti-Begging Regulations." *American Journal of Economics and Sociology* 64: 549–77.

Smith, Robert C. 2006. *Mexican New York: Transnational Lives of New Immigrants*. Berkeley: University of California Press.

Smothers, Ronald. 1986. "Black Leaders Say Queens Attack Is Evidence of 'Pervasive Problem.' " *New York Times*, December 23.

Soffer, Jonathan. 2010. *Ed Koch and the Rebuilding of New York City*. New York: Columbia University Press.

Sohn, Amy. 2009. *Prospect Park West*. New York: Simon and Schuster.

Sorkin, Michael. 2009. *Twenty Minutes in Manhattan*. New York: Reaktion Books.

Sorkin, Michael, and Sharon Zukin, eds. 2002. *After the World Trade Center: Rethinking New York*. New York: Routledge.

Sotomayor, Sonia. 2013. *My Beloved World*. New York: Alfred A. Knopf.

Souljah, Sister. 1999. *The Coldest Winter Ever*. New York: Pocket Books.

Steinberg, Stephen. 1981. *The Ethnic Myth: Race, Ethnicity, and Class in America*. New York: Atheneum.

Stelloh, Tim. 2011. "Not Quite a Reporter, but Raking Muck and Reaping Wrath." *New York Times*, January 24.

Sterba, James P. 1978. "'I Love New York' Campaign Going National." *New York Times*, July 7.

Stern, Robert A. M., David Fishman, and Thomas Mellins. 1997. *New York 1960: Architecture and Urbanism between the Second World War and the Bicentennial*. New York: Monacelli Press.

Stern, Robert A. M., David Fishman, and Jacob Tilove. 2006. *New York 2000: Architecture and Urbanism between the Bicentennial and the Millennium.* New York: Monacelli Press.

Stern, Robert A. M., Gregory F. Gilmartin, and John Massengale. 1983. *New York 1900: Metropolitan Architecture and Urbanism, 1890–1915.* New York: Rizzoli.

Stern, Robert A. M., Gregory F. Gilmartin, and Thomas Mellins. 1987. *New York 1930: Architecture and Urbanism between the Two World Wars.* New York: Rizzoli.

Stern, Robert A. M., Thomas Mellins, and David Fishman. 1999. *New York 1880: Architecture and Urbanism in the Gilded Age.* New York: Monacelli Press.

Stoddard, Grant. 2007. "Castaway." *New York Magazine,* June 25.

Stoll, David. 2009. "Which American Dream Do You Mean?" *Society* 46: 398–402.

Stoller, Paul. 2002. *Money Has No Smell: The Africanization of New York City.* Chicago: University of Chicago Press.

Storper, Michael, and Richard A. Walker. 1983. "The Theory of Labor and the Theory of Location." *International Journal of Urban and Regional Research* 7: 1–43.

Stout, Hilary. 2010. "The March of the Conversions." *New York Times,* Real Estate Section, July 8.

"Subway Concerts Music to Fight/Switch By." 1985. *New York Times,* Opinion, September 15.

Sugrue, Thomas J. 1996. *The Origins of the Urban Crisis.* Princeton, NJ: Princeton University Press.

Sullivan, C. J., and Wilson Dizard. 2010. "They'll Take Manhattan over Bronx." *New York Post,* October 22.

Sullivan, Robert. 2010. "The Concrete Jungle." *New York Magazine,* September 12.

Sulzberger, A. G., and Stacey Solie. 2010. "Guatemalans, in Brooklyn for Work, Keep Bonds of Home." *New York Times,* February 2.

Suro, Roberto. 2010. "New York: Teetering on the Heights." In *Hispanic New York: A Sourcebook,* edited by Claudio Iván Remeseira, 123–42. New York: Columbia University Press.

Suttles, Gerald D. 1972. *The Social Construction of Communities.* Chicago: University of Chicago Press.

Tanenbaum, Susie. 1995. *Underground Harmonies: Music and Politics in the Subways of New York.* Ithaca, NY: Cornell University Press.

Tavernise, Sabrina. 2011. "Outside Cleveland, Snapshots of Poverty's Surge in the Suburbs." *New York Times,* October 25.

Taylor, Marvin J., ed. 2005. *The Downtown Book: The New York Art Scene, 1974–1984.* Princeton, NJ: Princeton University Press.

Taylor, Monique M. 2002. *Harlem between Heaven and Hell.* Minneapolis: University of Minnesota Press.

Thabit, Walter. 2003. *How East New York Became a Ghetto.* New York: New York University Press.

Thompson, Clive. 2005. "The Rise of the Microneighborhood." *New York Magazine,* May 21.

Tissot, Sylvie. 2011. "Of Dogs and Men: The Making of Spatial Boundaries in a Gentrifying Neighborhood." *City & Community* 10: 265–84.

Tomasky, Michael. 2008. "The Day Everything Changed." *New York Magazine*, September 28.

Toth, Jennifer. 1993. *The Mole People: Life in the Tunnels beneath New York City*. Chicago: Chicago Review Press.

Toy, Vivian S. 2009a. "The Diaper District." *New York Times*, Real Estate Section, February 22.

———. 2009b. "Edgewater Park and Silver Beach Gardens, the Bronx: Co-ops Galore, but Not a High Rise in Sight." *New York Times*, Real Estate Section, August 2.

Traore, Rosemary L. 2004. "Colonialism Continued: African Students in an Urban High School in America." *Journal of Black Studies* 34: 348–69.

Trump, Donald J. (with Tony Schwartz). 1987. *Trump: The Art of the Deal*. New York: Random House.

Tuan, Mia. 2005. *Forever Foreigners or Honorary Whites?: The Asian Ethnic Experience Today*. New Brunswick, NJ: Rutgers University Press.

Turhan, Suna. 2012. "Bay Rich: Turks and More in Bay Ridge." Research paper. Department of Sociology, City University of New York Graduate Center.

Turner, Bryan. 1987. "A Note on Nostalgia. *Theory, Culture, and Society* 4: 147–56.

Tyler, Gus. 1987. "A Tale of Three Cities." *Dissent* (Fall): 463–70.

Tzou, Alice. 2011. "The Spirit of East Harlem: Beautiful but Misunderstood." Research paper. Department of Sociology, City University of New York Graduate Center.

Ukeles, Jacob B., and David A. Grossman. 2004. *Report on Jewish Poverty*. New York: Metropolitan Council on Jewish Poverty.

Ultan, Lloyd. 1997. "Shorehaven." *Bronx Roots-L-Archives*, August 7. Online publication.

Ultan, Lloyd, and Barbara Unger. 2000. *Bronx Accent: A Literary and Pictorial History of the Borough*. New Brunswick, NJ: Rivergate Books.

"Unfamiliar Names on Familiar Streets." 2007. *New York Times*, Letters to the Editor, April 29.

U.S. Census Bureau. 1990. *U.S. Census*. Washington, DC: Bureau of the Census.

———. 2000. *U.S. Census*. Washington, DC: Bureau of the Census.

———. 2004 (March.) *Current Population Survey*. Washington, DC: Bureau of the Census.

———. 2010. *U.S. Census*. Washington, DC: Bureau of the Census.

Vaisey, Stephen. 2007. "Structure, Culture, and Community: The Search for Belonging in 50 Urban Communes." *American Sociological Review* 72: 851–73.

Vandam, Jeff. 2008. "Condos Flood In; Hipness Stays Afloat." *New York Times*, Real Estate Section, December 21.

———. 2009. "History, with Hipper Retailing in Bed-Stuy." *New York Times*, Real Estate Section, August 23.

———. 2010. "The Bigger Little Italy." *New York Times*, Real Estate Section, February 3.

Vanderkam, Laura. 2011. "Where Did the Korean Greengrocers Go?" *City Journal* (Winter): 54–61

Vedantam, Shankar. 2010. "Shades of Prejudice." *New York Times*, January 19.

Venkatesh, Sudhir. 2008. *Gang Leader for a Day: A Rogue Sociologist Takes to the Streets*. New York: Penguin Books.

Vergara, Camilo José. 2009. "125th and Lex." *Slate*, December 3. Online.

Vesselinov, Elena, Matthew Cazessus, and William Falk. 2007. "Gated Communities and Spatial Inequality." *Journal of Urban Affairs* 29: 109–27.

Vigdor, Jacob L. 2002. "Does Gentrification Harm the Poor?" *Brookings-Wharton Papers on Urban Affairs* 3: 133–73.

Vitale, Alex S. 2008. *City of Disorder: How the Quality of Life Campaign Transformed New York Politics*. New York: New York University Press.

Vitello, Paul. 2009. "Pastor at Riverside Church Ends Stormy Tenure with Unexpected Resignation." *New York Times*, July 1.

Viteritti, Joseph. 1992. "Should Staten Island Leave the City?" *City Journal* (Autumn): 9–12.

Waldinger, Roger D. 1986. *Through the Eye of the Needle: Immigrants and Enterprise in New York's Garment Trades*. New York: New York University Press.

———. 1996a. *Still the Promised City?: African-Americans and New Immigrants in Post-Industrial New York*. Cambridge, MA: Harvard University Press.

———. 1996b."From Ellis Island to LAX: Immigrant Prospects in the American City." *International Migration Review* 30: 1078–86.

———. 2001. *Strangers at the Gates: New Immigrants in Urban America*. Berkeley: University of California Press.

———. 2011. "Immigration: The New American Dilemma." *Daedalus* 140: 215–25.

Walsh, Kevin. 2006. *Forgotten New York: Views of a Lost Metropolis*. New York: HarperCollins.

Way, Christina Halsey, ed., and Mary Delaney Krugman. 1998. *The Architectural and Historical Resources of Riverdale, the Bronx, New York: A Preliminary Survey*. Riverdale Nature Preservancy.

Wayne, Leslie. 1987. "5-Year Stock Rally: The Far-Reaching Impact." *New York Times*, August 3.

Weidman, Jerome. 1974. *Tiffany Street*. New York: Random House.

Weinstein, Emily. 2009. "One in a Million: The Religious Runaway." *New York Times*, Metropolitan Section, May 24.

Weisbord, Robert G., and Arthur Stein. 1972. *Bittersweet Encounter: The Afro-American and the American Jew*. New York: Schocken Books.

Wellman, Barry. 1988. "The Community Question Re-evaluated." In *Power, Community, and the City*, edited by Michael P. Smith, 81–107. New Brunswick, NJ: Transaction Books.

White, Norval, and Elliot Willensky. 2000. *AIA Guide to New York City*. New York: Crown.

Whitman, Walt. 1954. *Leaves of Grass*. New York: Signet Classics.

Whyte, William H. 1988. *City: Rediscovering the Center*. New York: Doubleday.

Wichmann, Moritz. 2012. "From Pit Bull to Terrier: Continuities and Change—The Gentrification of East Harlem." Research paper. Department of Sociology, City University of New York Graduate Center.

Williams, Terry, and William Kornblum. 1994. *The Uptown Kids: Struggle and Hope in the Projects*. New York: Grosset/Putnam.

Williams, Timothy. 2008. "Mixed Feelings on 125th Street." *New York Times*, June 13.

Wilson, Claire. 2001."About an Island That's Worth Remembering." *New York Times*, August 17.

Wilson, Michael. 2011. "On Quiet Roosevelt Island, Unease Pays a Sudden Visit." *New York Times*, December 10.

Wilson, William Julius, and Anmol Chaddha. 2009. "The Role of Theory in Ethnographic Research." *Ethnography* 10: 549–64.

Wines, Michael. 2011. "Picking the Pitch-Perfect Brand Name in China." *New York Times*, November 12.

Winnick, Louis. 1991. "Letter from Sunset Park." *City Journal* (Winter): 75–77.

Winston, Hella. 2006. *Unchosen: The Hidden Lives of Hasidic Rebels*. Boston: Beacon Press.

Wolfe, Tom. 1987. *The Bonfire of the Vanities*. New York: Farrar, Straus, Giroux.

Wolff, Kurt H., ed. and trans. 1950. *The Sociology of Georg Simmel*. New York: Free Press.

Woods, Vidal. 2010. "Kips Bay Clubhouse Welcomed by Residents." *Bronx Youth Heard*, July 12.

Wright, Christian L. 2011. "An Avenue Arrives, Tourists and All." *New York Times*, Real Estate Section, November 12.

Wright, Kai. 2008. "Where Murder Won't Go Quietly." *New York Magazine*, January 7.

Wright, Talmadge. 1997. *Out of Place: Homeless Mobilizations, Subcities, and Contested Landscapes*. Albany: State University of New York Press.

Wyly, Elvin, and James DeFilippis. 2010. "Mapping Public Housing: The Case of New York City." *City & Community* 9: 61–86.

Wynn, Jonathan R. 2011. *The Tour Guide: Walking and Talking New York*. Chicago: University of Chicago Press.

Xu, Fang. 2010. "The New Lower East Side: A Hipstoic Neighborhood." Research paper. Department of Sociology, City University of New York Graduate Center.

Yardley, Jim. 1999. "Perils amid Lure of Gentrification: Slaying Brings Shock to Gentrified Neighborhood." *New York Times*, March 11.

Yost, Mark. 2010. "A Piece of Handball Heaven." *Wall Street Journal*, May 29–30.

Young, Alford, Jr. 2006. *The Minds of Marginalized Black Men: Making Sense of Mobility, Opportunity, and Future Life Chances*. Princeton, NJ: Princeton University Press.

Yukich, Grace. 2010. "Boundary Work in Inclusive Religious Groups: Constructing Identity at the New York Catholic Worker." *Sociology of Religion* 71: 172–96.

Yungreis, Esther. 1978. "Rebbetzin's Viewpoint." *Jewish Press*, December 1.

Zeitz, Joshua M. 2007. *White Ethnic New York: Jews, Catholics, and the Shaping of Postwar Politics*. Chapel Hill: University of North Carolina Press.

Zengerle, Jason. 2009. "Repeat Defender." *New York Magazine*, November 22.

Zentella, Ana Celia. 2010. "Spanish in New York." In *Hispanic New York: A Sourcebook*, edited by Claudio Iván Remeseira, 321–53. New York: Columbia University Press.

Zhang, Xinyu. 2012. "An Urban Arcadia: Forest Hills in New York City." Research paper. Department of Sociology, City University of New York Graduate College.

Zhou, Min. 1992. *Chinatown: The Socioeconomic Potential of an Urban Enclave*. Philadelphia: Temple University Press.

———. 2009. *Contemporary Chinese America: Immigration, Ethnicity, and Community Transformation*. Philadelphia: Temple University Press.

Zimring, Franklin E. 2012. *The City That Became Safe*. New York: Oxford University Press.

Zipp, Samuel. 2010. *Manhattan Projects: The Rise and Fall of Urban Renewal in Cold War New York*. New York: Oxford University Press.

Zukin, Sharon. 1982. *Loft Living: Culture and Capital in Urban Change*. Baltimore, MD: Johns Hopkins University Press.

———. 1987. "Gentrification and Capital in the Urban Core." *Annual Review of Sociology* 13: 129–47.

———. 1995. *The Cultures of Cities*. Cambridge, MA: Blackwell.

———. 2002. "What's Space Got to Do with It?" *City & Community* 1: 345–48.

———. 2010a. *Naked City: The Death and Life of Authentic Urban Places*. New York: Oxford University Press.

———. 2010b. "How the City Lost Its Soul: American Cities Are Safer Than Ever Before—But They're Deader Too." *Playboy*, April.

Zukin, Sharon, and Ervin Kosta. 2004. "Bourdieu Off-Broadway: Managing Distinction on a Shopping Block in the East Village." *City & Community* 3: 101–114.

Zukin, Sharon, Valerie Trujillo, Peter Frase, Danielle Jackson, Tim Recuber, and Abraham Walker. 2009. "New Retail Capital and Neighborhood Change: Boutiques and Gentrification in New York City." *City & Community* 8: 47–64.

NOTE: The *New York Times* references are from either the online or the newspaper editions. The online edition has a slightly different title and date. In either case, the reader should have no trouble locating them in the online Times Archives. *New York Magazine* articles are from the online edition.

INDEX

Abrahamson, Mark, 374n14
Adam-Ovide, Marie, 312
Adopt-a-Monument Program, 214
adult and senior programs, 120–22. *See also* senior citizens
African Americans. *See* blacks
Africans: and African Market in Harlem, 39–40, 382n7; coalitions of, 70; differences within groups of, 62–63, identification of, 55–56, 393n31; Ivoirians, 55–56; Liberians, 393n31; and networks, 39–40, Nigerians: 58, 63; politics of, 55–56; religion of, 58; Senegalese, 62
AIDS, 339
Akwaaba Mansion, 177
Alba, Richard, 340–41, 371n26
Alvarez, Lizette, 375n16
American flags, flying of, 380n47
American Gangster, 115
American Legion, 206
Anderson, Elijah, 15, 80, 184,185, 268, 310, 369n7
Apollo Theater, 248
Armando's Pollo Rico, 296
art: galleries, 241–42, 376n26; grafitti; 201–4; on sidewalk surfaces, 185–86; sponsors; 214
artists: as vanguard for gentrification, 237, 247
Ascension Episcopal Church, 244
Asians: and basketball, 343–45; coalitions of, 69–70; and entertainment, 140–43; physical appearance of, 328; politics of, 29, 343–45, population in New York City, 29, 298; racial intermarriage, 297–98; relations with other groups, 140–41; as role models, 43, 344–45, 393n25; and Sunset Park, 158–59. *See also* Bhutanese; Chinese; conflict; ethnicity; Filipinos; Indians; Japanese; Koreans; Nepalese; politics; religion; Sri Lankans
Astoria (Queens), 371n24
Atlantic Development Group, 271–72
Atlantic Yards, 123, 279–80
authenticity, 147–48, 376n27, 382n7

Ballon, Hilary, 384n14
Barretto Point Park, 175
Battery Park, 177
Bay Plaza Theater, 120–21
beaches, 162–63
Beacon Mews, 278
Beastie Boys, 112
Bedford-Stuyvesant (Brooklyn), 236, 283, 286–87, 293–94, 311
Bed-Stuy. *See* Bedford-Stuyvesant
Beechhurst (Queens), 310
beer gardens, 381n19
Belafonte, Harry, 204
Bellafante, Ginia, 277, 380n45
Belmont/Arthur Avenue section (Little Italy of the Bronx), 251–52, 272
Bensonhurst (Brooklyn), 43–44, 164–65, 208–10, 325–26, 329
Berger, Joseph, 31, 374n14, 386n6
Bernstein, Fred, 282
Berrigan, Daniel, 250
Betances Houses, 129
Betances Senior Center, 121
Beyond the Melting Pot, 32–33
Bhutanese: as smallest immigrant group, 375n14
bicycle: as nuisance, 267, and races, 71; riding of, 369n4
"bike boys," 267
Bilefsky, Dan, 371n24
Bitterman, Marilyn, 110
blacks: and chess, 153–55; differences within group, 293–94, 312; and entertainment, 139–41; and history, 113, 177; and identity, 113, 332, 335–36; and Jews, 335–36, 393n30; and lodges and fraternal orders, 378n38; population in New York City, 298; and poverty, 340; and prejudice, 309–10, 313–14, 378n35, 391n7; in prison, 340; racial intermarriage, 341; relations with other groups, 93–94, 140–41, 285, 335, 392n10, 393n30; school performance, 379n41; success rates compared to immigrants, 370n8; success rates compared to Puerto

blacks (cont'd)
    Ricans, 372n38. *See also* conflict; educa-
    tion; ethnicity; politics; religion
Blarney Bar, the, 286
Blauner, Robert, 370–71n8
block associations, 116
Bloom, Nicholas Dagen, 129
Bloomberg, Michael R., 6; and commu-
    nity gardens, 377n29; and developers,
    262, 280; and gentrifiers, 262–63; and
    High Line Park, 178; and progressive
    policies, 178, 181, 262–64, 312, 369n8,
    390n51; and street use, 180–81; and
    undocumented immigrants, 34–35. *See
    also* politics
Blurring the Color Line, 340
B'nai Brith Lodges, 164
Bnei Baruch Kabbalah Center, 325–26
boat use by New Yorkers, 376n25, 383n8
Boerum Hill (Brooklyn), 125, 245, 256,
    267, 387n28
Bohemian Hall and Beer Garden, 381n19
Bookmobile, the, 378n36
Boone Street, 203–4
Borough Park (Brooklyn), 67–68, 269,
    321, 376n26
botanicas, 372n28
Bowery Hotel, 268
Bowery House, 252
Box House Hotel, 176–77
Bradhurst Avenue (W.E.B. DuBois Avenue),
    274–76
Bratton, William, 87
Brevoort, the, 173
Bronx, the: as a gentrifying area, 277–78,
    389n48; Yankees and, 94–95
Bronx Botanical Gardens, 272
Bronx Zoo, 272
Brooklyn Bridge Park, 253
Brooklyn Center for the Musical Arts, 43
Brooklyn culture and history, 208–10,
    329–30
Brooklyn Heights, 239
Brotherhood/SisterSol, 118
Brown, Lee, 87
Brownsville (Brooklyn), 276–77, 310,
    389n49
Bruni, Frank, 339
Buckley, Cara, 391n7
Bukharians. *See* Russians
buses, 105, 169–70, 297

Bushwick (Brooklyn), 75, 79, 166, 210–11,
    237, 247, 269, 386n3
"Bushwood," 237

Café Clementine, 173
Cambria Heights (Queens), 310–11
camera surveillance, 6, 89, 179–80,
    374n12, 384n16
Canarsie (Brooklyn), 75–76, 299–300,
    309–10, 313–14
Caplow, Theodore, 268–69
Carnegie Hill (Manhattan), 333
Carnes, Tony, 392n15
Caro, Robert, 384n14
Carroll Gardens (Brooklyn), 267
Casso, Anthony "Gaspipe," 196
Castellano, Paul, 173
Catholic Worker, 250
Catholics: and botanicas, 372n28; and
    exorcisms, 101–2, 375n22; and gays,
    339–40, 394n37; and identity, 317–18;
    and immigrants, 59; and Pope John Paul
    II, 331; and relations with other groups,
    68–69, 145–48, 303
Central Park, 19, 99, 149, 177
Chabad/Lubavitch Center, 243
change in neighborhoods: social and physi-
    cal, 102, 208, 211–13, 265–83, 366–67
cemeteries, 211–12
Chang, Jerry W., 328
Chaszar, Moses, 21–22
Chelsea (Manhattan), 338
Childs, Donald. *See* Halem (Harlem) Bike
    Doctor
Chinatown (Manhattan), 370n2, 387n12
Chinese: areas of residence, 370n2; and art
    galleries, 241–42; and basketball, 343–
    45; differences within group, 62–63,
    370n2; and economic status, 370n2; and
    education, 370n2; and entertainment,
    142–43; networks of, 39, 394n45; physi-
    cal appearance of, 328; politics of, 343,
    394n45; population changes among, 31;
    relations with other groups, 121, 302–3,
    393n25; and religion, 332–33; as role
    models, 43, 344–45, 393n25; school per-
    formance of, 379n41. *See also* conflict;
    ethnicity; immigration; politics; religion
Chinese Scholars Garden, 160
Chittenden Avenue, 214
Christian Faith Cathedral, 318